Guide to
UNIX Using Linux
Second Edition

Michael Palmer, Jack Dent, Tony Gaddis

THOMSON

COURSE TECHNOLOGY

Australia • Canada • Mexico • Singapore • Spain • United Kingdom • United States

Guide to UNIX Using Linux, Second Edition

by Michael Palmer, Jack Dent, and Tony Gaddis

Associate Publisher:
Steve Elliot

Acquisitions Editor:
Will Pitkin

Senior Editor:
Lisa Egan

Product Manager:
Amy M. Lyon

Developmental Editor:
Jill Batistick

Production Editor:
Kristen Guevara

Technical Editors:
Ross Brunson, Randy Weaver

Quality Assurance Technical Lead:
Nicole Ashton

Associate Product Manager:
Tim Gleeson

Editorial Assistant:
Nick Lombardi

Marketing Manager:
Jason Sakos

Cover Design:
Steve Deschene

Compositor:
GEX Publishing Services

BRIEF

Contents

TABLE OF
Contents

Preface

Guide to UNIX Using Linux gives you a solid grounding in the fundamentals of the UNIX operating system. The concepts you learn in this book help prepare you to use UNIX on all types of computer systems, including PCs, workstations, and mainframe computers.

Today UNIX is found in all areas of computer use from the Internet to desktop PCs to industrial-strength servers. Chances are that the next time you access an Internet server, your host will be using a version of UNIX.

Taking a hands-on, practical approach, this book guides you through the basics of the UNIX system and programming concepts. You practice these basic concepts and programming techniques using Linux, a PC-compatible clone of UNIX that is an ideal tool for teaching. Linux is storming the computer scene as a popular server and desktop operating system. Throughout the book, your learning is facilitated by a proven combination of tools that powerfully reinforce both concepts and real-world experience.

This book includes:

- Red Hat Linux 7.2 Publisher's Edition and complete installation instructions
- Step-by-step, hands-on instructions to learn UNIX commands and utilities, UNIX shell programming, data management, text editing, Perl scripts, CGI scripts, Web programming, and C and C++ programming
- Comprehensive review and end-of-chapter materials, including point-by-point summaries, Command Summaries, Review Questions, and Discovery Exercises—all of which reinforce your learning and enable you to practice and master UNIX skills
- Presentation of the X Window graphical user interface, with a focus on the popular GNOME desktop and applications
- Review of UNIX security for all types of situations
- Extensive screen captures and graphics to visually reinforce the text and hands-on exercises

The Intended Audience

This book is designed to serve anyone who wants to learn UNIX and how to use the programming features built into UNIX. It provides a solid beginning for general UNIX users, programmers, and system administrators. General users will appreciate learning how to use UNIX utilities, how to employ command line commands, and how to use the

X Window-based GNOME interface. Programmers and system administrators will be interested in learning how to use all types of powerful programming capabilities in UNIX. When you finish this book, you will have a valuable foundation of UNIX skills on which to build for general or professional use.

Chapter Descriptions

The chapter coverage is balanced, with each chapter building on the skills and knowledge acquired in the preceding chapters. Here is a summary of what you will learn in each chapter:

- **Chapter 1: The Essence of UNIX** gives you a basic introduction to UNIX and Linux, including how to access a UNIX system, how to use basic UNIX commands, and how to choose a shell in which to work. You also learn about the roles of general users and system administrators.

- **Chapter 2: Exploring the UNIX File System and File Security** introduces you to the standard tree structure of files and directories, how to navigate the file system, and how partitions are deployed. You also gain hands-on experience with basic UNIX utilities to create files and directories, manage them, and make them secure.

- **Chapter 3: The UNIX Editors** enables you to learn the most commonly used UNIX editors, vi and Emacs. After you learn how to use these editors, you employ them in later chapters to process data, create scripts, and write programs.

- **Chapter 4: UNIX File Processing** gives you basic techniques for handling data stored in files and for manipulating files. You use file creation and manipulation utilities, including the following: input, output, and error redirection utilities; utilities for creating, finding, moving, and deleting files; utilities for cutting, pasting, and sorting file contents; and the join and awk utilities for file processing.

- **Chapter 5: Advanced File Processing** builds on the knowledge you learned in Chapter 4, while introducing a more advanced range of file-processing utilities that include selection commands, manipulation and formatting commands, and file processing commands.

- **Chapter 6: Introduction to Shell Script Programming** gives you an introduction to using shell scripts, which are powerful files containing commands that can be executed as a group. You begin creating shell scripts that use different forms of programming logic to create a menu, a simple database, and a report. You also learn how to debug scripts.

- **Chapter 7: Advanced Shell Programming** builds on the skills you learned in Chapter 6 and enables you to add more functionality to the scripts you have created. You learn advanced techniques for managing data files, testing scripts, formatting screens, and creating shell functions.

- **Chapter 8: Exploring the UNIX Utilities** summarizes many of the utilities you have already learned and introduces you to new utilities for processing files, storing data on floppy disks, managing disk usage, monitoring the system status, and working with text files.

- **Chapter 9: Perl and CGI Programming** gives you a taste of how to program in Perl, CGI, and HTML to manipulate data, access disk files, and create an interactive Web page.

- **Chapter 10: Developing UNIX Applications in C and C++** is an introduction to writing C and C++ programs in UNIX. You build on knowledge of data and logic structures that you have learned earlier in the book and put it to work creating C and C++ programs.

- **Chapter 11: The X Window System** enables you to learn about the UNIX X Window graphical interface. In this chapter, you discover how to use the X Window GNOME desktop and its built-in applications.

- **Appendix A: How to Access a UNIX/Linux System** shows you how to access a UNIX/Linux system using a dumb terminal, a computer running a Microsoft Windows operating sytem, or a computer running UNIX or Linux.

- **Appendix B: Syntax Guide to UNIX Commands** provides a quick reference and review of the utilities and commands you have learned in this book, including the commands for the vi and Emacs editors.

- **Appendix C: How to Install Red Hat Linux 7.2** shows you how to install a Linux system from scratch. In addition, you learn how to install Apache Web Server, which allows you to use it as a web server for your intranet or local workgroup.

- **Appendix D: UNIX Variants** provides an overview of some of the most popular UNIX variants and helps you become familiar with the reasons why so many exist. In the process, you'll learn about the Berkeley System Distribution (BSD) standard and the System V release 4 (SVR4) standard.

- **Appendix E: Linux Security: Network and Internet Connectivity** provides a discussion about running a powerful and flexible system, and the responsibility of ensuring that the system is not easily broken into and misused. This appendix informs you about the security risks of running a standard Linux installation and the steps you can take to make your computer more secure.

Features

To ensure a successful learning experience, this book includes the following pedagogical features:

- **Chapter Objectives**. Each chapter in this book begins with a detailed list of the concepts to be mastered within that chapter. This list provides you with a quick reference to the contents of that chapter, as well as a useful study aid.

- **Chapter Lessons**. Every chapter is divided into two lessons to provide a gradual introduction of the topics and flexibility for covering the topics in a classroom environment.

- **Screen Captures, Illustrations, and Tables**. Numerous reproductions of screens and illustrations of concepts aid you in the visualization of theories, concepts, and how to use commands and desktop features. In addition, many tables provide details and comparisons of both practical and theoretical information and can be used for a quick review of topics.

- **Hands-on Projects**. One of the best ways to reinforce learning about UNIX is to practice its commands, utilities, and programming features. Each chapter in this book contains many Hands-on Projects that give you experience implementing what you have learned.

- **Case Approach**. Each chapter opens with a hypothetical case that you follow throughout the book. The running case helps to anchor what you are learning in a real-world context.

- **End of Chapter Material**. The end of each chapter includes the following features to reinforce the material covered in the chapter:

    Summary. A bulleted list gives a thorough point-by-point summary of the chapter, which can be used as a valuable study aid.

    Command Summary. Some chapters, in which many commands are introduced, feature a command summary table. The table lists the commands, their purpose, and any command options covered in the chapter.

    Review Questions. A list of review questions tests your knowledge of the most important concepts covered in the chapter.

    Discovery Exercises. Each chapter concludes with Discovery Exercises, which provide students with additional hands-on practice using the skills and concepts they learned in the chapter.

Text and Graphic Conventions

Wherever appropriate, additional information and exercises have been added to this book to help you better understand what is being discussed in the chapter. Icons throughout the text alert you to additional materials. The icons used in this textbook are as follows:

The Note icon is used to present additional helpful material related to the subject being described.

Each Hands-on Project in this book is preceded by the Hands-on icon.

Tips are used to present extra information about how to use a command or how to address a particular need.

The cautions are provided to help you anticipate potential problems or mistakes so that you can prevent them from happening.

Instructor's Materials

The following supplemental materials are available when this book is used in a classroom setting. All of the supplements available with this book are provided to the instructor on a single CD-ROM.

Electronic Instructor's Manual. The Instructor's Manual that accompanies this textbook includes:

- Additional instructional material to assist in class preparation, including suggestions for classroom activities, discussion topics, quizzes, and additional exercises.
- Solutions to all end-of-chapter materials, including the Review Questions and Discovery Exercises.

ExamView®. This textbook is accompanied by ExamView, a powerful testing software package that allows instructors to create and administer printed, computer (LAN-based) and Internet exams. ExamView includes hundreds of questions that correspond to the topics covered in this text, enabling students to generate detailed study guides that include page references for further review. The computer-based and Internet testing components allow students to take exams at their computers and save the instructor time by grading each exam automatically.

PowerPoint presentations. This book comes with Microsoft PowerPoint slides for each chapter. These are included as a teaching aid for classroom presentation, to make available to students on the network for chapter review, or to be printed for classroom distribution. Instructors, please feel at liberty to add your own slides for additional topics you introduce to the class.

Figure files. All of the figures and tables in the book are reproduced on the Instructor's Resource CD, in bit map format. Similar to the PowerPoint presentations, these are included as a teaching aid for classroom presentation, to make available to students for review, or to be printed for classroom distribution.

Hands-on Project files. The program and data files for the Hands-on Projects are included for instructors to help reduce the time it takes to reproduce them. Having these files can be valuable for class discussions, presentations about specific topics, and reviewing students' work.

System Requirements

To install Red Hat Linux 7.2, your computer should meet the following minimum requirements:

- A Pentium II computer or above that operates at 200 MHz or faster
- 64 MB of RAM
- At least 1.8 GB of disk space (to install X Windows desktops)
- 3.5-inch floppy drive
- CD-ROM drive
- Mouse or pointing device

To access a UNIX/Linux host on a local area network to which your computer is connected, you need the following software and information:

- Telnet program
- Either an IP address or the host and domain name of the UNIX system

To access a UNIX/Linux host via the Internet, you need the following software and information:

- Dial-up connection to an Internet service provider (ISP)
- Telnet program
- Either an IP address or the host and domain name of the UNIX system

Read This Before You Begin

There are several ways to set up a lab for the hands-on activities in this text. One is to provide students with their own PCs equipped with Red Hat Linux 7.2. This enables students to have the full experience of working with UNIX, including access to the X Window interface and the GNOME desktop.

Another way to perform the hands-on activities in this book is to provide students with access to a computer running Red Hat Linux 7.2 or later that is configured as a server and connected to a network. Students can access the server remotely from a networked lab equipped with computers running Windows 95/98, Windows NT 4.0, Windows 2000, Windows XP, Mac OS X, or UNIX and using the Telnet capabilities built into these systems. Students can also use computers with any of these operating systems and access the Red Hat Linux server over an Internet connection from a lab or from home. **One limitation to this method is that students cannot perform the X Window hands-on activities in Chapter 11 and certain other activities that require physically manipulating the system, such as when creating floppy disks**.

Yet another way to perform the hands-on activities is from a terminal that is directly connected to a Red Hat Linux server or connected through a network terminal or access server.

Acknowledgments

Many talented people have participated in the creation of this book. We want to thank Acquisitions Editor Will Pitkin for making the work on this book possible. Also, two people have been especially important in turning this book into reality, Product Manager Amy Lyon and Developmental Editor Jill Batistick. Amy Lyon has provided decision support, coordinated resources, and given moral support. Jill Batistick has gone beyond the call of duty to help in many ways through experienced and talented editing and encouragement.

Our thanks also go to the technical editors Ross Brunson and Randy Weaver, as well as the peer reviewers Denny Brown, Ozarks Technical Community College; Judy Dunn, Laramie County Community College; Rick Menking, Hardin-Simons University; and Carson Reid, Herzing College. Further, we want to thank the Production Editor, Kristen Guevara, for her dedication and creativity. In addition, Nicole Ashton's Quality Assurance team has spent many hours testing all of the hands-on exercises and validating the text.

Dedication

I dedicate this book to Don and Faire Snapp for the many ways in which they give to others.

—Michael Palmer

RED HAT LINUX 7.2 PUBLISHER'S EDITION

This book includes a copy of the Publisher's Edition of Red Hat® Linux® from Red Hat, Inc., which you may use in accordance with the license agreement. Official Red Hat® Linux®, which you may purchase from Red Hat, includes the complete Red Hat® Linux® distribution, Red Hat's documentation, and may include technical support for Red Hat® Linux®. You also may purchase technical support from Red Hat. You may purchase Red Hat® Linux® and technical support from Red Hat through the company's web site (www.redhat.com) or its toll-free number 1.888.REDHAT1. There is a sticker on the top of the envelope containing the Red Hat® Linux® CD-ROMs (this sticker may also be on the inside back cover of the text). By ripping this seal, you agree to the terms listed above.

1

THE ESSENCE OF UNIX

Dominion Consulting specializes in management systems for large hotels and resorts. Dominion's founders, Eli Addison and Carmen Scott, recognize the need for an in-house computer system that lets their employees work as a team. UNIX is an operating system designed for collaborative development of software, allowing people to work together and share information in controlled ways. Dominion has offered you a position as a UNIX system trainee. Your managers want you to understand the basics of operating systems in general, and UNIX in particular. They ask you to log in to UNIX and learn how to use some basic commands.

This chapter introduces the UNIX operating system and a few of its basic commands. It also explains how you can use Linux to learn UNIX. As a variant of UNIX, Linux runs on PCs with Intel processors, but uses the same file systems and commands as other UNIX versions. Linux can be run from an individual PC workstation or as a server operating system that is accessed through a network. When you access it through a network, you may use an old fashioned UNIX terminal, a UNIX or Linux workstation, or a Windows-based workstation. There are several versions of Linux, but this book uses Red Hat Linux, which is one of the most popular.

After you explore essential background information in this chapter, you begin to work with UNIX. If you're familiar with operating systems in general, then some background material may be review for you. This chapter also provides plenty of opportunity for hands-on practice of UNIX commands, primarily in the context of the opening case. The case study reflects a realistic scenario for the tasks you complete in this chapter. You learn to use a variety of basic commands to meet the goals of the scenario.

◀ LESSON A ▶

GETTING STARTED WITH UNIX

After completing this lesson, you should be able to:

♦ Define operating systems in general and the UNIX operating system in particular
♦ Describe Linux as it relates to UNIX
♦ Explain the function of UNIX shells
♦ Describe the options for connecting to a UNIX system
♦ Define the syntax used for entering UNIX commands
♦ Use the date, cal, who, man, whatis, and clear commands
♦ Perform basic command-line editing operations
♦ Enter multiple commands on a single command line
♦ Recall a command from the command history
♦ Log in to and log out of UNIX

UNDERSTANDING OPERATING SYSTEMS

An **operating system** (OS) is the most important program that runs on a computer. Operating systems enable you to store information, process raw data, use application software, compile your own programs, and access all hardware attached to a computer, such as a printer or keyboard. In short, the operating system is the most fundamental computer program. It controls all the computer's resources and provides the base upon which application programs can be used or written. Figure 1-1 shows the relationship between an operating system and other parts of a computer system.

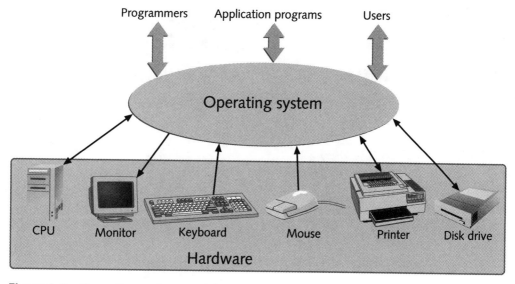

Figure 1-1   Operating system model

Different computer systems may have different operating systems. For example, the most common operating systems for desktop personal computers are Microsoft Windows, Mac OS, and Linux. Popular server computer operating systems are Microsoft Windows NT/2000/.NET, UNIX/Linux, NetWare, and Mac OS Server. Mainframe computers may use Digital Equipment's OpenVMS (Open Virtual Memory System) operating system or IBM's MVS (Multiple Virtual Storage) operating system. Networks also have operating systems, such as Novell NetWare, UNIX/Linux, Windows NT, Windows 2000/XP, and Windows .NET Server. UNIX is the leading operating system for workstations, which are powerful computers linked together on a local area network.

PC Operating Systems

A **personal computer** system or **PC** is usually a stand-alone machine, such as a desktop or laptop computer. A PC operating system conducts all the input, output, processing, and storage operations on a single computer. Figure 1-2 identifies some popular PC operating systems.

Microsoft Windows

Linux

Apple Mac OS

Microsoft DOS

Figure 1-2   Common PC operating systems

Mainframe Operating Systems

A mainframe operating system controls a **mainframe system**, a large computer system with multiple processors that conducts input, output, processing, and storage operations for many users. Historically, mainframe systems have been popular in large corporations and industrial computing. Figure 1–3 shows some recognized mainframe operating systems and their manufacturers.

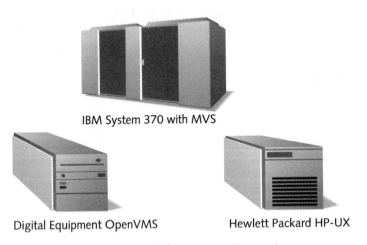

IBM System 370 with MVS

Digital Equipment OpenVMS

Hewlett Packard HP-UX

Figure 1-3   Common mainframe operating systems

Network Operating Systems

A computer **network** combines the convenience and familiarity of the personal computer with the processing power of the mainframe. A network lets multiple users share computer resources and files. A **network operating system** controls the operations of a **server** computer, sometimes called a **host** computer, which accepts requests from user programs running on other machines, called **clients**. Figure 1-4 shows the relationship of servers and clients on a network.

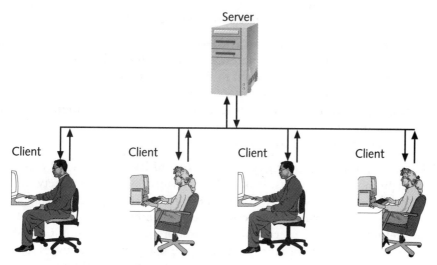

Figure 1-4   Relationship of servers and clients on a network

In a centralized approach, all the users' data and applications reside on the server. This type of network is called a **server-based network**. The system administrator secures all the information on the network by securing the server. The system administrator easily maintains the users' applications and performs back-up operations directly on the server. If the server fails, however, the entire network fails.

Peer-to-peer networks, which work best for small networks, are more distributed than server-based networks. In a peer-to-peer configuration, each system on the network is both a server and a client. There is no central server that manages user accounts, because each peer offers its own shared resources and controls access to those resources, such as through a workgroup of designated members or through accounts created on that peer workstation. Data and applications are not centrally located, but reside on the individual systems in the network. Software upgrades and back-up operations must be performed locally at each computer. Security, which is implemented on each computer, is not uniform. Each user of the network is, to some degree, responsible for administering his or her own system. Despite the disadvantages a peer-to-peer network presents to the system administrator, the individual users do not depend on a central server. If one computer in the network fails, the other systems continue to operate.

Introducing the UNIX Operating System

UNIX is a multi-user, multitasking operating system with built-in networking functions. It can be used on systems functioning as:

- Dedicated servers in a server-based network
- Client workstations connected to a server-based network
- Client/server workstations connected to a peer-to-peer network
- Stand-alone workstations not connected to a network

UNIX is a **multi-user system,** which lets many people simultaneously access and share the resources of a server computer. Users must **log in** by typing their user name and a password before they are allowed to use a multi-user system. This validation procedure protects each user's privacy and safeguards the system against unauthorized use. A **multitasking system** lets one user execute more than one program at a time. For example, on a multitasking system, you can update records in the foreground while your document prints in the background.

UNIX is also a portable operating system. Its **portability** means it can be used in a variety of computing environments. In fact, UNIX runs on a wider variety of computers than any other operating system. It also connects to the Internet, executing popular programs such as **File Transfer Protocol (FTP)**, an Internet protocol used for sending files; and **Telnet**, an Internet terminal emulation program. Dominion Consulting chose UNIX as the OS for its computer system because many of its employees must work on a range of computers performing a variety of tasks at the same time.

A Brief History of UNIX

A group of programmers at Bell Labs originally developed UNIX in the early 1970s. Bell Labs distributed UNIX in its source code form, so anyone who used UNIX could customize it as needed. Attracted by its portability and low cost, universities began to modify the UNIX code to make it work on different machines. Eventually, two standard versions of UNIX evolved: AT&T produced System V, and the University of California at Berkeley developed BSD (Berkeley Software Distribution). Using features of both versions, Linux may be a more integrated version of UNIX than its predecessors. Currently, the Portable Operating System Interface for UNIX (POSIX) project, a joint effort of experts from industry, academia, and government, is working to standardize UNIX.

UNIX Concepts

UNIX pioneered concepts that have been applied to other operating systems. For example, Microsoft DOS and Microsoft Windows adopted original UNIX design concepts, such as the idea of a **shell**, which is an interface between the user and the operating system, and the hierarchical structure of directories and subdirectories.

The concept of layered components that make up an operating system also originated with UNIX. Layers of software surround the computer system's inner core to protect its vital hardware and software components and to manage the core system and its users. Figure 1-5 shows how the layers of a UNIX system form a pyramid structure.

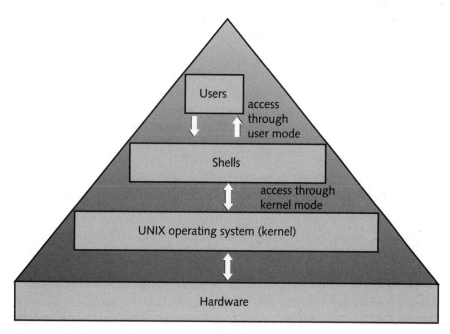

Figure 1-5   Layers of a UNIX system

At the bottom of the pyramid is the hardware. At the top are the users. The layers between them provide insulation, assuring system security and user privacy. The **kernel** is the base operating system, and it interacts directly with the hardware, software services, application programs, and user-created scripts (which are files containing commands to execute). It is accessible only through **kernel mode**, which is reserved for the system administrator. This prevents unauthorized commands from invading the **foundation layer** or the hardware that supports the entire UNIX structure. **User mode** provides access to higher layers where all application software resides.

This layered approach, and all other UNIX features, were designed by programmers for use in complex software development. Because the programmers wrote UNIX in the C programming language, UNIX can be installed on any computer that has a C compiler. Its portability, flexibility, and power make UNIX a logical choice for network operating systems. In addition, with the growth in popularity of Linux, the general popularity of UNIX is increasing.

Linux and UNIX

Linux is a UNIX-like operating system, because it is not written from the traditional UNIX code. Instead, it is original code (the kernel) created to look and act like UNIX, but with enhancements that include the POSIX standards. Linus Torvalds, who released it to the public, free of charge, in 1991, originally created Linux. A number of companies now offer commercial distributions or versions of Linux.

Linux offers all the complexity of UNIX at no cost; or for a relatively small amount of money, you can purchase commercial versions that have specialized tools and features. With all the networking features of commercial UNIX versions, Linux is robust enough to handle large tasks. You can install Linux on your PC, where it can coexist with other operating systems, and test your UNIX skills. All these features make Linux an excellent way to learn UNIX, even when you have access to other computers running UNIX.

INTRODUCING UNIX SHELLS

The shell is a UNIX program that interprets the commands you enter from the keyboard. UNIX provides several shells, including the Bourne shell, the Korn shell, and the C shell. Stephen Bourne at AT&T Bell Laboratories developed the **Bourne shell** as the first UNIX command processor. Another Bell employee, David Korn, developed the Korn shell. Compatible with the Bourne shell, the **Korn shell** includes many extensions, such as a history feature that lets you use a keyboard shortcut to retrieve commands you previously entered. The **C shell** is designed for C programmers' use. Linux uses the freeware **Bash shell** as its default command interpreter. Its name is an acronym for "Bourne Again Shell," and it includes the best features of the Korn and Bourne shells. No matter which shell you use, your initial communications with UNIX always take place through a shell interpreter. Figure 1-6 shows the role of the shell in the UNIX operating system.

Figure 1-6   Shell's relationship to the user and the hardware

Choosing Your Shell

Before working with a UNIX system, you need to determine which shell to use as your command interpreter. Shells do much more than interpret commands: each has extensive built-in commands that, in effect, turn the shells into first-class programming languages. (You pursue this subject in depth in Chapters 6 and 7.) A default shell is associated with your account when it is created, but you have the option to switch to a different shell after you log in. Bash is the default shell in Linux, and it is the shell many users prefer. Here is a list of shells:

- Bourne
- Korn (ksh)
- C shell (csh)
- Bash
- ash (a freeware shell derived from the Bourne and C shells)
- tcsh (a freeware shell derived from the C shell)
- zsh (a freeware shell derived from the Korn shell)

Switching from Shell to Shell

After you choose your shell, the system administrator stores your choice in your account record, and it becomes your assigned shell. UNIX uses this shell any time you log in. However, you can switch from one shell to another by typing the shell's name (such as tcsh, bash, or ash) on your command line. You work in that shell until you log in again or type another shell name on the command line. Users often use one shell for writing shell scripts (programs) and another for interacting with a program.

CHOOSING USER NAMES AND PASSWORDS

Before you can work with UNIX and its programs, you must log in by providing a unique user name and password. Decide on a name you want to use to identify yourself to the UNIX system, such as "aquinn." This is the same name others on the UNIX system use to send you electronic mail. Some UNIX versions recognize only the first eight characters of a user name, while others, such as Red Hat Linux 7.2, recognize up to 32 characters.

You must also choose a password, which must contain six or more characters when using newer versions of UNIX, such as Red Hat Linux 7.2. The password should be easy for you to remember but difficult for others to guess, such as a concatenation of two or more words that have meaning to you—a combination of hobbies or favorite places, for example—written in a mix of uppercase and lowercase letters, numbers, and hyphens. The password can contain letters, numbers, and punctuation symbols, but not control characters, such as Ctrl+X.

 The default minimum password length depends on your version of UNIX. Some earlier versions of Linux have a minimum length of five characters, but Red Hat Linux 7.2 and later require a minimum length of six characters, which is the practice used in this book.

You can log in to any UNIX or Linux system as long as you have a user account and password on the workstation or host (server) computer. A UNIX system administrator creates your account by adding your user name (also called a login name or user id) and your password. To use this book and the hands-on tutorials, you must have an account on a UNIX or Linux system along with some means to connect to that system. Some of the common ways to connect are:

- Through a Telnet connection to a remote computer, such as from another UNIX/Linux or a Windows-based operating system

- Through client software on a UNIX/Linux client/server network

- As a peer on a peer-to-peer, local area network in which each computer has the UNIX/Linux operating system installed

1

- On a stand-alone PC that has the Linux operating system installed
- Through a dumb terminal, such as a Wyse terminal, connected to a communication port on a UNIX/Linux host

The steps you take to connect to a UNIX system vary according to the kind of connection you use. Connecting via a dumb terminal or accessing UNIX through a stand-alone system are two of the easiest methods. In both cases, you turn on the terminal or stand-alone computer and log into your account. Connecting by using client software for a client/server network may take special instructions or training from a network administrator.

If you connect on a peer-to-peer network, you can use Telnet. Connecting through Telnet is one of the most common methods and is described in the next section. You can use Telnet to access a UNIX peer or server computer over a local area network and through the Internet. Appendix A also discusses how to connect over a network using different methods.

CONNECTING TO UNIX USING TELNET

Telnet is a terminal emulation program. It runs on your computer and connects your PC to a server, or host, on the network. The PC from which you connect can be running UNIX, Linux, a Windows-based operating system, or Mac OS. You can then log in to a UNIX host and begin working with UNIX. Most UNIX versions include Telnet, as do most versions of Microsoft Windows and later versions of Mac OS. Each computer on the Internet has an **Internet Protocol (IP) address**. An IP address is a set of four numbers separated by periods, such as *172.16.1.61*. Most systems on the Internet also have a **domain name**, such as *Lunar.campus.edu*. Both the IP address and the domain name identify a system on the network. Programs such as Telnet use IP addresses or domain names to access remote systems.

To access a UNIX host via Telnet:

1. Find the remote host's IP address or domain name.

2. Connect to the Internet, if necessary. If you use a PPP connection to dial into an ISP, make that connection. If you use a full-time Internet connection at work or school, ignore this step.

3. Start your Telnet program, and connect to the UNIX system.

4. Follow the instructions in your Telnet program to connect to a remote host. Usually, you must provide the host name or IP address to connect to a UNIX system. For example, you can type the following command after the prompt in a Windows 95/98/Me MS-DOS Prompt window or in a Windows NT/2000/XP Command Prompt window to gain access to the system *Lunar.campus.edu*:

```
telnet Lunar.campus.edu
```

To access Telnet in Red Hat Linux with the GNOME interface, click the icon for the Terminal emulation program in the Panel at the bottom of the screen (you learn more about how to access the command line later in this chapter); then type telnet plus the hostname or IP address of the computer to which you want to connect.

To access Telnet in Windows 95/98, click Start, point Programs, click MS-DOS Prompt, and type telnet plus the hostname or IP address. In Windows Me, click Start, point to Programs, point to Accessories, click MS-DOS Prompt, and type telnet *hostname* or *IP address*. In Windows NT, click Start, point to Programs, click Command Prompt, and type telnet *hostname* or *IP address*. For Windows 2000, click Start, point to Programs, point to Accessories, click Command Prompt, and type telnet *hostname* or *IP address*. In Windows XP, click Start, click All Programs, point to Accessories, click Command Prompt, and type telnet *hostname* or *IP address*. In Mac OS X, open Macintosh HD, double-click Applications, double-click Utilities, double-click Terminal, and type telnet *hostname* or *IP address*.

Logging In to UNIX

After you boot or connect to a UNIX system, you must log in by entering your user name and password. You see a prompt or a login box if you are using a **graphical user interface (GUI)**—requesting your login or user account name and your password. For security reasons, the password does not appear on the screen as you type it.

When you connect through the network or by using a dumb terminal, you log in and execute commands using a command-line screen. If you are on a stand-alone PC, the system may be configured to use only the command-line (text) mode, or it may be configured using a GUI. In UNIX, the foundation of a GUI is called the X Window interface. The X Window interface can have a different look and feel depending on what desktop environment is used with it. The Red Hat Linux examples in this text use the popular (and free) GNU Network Object Model Environment (GNOME) desktop. GNU stands for "Gnu's Not Unix," which was an endeavor started in 1983 to develop a free, open-standards, UNIX-like operating system (and additional operating system utilities). They were typically written in the C language.

You cannot log in without an authorized user account. If your password fails, or if you wait too long before entering your name and password, contact your system administrator for help.

After you log in, you are ready to begin using the system. If you access UNIX through a network or a dumb terminal—or if your stand-alone system is configured for the command-line text mode—you can immediately enter commands at the command prompt. However, if you are using a stand-alone computer and an X Window desktop such as GNOME, you must open a terminal window to access the command prompt.

To open the GNOME Terminal emulation program:

1. Click the icon in the Panel, which is the bar at the bottom of the screen that looks like a computer monitor with the bottom of a foot in front of it. If you are not sure of which icon to click, slowly move your cursor over each icon in the Panel until you see an information box that says "Terminal emulation program."

2. Notice the command-line prompt in the terminal window in Figure 1-7. The prompt in the line follows this format [*myname@localhost myname*]$. You can enter commands after the prompt in this window.

Figure 1-7 GNOME terminal window

3. Close the terminal window by typing **exit** and then press **Enter**.

ENTERING COMMANDS

To interact with UNIX, you enter a **command**, which is text you type after the command prompt. When you finish typing the command, press Enter. UNIX is **case-sensitive**; that is, it distinguishes between uppercase and lowercase letters, so John differs from john. You type most UNIX commands in lowercase.

Commands are divided into two categories: user-level commands that you type to perform tasks, such as retrieve information or communicate with other users; and system-administration commands, which the system administrator uses to manage the system.

You must know a command's syntax to enter it properly. **Syntax** refers to a command's format and wording, as well as the options and arguments you can use to extend and modify its functions. Most commands are single words, such as the command "clear." If you enter a command using correct syntax, UNIX executes the command. Otherwise, you receive a message that UNIX cannot interpret your command.

Appendix B, "Syntax Guide to UNIX Commands," alphabetically lists all the commands in this book, and tells you how to enter each command and use its options.

The place on the screen where you type the command is called the **command line**. Commands use the following syntax:

Syntax **command_name** [-option] [*argument*]

Dissection

- The **command_name** specifies what operation to perform. In the syntax illustrations in this book, command names appear in boldface.

- Command options are ways to request that UNIX carry out a command in a specific style or variation. Options follow command names, separated by a space. They usually begin with a hyphen (-). Options are also case-sensitive. For example, -R differs from -r. You do not need to type an option after every command; however, some commands do not work unless you specify an option. The syntax illustrations in this book list options in square brackets ([ ]) when the command does not require them.

- Command *arguments* follow command options, separated by white space. Command arguments are usually file and directory names. In the syntax illustrations in this book, arguments appear in italics. Square brackets surround arguments if the command does not require them.

The date Command

Use the UNIX date command to display the system date, which the system administrator maintains. Because the date and time on a multi-user system are critical for smooth processing, only the system administrator can change the date. You start your UNIX training at Dominion Consulting by checking the system date.

To display your system date:

1. Type **date** in the command line, and press **Enter**.

   A date like the one below appears:

   `Mon Apr 20 21:30:08 EST 2004`

   You may see the abbreviation EDT (eastern daylight time) instead of EST (eastern standard time), or another time zone abbreviation, such as PDT (Pacific daylight time) or CST (central standard time). Notice also that UNIX uses a 24-hour clock.

2. Type **Date** in the command line, and press **Enter**. You see the following system error message:

```
bash: Date: command not found
```

The system error message appears because you must enter the date command, like most UNIX commands, in lowercase letters.

The date command has an option, -u, which displays the time in Greenwich Mean Time (GMT). GMT is also known as Universal Coordinated Time, for which the abbreviation is UTC. UTC is considered the international time standard. To learn more about UTC, visit NASA's Web page, at *www.ghcc.msfc.nasa.gov/utc.html*.

To display your system date in UTC:

1. Type **date -u** in the command line, and press **Enter**.

A date like the one below appears:

```
Mon Apr 20 23:43:148 UTC 2004
```

The cal Command

Use the cal command to show the system calendar. Your manager at Dominion, Rolfe Williamson, advises you that this is the command commonly used to schedule tasks and events.

To display your system's default calendar:

1. Type **cal** in the command line, and press **Enter**. Without an option, the cal command shows a calendar of the current month. Assuming the current month is January of the year 2004, you see the default calendar shown in Figure 1-8.

2. Type **cal -j 2004** in the command line, and press **Enter**.

The -j option displays the Julian date format. In other words, it shows the days as numbers starting with 1 and ending with 366 (a leap year in this example), as shown in Figure 1-9.

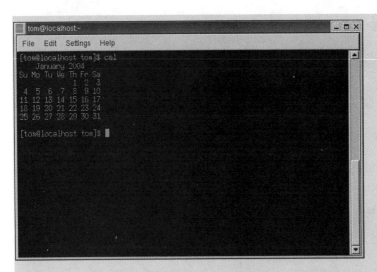

Figure 1-8   Example of cal (current month) command

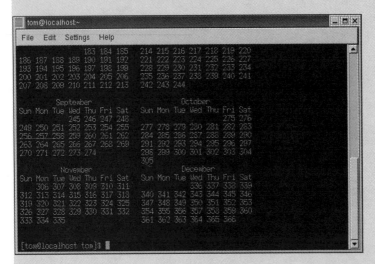

Figure 1-9   Example of cal command showing a full year of Julian dates

3. To determine the day of the week when the Declaration of Independence was signed, type **cal 7 1776** in the command line, and press **Enter**. You should see a calendar similar to the one in Figure 1-10. In this case, the month and year are the command arguments.

If you type cal may 1999, you see an error message similar to the following because you must use numbers, such as 5, to indicate months, such as May.

`cal: illegal month value: use 1-12`

1

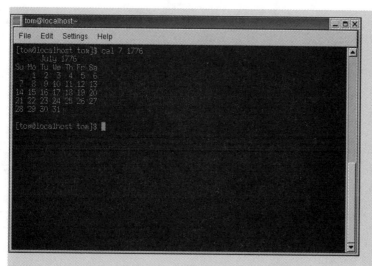

Figure 1-10 Example of cal command (July 1776)

The who Command

In a multi-user system, knowing who is logged in to the system may be helpful. Use the who command to see who is using the system and their current location. At Dominion, who is a useful command for getting to know your co-workers.

To use the who command to determine who is logged into the system:

1. Type **who** in the command line, and press **Enter**.

2. You see a list like the one below showing user names, the terminals they are using, and the dates and the times they logged in.

```
root    tty1    Aug 12 07:56
ellen   tty1    Aug 12 08:15
john    tty2    Aug 12 08:15
jerry   tty3    Aug 12 08:21
```

3. To display a line of column headings with the who command's output, type **who -H** and press **Enter**. You see a list like the one below.

```
USER    LINE    LOGIN-TIME      FROM
root    tty1    Aug 12 07:56
ellen   tty1    Aug 12 08:15
john    tty2    Aug 12 08:15
jerry   tty3    Aug 12 08:21
```

If any current users are logged in from a remote host, the FROM column shows the name of the host.

4. Idle time is the amount of time that has elapsed with no activity in a user's session. Type **who –i** and press **Enter** to see each user's idle time. You see a list similar to the one below.

```
root    tty1    Aug 12 07:56    00:29
ellen   tty1    Aug 12 08:15    .
john    tty2    Aug 12 08:15    00:01
jerry   tty3    Aug 12 08:21    old
```

The output shows that the person logged in as *root* has performed no activity in the last 29 minutes, and John's session has been idle for one minute. The period on Ellen's line indicates that her session has been active in the last minute. The word "old" on Jerry's line indicates no activity in the past 24 hours.

5. If you wish to use multiple options on the same command line, type them all after a single hyphen. For example, type **who –iH** and press **Enter** to see a list of users with idle times and column headings. You see a list similar to the one below.

```
USER    LINE    LOGIN-TIME      IDLE        FROM
root    tty1    Aug 12 07:56    00:29
ellen   tty1    Aug 12 08:15    .
john    tty2    Aug 12 08:15    00:01
jerry   tty3    Aug 12 08:21    old
```

6. Type **who –q** and press **Enter** to see a quick list of current users. You see a list similar to the one below, which shows only login names and the total number of users on the system.

```
root ellen john jerry
# users=4
```

7. To determine which terminal you are using or what time you logged in, type **who am I** in the command line, and press **Enter**. You see a line similar to the one below. It shows your user name, terminal, and the date and time you logged in.

```
lucky.campus.edu!ellen    tty1    Aug 12 08:15
```

The output above shows that you are logged in to the system lucky.campus.edu as the user ellen. Another option is to type whoami as one word, which displays your account name (called the userid).

Any time you provide two arguments to the who command, you see the output described in Step 7. For example, you can type "who are you" or "who x x" to see the same information. Traditionally, UNIX users type "who am I" to see information describing their session.

Another command that is similar to who is the w command. System administrators often use the w command to see not only who is logged in, but also to see what system resources, such as CPU resources, are being used.

Command-line Editing

Shells support certain keystrokes for performing command-line editing. For example, Bash (which is the default Linux shell) supports the left and right arrow keys, which move the cursor on the command line. Other keys, used in combination with the Ctrl or Alt key, are used for other editing operations.

Not all shells support command-line editing in the same manner. The following steps work with the Bash shell.

To edit a command typed on the command line:

1. To determine which shell you are using, type **echo $SHELL** and press **Enter**. If you are using the Bash shell, you see the following output:

   ```
   /bin/bash
   ```

   If you are not using the Bash shell, type **bash** and press **Enter**.

2. Type **who am I** but do *not* press Enter.

3. Press the **left arrow** key to move the cursor to the letter **a** in the word "am".

4. Press **Alt+D** to delete the word "am".

5. Press **Ctrl+K** to delete the command line from the current cursor position.

6. Press **Ctrl+A** to move the cursor to the beginning of the command line.

7. Press **Ctrl+K** again to delete the command line.

8. Retype the command **who am I** but do *not* press Enter.

9. Press **Alt+B** three times. Watch the cursor move to the first character of the previous word each time you press the key combination. The cursor should be positioned at the beginning of the line.

10. Press **Alt+F** three times. Each time you press the key combination, the cursor moves to the position just before the first character of the next word.

11. Press **Ctrl+A**, and then press **Ctrl+K** to clear the command line.

Multiple Command Entry

You may type more than one command on the command line by separating each command with a semicolon (;). When you press Enter, UNIX executes the commands in the order in which you entered them.

To enter multiple commands on the command line:

1. Type **date ; who -iH** and press **Enter**. You see information similar to the following:

```
Mon Apr 20 21:35:09 EST 2004
USER   LINE   LOGIN-TIME   IDLE    FROM
root   tty1   Apr 20 07:56  00:29
ellen  tty1   Apr 20 08:15   .
john   tty2   Apr 20 08:15  00:01
jerry  tty3   Apr 18 08:21   old
```

The date command produces the first line of the output shown above. The remainder of the output is the result of the who command.

The w -u command produces information similar to who -iH, but with additional information about system resource use.

The clear Command

As you continue to enter commands, your screen may become cluttered. Unless you need to refer to commands you previously entered and their output, you can use the **clear** command to clear your screen. It has no options or arguments.

To clear the screen:

1. Type **clear** on the command line, and press **Enter**. The command prompt is now in the upper-left corner of your screen.

The Command-line History

Often you find yourself entering the same command several times within a short period of time. Most shells keep a list of your recently used commands and allow you to recall a command without retyping it. You can access the command history with the up and down arrow keys. Pressing the up arrow key once recalls the most recently used command. Pressing the up arrow key twice recalls the second most recently used command. Each time you press the up arrow key, you recall an older command. Each time you press the down arrow key, you scroll forward in the command history. When you locate the command you want to execute, press Enter.

To use the command-line history:

1. Type **date** and press **Enter**.

2. Type **who** and press **Enter**.

3. Type **who -iH** and press **Enter**.

1

4. Type **clear** and press **Enter**.

5. Press the **up arrow** key four times. The date command is recalled to the command line. Do *not* press Enter.

6. Press the **down arrow** key twice. The who –iH command is recalled to the command line. Press **Enter** to execute the command.

The man Program

For reference, UNIX includes an online manual that contains all commands, including their options and arguments. The man program in UNIX displays this online manual, called the man pages, for command-line assistance. Although the man pages for some commands contain more information than others, most man pages list the following items.

- *Name*—the name of the command and a short statement describing its purpose

- *Synopsis*—a syntax diagram showing the usage of the command

- *Description*—a more detailed description of the command than the name item gives

- *Options*—a list of command options and their purposes

- *See Also*—other commands or man pages that provide related information

- *Bugs*—a list of the command's known bugs

The man program usually accepts only one argument—the name of the command about which you want more information. The online manual shows the valid command formats that your system accepts. To close the online manual, type q.

You decide to display information about the who command and the man program for yourself and others at Dominion.

To display online help for commands:

1. Type **man who** in the command line, and press **Enter**. You see the explanation of the who command illustrated in Figure 1-11.

2. Press **Enter** one or more times to view additional lines of text. Next press the **Spacebar** to view additional pages of documentation.

3. Type **q** to exit the man program.

4. Type **man man** and press **Enter**. You see the man pages describing the man command.

5. Type **q** to exit the man program.

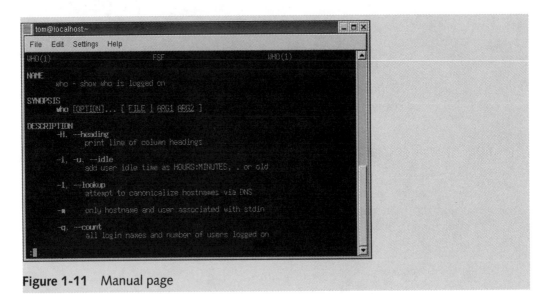

Figure 1-11   Manual page

The whatis Command

Sometimes you find that the man pages contain more information than you want to see. To display a brief summary of a command, use the whatis command. The whatis command shows only the name and brief description that appears near the top of a command's man page.

The whatis command relies on information stored in a database. On some UNIX systems, the administrator must execute the makewhatis command, which creates the database, before the whatis command operates properly. On other systems, such as Red Hat Linux, the whatis database is automatically built during installation.

To display a brief description of a command with the whatis command:

1. Type **whatis who** and press **Enter**.

2. You see a summary of the who command, as shown below.

```
who              (1)   - show who is logged on
```

LOGGING OUT OF UNIX

When you finish your day's work or leave your terminal for any reason, log out of the UNIX system. **Logging out** ends your current process and indicates to UNIX that you are finished. How you log out depends on the shell you are using. For the Bourne, Korn, or Bash shells, type exit on the command line or press Ctrl+D. In the C shell, type logout on the command line.

To log out of UNIX:

1. In the command line, type **exit** and press **Enter**.

If you are working in an X Window desktop environment, such as GNOME, typing exit and pressing Enter only closes the terminal window. To log out, use the Log out option. For example, if you are using GNOME, click the Main Menu (foot) icon in the Panel at the bottom of the screen, click Log out on the menu, select Logout in the dialog box, and then click Yes.

◀ LESSON B ▶

ROLES OF THE SYSTEM ADMINISTRATOR AND ORDINARY USERS

After completing this lesson, you should be able to:
- Discuss the role of the system administrator
- Identify the system administrator's and the ordinary user's command prompts
- Change your personal password
- View files on your screen using the cat, more, less, head, and tail commands
- Redirect output to a file

UNDERSTANDING THE ROLE OF THE UNIX SYSTEM ADMINISTRATOR

There are two types of users on a UNIX system: system administrators and ordinary users. As the name suggests, a **system administrator** manages the system by adding new users, deleting old accounts, and ensuring that the system performs services well and efficiently for all users. **Ordinary users** are all other users. The system administrator is also called the **superuser**, because the system administrator has unlimited permission to alter the system. UNIX grants this permission when the operating system is initially installed. The system administrator grants privileges and permissions to regular users.

The system administrator has a unique user name: **root**. This account has complete access to a UNIX system. The password for the root account is confidential; only the system administrator and a back-up person know it. If the root's password is lost or forgotten, the system administrator uses an emergency rescue procedure to reset the password.

The System Administrator's Command Line

While ordinary users type their commands after the $ (dollar sign) command prompt, the system administrator's prompt is the # (pound) symbol. The UNIX system generates a default setting for the command prompt for the system administrator in the following format:

```
[root@hostname root]#
```

In the prompt, *hostname* is the name of the computer the system administrator logged into. In addition, the second instance of root refers to the default home directory for the root account. (You will learn more about home directories later in this book.)

The Ordinary User's Command Line

The $ (dollar sign) is traditionally associated with ordinary users. The UNIX system generates a default setting for the command prompt for ordinary users. The following format is common on Linux systems:

```
[username@hostname username]$
```

In the prompt, *username* is the user's login name, such as jean, and *hostname* is the name of the computer the user is logged into. The second instance of the username refers to the name of the user's home directory.

CHANGING PASSWORDS

Your user name, or login name, identifies you to the system. You can choose your own user name and give it to the system administrator, who then adds you as a new user. As mentioned, some UNIX versions recognize up to eight characters, while other versions, such as Red Hat Linux 7.2, recognize up to 32 characters in your user name—which is often your first name or nickname.

A user name is unique, but not confidential, and may be provided to other users. The password, on the other hand, is confidential and secures your work on the system. You can change your password, if necessary, by using the passwd command. If you do not have a password, use the passwd command to create one.

UNIX lets you change your password only if the new one differs from the old password by at least three characters; has six or more characters, including at least two letters and one number; and is different from your user name.

The password you chose for the Dominion system, Gscott956, is too similar to another password on the system, so the system administrator asks you to change it.

To change your password:

1. Type **passwd** after the command prompt, and press **Enter**.

2. Type your current password, and press **Enter**.

> 3. Type your new password, and press **Enter**. Your new password does not appear on the screen as you type.
>
> 4. Retype your new password, and press **Enter** so that UNIX can confirm the new password.

If the password you retype as confirmation does not match your new UNIX password, UNIX asks you to enter the password again. UNIX may also ask you to choose a different password because you chose one that is too short or too easily guessed, such as *password*.

After changing your password, you should log out and log in again to make sure UNIX recognizes your new password.

Remember your password! You need your password every time you log into UNIX.

VIEWING FILES USING THE CAT, MORE, LESS, HEAD, AND TAIL COMMANDS

Three UNIX commands let you view the contents of files: cat, more, and less. The more and less commands display a file, one screen at a time. More scrolls only down, while less enables you to scroll down and up. The cat command displays the whole file at one time. Two other commands, head and tail, let you view the first few or last few lines of a file.

The cat command gets its name from the word **concatenate**, which means to link. You can display multiple files by entering their file names after the cat command and separating each with a space. UNIX then displays the files' contents in the order you entered them.

Your system administrator at Dominion mentions that you can use the cat command to view a file called shells that resides in the /etc directory. This file contains a list of valid shell programs on the system.

To view the shells file:

> 1. Type **cat /etc/shells** after the command prompt, and press **Enter**.
>
> (The forward slash (/) is used to indicate a directory or folder change.) You see a list of the available shells, including /bin/sh, /bin/bash, /bin/bash2, bin/ash, /bin/bsh, /bin/tcsh, and /bin/csh.
>
> Sometimes it is helpful to see a file's contents displayed with line numbers. The -n option causes the cat command to display a number at the beginning of each line of output.
>
> 2. Type **cat -n /etc/shells** and press **Enter**. You see the same list of shells as before, but this time a number precedes each line.

You can also view another file in the /etc directory called termcap. This multiple-page file contains many specifications about all terminals supported on the Linux system. The cat command is not a practical way to view this file, which is longer than one screen. However, you can use the more and less commands to read a large file, screen by screen.

To view the contents of large files on the screen with the more command:

1. Type **more /etc/termcap** after the command prompt, and press **Enter**.

2. Press the **Spacebar** to scroll to the next screen.

3. Terminate the display by typing **q** (for quit).

To view the contents of large files on the screen with the less command:

1. Type **less /etc/termcap** after the command prompt, and press **Enter**. You see a long file of text on your screen.

2. Press the **down arrow** key several times to scroll forward in the file one line at a time.

3. Press the **up arrow** key several times to scroll backward in the file one line at a time.

4. Press **Pg Dn**, **Spacebar**, **z**, or **f** to scroll forward one screen.

5. Press **Pg Up** or **b** to return to a previous screen.

6. Terminate the display by typing **q** (for quit) when you see a colon (:) at the bottom of a screen.

Sometimes you only need to glimpse part of a file's contents to determine what is stored in the file. The head command shows you the first few lines of a file; by default, it is the first 10 lines.

To view the first or last few lines of a file:

1. Type **head /etc/termcap** and press **Enter** to see the first 10 lines of the /etc/termcap file.

2. The -n option specifies the number of lines the head command displays. Type **head -n 5 /etc/termcap** and press **Enter**. You see the first five lines of the /etc/termcap file.

3. The tail command shows you the last few lines of a file. Like the head command, tail displays 10 lines by default. Type **tail /etc/termcap** and press **Enter** to see the last 10 lines of the /etc/termcap file.

4. The -n option specifies the number of lines the tail command displays. Type **tail -n 5 /etc/termcap** and press **Enter**. You see the last five lines of the /etc/termcap file.

REDIRECTING OUTPUT

In UNIX, the greater than sign (**>**) is called a redirection symbol. You can use this **redirection symbol** to create a new file or overwrite an existing file by attaching it to a command that produces output. In effect, you redirect the output to a disk file instead of the monitor. You already used the who command to find out who was logged into the system at Dominion. Now you can use the same command with the > redirection symbol to save this information in a text file. (You learn about other redirection symbols later in this book.)

To save to a file that lists persons logged into the system:

1. Type **who > current_users** after the command prompt, and press **Enter**. The who command output does not appear on the screen, but is redirected to a new disk file called current_users. UNIX places this text file in the active directory (the folder on the disk where you are currently using the system).

2. Type **cat current_users** after the command prompt, and press **Enter** to see a list of users currently using the system, similar to the one below.

```
jean     tty1     Feb 7   07:15
joseph   tty2     Feb 7   07:15
becky    tty3     Feb 7   08:05
```

You can also use the redirection symbol with the cal command to save a calendar in a text file. For example, you are involved in a Dominion development project with a projected deadline in the year 2004. You can save the calendar in a text file.

To save the year 2004 calendar in a file:

1. Type **cal 2004 > year_2004** after the command prompt, and press **Enter**. This creates a text file called year_2004.

2. Type **less year_2004** and press **Enter** to see the calendar created by the previous command. Use the arrow keys, Pg Dn, Pg Up, and other keys to scroll through the file.

3. Terminate the display by typing **q** (for quit).

You can also use the cat command to create files from information you type at the keyboard. Type cat > *filename* after the command prompt, where *filename* is the name of the file you are creating. Enter the data in the file, and then press Ctrl+D to end data entry from the keyboard.

Use the redirection symbol (>) to send output to a file that already exists only if you want to overwrite the current file. To append output to an existing file, use two redirection symbols (>>). This adds information to the end of an existing file without overwriting that file.

As you work with UNIX, you remember that Rolfe, your supervisor, asked you to complete a few tasks by the end of the week. You decide to create a notes file of task reminders.

To create a new file:

1. Type **cat > notes** after the command prompt, and press **Enter**.

2. Type the following: **Remember to order a new CD-ROM, and send the report by Thursday** and press **Enter**.

3. Press **Ctrl+D**.

4. To review the file you just created, type **cat notes** after the command prompt, and press **Enter**. The sentence you typed in Step 2 appears on the screen.

After you create the notes file, you remember that Rolfe asked you to complete another task. You can append the reminder to the existing notes file. You also want to include the appropriate monthly calendar in the file for reference.

To add information to an existing file:

1. Type **cat >> notes** after the command prompt, and press **Enter**.

2. Type the following: **Also remember to make reservations for Sept. conference** and press **Enter**.

3. Press **Ctrl+D**.

4. To add the calendar to your notes, type **cal 9 2004 >> notes**.

5. Type **less notes** and then press **Enter** to review the file.

6. Type **q** to exit the file.

CHAPTER SUMMARY

❑ The operating system is the most fundamental computer program. It controls all computer resources and provides the base upon which application programs can be used or written.

❑ A server-based network is centralized. All the users' data and applications reside on the server, which is secured, maintained, and backed up by the system administrator. Each computer in a server-based network relies on the server. All systems in a peer-to-peer network function as both server and client. The security and maintenance of the network is distributed to each system. If one of the systems in a peer-to-peer network fails, the other systems continue to function.

❑ The UNIX operating system is a multi-user system that lets many people access and share the computer simultaneously. It is also a multitasking operating system; it can perform more than one task at one time.

❑ UNIX systems may be configured as dedicated servers in a server-based network, client workstations in a server-based network, client/server workstations in a peer-to-peer network, or stand-alone workstations connected to no network.

❑ The concept of the layered components that make up an operating system originated with UNIX. Layers of software surrounding the computer system's inner core protect the vital hardware and software components and manage the core system for users.

❑ Linux is a UNIX-like operating system that you install on your PC. It coexists with other operating systems such as Windows and MS-DOS.

❑ In UNIX, you communicate with the operating system programs through an interpreter called the shell, which interprets the commands you enter from the keyboard. UNIX provides several shell programs, including the Bourne, Korn, and C shells. The Bash shell provides enhanced features from the Bourne and the Korn shells. It is the most popular shell on the Linux system.

❑ In UNIX, the system administrator sets up accounts for ordinary users. To set up your account and to protect the privacy and security of the system, you select and give the system administrator your user name and password. You can log into any UNIX or Linux system anywhere as long as you have a user account and password on the host (server) computer. You can also use UNIX/Linux, Microsoft Windows, and Mac OS Telnet programs to log into a remote UNIX system.

❑ The commands you type to work with UNIX have a strict syntax that you can learn by referring to the online manual called the man pages. Use the man program to display the syntax rules for a command. Use the whatis command to see a brief description of a command. Use the who command to list who is logged in and where they are located. Use the cal command to display the system calendar for all or selected months. To log out when you decide to stop using UNIX, use the exit or logout command.

❑ Most shells provide basic command-line editing capabilities and keep a history of your most recently used commands. Use the up and down arrow keys to scroll backward and forward through the list of recently used commands. You may enter multiple commands on a single command line by separating them with a semi-colon. UNIX executes the commands in the order in which you enter them.

❑ You can use the view commands to view the contents of files. Use the cat command to create a file by typing information from the keyboard. Use the less and more commands to display multi-page documents. Use the head and tail commands to view the first or last few lines of a file.

COMMAND SUMMARY

Review of Chapter 1 Commands		
Command	Purpose	Options Covered in This Chapter
cal	Show the system calendar	-j displays the Julian date format
cat	Display multiple files	-n displays line numbers
clear	Clear the screen	
date	Display the system date	-u displays the time in Greenwich mean time
exit or logout	Exit UNIX	
head	Display the first few lines of a file	-n displays the first n lines of the specified file
less	Display a long file one screen at a time and scroll up and down	
man	Display the online manual for the specified command	
more	Display a long file one screen at a time and scroll down	
passwd	Change your UNIX password	
tail	Display the last few lines of a file	-n displays the last n lines of the specified file
whatis	Display a brief description of a command	
who	See who is logged in	-H displays column headings -i displays session idle times -q displays a quick list of users

REVIEW QUESTIONS

1. You have typed the command Cal 2005, but instead of displaying the calendar for the year 2005, your computer displays an error message. What is wrong?

    a. You must type the command as CAL 2005, because UNIX is case sensitive.

    b. You must type the command as cal 2005, because UNIX is case sensitive.

    c. The UNIX Cal command does not work unless you enter only the last two digits of the year, such as Cal 05.

    d. You must run the UNIX calendar generator, Calgen, before you can view a calendar.

2. In which order are the components of a UNIX command given?

   a. name, arguments, options

   b. name, options, arguments

   c. options, name, arguments

   d. arguments, options, name

3. Which of these statements is false?

   a. Linux is compatible with UNIX.

   b. Ordinary users can change the system date.

   c. The UNIX operating system includes a kernel.

   d. You can change the shell after you select one.

4. In a network that is exclusively _____, shared data files are distributed among individual user's workstations making them available to other network users.

   a. peer-to-peer

   b. server-based

   c. stand-alone

   d. workstation

5. UNIX may be configured to run as _____.

   a. a server in a server-based network

   b. a client workstation in a server-based network

   c. a client/server workstation in a peer-to-peer network

   d. all of the above

6. What is required to log into a computer running UNIX or Linux?

   a. a user name and password

   b. only a password

   c. a kernel

   d. a shell

7. Use the UNIX date command to _____.

   a. display the system calendar

   b. display any date in the future

   c. reset the system date

   d. display the system date

8. The _____ program provides online command syntax documentation.

   a. man

   b. comhelp

    c. get

    d. head

9. The whatis command provides _____.

    a. a brief description of a command

    b. a page-by-page detailed description of a command with several examples showing how to use the command

    c. a description of a hardware device attached to the system

    d. an online tutorial on the UNIX operating system

10. When you type the _____ command, you see the date plus the time in Greenwich Mean Time (GMT).

    a. date –j

    b. cal –g

    c. date –u

    d. year –dg

11. Which of the following best describes UNIX?

    a. It is a multi–user, multitasking operating system.

    b. It is an operating system that cannot operate on a stand–alone PC.

    c. It is an operating system tied to a graphical user interface.

    d. It is a portable, single–user operating system.

12. Why is the UNIX operating system designed with layers?

    a. to increase its speed

    b. to permit networking

    c. to allow other operating systems to communicate with it

    d. to control access to the core system from the user environment

13. When viewing a file with the cat command, you can _____.

    a. edit the file

    b. only view the file

    c. spell check the file

    d. delete the file

14. After creating a file with the cat > *filename* command, if you use the command again with the same filename, you _____.

    a. append new information to the file

    b. overwrite the file

    c. create a new file

    d. delete the file

15. Which of the following is a shell available in UNIX?

    a. Bourne

    b. C

    c. Korn

    d. all of the above

    e. only a and c

16. When you connect to a UNIX computer through Telnet, you must provide the _____ for that computer.

    a. hard-coded device address

    b. IP address or domain name

    c. security id and network id

    d. serial number

17. Using the -H option with the who command displays _____.

    a. your login name

    b. who is logged in with the information in column headings

    c. user idle time information

    d. help information for the who command

18. A password should not contain _____.

    a. numbers

    b. uppercase letters

    c. control characters

    d. the underscore character

19. True or False: The > symbol may be combined with the who command to create an output file.

20. You want to view only the last eight lines of the /etc/termcap file. Which of the following commands enables you to accomplish this?

    a. less –n 8 /etc/termcap

    b. cat –8 l /etc/termcap

    c. viewend –l 8 /etc/termcap

    d. tail –n 8 /etc/termcap

21. Multiple commands entered on the same command line must be separated by a _____.

    a. space

    b. semicolon (;)

    c. colon (:)

    d. comma (,)

22. The _____ command enables you to view the contents of a file one screen at a time and either scroll up or down through the contents.

    a. list

    b. log incat

    c. display

    d. less

23. The symbol that ordinary users see as their command prompt is the _____.

    a. colon (:)

    b. pound sign (#)

    c. slash character (/)

    d. dollar sign ($)

24. True or False: If you are using a GUI on a UNIX system, you are probably using a desktop, such as GNOME, built on the X Window interface.

25. True or False: Your password must be different from your user name.

26. In newer versions of Linux, such as Red Hat 7.2, a password must contain at least _____ character(s).

    a. six

    b. eight

    c. twelve

    d. one

27. When you change your password using the passwd command, you _____.

    a. must first review a list of passwords that cannot be used in UNIX

    b. enter the new password and then verify it by entering it again

    c. must specify if this new password can be used again at a later date

    d. automatically send the system administrator an e-mail message showing that you changed the password

28. When using the cat > *filename* command, you must enter _____ to end keyboard input.

    a. *

    b. Ctrl+D

    c. q

    d. exit

29. The _____ command clears the screen.

    a. *

    b. #

    c. clear

    d. who –c

30. What is the default shell in Linux?

    a. Bin

    b. Korn

    c. Bash

    d. C

DISCOVERY EXERCISES

1. Use the cat command to view the contents of the file /etc/profile.

2. Use the more command to view the contents of /etc/profile.

3. Use the cal command to determine on what day of the week you were born.

4. Use the cal command to discover on what day of the week the Declaration of Independence was signed.

5. Use the cal command to discover what is unusual about the year 1752.

6. Clear the screen, and view the online manual for the cal command. What is the explanation for the year 1752?

7. Determine the current UTC.

8. Create a file called *today* containing today's date.

9. Create a file called *manual_for_date* containing the online manual for the date command.

10. Use the who command to append a quick list of current users to the today file that you created in Discovery Exercise 8.

11. View the files today and manual_for_date:

    ❑ individually

    ❑ in sequence

12. View the files today and manual_for_date in sequence by using:

    ❑ the less command

    ❑ the more command

13. Create a file containing the calendar for next year, and use the more command to view the file, and scroll forward through it.

14. Use the less command to view the file you created in Discovery Exercise 13, and scroll backward through it.

15. Use the tail command to view the last 10 lines of the file you created in Discovery Exercise 13.

16. Create a file listing two tasks on your to-do list.

17. Add another task to the list in the file you created in Discovery Exercise 16.

18. Practice viewing documentation for the passwd command.

19. Find documentation about the who command, and then find documentation about a new command called finger. On the basis of the documentation, compare how you would use these two commands.

20. Use one command line to run both the who and finger commands so that you can compare their output back-to-back.

21. Use the option for the who command that displays a heading for the information displayed.

22. Combine the cat and cal commands to create a file, called **memo**, that contains a memo about a meeting to review a new hotel management program. Attach a calendar for August of 2004 to your memo, and remind the memo's recipients of the meeting dates for Monday, Tuesday, and Wednesday of the second week of the month.

23. Append the calendar for September to the end of the memo file you created in Discovery Exercise 22.

24. Use the head command to view the first six lines of the file you created in Discovery Exercise 22.

25. Repeat the command you used in Discovery Exercise 23, but redirect the output to another file. What is stored in the file you created?

26. Your system administrator at Dominion mentions that you can also specify the number of bytes you wish to view with the head and tail commands. Use the man program to discover how this is done. Perform the proper commands to view the first and last 10 characters of the memo file you created in Discovery Exercise 22.

2

EXPLORING THE UNIX FILE SYSTEM AND FILE SECURITY

Dominion Consulting is creating a centralized telephone database that will contain each employee's name and phone number information. Currently each department maintains this information and stores it in multiple files located in separate directories. Your job is to consolidate this information into a single master database that everyone in the company can access.

In Lessons A and B of this chapter, you explore the UNIX file system, including the basic concepts of files and directories and their organization in a hierarchical tree structure. After you learn to navigate the file system, you practice what you've learned by creating directories and files and copying files from one directory to another. You also have the opportunity to set file permissions, which is vital for security in a multi-user system such as UNIX.

◀ LESSON A ▶

UNDERSTANDING FILES AND DIRECTORIES

After completing this lesson, you should be able to:

- ♦ Discuss and explain the UNIX file system
- ♦ Define a UNIX file system partition
- ♦ Use the mount command to mount a file system
- ♦ Discuss relative and absolute path addressing
- ♦ Diagram the UNIX file system hierarchy
- ♦ Navigate the file system

UNDERSTANDING THE UNIX FILE SYSTEM

In UNIX, a **file** is the basic component for data storage. UNIX considers everything it interacts with a file, even attached devices such as the monitor, keyboard, and printer. A **file system** is the UNIX system's way of organizing files on mass storage devices such as hard and floppy disks. A **physical file system** is a section of the hard disk that has been formatted to hold files. UNIX consists of multiple file systems that form virtual storage space for multiple users. The file system's organization is a hierarchical structure similar to an inverted tree; that is, it is a branching structure where top-level files contain other files, which in turn contain other files. Figure 2-1 illustrates a typical UNIX directory.

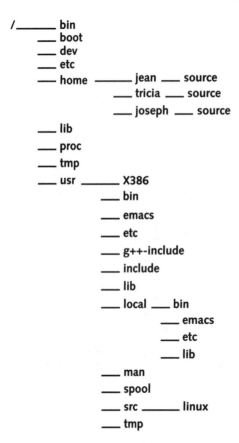

Figure 2-1 Typical UNIX directory

Understanding the Standard Tree Structure

The tree-like structure for UNIX file systems starts at the root level. Root is the name of the file at this basic level, and it is denoted by the slash character (/). The slash represents the **root directory**.

2

A **directory** is a special kind of file that can contain other files and directories. Regular files store information, such as records of employee names and addresses or payroll information, while directory files store the names of regular files and the names of other directories, which are called **subdirectories**. The subdirectory is considered the **child** of the **parent** directory because the child directory is created within the parent directory. In Figure 2-1, the root directory (/) is the parent of all the other directories. The home directory, as a further example, is the parent of the jean, tricia, and joseph subdirectories.

USING UNIX PARTITIONS

The section of the disk that holds a file system is called a **partition**. One disk may have many partitions, each separated from the others so that it remains unaffected by external disturbances such as structural file problems associated with another partition. When you install UNIX on your computer, one of your first tasks is deciding how to partition your hard drive.

UNIX partitions are identified with names: for example, Linux uses "hda1" and "hda2" for some types of disks. In this case, the first two letters tell UNIX the device type; "hd," for instance, identifies the commonly used IDE type of hard disk. The third letter, "a," in this case, indicates whether the disk is the primary or secondary disk (a=primary, b=secondary).

Partitions on a disk are numbered starting with 1. The name "hda1" tells UNIX that this is the first partition on the disk, and the name "hda2" indicates it is the second partition on the same disk. If you have a second hard disk with two partitions, the partitions are identified as "hdb1" and "hdb2."

Computer storage devices such as hard disks are called peripheral devices. Computer **peripherals**, like hard disks, connect to the computer through **electronic interfaces**. The two most popular hard disk interfaces are **IDE** (Integrated Drive Electronics) and **SCSI** (Small Computer System Interfaces). On PCs, IDE hard disk drives (identified as hd*x*) are more common than SCSI (pronounced "scuzzy"). SCSI is faster and more reliable. It is often used on servers. If you have a primary SCSI hard disk with two partitions, the two partitions are named "sda1" and "sda2." Figure 2-2 shows two partition tables: one with an IDE drive and the other with a SCSI drive.

Note that the first table in Figure 2-2 identifies "hda" as the device, which indicates an IDE drive. The second table identifies "sda" as the device, which indicates a SCSI drive.

Red Hat Linux 7.2 has an Automatic Partitioning option that you can select as you are installing the system. This tool automatically allocates space to create the swap, /boot, and root partitions described in the next section of this text.

```
Disk/dev/hda: 128 heads, 63 sectors, 767 cylinders
Units = cylinders of 8064 * 512 bytes

Device    Boot  Begin   Start    End    Blocks  Id  System
/dev/hda1   *      1       1     242   975712+   6  DOS 32-bit >=32M
/dev/hda2         243     243    767  2116899    5  Extended
/dev/hda3         243     243    275   127024+  83  Linux native
/dev/hda6         276     276    750  1028224+  83  Linux native
/dev/hda7         751     751    767    68512+  82  Linux swap

Command (m for help):  _
```

This partition table is from a Linux system with an IDE drive

```
Disk /dev/sda: 255 heads, 63 sectors, 1106 cylinders
Units = cylinders of 16065 * 512 bytes

Device    Boot  Begin   Start    End    Blocks  Id  System
/dev/sda1            1       1     64   514048+  83  Linux native
/dev/sda2           65      65   1106  8369865    5  Extended
/dev/sda5           65      65   1084  8193118+  83  Linux native
/dev/sda6         1085    1085   1100   128488+  82  Linux swap

Command (m for help):  _
```

This partition table is from a Linux system with a SCSI drive

Figure 2-2   Two partition tables

Setting Up Hard Disk Partitions

Partitioning your hard disk provides organized space to contain your file systems. If one file system fails, you can work with another. This section provides general guidelines on how to partition hard disks. These recommendations are suggestions only. How you partition your hard drive may vary depending on your system's configuration, number of users, and planned use. Partition size is measured in megabytes (MB, about a million characters) or gigabytes (GB, about a billion characters). Some UNIX vendors, such as Red Hat, recommend at least three partitions, root, swap, and /boot.

You can begin the process by setting up a partition for the root file system, which holds the root directory (referred to as "/"). A partition must be mounted before it becomes part of the file system. The kernel mounts the root file system when the system starts.

The size of the root partition depends on the type of installation you are performing. For example, in Red Hat Linux 7.2, the root partition must be a minimum of 1.2 GB to load the basic operating system required for a workstation or portable computer installation. If you are setting up a server or are loading the full complement of software packages that come with Red Hat Linux, then consider a partition of about 3.5–4 GB.

To install the operating system, X Window interface, desktops, and most of the software for a Red Hat Linux 7.2 installation, you need a minimum of about 3 GB of disk space. However, if you install a minimum workstation configuration for a desktop or portable computer, and you include the operating system, X Window interface, and one desktop, such as GNOME, you need about 1.5 GB of space.

After creating the root partition, you should set up the **swap** partition. The swap partition acts like an extension of memory, so that UNIX has more room to run large programs. Linux distributors, such as Red Hat, suggest that your swap space be a minimum of 32 MB and at least match the size of the amount of internal memory (RAM) in the computer. However, for better performance, it is a good idea to set the swap space at twice the size of the RAM. For example, if your computer has 64 MB of RAM, consider allocating 128 MB for the swap partition.

A swap partition enables **virtual memory**. Virtual memory means you have what seems to be unlimited memory resources. Swap partitions accomplish this by providing swap space on a disk and treating it like an extension of memory (RAM). It is called swap space because the system can use it to swap information between disk and RAM. Setting up swap space makes your computer run faster and more efficiently.

You can create and use more than one swap partition on Linux. Having multiple swap partitions spread across several hard disks can sometimes improve application performance on busy systems.

The **/boot** partition is used to store the operating system files that compose the kernel. The size of this partition depends on how much space is needed for the operating system files in your version of UNIX. For example, if you are installing Red Hat Linux 7.2 (or higher), consider a /boot partition that is 50–60 MB in size.

If you plan to have multiple users accessing your system, you may want to create a **/usr** partition in which to store some or all of the nonkernel operating system programs that are accessed by users. These programs include software development packages that support computer programming, networking, Internet access, graphical screens (including X Window), and the large number of UNIX **utilities** (programs that perform utilitarian operations like copying files, listing directories, and communicating with other users). The /usr partition should be large enough—such as 1 GB or more—to accommodate all of the software that you install.

If you plan on having multiple users access the system, you can create a **/home partition**, which is the home directory for all users' directories. Having separate /usr and /home partitions makes many system administration tasks, such as backing up only software or only data, much easier.

The /home partition is the storage space for all users' work. If the root partition (or any other partition) crashes, having a /home partition ensures that you do not lose all the users' information. Although regular user accounts are restricted from reading information in other partitions, you own and can access most files in your home directory. You can grant or deny access to your files as you choose. See "Setting File Permissions" later in this chapter for more information on file ownership.

To prepare for a new software system to hold human resources information, Dominion Consulting sets up a UNIX workstation that has 256 MB of RAM and 60 GB of hard disk space to be accessed by 10 users. Dominian Consulting allows 3.5GB for the root partition (particularly for the GNOME desktop), 50 MB for the /boot partition, 512 MB for the swap partition, 15 GB for the /usr partition, and about 41 GB for the /home partition.

EXPLORING THE ROOT FILE SYSTEM

The root (/) file system is mounted by the kernel when the system starts. To **mount** a file system is to connect it to the directory tree structure. The system administrator uses the mount command to mount a file system. The syntax of the mount command is:

Syntax **mount** *device-name mount-point*

Dissection

- *device-name* identifies the partition (file system) to **mount**

- *mount-point* identifies the directory where you want to mount the filesystem

---

See "Using the mount Command" later in this chapter for more information about the mount command.

UNIX must mount a file system before any programs can access files on that file system. After mounting, the root file system is accessible for reading only during the initial systems check and bootup sequence—after that, it is remounted as read and write. The root file system contains all essential programs for file system repair, restoring from a backup, starting the system, and initializing all devices and operating resources. It also contains the information for mounting all other file systems. Nothing beyond these essentials should reside in the root partition.

 You can restore a crashed root partition using rescue files stored on floppy disks or tape. The installation media that comes with Red Hat Linux can be used to create rescue disks.

The root directory itself generally contains subdirectories that contain files. The next sections describe the more frequently referenced subdirectories of the root file system.

The /bin Directory

The /bin directory contains **binaries**, or **executables**, which are the programs needed to start the system and perform other essential system tasks. This directory holds many programs that all users need to work with UNIX.

The /boot Directory

The /boot directory normally contains the files needed by the **bootstrap loader** (the utility that starts the operating system); it also contains the kernel (operating system) images.

The /dev Directory

Files in /dev reference system devices. They access system devices and resources such as hard disks, the mouse, printers, consoles, modems, memory, floppy disks, and the CD-ROM drive. All UNIX versions include many device files in the /dev directory to accommodate separate vendor devices that can be attached to the computer. The device files are divided into two major classifications: block types and character types. The type indicates the method of data transmission on the device, either as a block of characters or as a serial flow of characters. You can see the list of device files by typing ls –l /dev after the command prompt. (See "Listing Directory Contents" later in this chapter for more information on the ls command.) The far-left character on the list tells you whether the file is a character device (c) or a block device (b), as shown in Figure 2-3.

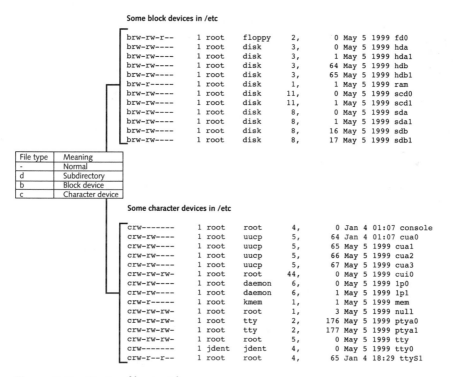

Some block devices in /etc

```
brw-rw-r--   1 root   floppy   2,    0 May 5 1999 fd0
brw-rw----   1 root   disk     3,    0 May 5 1999 hda
brw-rw----   1 root   disk     3,    1 May 5 1999 hda1
brw-rw----   1 root   disk     3,   64 May 5 1999 hdb
brw-rw----   1 root   disk     3,   65 May 5 1999 hdb1
brw-r-----   1 root   disk     1,    1 May 5 1999 ram
brw-rw----   1 root   disk    11,    0 May 5 1999 scd0
brw-rw----   1 root   disk    11,    1 May 5 1999 scd1
brw-rw----   1 root   disk     8,    0 May 5 1999 sda
brw-rw----   1 root   disk     8,    1 May 5 1999 sda1
brw-rw----   1 root   disk     8,   16 May 5 1999 sdb
brw-rw----   1 root   disk     8,   17 May 5 1999 sdb1
```

File type	Meaning
-	Normal
d	Subdirectory
b	Block device
c	Character device

Some character devices in /etc

```
crw-------   1 root   root     4,    0 Jan 4 01:07 console
crw-rw----   1 root   uucp     5,   64 Jan 4 01:07 cua0
crw-rw----   1 root   uucp     5,   65 May 5 1999 cua1
crw-rw----   1 root   uucp     5,   66 May 5 1999 cua2
crw-rw----   1 root   uucp     5,   67 May 5 1999 cua3
crw-rw-rw-   1 root   root    44,    0 May 5 1999 cui0
crw-rw----   1 root   daemon   6,    0 May 5 1999 lp0
crw-rw----   1 root   daemon   6,    1 May 5 1999 lp1
crw-r-----   1 root   kmem     1,    1 May 5 1999 mem
crw-rw-rw-   1 root   root     1,    3 May 5 1999 null
crw-rw-rw-   1 root   tty      2,  176 May 5 1999 ptya0
crw-rw-rw-   1 root   tty      2,  177 May 5 1999 ptya1
crw-rw-rw-   1 root   root     5,    0 May 5 1999 tty
crw-------   1 jdent  jdent    4,    0 May 5 1999 tty0
crw-r--r--   1 root   root     4,   65 Jan 4 18:29 ttyS1
```

Figure 2-3   Device files in /dev

Explanations of the items listed in Figure 2-3 follow:

- **console** refers to the system's console, which is the monitor connected directly to your system.

- **ttyS1** and **cua1** are devices used to access serial ports. For example, /dev/ttyS1 refers to COM2, the communication port on your PC.

- **cua** devices are callout devices used in conjunction with a modem.

- Device names beginning with **hd** access IDE hard drives.

- Device names beginning with **sd** are SCSI drives.

- Device names beginning with **lp** access parallel ports. The lp0 device refers to LPT1, the line printer.

- **null** is a "black hole;" any data sent to this device is gone forever. Use this device when you want to suppress the output of a command appearing on your screen. Chapters 6 and 7 discuss this technique.

- Device names beginning with **tty** refer to terminals or consoles. Several "virtual consoles" are available on your Linux system. (You access them by pressing Alt+F1, Alt+F2, and so on.) Device names beginning with **pty** are "pseudoterminals." They are used to provide a terminal to remote login sessions. For example, if your machine is on a network, incoming remote logins would use one of the pty devices in /dev.

The /etc Directory

The /etc directory contains configuration files that the system uses when the computer starts. Most of this directory is reserved for the system administrator, and it contains system-critical information stored in files:

- *passwd*—the user information file

- *rc*—scripts or directories of scripts to run when the system starts

- *fstab*—mapping information about file systems to devices (such as hard disks and CD-ROMs)

- *group*—the user group information file

- *inittab*—the configuration file for the **init** program that performs essential chores when the system starts

- *motd*—the message of the day file

- *printcap*—the printer capability information file

- *termcap*—the terminal capability information file

- *profile* and *bashrc*—files executed at logon that let the system administrator set global defaults for all users

- *login.defs*—the configuration file for the login command

The /lib Directory

This directory houses kernel modules, security information, and the **shared library images**, which are files that programmers generally use to share code in the libraries rather than creating copies of this code in their programs. This makes the programs smaller. Many files in this directory are symbolic links to other library files. A **symbolic link** is a name that points to and lets you access a file located in a directory other than the current directory. In the directory's long listing, *l* in the far-left position identifies files that are symbolic links.

The /mnt Directory

Mount points for temporary mounts by the system administrator reside in the /mnt directory. This directory is often divided into subdirectories such as /mnt/cdrom and /mnt/floppy, to clearly specify device types.

The /proc Directory

The /proc directory occupies no space on the disk; it is a **virtual file system** allocated in memory only. Files in /proc refer to various processes running on the system, as well as details about the operating system kernel.

The /root Directory

The /root directory is the home directory for the root user—the system administrator.

The /sbin Directory

The /sbin directory is reserved for the system administrator. Programs that start the system, programs needed for file system repair, and essential network programs are stored here.

The /tmp Directory

Many programs need a temporary place to store data during processing cycles. The traditional location for these files is the /tmp directory.

The /var Directory

The /var directory holds subdirectories which have sizes that often change. These subdirectories contain files such as error logs and other system performance logs that are useful to the system administrator. The /var/spool/mail subdirectory can contain incoming mail from the network, for example. Another example is the /var/spool/lpd directory, which is the default directory for holding print files until they are fully transmitted to a printer.

USING THE MOUNT COMMAND

As you learned, UNIX uses the mount command to connect the file system partitions to the directory tree when the system starts. Users can access virtually any file system that has been mounted and to which they have been granted permission. Additional file systems can be mounted at any time using the mount command. The floppy disk and CD-ROM drive are the file system devices beyond the hard disk that are most commonly mounted.

 To ensure security on the system, only the root user can normally use the mount command. Ordinary users can sometimes mount and unmount file systems located on floppy disks and CDs.

Suppose you want to access files on a CD for the Dominion Consulting database. The system administrator mounts a CD-ROM by inserting a disk in the drive, and then uses the following mount command:

```
mount -t iso9660 /dev/cdrom /mnt/cdrom
```

This command mounts the CD on a device called "cdrom" located in the /dev directory. The actual mount point in UNIX is /mnt/cdrom, a directory that references the CD-ROM device. After the CD is mounted, you can access its files through the /mnt/cdrom directory.

UNIX supports several different types of file systems. The type of file system is specified with the -t option. CD-ROMs are classified as iso9660 devices, so the system administrator types -t, followed by the argument iso9660 to specify the file system for CD-ROMs.

 After a CD-ROM is mounted, you can view the device paths, file system, and permissions by typing the following at the command prompt: cat /etc/fstab.

You also want to store back-up files on a floppy disk. The system administrator mounts a floppy disk in the floppy drive using this command:

```
mount -t filesystem /dev/fd0 /mnt/floppy
```

This command mounts the floppy in the first floppy drive, which is the device /dev/fd0, to the mount point, /mnt/floppy, in the UNIX file structure. Any files stored in the directory /mnt/floppy are written to the floppy. On most UNIX systems, you can specify a few different floppy disk file systems, such as vfat for MS-DOS and Windows-based systems that use the FAT file system (which supports long filenames).

 If you don't specify the -t option with a file system type when you mount a floppy disk, the mount command automatically detects the type of file system, as with a floppy disk preformatted for FAT.

After accessing manually mounted file systems, the system administrator unmounts them using the umount command before removing the storage media, as in these examples:

```
umount /mnt/floppy
umount /mnt/cdrom
```

See Appendix B, "Syntax Guide to UNIX Commands," for a brief description of the mount and umount commands.

UNDERSTANDING PATHS AND PATHNAMES

As you learned, all UNIX files are stored in directories in the file system, starting from the root directory. To specify a file or directory, use its **pathname**, which follows the branches of the file system to the desired file. A forward slash (/) separates each directory name. For example, suppose you want to specify the location of the file phones.502. You know that it resides in the source directory in Jean's home directory, /home/jean/source, as illustrated in Figure 2-1. You can specify this file's location as /home/jean/source/phones.502.

Using Your Command-line Prompt

The UNIX command prompt may indicate your location within the file system. For example, the prompt [jean@localhost jean]$ is the **default prompt** that the system generated when the system administrator first created the login account. The prompt [jean@localhost jean]$ means that "jean" is the user working on the host machine called "localhost" in her home directory, which bears her user name, "jean." In other words, "jean is at localhost in her home directory." When Jean changes her location to /home/jean/source, her prompt looks like:

```
[jean@localhost source]$
```

When the system is initially installed, the default root prompt looks like this: [root@localhost root]#. To simplify the meaning of the command prompts in this book, the steps use $ to represent the ordinary user's command prompt and # to represent the system administrator's command prompt.

Customizing Your Prompt

Your login prompt is configured automatically when you log in. An environment variable, PS1, contains special formatting characters that determine your prompt's configuration.

To see the contents of the PS1 environment variable:

1. Type **echo $PS1** and press **Enter**.

2. You see the contents of the PS1 variable, which may appear as:

   [\u@\h \W]\$

Characters that begin with \ are special Bash shell formatting characters. \u prints the user name, \h prints the system host name, and \W prints the name of the working directory. The \$ character prints either a # or a $, depending on the type of user logged in. The brackets, [and], and the space that separates \h and \W, are not special characters, so they are printed just as they appear. When Jean is logged into the system local-host and working in her home directory, her prompt appears as [jean@localhost jean]$ in the format shown previously.

Table 2-1 shows other formatting characters for configuring your Bash shell prompt.

Table 2-1   Formatting characters for configuring a Bash shell prompt

Formatting Character	Purpose
\d	Displays the date
\h	Displays the host name
\n	Displays a new line
\nnn	Displays the ASCII character that corresponds to the octal number *nnn*
\s	Displays the shell name
\t	Displays the time
\u	Displays the user name
\w	Displays the path of the working directory
\W	Displays the name of the working directory without any other path information
\!	Displays the number of the current command in the command history
\#	Displays the number of the command in the current session
\$	Displays a # if root is the user, otherwise displays a $
\$PWD	Displays the path of the current working directory
\[	Marks the beginning of a sequence of nonprinting characters, such as a control sequence
\]	Marks the end of a sequence of nonprinting characters
\\	Displays a \ character

To configure your Bash shell prompt:

1. To change your prompt to display the date and time, type **PS1='\d \t>'** and press **Enter**. Type the command with no spaces between the characters. Your prompt now looks similar to:

   ```
   Tue Jul  5 09:18:33>
   ```

2. To change your prompt to display the current working directory, type **PS1='\w>'** and press **Enter**. Your prompt now looks similar to:

   ```
   ~>
   ```

   The \w formatting character displays the ~ to represent the user's home directory.

   To change your prompt to display the full path of the current working directory, you must use another environment variable, PWD. The PWD variable contains the full pathname of the current working directory.

3. To display the PWD variable in the prompt, type **PS1='$PWD>'** and press **Enter**. (Notice that you must place the $ in front of the environment variable name to extract its contents.) Your prompt now looks similar to:

   ```
   /home/jean>
   ```

4. Log out of the system, and log back on to reset your prompt to its default configuration.

The pwd Command

You can use the UNIX pwd command to display your current path (pwd stands for **print working directory**).

To display your current path:

1. After the $ command prompt, type **pwd** and press **Enter**. The system displays the path of your current working directory.

NAVIGATING THE FILE SYSTEM

To navigate the UNIX directory structure, use the cd (change directory) command. Its syntax is:

Syntax **cd** *directory*

Dissection

- *directory* is the name of the directory to which you want to change. The directory name is expressed as a path to the destination, with slashes (/) separating subdirectory names.

When you log in, you begin in your home directory, which is under the /home directory. When you change directories and then want to return to your home directory, type cd, and press Enter. (Some shells also use the tilde character (~) to denote the user's home directory.)

You want to go to the mail subdirectory to see if Dominion employees sent you e-mail.

To change directories:

1. First, change your prompt so that you can view the directory path. At the $ command prompt, type **PS1='$PWD>'** and press **Enter**.

2. Type **cd /var/spool/mail** and press **Enter**. This moves you to the /var/spool/mail subdirectory.

3. Type **cd** and press **Enter**. The change directory command (cd) without arguments returns you to your home directory.

UNIX refers to a path as either an absolute path or a relative path. An **absolute path** begins at the root level and lists all subdirectories to the destination file. For example, assume that Becky has a directory named lists, located under her home directory. In the lists directory, she has a file called todo. The absolute path to the todo file is /home/becky/lists/todo. The path lists each directory that lies in the path to the todo file.

> Any time the / symbol is the first character in a path, it stands for the root directory. All other / symbols in a path serve to separate the other names.

A **relative path** takes a shorter journey. You can enter the relative path to begin at your current working directory and proceed from there. In Figure 2-1, Jean, Tricia, and Joseph each have subdirectories located in their home directories. Each has a subdirectory called "source." Because Jean is working in her home directory, she can change to her source directory by typing the following command and pressing Enter:

```
cd source
```

Jean is changing to her source directory directly from her home directory, /home/jean. This example uses relative path addressing. Her source directory is one level away from her current location, /home/jean. As soon as she enters the change directory command, cd source, the system takes her to /home/jean/source, because it is relative to her current location.

If Tricia, who is in the /home/tricia directory, enters the command cd source, the system takes her to the /home/tricia/source directory. For Tricia to change to Jean's source directory, she can enter:

```
cd /home/jean/source
```

This example uses absolute path addressing, because Tricia starts from the root directory and works through all intervening directories.

To navigate directories:

1. If you are not in your home directory, type **cd** and press **Enter**.

2. The parent directory of your home directory is /home. /home is an absolute path name. Type **cd /home** and press **Enter**. The system takes you to the /home directory.

   You may now use the relative path with the cd command to return to your home directory. For example, if your user name is phillip, you can type cd phillip.

3. Type the **cd** command followed by your user name, and press **Enter**. The system takes you to your home directory.

Using Dot and Dot Dot Addressing Techniques

UNIX interprets a single **dot** character to mean the current directory, and **dot dot** (two consecutive dots) to mean the parent directory. Entering the following command keeps you in the current directory:

```
cd .
```

If you use two dots (known as dot dot), you move back to the parent directory. Do not type a space between the two dots. The next example shows how the user, jean, who is currently in the /home/jean/source directory, returns to her home directory, which is /home/jean:

```
cd ..
```

Assume you are Jean in her home directory, and want to go to Tricia's source directory. Use the following command:

```
cd ../tricia/source
```

You must always use a space after a UNIX command before including arguments to that command.

In the previous example, the dot dot tells the operating system to go to the parent directory, which is /home. The first / separator followed by the directory name tells the operating system to go forward to the tricia subdirectory. The second / separator followed by the directory name tells UNIX to go forward to the source subdirectory, the final destination. If no name precedes or follows the slash character, UNIX treats it as the root directory. Otherwise, / separates one directory from another.

To use dot and dot dot to change your working directory:

1. If you are not in your home directory, type **cd** and press **Enter**.

2. Type **cd .** and press **Enter**. Because the . (dot) references your current directory, the system did not change your working location.

3. Type **cd ..** and press **Enter**. The system takes you to the parent directory, which is /home.

4. Type **cd ..** and press **Enter**. The system takes you to the root (/) directory.

5. Type **cd** and press **Enter**. The system takes you to your home directory.

Listing Directory Contents

Use the ls (list) command to display a directory's contents, including files and other directories. When you use the ls command with no options or arguments, it displays the names of regular files and directories in your current working directory.

To see a list of files and directories in your current working directory:

1. Type **ls** and press **Enter**.

   You see a list of file and/or directory names.

You can provide an argument to the ls command to see the listing for a specific file or to see the contents of a specific directory.

To see a listing for a specific file or directory:

1. If you are not in your home directory, type **cd** and press **Enter**.

2. In Chapter 1, you used the cat command to create a notes file. You should still have that file in your home directory. Type **ls notes** and press **Enter**. The system displays the listing for the notes file.

3. To see the contents of a directory other than your current working directory, give the directory name as an option to the ls command. For example, to see the contents of the /var directory, type **ls /var** and press **Enter**. You see a listing similar to the one below.

   ```
   cache  gdm   local  log    nis   preserve   spool  yp
   db     lib   lock   mail   opt   run        tmp
   ```

You can also use options to display specific information or more information than the command alone provides. The –l option for the ls command generates a long directory listing, which includes more information about each file. You decide to print a long listing of the /etc and /home directories for the Dominion system.

To use the ls command with the -l option:

1. Type **ls -l /etc** and press **Enter**.

   You see information similar to that in Figure 2-4.

Figure 2-4   Contents of the /etc directory

2. Type **ls -l /** and press **Enter**.

   You see information similar to that in Figure 2-5.

Figure 2-5   Contents of the /directory

As you can see from the figures, the ls -l command provides more information about each item in the listing than a simple ls command. For example, look at the first item listed in Figure 2-5:

```
drwxr-xr-x    2 root    root        4096 Jan 17  09:11 bin
```

If you look in the far-right column, you see bin, the name of a file. All the columns to its left contain information about the file bin. Here is a description of the information in each column, from left to right.

- *File Type and Access Permissions*—The first column of information shown is the following set of characters:

  drwxr-xr-x

  The first character in the list, d, indicates the file is actually a directory. If bin were an ordinary file, a hyphen (–) would appear instead. The remainder of the characters indicate the file's access permissions. You learn more about these later in this chapter, in the section "Setting File Permissions."

- *Number of Links*—The second column is the number of files that are hard linked to this file. (You learn about links in Chapter 5.) If the file is a directory, this is the number of subdirectories it contains. The listing for bin shows it contains two entries. (A directory always contains at least two entries: dot and dot dot.)

- *Owner*—The third column is the owner of the file. The root user owns the bin directory.

- *Group*—The fourth column is the group that owns the file. The root group owns the bin directory.

- *Size*—The fifth column shows the size of the file in bytes.

- *Date and Time*—The sixth and seventh columns show the date and time the file was last modified.

- *Name*—The eighth column shows the file's name.

You can also use the -a option with the ls command to list **hidden files**, those with names that begin with a dot. The operating system normally uses hidden files to keep configuration information and for other purposes. The system administrator at Dominion tells you that your home directory contains a number of hidden files. You can list them using the -a option with the ls command.

To list hidden files in your home directory:

1. Type **ls -a** after the command prompt, and press **Enter**.

   You see a list similar to the one in Figure 2-6.

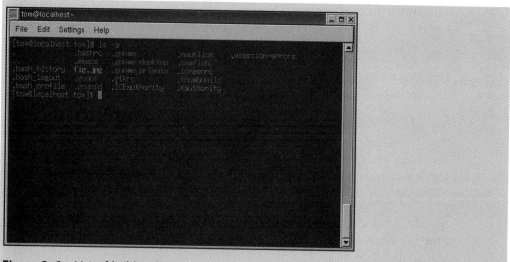

Figure 2-6   List of hidden files in the user's home directory

See Appendix B, "Syntax Guide to UNIX Commands," for a brief description of the ls command.

Using Wildcards

A wildcard is a special character that can stand for any other character or, in some cases, a group of characters. Wildcards are useful when you wish to work with several files whose names are similar or with a file whose exact name you cannot remember. UNIX supports several wildcard characters. In this section, you learn about two: * and ?.

The * wildcard represents any group of characters in a filename. For example, assume Becky has these nine files in her home directory:

```
friends
instructions.txt
list1
list2
list2b
memo_to_fred
memo_to_jill
minutes.txt
notes
```

If she enters ls *.txt and presses Enter, she sees the following output:

```
instructions.txt   minutes.txt
```

The argument *.txt causes ls to display the names of all files that end with .txt. If she enters ls memo*, she sees the following output:

```
memo_to_fred  memo_to_jill
```

If she enters the command ls *s and presses Enter, ls displays all filenames that end with "s". She sees the output:

```
friends  notes
```

The ? wildcard takes the place of only a single character. For example, if Becky types ls list? and presses Enter, ls displays all files whose names start with "list" followed by a single character. She sees the output:

```
list1  list2
```

She does not see the listing for the file list2b, because two characters follow the word "list" in its name.

To work with wildcards:

1. To practice using wildcards, you first must create a set of files with similar names. In Chapter 1, you used the cat command to create the notes file. Use the cat command now to create these five files:

   - first_name: a file containing your first name
   - middle_name: a file containing your middle name
   - last_name: a file containing your last name
   - full_name1.txt: a file containing your full name
   - full_name22.txt: another file containing your full name

2. Type **ls *name** and press **Enter.** You see first_name, last_name, and middle_name listed.

3. Type **ls full_name?.txt** and press **Enter.** You see full_name1.txt listed.

◀ LESSON B ▶

WORKING WITH FILES, DIRECTORIES, AND SECURITY

After completing this lesson, you should be able to:
♦ Create new directories to store files
♦ Copy files from one directory to another
♦ Set file permissions to let other users access your directory and files

CREATING DIRECTORIES AND FILES

As part of your work to create Dominion's centralized telephone database, your manager at Dominion, Rolfe Williamson, asks you to create directories for departments 4540 and 4550, and then create files of department phone numbers to store in those directories. You can use the mkdir (make directory) command to create a new directory, and then use the cat command to create the phone files.

To create new directories and phone files:

1. Type **cd** and press **Enter** to make sure you are in your home directory.

2. Type **mkdir dept_4540** and press **Enter** to make a new directory called dept_4540.

3. Type **ls** and press **Enter**. You see the dept_4540 directory in the listing.

4. Type **cd dept_4540** and press **Enter** to change to the new directory. Now you can use the cat command to create a file called phones1. The phones1 file contains fields for area code, phone prefix, phone number, last name, and first name. A colon (:) separates each field.

5. Type these commands, pressing **Enter** at the end of each line:

   cat > phones1
   219:432:4567:Harrison:Joel
   219:432:4587:Mitchell:Barbara
   219:432:4589:Olson:Timothy

6. Press **Ctrl+D**.

7. Type **cd** and press **Enter** to return to your /home directory.

8. Type **mkdir dept_4550** and press **Enter** to make a new directory called dept_4550.

9. Type **ls** and press **Enter**. You see the dept_4550 directory in the listing.

10. Type **cd dept_4550** and press **Enter** to change to the new directory. Now you can use the cat command to create the file phones2, which contains the same fields as the phones1 file.

11. Type these commands, pressing **Enter** at the end of each line:

    cat > phones2
    219:432:4591:Moore:Sarah
    219:432:4567:Polk:John
    219:432:4501:Robinson:Lisa

12. Press **Ctrl+D**.

You created two new directories using the mkdir command, and then created two files of phone number information using the cat command.

You can delete empty directories by using the remove directory (rmdir) command. First, use the cd command to change to the parent directory of the subdirectory you want to delete. For example, if you want to delete the old directory in /home/old, first change to the home directory. Then type rmdir *directory*, as in rmdir old, and press Enter.

COPYING FILES

You use the UNIX copy command, cp, to copy files from one directory to another. The -i option warns you that the cp command overwrites the destination file. You can also use the dot notation (current directory) as shorthand to specify the destination of a cp command.

After you create the phone file, Rolfe wants you to create a new central directory for Dominion called corp_db, and then copy the phones1 file into it. You can use the tilde character (~) to represent the location of your home directory.

To copy the phones1 file into a new directory, corp_db:

1. Type **cd** and then press **Enter** to return to your home directory.

2. Type **mkdir corp_db** and press **Enter** to make a new directory.

3. Type **cd corp_db** and press **Enter** to change to the new directory.

4. To copy the phones1 file from the dept_4540 directory to the current directory, type **cp ~/dept_4540/phones1 .** and press **Enter**.

5. To copy the phones2 file from the dept_4550 directory to the current directory, type **cp ~/dept_4550/phones2 .** and press **Enter**.

Now the Dominion central database contains two files. You can use the cat command to combine the two files, and redirect (>) the output to the corp_phones file, which lists all phone number information for the company.

To concatenate two files to one:

1. Type **cat phones1 phones2 > corp_phones** and press **Enter** to add the contents of the two phone files to one new file called corp_phones.

2. Type **more corp_phones** and press **Enter** to view the new file's contents.

As you recall from Chapter 1, the more command, which lets you display files one screen at a time, is especially useful for reading long files.

To delete files you do not need, use the remove (rm) command. First, use the cd command to change to the directory containing the file you want to delete. Then type rm *filename*. For example, to delete the file "old" in the current directory, type rm old. You may or may not receive a warning before the file is deleted. Be sure you want to remove a file permanently before using this command. You learn more about the rm command in Chapter 4.

SETTING FILE PERMISSIONS FOR SECURITY

Because UNIX is a multi-user system, users can set permissions for files they own so that others can read, write, or execute their files. The original owner of a file is the account that created it; however, file ownership can be transferred to another account. The permissions the owner sets are listed as part of the file description. Figure 2-7 shows directory listings that describe file types.

Notice the long listing of the two directories. (Remember that the directory is just another file.) An earlier section of this chapter, "Listing Directory Contents," describes the information presented in a long listing. Now you can look closer at the file permissions. For the first file described, the column on the far left shows the string of letters drwxr-xr-x. You already know the first character indicates the file type. The characters that follow are divided into three sections of file permission specifiers. There are three specifiers in each section, as illustrated in Figure 2-8.

File type	Meaning
-	Normal file
d	Subdirectory
l	Symbolic link
b	Block device file
c	Character device file

```
Excerpt from ls -l /etc

drwxr-xr-x   16 root    root         4096  Jan  17   9:29   X11
-rw-r--r--    1 root    root           46  Jan  15  19:11   adjtime
drwxr-xr-x    1 root    root         1024  Feb  27   2004   cron.daily
```

```
Excerpt from ls -l /home/jean/source

rw-rw-r--     1 jean    jean          387  Dec  12  23:11   phones.502
```

Figure 2-7   File types described in directory listings

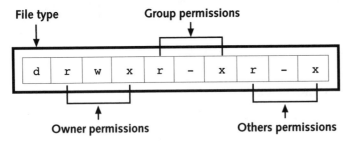

Figure 2-8   Example of file type and file permissions for a file

The first section of file permission specifiers indicates the owner's permissions. The owner, like all users, belongs to a group of users. The second section indicates the group's permissions. This specification applies to all users (other than the owner) who are members of the owner's group. The third section indicates all others' permissions. This specification applies to all users who are not the owner and not in the owner's group. In each section, the first character indicates read permissions. If an "r" appears there, that category of users has permission to read the file. The second character indicates write permission. If a "w" appears there, that category of user has permission to write to the file. The third character indicates execute permission. If an "x" appears there, that category of user has permission to execute the file. If a dash (-) appears in any of these character positions, that type of permission is denied.

If a user is granted read permission for a directory, the user can see a list of its contents. Write permission for a directory means the user can rename and delete files in the directory. Execute permission for a directory means the user can make the directory the current working directory.

From left to right, the letters rwxr-xr-x mean:

r   File's owner has read permission

w   File's owner has write permission

x   File's owner has execute permission (can run the file as a program)

r   Group has read permission

-   Group does not have write permission

x   Group has execute permission

r   Others have read permission

-   Others do not have write permission

x   Others have execute permission

You can change the pattern of permission settings by using the chmod command. For example, setting others' permissions to - - - removes all permissions for others. They cannot read, write, or execute the file. In the first line of Figure 2-7, notice that the owner has read, write, and execute (rwx) permissions for the subdirectory X11. The first character is the file type, in this case, a "d" for a subdirectory. The rwx gives the owner read, write, and execute permissions. The next r-x indicates that the group of users that shares the same group id as the owner has only read and execute permissions; the final r-x gives read and execute permissions to others. The system administrator assigns group ids when he or she adds a new user account. **Group ids** give a group of users equal access to files that they all share. Others are all other users who are not associated with the owner's group by a group id, but who have read and execute permissions.

Use the UNIX chmod command to set file permissions. In its simplest form, the chmod command takes as arguments a symbolic string followed by one or more file names. The symbolic string specifies permissions that should be granted or denied to categories of users. Here is an example: ugo+rwx. In the string, the characters ugo stand for user (same as owner), group, and others. These categories of users are affected by the chmod command. The next character, the + sign, indicates that permissions are being granted. The last set of characters, in this case rwx, indicates the permissions being granted. The symbolic string ugo+rwx indicates that read, write, and execute permissions are being granted to the owner, group, and others. Here is an example of how the symbolic string is used in a command, to modify the access permissions of myfile:

```
chmod ugo+rwx myfile
```

Here is a command that grants group read permission to the file "customers":

```
chmod g+r customers
```

It is also possible to deny permissions with a symbolic string. The following command denies the group and others write and execute permissions for the file account_info.

```
chmod go-wx account_info
```

The octal permission format is another way to assign permissions, but is more complex because it assigns a number on the basis of the type of permission and on the basis of owner, group, and other. Execute permission is assigned 1, write is 2, and read is 4. These permission numbers are added together for a value between 0 and 7. For instance, a read and write permission is a 6 (4+ 2) while read and execute is a 5 (4 + 1).

There are three numeric positions (xxx) after the chmod command. The first position gives the permission number of the owner, the second gives group permissions, and the last position gives the permission number of other. For example, the command chmod 755 myfile assigns read, write, and execute permissions to owner (7) for myfile; it assigns read and execute permissions to both group and other (5 in both positions).

If you want to set security on a directory to ensure that users must know the exact path to a file in that directory—so they can execute a program, but not snoop—configure the directory to have 711 permissions. This gives all permissions to the owner (you) and only execute permissions to group and others.

See Appendix B, "Syntax Guide to UNIX Commands," for a brief description of the chmod command.

Some versions of UNIX include the umask command, which enables you to set permissions on multiple files at one time. This command is even more complex than using chmod octal commands, but can save time for system administrators. For example, umask 022 grants rwx permissions for all users. However, you can also grant permissions on multiple files by using the wildcard asterisk (*) with chmod. For example, chmod 777 * grants full permission on all files in the current directory to all users and groups.

Rolfe wants all users to have access to the corp_phones file. To make that possible, he asks you to change the file permissions. First, permit access to your home directory. Next, allow access to the corp_db directory, and then set the permissions for everyone to read the corp_phones file. You can use the chmod command with the x argument to grant access to directories.

To change file and directory permissions:

1. Make sure that you are in your home directory.

2. Type **chmod go+x ~** and press **Enter** to allow access to your home directory.

   This command means "make your home directory (~) accessible (+x) to the group (g) and others (o)."

3. Type **chmod ugo+x ~/corp_db** and press **Enter** to allow access to the corp_db directory.

2

This command means "make the corp_db directory accessible (+x) for the owner (u), group (g), and others (o)."

4. Type **chmod ugo+r ~/corp_db/corp_phones** and press **Enter** to set permissions so everyone can read the file.

This command means "make the corp_phones file readable (+r) for the owner (u), group (g), and others (o)."

 From your home directory, you can create any subdirectory and set permissions for it. However, you cannot create subdirectories outside your home directory unless the system administrator makes a special provision.

You used the appropriate UNIX commands to create new directories to store files and set up a central directory for all users, and then you transferred files from other directories to the central directory. Finally, you changed file permissions so other users can access the directories and files you created.

CHAPTER SUMMARY

- ❏ In UNIX, a file is the basic component for data storage. UNIX considers everything to be a file, even attached devices such as the monitor, keyboard, and printer.

- ❏ A file system is the UNIX system's way of organizing files on mass storage devices such as hard and floppy disks. Files are stored on a file system, which is a hierarchical structure like a tree where top-level directories contain other directories, which in turn contain other directories. Every file can be located by using a correct and unique pathname; that is, a listing of names of directories leading to a particular file.

- ❏ The standard tree structure starts with the root (/) directory, which serves as the foundation for a nested group of other directories and subdirectories.

- ❏ The section of the disk that holds a file system is called a partition. One disk may have many partitions, each separated from the others so that it remains unaffected by external disturbances such as structural file problems associated with another partition. The UNIX file system is designed to allow access to multiple partitions after they are mounted in the tree structure.

- ❏ A path, as defined in UNIX, serves as a map to access any file on the system. An absolute path is one that always starts at the root level. A relative path is one that starts at your current location.

- ❏ You may customize your command prompt to display the current working directory name, the date, time, and several other items.

- ❏ The ls command displays the names of files and directories contained in a directory. The ls -l command and its options display all file information on the screen. This display is often called a long listing. The ls -a command shows hidden files.

❑ Wildcard characters can be used in a command, such as ls, and take the place of other characters in a file name. The * wildcard can take the place of any string of characters, and the ? wildcard can take the place of any single character.

❑ You can use the mkdir command to create a new directory as long as you own the parent directory. A file's original owner is the person who creates it, and he or she becomes the one who controls access to it (although the root account also can control access).

❑ You can use the chmod command to set permissions for files that you own. The permissions settings are rwx, which mean read, write, and execute, respectively. File permissions are set to control file access by three types of users: the owner, the group, and others. You must remember to change permission settings on any directories you own if you want others to access information in those directories. You use the execute permission (x) command to grant access to directories.

❑ You can use the cp command to copy a source file to a destination file. UNIX overwrites the destination file without warning unless you use the –i option. The dot notation (current directory) is a shorthand way to specify the destination in a cp command.

COMMAND SUMMARY

Review of Chapter 2 Commands		
Command	**Purpose**	**Options Covered in This Chapter**
cd	Change directories	
chmod	Set file permissions for specified files	
cp	Copy files from one directory to another	-i prevents overwriting of the destination file without warning
ls	Display a directory's contents, including its files and subdirectories	-a lists the hidden files -l (lowercase L) generates a long listing of the directory
mkdir	Make a new directory	
mount	Connect the file system partitions to the directory tree when the system starts; and mount additional devices, such as the CD-ROM and floppy drives	-t specifies the type of file system
pwd	Display your current path	
rm	Remove a file	
rmdir	Remove an empty directory	
umask	Set file permissions for multiple files	
umount	Disconnect the file system partitions from the directory tree	

REVIEW QUESTIONS

1. The purpose of a UNIX file system is to _____.
   a. organize files on mass storage
   b. offer hierarchical storage space for one or more users
   c. enable users to create directories
   d. all of the above
   e. only a and c

2. The standard tree structure starts at the _____ directory.
   a. home
   b. user
   c. bin
   d. root

3. For a regular user, an absolute path must always start at the _____.
   a. current directory
   b. root directory
   c. first allocated partition
   d. home directory

4. A disk partition is used to _____.
   a. allocate space for a file system
   b. compress space on a disk
   c. set permissions on files
   d. eliminate the need for home directories

5. A partition named hdb1 is the _____.
   a. first partition on IDE hard drive number 1
   b. second partition on SCSI hard drive number 2
   c. second partition on the primary SCSI hard drive
   d. first partition on IDE hard drive number 2

6. A partition named sda2 is the _____.
   a. first partition on IDE hard drive number 2
   b. first partition on the primary SCSI hard drive
   c. second partition on SCSI hard drive number 1
   d. second partition on IDE hard drive number 2

7. When you set up partitions, begin by setting up the ———————— partition, which is critical for a UNIX system.

   a. root

   b. /usr

   c. /home

   d. bin

8. Red Hat Linux operating system files and programs typically are stored in ————————.

   a. /proc

   b. /home

   c. /boot

   d. /usr

9. The ———————— partition is the storage space for users' personal files.

   a. /home

   b. /

   c. /root

   d. /bin

10. A path is a ————————.

   a. tree structure

   b. long directory listing

   c. map of partitions

   d. map to access any file on the system

11. Which of the following partitions serves as virtual memory?

   a. swap

   b. /root

   c. /etc

   d. /usr

12. The ———————— directory contains the files that hold the user account information and the user group information.

   a. /mnt

   b. /etc

   c. /lib

   d. /proc

2

13. When you type cd. and press Enter, what directory do you access?
    a. the parent directory
    b. your current directory
    c. your home directory
    d. the child directory

14. When you type cd and press Enter, what directory do you access?
    a. the parent directory
    b. your current directory
    c. your home directory
    d. the child directory

15. Which of these statements is false?
    a. You can create a child directory only in a parent directory you own.
    b. You must set the x permission for all directories that you want to access.
    c. You can use the cd .. command to move up one directory in the directory tree.
    d. The dot dot (..) refers to the parent directory.

16. By default, the ~ is shorthand for _____ directory.
    a. the parent
    b. the child
    c. your current
    d. your home

17. The \s formatting character, which is used to customize the prompt, causes the
    _____ to be displayed.
    a. time in 24–hour format
    b. host name
    c. shell name
    d. home directory name

18. The ls –l command is useful for checking file _____.
    a. permissions
    b. type
    c. size
    d. all of the above

19. When you fully view the contents of a directory, including the permissions, the _____ file type designation represents a subdirectory.

    a. f

    b. d

    c. –

    d. space

20. Which of these grants the group read and write access to the accounts file?

    a. chmod g+rw accounts

    b. chmod g+rx accounts

    c. chmod o+rx accounts

    d. chmod g–rw accounts

21. Which command enables you to view the current directory path?

    a. ls

    b. rwx

    c. pwd

    d. rm

22. The _____ environment variable stores the command–line prompt.

    a. PWD

    b. PROMPT

    c. PATH

    d. PS1

23. When you use the cp command, you should be aware that _____.

    a. the dot destination places the file in the parent directory

    b. the destination file overlays a file with the same name

    c. it destroys the source file

    d. the source file cannot be relatively addressed

24. The remote directory is in the user's home directory. To copy a file from the remote directory to the current directory, type _____.

    a. cp ~/remote/*filename* .

    b. cp +/*filename*

    c. cp > /remote/*filename*

    d. cp/remote/*filename*

25. The –i option, used with the cp command, causes the cp command to
_____.

    a. ignore any requests not to overwrite the destination file, if it already exists

    b. insert the file being copied into the existing destination file

    c. warn you that it overwrites the destination file

    d. none of the above

DISCOVERY EXERCISES

1. Use the cd command to access the /mnt directory.

2. After you access the /mnt directory in Discovery Exercise 1, type ls –l to view its contents. What files do you see listed?

3. Use the cd command to return to your home directory, and then use pwd to verify that you are in your home directory.

4. The file notice.txt is in the directory notices, which is in the directory public. The public directory is in Tom's home directory. (Tom's user name is tom.) What is the absolute path to the notice.txt file?

5. If your current working directory is the notices directory (under Tom's home directory), what is the relative path to the notices.txt file?

6. List an example of the cd command showing how to use absolute path addresses.

7. List an example of the cd command showing how to use relative path addresses. Log in and display the directories in /bin, /sbin, and /etc.

8. List the chmod symbolic string that grants read, write, and execute permission to a file's owner and group.

9. List the chmod symbolic string that denies a file's read, write, and execute permission to all users who are not the owner or not in the owner's group.

10. Create a file in your home directory using the cat command. Change permissions so that no one can access that file.

11. Log in as another user, and try to access the files you previously created. Log in again under your account, and modify the files so they are accessible. (To complete this exercise, ask your instructor for another account and password that you can use.)

12. Change your prompt to display the time.

13. Use the chmod command to protect your home directory from access by anyone but you.

14. Use the ls command option to list hidden files in your home directory.

15. Use the absolute path to change to the /etc directory. From the /etc directory, change to the X11 directory using the relative path. Now list the .bashrc file in your home directory using the ls command. (Stay in the current location to do this.)

16. In the command line, type cd ~/../.. and press Enter. Where are you now located in the tree structure? Explain how you got there.

17. In the command line, type cd ~/../../etc/X11 and press Enter. Where are you now located in the tree structure? Explain how you got there.

18. Using the relative path from your home directory, enter the cat command to display the contents of the /etc/passwd file.

19. Use the cd command to return to your home directory. Redirect the output of the date command to a file named chap2info. Use the ls command to get a long listing for this file. What permissions do the owner, group, and others have?

20. Change the permissions for the chap2info file to read and write for the owner, and deny permissions for anyone else. Look at a long listing to confirm that the changes took effect.

21. Modify your command prompt so that it always displays the absolute path of your current working directory.

22. Create a directory called tempdir, in your home directory. Use the cd command to switch to the tempdir directory. Use the cat command to create a file, called tempfile, in your tempdir directory. Go back to your home directory, and try to delete the tempdir directory. What happens? Use the man command to see if you can find a way to delete the tempdir directory without first deleting the tempfile within it.

23. Use the mount command with no options to see what devices and file systems are mounted.

3

THE UNIX EDITORS

All employees at Dominion Consulting write weekly memos summarizing their activities and accomplishments. They write these memos using a UNIX text editor, which lets them create and modify simple text-based documents. UNIX includes at least two text editors—vi editor and Emacs. As part of your UNIX training, your manager at Dominion Consulting, Rolfe Williams, asks you to use these editors to create two versions of the same memo summarizing basic features of text files.

This chapter introduces two UNIX editors. An **editor** is a program for creating and modifying computer documents such as programs and data files. Files may contain notes, memos, or program source code, for example. A **text editor** is like a simplified word processing program; you can use a text editor to create and edit documents, but you cannot format them using bold-faced, centered text or other features. All operating systems have a standard editor; many also include alternate editors. In UNIX systems, you nearly always find two popular editors, the vi editor and the Emacs editor. Linux contains both editors, with users often preferring to use the vi editor.

◀ LESSON A ▶

THE vi EDITOR

> **After completing this lesson, you should be able to:**
> - Describe an ASCII text file
> - Explain why operating system editors use ASCII files
> - Create and edit simple documents using the vi editor

UNDERSTANDING UNIX FILES

Almost everything you create in UNIX is stored in a file. All information stored in files is in the form of binary digits. A **binary digit**, called a **bit** for short, is in one of two states. The states are 1 (on) and 0 (off). They can indicate, for example, the presence or absence of a voltage in an electronic circuit. Because the computer consists of electronic circuits that are either in an on or off state, binary numbers are perfectly suited to report these states. The exclusive use of 0s and 1s as a way to communicate with the computer is known as **machine language**. The earliest programmers had to write their programs using machine language, a tedious and time-consuming process.

ASCII Text Files

To make information stored in files accessible, computer designers established a standard method for translating binary numbers into plain English. This standard uses a string of eight binary numbers, called a **byte,** which is an acronym for "binary term." A byte can be configured into fixed patterns of bits, and these patterns can be interpreted as an alphabetic character, decimal number, punctuation mark, or a special character, such as &, *, or @. Each byte, or **code**, has been standardized into a set of bit patterns known as ASCII codes. **ASCII** stands for the American Standard Code for Information Interchange. Computer files containing nothing but printable characters are called **text files**, and files that contain nonprintable characters, such as machine instructions, are called **binary files**. Figure 3-1 lists the printable and nonprintable ASCII characters.

Binary Files

Computers are not limited to processing ASCII codes. To work with graphic information, such as icons, illustrations, and other images, binary files can include strings of bits representing white and black dots, where each black dot represents a 1 and each white dot a 0. Graphics files include bit patterns—rows and columns of dots called a **bitmap**—that must be translated by graphics software, commonly called a graphics viewer, which transforms a complex array of bits into an image.

Printing Characters (Punctuation Characters)

Dec	Octal	Hex	ASCII
32	040	20	(Space)
33	041	21	!
34	042	22	"
35	043	23	#
36	044	24	$
37	045	25	%
38	046	26	&
39	047	27	'
40	050	28	(
41	051	29	)
42	052	2A	*
43	053	2B	+
44	054	2C	,
45	055	2D	-
46	056	2E	.
47	057	2F	/

(Decimal Numbers—Print)

Dec	Octal	Hex	ASCII
48	060	30	0
49	061	31	1
50	062	32	2
51	063	33	3
52	064	34	4
53	065	35	5
54	066	36	6
55	067	37	7
56	070	38	8
57	071	39	9

Printing Characters (Alphabet—Upper Case)

Dec	Octal	Hex	ASCII
65	101	41	A
66	102	42	B
67	103	43	C
68	104	44	D
69	105	45	E
70	106	46	F
71	107	47	G
72	110	48	H
73	111	49	I
74	112	4A	J
75	113	4B	K
76	114	4C	L
77	115	4D	M
78	116	4E	N
79	117	4F	O
80	120	50	P
81	121	51	Q
82	122	52	R
83	123	53	S
84	124	54	T
85	125	55	U
86	126	56	V
87	127	57	W
88	130	58	X
89	131	59	Y
90	132	5A	Z

Printing Characters (Alphabet—Lower Case)

Dec	Octal	Hex	ASCII
97	141	61	a
98	142	62	b
99	143	63	c
100	144	64	d
101	145	65	e
102	146	66	f
103	147	67	g
104	150	68	h
105	151	69	i
106	152	6A	j
107	153	6B	k
108	154	6C	l
109	155	6D	m
110	156	6E	n
111	157	6F	o
112	160	70	p
113	161	71	q
114	162	72	r
115	163	73	s
116	164	74	t
117	165	75	u
118	166	76	v
119	167	77	w
120	170	78	x
121	171	79	y
122	172	7A	z

(Special Characters—Print)

Dec	Octal	Hex	ASCII
58	072	3A	:
59	073	3B	;
60	074	3C	<
61	075	3D	=
62	076	3E	>
63	077	3F	?
64	080	40	@

Nonprinting Characters (Abridged)
Control Characters

Dec	Octal	Hex	ASCII
0	000	00	^@ (Null)
7	007	07	Bell
8	010	08	Backspace
9	011	09	Tab
10	012	0A	LineFeed, Newline
11	013	0B	Vertical Tab
12	014	0C	Formfeed
13	015	0D	Carriage return

Figure 3-1   ASCII characters

Executable Program Files

Many programmers develop source code for their programs by writing text files; then they compile these files to convert them into executable program files. Programmers and users also develop scripts, which are files containing commands. Scripts are typically not compiled into machine code prior to running, but are executed through an interpreter.

At the time the script is run, the interpreter looks at each line and converts the commands on each line into action taken by the computer. Scripts are interpreted program files that are executable.

Compiled and interpreted files that can be run are called **executable program files**. These files can be run from the command line.

Using Editors

Editors let you create and edit ASCII files. UNIX normally includes the two editors vi and Emacs. They are **screen editors**: they display the text you are editing one screen at a time, and let you move around the screen to change and add text. You can also use a line editor to edit text files. A **line editor** lets you work with only one line or group of lines at a time. Although line editors do not let you see the context of your editing, they are useful for general tasks such as searching, replacing, and copying blocks of text.

Using the vi Editor

The vi editor is so called because it is visual—it immediately displays on screen the changes you make to text. It is also a **modal editor**; that is, it works in three modes: insert mode, command mode, and extended (ex) command set mode. **Insert mode**, which lets you enter text, is accessed by typing the letter i after the vi editor is started. **Command mode**, which is started by pressing Esc, lets you enter commands to perform editing tasks, such as moving through the file and deleting text. The **ex mode** employs an extended set of commands that were initially used in an early UNIX editor called ex. You can access this mode by pressing Esc to enter the command mode, and then type colon (:) to enter extended commands at the bottom of the screen.

Now you're ready to write your first memo using the vi editor. To do so, you complete the following tasks:

- Create a new file in the vi editor
- Insert, edit, and delete text
- Search and replace text
- Add text from other files
- Copy, cut, and paste text
- Print a file
- Save a file, and exit vi

There are different versions of the vi editor included in different versions of UNIX. The commands described in this chapter generally apply to most UNIX vi editor versions. However, they particularly apply to the vi editor in Red Hat Linux, which is technically called the vim (vi improved) editor.

Creating a New File in the vi Editor

Start by creating a file called temp to hold your first memo summarizing the basic features of text files. To start vi and create a new file, you type vi followed by the new file's name.

To enter vi and create a new file:

1. After the $ command prompt, type **vi temp** and press **Enter**. This starts vi and begins editing a new file called temp. Your screen should look similar to Figure 3-2.

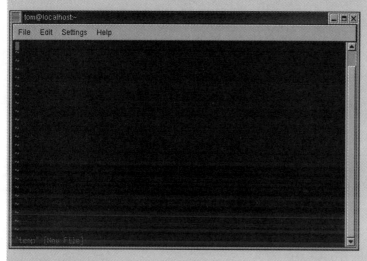

Figure 3-2   vi editor's opening screen

In the upper-left corner of your screen, you see the cursor, shown in Figure 3-2 as a solid block. The cursor indicates your current location in the file.

The line containing the cursor is the **current line**. Lines containing tildes (~) are not part of the file; they indicate lines on the screen only, not lines of text in the file.

Inserting Text

When you start the vi editor, you're in command mode. This means that the editor interprets anything you type on the keyboard as a command. Before you can insert text in your new file, you must use the i (insert) command.

To insert text in the temp file:

1. Type **i** (but do not press Enter).

   Like most vi commands, the i command does not appear (or echo) on your screen. The command switches you from command mode to insert mode; you don't need to press Enter to signal the command's completion.

2. Type the text shown in Figure 3-3.

   If you need to delete characters, press the **Backspace** key. Press **Enter** at the end of each line to move to the next line.

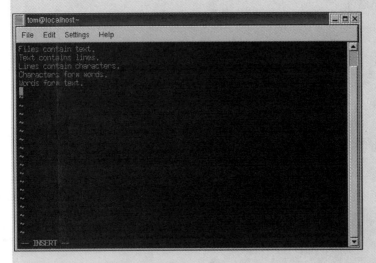

Figure 3-3   Inserting text with the vi editor

In insert mode, every character you type appears on the screen. To switch to command mode, press Esc.

Repeating a Change

Use the repeat (.) command to repeat the most recent change you made. Because you just inserted text, the repeat command repeats the insertion, duplicating the inserted text. You can add the next item in your memo by repeating the previous line, and then editing it.

To repeat your last edit command:

1. Press **Esc** to switch to command mode.

2. Type **.** (period).

The vi editor inserts the last text you typed below the current line. Your screen should look similar to the one in Figure 3-4.

3

```
tom@localhost~
File  Edit  Settings  Help
Files contain text.
Text contains lines.
Lines contain characters.
Characters form words.
Words form text.
Files contain text.
Text contains lines.
Lines contain characters.
Characters form words.
Words form text.
~
~
~
~
~
~
~
~
```

Figure 3-4 Repeating a command in the vi editor

Now you're ready to edit the text you just inserted. Start by moving the cursor around the screen, and then deleting unnecessary text.

Moving the Cursor

You can move the cursor when you are in command mode. Start by moving around the screen to get a feel for the commands, and then move to the particular line you want to edit.

To move the cursor around the screen:

1. Press **Esc** to make sure you are in command mode.

2. Press the arrow keys to move up, down, left, and right one character at a time.

3. Type **H** to move the cursor to the upper-left corner of the screen.

   (*Hint*: Make sure you type capital letters as indicated in these steps.)

4. Type **L** to move the cursor to the last line on the screen.

5. Type **G** to go to the beginning of the last line. This is the go to command. You can include a number before the G to indicate the line to which you want to move.

6. Type **2G** to move to the beginning of the second line.

In addition to these commands, you can use other commands to move the cursor. Table 3-1 summarizes the vi editor's cursor movement keys.

Table 3-1   vi editor's cursor movement keys

Key	Movement
h or left arrow	Left one character position
l or right arrow	Right one character position
k or up arrow	Up one line
j or down arrow	Down one line
H	Upper-left corner of the screen
L	Last line on the screen
nG	Go to the line specified by a number, n
w	Forward one word
b	Back one word
0 (zero)	To the beginning of the current line
$	To the end of the current line
Ctrl+U	Up one-half screen
Ctrl+D	Down one-half screen
Ctrl+F or Pg down	Forward one screen
Ctrl+B or Pg up	Back one screen

Remember that the control key combinations and the letter keys shown in Table 3-1 are designed to work in command mode. The arrow keys, which are used for moving around text, work in both command and insert mode.

 Using the letter keys to move the cursor dates back to the days when UNIX used teletype terminals that had no arrow keys. Designers of vi chose the letter keys because of their relative position on the keyboard.

Deleting Text

Now that you know how to insert text and move around a file, you are ready to delete text. To do so, move to a character, and then type x to delete that character. You can also combine many delete commands with cursor movement commands to delete more than one character. Table 3-2 summarizes the most common delete commands.

Table 3-2   vi editor's delete commands

Command	Purpose
x	Delete the character at the cursor
dd	Delete the current line
dw	Delete the word starting at the cursor; if the cursor is in the middle of the word, delete from the cursor to the end of the line
d$ or D	Delete from the cursor to the end of the line
d0	Delete from the cursor to the start of the line

Now you can use the delete commands and the cursor movement keys to edit text you inserted in your memo.

To edit the temp file by deleting text:

1. Press **Esc** to make sure you are in command mode.

2. Type **1G** to move to the first line of the file. You want to delete this line.

3. To delete the first line, type **dd** (but do not press Enter).

   Your file should now look like Figure 3-5.

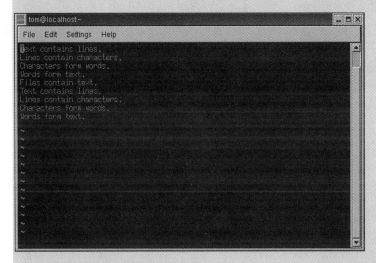

Figure 3-5   Memo after deleting the first line

4. Press **w** to go to the next word, "contains."

5. Type **dw** to delete the current word (so the line now reads "Text lines"), and then type **i** to enter insert mode.

6. Type **consistss of** between "Text" and "lines." Be sure to include the extra "s."

7. Press the arrow keys to move the cursor to the extra "s" in "consistss," and then press **Esc** to switch to command mode.

8. To delete the current character (the extra "s"), type **x** (but do not press Enter).

   Your memo should now look like the one in Figure 3-6.

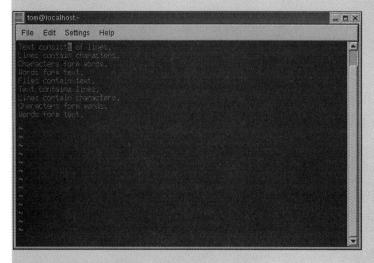

Figure 3-6 Memo after editing

Now you want to edit the sentence, "Files contain text," by deleting the last word.

9. Press the arrow keys to move to the sentence, "Files contain text," and then move to the "c" in "contain."

10. Type **d$** to delete the text from the cursor to the end of the line, and then type **i** to switch to insert mode.

11. Type **consist of words.** to complete the sentence.

    Now you can edit the next sentence by replacing the first word.

12. Press the arrow keys to move to the next line in the file, move to the initial character in the word "lines," and then press **Esc** to switch back to command mode.

13. Type **d0** to delete the text from the cursor to the beginning of the line, and then type **i** to enter insert mode.

14. Type **Words form** to insert that text at the beginning of the sentence.

15. Your completed memo should look like the one in Figure 3-7.

3

Figure 3-7   Completed memo after editing

The vi editor offers you alternatives for copying, cutting, and pasting text.

 The delete line command, dd, actually places deleted lines in a buffer. You can then use the paste command, p, to paste deleted (cut) lines elsewhere in the text. (Position the cursor where you want to paste them.) To copy and paste text, use the yank command, yy, to copy the lines. After yanking the lines you want to paste elsewhere, move the cursor, and type p to paste the text in the current location.

Undoing a Command

If you complete a command and then realize you want to reverse its effects, you can use the undo command. For example, if you delete a few lines from a file by mistake, type u to restore the text.

Searching for a Pattern

You can search forward for a pattern of characters by typing a forward slash (/), typing the pattern you are seeking, and then pressing Enter. For example, suppose you want to know how many times you used the word "consist" or "consists" in your memo.

 To search for a pattern of text to find either word:

1. Press **Esc** to make sure you are in command mode.

2. Type **H** to move the cursor to the top of the screen.

3. Type **/cons** to search for the string "cons."

4. Press **Enter**. The cursor moves to the beginning of the word "consists" on line 1.

5. To search for the next occurrence of "cons," press **n** (for next). The cursor moves to the beginning of the word "consist" on the fifth line.

   If you had searched for "/con," you would have first found "consist" on line 1 and then "contain" on line 2.

6. To see file status information, press **Ctrl+g** (or **Ctrl+G** this is one instance in which you can use uppercase or lowercase in UNIX). Your screen should look like the one in Figure 3-8.

Figure 3-8   vi status line

The **status line** at the bottom of the screen displays information, including line-oriented commands (explained later in this lesson) and error messages.

Searching and Replacing

Let's say you want to change all occurrences of "text" in your memo to "documents." Instead of searching for "text," and then deleting and inserting "documents," you can search and replace with one command. The commands you learned so far are screen-oriented. Commands that can perform more than one action (searching and replacing) are **line-oriented commands** and they operate in the ex mode.

3

Screen-oriented commands execute at the location of the cursor. You do not need to tell the computer where to perform the operation: it takes place relative to the cursor. Line-oriented commands, on the other hand, require you to specify an exact location (an **address**) for the operation. Screen-oriented commands are easy to type, and their changes appear on the screen. Typing line-oriented commands is more complicated, but they can execute independently of the cursor and in more than one place in a file.

A colon (:) precedes all line-oriented commands. It acts as a prompt on the status line. Enter line-oriented commands on the status line, and press Enter when you complete the command.

In this chapter, all instructions for line-oriented commands include the colon as part of the command.

To search for a pattern of characters:

1. Press **Esc** to make sure you are in command mode.

2. Type **/form** and press **Enter**. This command instructs vi to search for the first occurrence of the word "form," and moves the cursor under that word.

3. Type **n** to repeat the search. vi locates the next occurrence of the word "form."

To search for "text" and replace it with "documents":

1. Press **Esc** to make sure you are in command mode.

2. Type **:1,$s/text/documents/g** (but do not press Enter). This command means "From the first line (1) to the end of the file ($), search for 'text' and replace it with 'documents' (s/text/documents/) everywhere it occurs on each line (g)."

3. Press **Enter**. Your screen should look like the one illustrated in Figure 3-9.

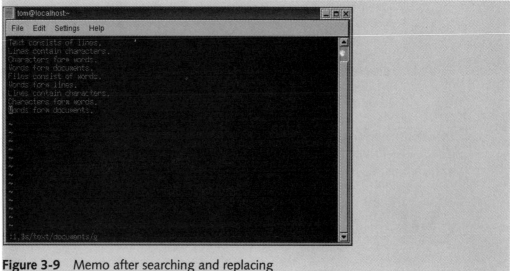

Figure 3-9   Memo after searching and replacing

Note that the word "Text" in line 1 remains unchanged because it is capitalized. By default, case matters in searches.

Saving a File and Exiting vi

As you edit a file, saving your changes is a good idea. You should always save the file before you exit vi; otherwise, you lose your changes.

To save the temp file:

1. Press **Esc**, if necessary, to enter the command mode.

2. Type **:x** and then press **Enter** to save your changes, exit the vi editor, and return to the UNIX shell.

While in command mode, you can also use :wq (write and quit) or ZZ to exit the editor after you save the file on disk. To save a file and continue working with the vi editor, type :w (but do not press Enter).

Adding Text from Another File

Sometimes the text you want to include in one file is already part of another file. For example, let's say you want a separate copy of the text in the file temp so you can use it to practice editing. Start by creating a new file called practice, and then add text from the temp file by using the line-oriented r (read) command.

To create a new file, and add text from another file:

1. Type **vi practice** and press **Enter** to create a new file.

2. Press **Esc** to make sure you are in command mode.

3. Type **:r temp** (but do not press Enter).

   Your file should look like the one illustrated in Figure 3-10. The status line provides information about the file you added, including its name and the number of lines and characters it contains.

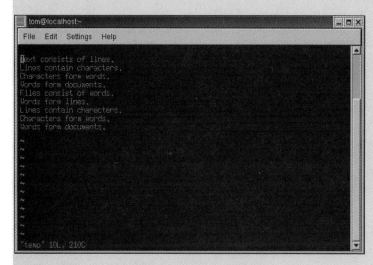

Figure 3-10   Adding text from another file

   The r command copied the text from temp, and put it in the current file, practice. Notice the blank line at the top of the file.

4. Move the cursor to the blank line, and type **dd** to delete it.

Leaving vi Temporarily

If you want to execute other UNIX commands while you work with vi, you can launch a shell or other commands from within vi. For example, let's say you are working on your memo for Dominion, and want to quickly check the current date.

To leave vi temporarily to find the current date and time:

1. Press **Esc** to enter the command mode.

2. Type **:!date** and press **Enter**.

   You see today's date and instructions for returning to command mode.

3. Press **Enter** to return to command mode.

When you want to run several command-line commands without first closing your vi session, use the Ctrl+z option to display the command line.

To access the command line to execute several commands:

1. Type **Ctrl+z** to access the command line.

2. Type **ls -l** to execute a command.

3. Type **fg** to return to your vi edit session.

Changing Your Display While Editing

Besides using the vi editing commands, you can also set options in vi to control editing parameters such as line number display and whether case matters in searches. Turn on line numbering when you want to work with a range of lines, for example, when you're deleting or cutting and pasting a block of text. Then you can refer to the line numbers to specify the text. You decide to delete the last three lines from your memo. Turn on line numbering first, and then use a delete command.

To use automatic line numbering:

1. Press **Esc** to be certain you are in the command mode.

2. Type **:set number** and press **Enter**.

   Your redrawn screen shows line numbers to the left of the text. Your screen should look like the one in Figure 3-11.

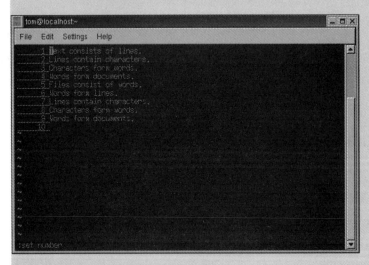

Figure 3-11 Changing your display

Line numbers are for reference only. They are not part of the file. Now you can use these reference numbers to delete the last three lines in the file.

3. Type **:7,9d** and press **Enter**.

You deleted the last three lines of the file.

Copying or Cutting and Pasting

You can use the yy command in vi to copy a specified number of lines from a file and place them on the clipboard. To delete the lines from the file and store them on the clipboard, use the dd command. Now you want to reorganize your document so that the first three lines are at the end of the file. You can use cut and paste commands to make this change.

To cut and paste text:

1. From the command mode, type **H** to move the cursor to the beginning of line 1.

2. Type **3dd** to cut the first 3 lines from the document and store them in the buffer.

3. Type **G** to move the cursor to the end of the file.

4. Type **p** to paste the three lines at the end of the file.

Printing Text Files

You can use the lpr (line print) shell command to print a file. Type !lpr and then type the name of the file you want to print.

To print a file:

1. Press **Esc**, if necessary, to return to command mode.

2. Type **:w** and press **Enter** to save the practice file.

3. Type **:!lpr practice** and press **Enter**. This prints the file practice in the current directory on the default printer.

You can also specify which printer you want to use with the -Pprinter option. For example, you may use two printers, lp1 and lp2. To print the practice file on lp2, type :!lpr-Plp2 practice and press Enter.

Canceling an Editing Session

If necessary, you can cancel an editing session, so that you discard all the changes you made. Another option is to save only the changes you made since last using the :w command. You decide to make one more change in the practice file, and then decide to exit without saving it.

To make an additional change, and then cancel without saving it:

1. Press **Esc** to access the command mode.

2. With the cursor at the beginning of the top line (type **H** if it is not), type **dd** (but do not press Enter).

3. Type **:q!** and press **Enter**.

4. Type **vi practice** and press **Enter**. Notice that the sentence "Words form documents." is back in the file on line 1 because your change in Step 2 was not saved.

5. Type **:q!** and press **Enter**.

You can access help documentation after you start the vi editor by typing Esc, then :, and then help. Type :q! to exit the help file.

◀ LESSON B ▶

THE EMACS EDITOR

After completing this lesson, you should be able to:

♦ Compare and contrast the features of Emacs and the vi editor

♦ Become familiar with the most important Emacs editor commands

♦ Create and edit simple documents using the Emacs editor

USING THE EMACS EDITOR

Emacs is another UNIX text editor that has gained popularity but, due to its complexity, continues to run second to the vi editor. Unlike vi, Emacs is not modal: it does not switch from command mode to insert mode. This means that you can type a command without verifying that you are in the proper mode. Although Emacs is more complex than vi, it is more consistent. For example, you can enter most commands by pressing Alt or Ctrl key combinations.

Emacs also supports a sophisticated macro language. A **macro** is a set of commands that automates a complex task. Think of a macro as a "super-instruction." Emacs has a powerful command syntax and is extensible. Its packaged set of customized macros lets you read electronic mail and news, and edit the contents of directories. Emacs is reputed to have more features than any other UNIX program. You can start learning Emacs by learning its common commands. Table 3-3 lists these commands.

Table 3-3   Common emacs commands

Alt Command	Purpose	Ctrl Command	Purpose
Alt+<	Move cursor to start of file	Ctrl+@	Mark the cursor location. After moving the cursor, you can move or copy text to the mark.
Alt+>	Move cursor to end of file	Ctrl+A	Move cursor to start of line
Alt+B	Move cursor back one word	Ctrl+B	Move cursor back one character
Alt+D	Delete current word	Ctrl+D	Delete the character under cursor
Alt+F	Move cursor forward one word	Ctrl+E	Move cursor to end of line
Alt+Q	Reformat current paragraph using word wrap so that lines are full	Ctrl+F	Move cursor forward one paragraph using word wrap so that lines are full
Alt+T	If the cursor is under the first character of the word, transpose the word with the preceding word; if the cursor is not under the first character, transpose the word with the following word	Ctrl+G	Cancel the current command
Alt+U	Capitalize all letters of the current word	Ctrl+H	Use online help
Alt+W	Scroll up one screen	Ctrl+K	Delete text to the end of the line
Alt+x doctor	Enter doctor mode to play a game in which Emacs responds to your statements with questions. Save your work first. Not all versions support this mode.	Ctrl+N	Move cursor to next line
		Ctrl+P	Move cursor to preceding line
		Ctrl+T	Transpose the character before the cursor and the character under the cursor
		Ctrl+V	Scroll down one screen
		Ctrl+W	Delete marked text. Press **Ctrl+Y** to restore deleted text.
		Ctrl+Y	Insert text from the file buffer, and place it after the cursor
		Ctrl+H, T	Run a tutorial about Emacs

3

Table 3-3   Common emacs commands (continued)

Alt Command	Purpose	Ctrl Command	Purpose
		Ctrl+X, Ctrl+C	Exit Emacs
		Ctrl+X, Ctrl+S	Save the file
		Ctrl+X, U	Undo the last change
		Ctrl+Del	Delete the character under the cursor

In most cases, Ctrl and Alt commands in Emacs are not case sensitive, so Alt+B and Alt+b are the same command.

You can use Emacs to duplicate your first memo for Dominion Consulting. To do so, you complete the following tasks:

- Create a new file in Emacs
- Edit and delete text
- Copy, cut, and paste text

Creating a New File in Emacs

You can start Emacs by typing the emacs command in the terminal window. If you type a filename after this command, Emacs creates a new, blank file with that name, or opens an existing file with that name. If you type emacs with no filename, Emacs displays the introductory list of a few important commands, shown in Figure 3-12. If the Emacs window exceeds the length of the screen, maximize the window by using the controls on the top border of the window.

If you are using the GNOME interface, open the Emacs editor by clicking the foot (Main Menu) icon, clicking Programs, clicking Applications, and then clicking Emacs.

Figure 3-12   Emacs opening screen (without a filename)

As Figure 3-12 illustrates, there is a menu bar at the top of the Emacs screen. When you click one of the items, such as Edit, a menu appears, as shown in Figure 3-13. The default menu bar has the following categories:

- *Buffers*—Enable you to open any of the editor's storage buffers that currently hold information, including the text that is already in the file

- *Files*—Used for operations such as opening a file, opening a directory, saving information in a buffer, killing a buffer, inserting information from another file, and going into the split window mode

- *Tools*—Used for printing a file, comparing or merging files, installing Emacs patches, reading and sending e-mail, and even compiling code

- *Edit*—Offers text editing functions such as undoing a change, cutting or copying text, pasting text, and so on (see Figure 3-13)

- *Search*—Provides all kinds of search options, plus the ability to place tags in a document so that you can easily return to a certain location or mark text to be copied

- *Mule*—Used to set the language environment, fonts, and the input method

- *Help*—Provides assistance through access to manuals, a tutorial, and in customizing the Emacs editor

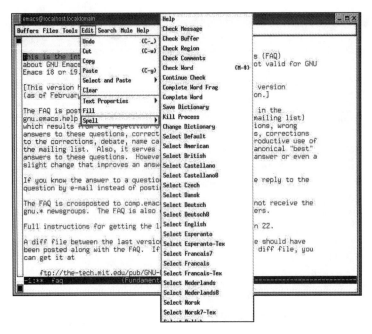

Figure 3-13   Emacs edit menu and spelling options

Start by creating a file called practice.fil that contains the same text as your original temp memo for Dominion Consulting.

To start Emacs, and create a file called practice.fil:

1. Type **emacs practice.fil** and then press **Enter**.

   You see the opening screen; its status bar indicates you are creating a new file.

2. To add text to the file, type the text you see in Figure 3-14.

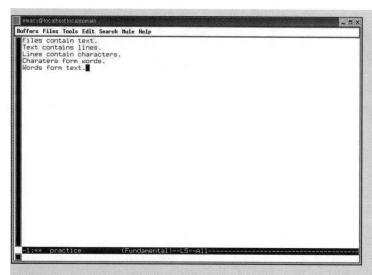

Figure 3-14 Creating a new file in Emacs

3. Press **Ctrl+x** and then **Ctrl+s** to save the file.

4. Press **Ctrl+x** and then **Ctrl+c** to exit the file.

In Emacs, you must press the two Ctrl key combinations to save and exit a file.

Editing an Emacs File

To navigate an Emacs file, you can use either the cursor movement keys—such as the arrow keys, Pg up, Pg down, Home, and End—or Ctrl key combinations. Before editing the file named practice.fil, move around the file a bit to get used to using the Ctrl and Alt key combinations (see Table 3-3) for moving the cursor to different places.

To navigate the practice file:

1. To return to Emacs via the command line and retrieve your file, type **emacs practice.fil** and press **Enter**.

2. Press **Ctrl+f** to move forward one character, and then press the **right arrow** key.

3. Press **Ctrl+b** to move back one character, and then press the **left arrow** key.

4. Use the **down arrow** and **up arrow** keys to move down and up through lines in the document. Place the cursor on the line that begins "Lines contain…"

To delete text and undo the deletion:

1. Press **Ctrl+k** to delete the current line.

2. Press **Ctrl+x** and then type **u** to undo the last change.

You can restore the text repeatedly, even after making many changes. Press Ctrl+x, and then u. Use this command to undo your editing commands in sequence.

In Emacs, you can insert text simply by typing. You can also insert text by copying and pasting, or by cutting and pasting. For instance, you can copy the first two lines of the practice file and paste them at the end of the file.

To copy and paste text in Emacs:

1. Move the cursor to the beginning of the sentence "Characters form words."

2. Press **Ctrl+Spacebar**. This marks the starting point for the block of text you want to copy. You see the words "Mark set" in the status bar.

3. Press the **down arrow** key twice to move the cursor to the first empty line below the text.

4. Press **Alt+w**. This marks the end of the text block to copy, briefly moves the cursor to the location you marked in Step 2, and then goes back down to the end of the text. You can also hold down Esc and press w to mark the end of the block.

5. Press **Ctrl+y** to paste the marked text from the clipboard into the buffer.

To cut and paste rather than copy and paste, press Ctrl+w when the cursor is at the end of the block you want cut.

Like the vi editor, Emacs lets you search for specific text. For example, suppose you want to find the text "on" in your practice document.

To search for specific words:

1. Press **Ctrl+s**. You see the "I-search" prompt in the status line. You can now type the text you are seeking.

2. Type **on** (but do not press Enter).

3. Press **Ctrl+s** to search for the next occurrence of "on." Press **Ctrl+s** again.

4. Press **Ctrl+r** to search backward for the previous occurrence of "on."

To search using the menu bar Search option:

1. Type **Alt+<** to move to the beginning of the file.

2. Click the **Search** menu.

3. Click **Search** on the menu, and notice that the cursor goes to the status line at the bottom of the screen.

4. Type **on** in the status line, and press **Enter**.

5. Click the **Search** menu, and click **Repeat Search** to locate the next occurrence of "on."

6. Click the **Search** menu, and click **Repeat Backwards** to search for "on" backwards.

3

To reformat the document to use word wrap:

1. Type **Alt+<** to move to the beginning of the file.

2. Press **Alt+Q** to reformat the file so the lines are full of text (words wrap around from one line to the next).

After working with the practice document, you're ready to exit Emacs. To do so, follow the instructions in the earlier section, "Creating a New File in Emacs." (Press Ctrl+x and Ctrl+s to save the file, and then press Ctrl+x and Ctrl+c to exit the file.)

Use the Emacs tutorial to learn more about the Emacs editor. Click the Help menu and click Emacs Tutorial; or in most versions of Emacs, type Ctrl+h and then type t.

CHAPTER SUMMARY

- Bytes are computer characters stored using numeric codes. A set of standardized codes known as ASCII codes is often used. ASCII stands for the American Standard Code for Information Interchange. Computer files that contain only ASCII characters (bytes) are called text files.

- The vi editor is a popular choice among UNIX users. Standard editors process text files. Text files are also called flat files or ASCII files. The vi editor is a modal editor, because it works in three modes: insert, command, and ex mode. Insert mode lets you enter text, while command mode lets you navigate the file and modify the text. The ex mode is used to access an extended set of commands, including the commands to save and exit a file.

- In the vi editor's insert mode, characters you type are inserted in the file. They are not interpreted as vi commands. To exit insert mode and re-enter command mode, press Esc.

❐ With vi, you initially edit a copy of the file placed in the computer's memory. You do not alter the file itself until you save it on disk.

❐ The Emacs editor is popular as an alternative to the vi editor, and along with vi, is included with most UNIX systems, including Linux.

❐ Unlike vi, Emacs is not modal. (That is, it does not switch between modes.) Emacs has a powerful command syntax, is extensible, and supports a sophisticated language of macro commands. A macro is a set of commands designed to simplify a complex task. Emacs' packaged set of customized macros lets you read electronic mail and news, and edit the contents of directories.

❐ You can start Emacs by typing emacs at the command line with or without a filename. If you enter this command and then type a filename, Emacs creates a new, blank file with that name, or opens an existing file with that name. If you type emacs with no filename, Emacs displays an introductory list of a few important commands. You can also start Emacs in the GNOME desktop by clicking the Main Menu, clicking Programs, clicking Applications, and then clicking Emacs.

❐ You can use either the cursor movement keys—such as the arrow keys, Pg up, Pg down, Home, and End—or Ctrl key combinations to navigate an Emacs file.

❐ You can undo your editing changes in sequence, even after you've made many changes.

❐ In Emacs, you can insert text simply by typing. You can also insert text by copying and pasting, or by cutting and pasting. Like the vi editor, Emacs lets you search for specific text.

COMMAND SUMMARY

Review of Chapter 3 Commands	
Command	**Purpose**
vi commands:	
. (repeat)	Repeat your most recent change
/	Search forward for a pattern of characters
:!	Leave vi temporarily
:q	Cancel an editing session
:r	Read text from one file and add it to another
:set	Turns on certain options, such as line numbering
:w	Save a file and continue working
:wq	Write changes to disk, and exit vi
:x	Save changes and exit vi
i	Switch to insert mode
p	Paste text from the buffer
u	Undo your most recent change
vi	Start the vi editor
yy	Copy (yank) text to the clipboard
ZZ	In command mode, save changes and exit vi
lpr	Print a file
Ctrl+z	Leave vi to temporarily access the command line
UNIX commands:	
:!lprfilename	Print a file
Emacs commands:	
See Table 3-3	

REVIEW QUESTIONS

1. What do you enter at the UNIX command line to start the vi editor?

    a. edit *filename*

    b. ed *filename*

    c. Ctrl+vi

    d. vi *filename*

2. While in the vi command mode, you can exit vi without saving your work by typing _____.

   a. !quit

   b. :q!

   c. :wq!

   d. :nosave

3. To issue a command in Emacs, press _____.

   a. and hold the Ctrl key, and then press a letter

   b. and hold the Alt key, and then press a letter

   c. the function keys (F1–F12)

   d. all of the above

   e. a and b

4. Which of these Ctrl key combinations lets you quit the Emacs editor and return to the command line?

   a. Ctrl+C, Ctrl+X

   b. Ctrl+X, Ctrl+C

   c. Ctrl+S, Ctrl+X

   d. Ctrl+X, Ctrl+E

5. Which of these best compares Emacs to the vi editor?

   a. The vi editor enables you to save a file without exiting, but Emacs does not.

   b. Both have an insert mode and a command mode.

   c. The Emacs editor has a sophisticated macro language, but vi does not.

   d. all of the above

   e. only b and c

6. To view vi help documentation while you are in the vi editor, press _____ in command mode.

   a. Ctrl+H

   b. Alt+H

   c. H

   d. :help

7. In the vi editor's command mode, what single character do you type to start searching for a text pattern?

   a. ?

   b. s

   c. /

   d. :

8. How can you start a tutorial about Emacs?

    a. Click the Help menu, and click Emacs Tutorial.

    b. Press Ctrl+T.

    c. Press Ctrl+E.

    d. Click the Tools menu, and click Tutorial.

9. Which of the following are Emacs menu bar options?

    a. Instruments

    b. Mule

    c. Search

    d. all of the above

    e. only b and c

10. In the vi editor, what does typing the x command (without a colon) do?

    a. inserts a letter

    b. goes to the end of the line

    c. deletes the letter under the cursor

    d. opens the bash shell screen so you can type a UNIX command

11. What happens when you type the H command in the vi editor?

    a. You go to the end of the current line.

    b. You go to the first letter of the top line.

    c. You delete the last line of text.

    d. You delete the first line of text.

12. Which of these vi commands enables you to insert text that is already stored in a vi buffer?

    a. Ctrl+P

    b. :p

    c. Ctrl+i

    d. p

    e. Ctrl+b

13. True or False: In most cases, the Ctrl and Alt commands in Emacs are case-sensitive; thus Ctrl+a is not the same command as Ctrl+A.

14. In Emacs, the _____ command marks the start of the block of text you want to copy.

    a. Ctrl+m

    b. Ctrl+Spacebar

    c. Ctrl+s

    d. none of the above

3

15. Which of these vi commands adds text from another file?

    a. r

    b. read

    c. :r

    d. :w

16. In the Emacs editor, the _____ command enables you to capitalize all letters in the word currently pointed at by the cursor.

    a. Alt+U

    b. Alt+C

    c. Ctrl+C

    d. Ctrl+N

17. The _____ command moves the cursor to the beginning of the file in the Emacs editor.

    a. Ctrl+<

    b. Ctrl+>

    c. Alt+<

    d. Alt+>

18. The _____ command enables you to scroll down a screen in the Emacs editor.

    a. Ctrl+S,C

    b. Ctrl+X,S

    c. Ctrl+V

    d. Ctrl+J

19. What will happen when you use the vi command 4,$s/green/orange/g?

    a. All instances of the words green and orange are highlighted, except on line 4.

    b. Beginning at line 4 to the end of the file, all instances of the word "green" are changed to the word "orange."

    c. Beginning at line 4 to the end of line 8, all instances of the word "orange" are changed to the word "green."

    d. Beginning at line 1 through line 4, all instances of the words "green" and "orange" are deleted.

20. Which of the following is accomplished by the d$ vi command?

    a. It deletes text from the cursor to the end of the line.

    b. It deletes all of the text in the document.

    c. It restores the text that was just deleted.

    d. It restores a vi document that has been deleted within the current logon session.

21. Which vi command enables you to move to the beginning of the 10th line in the vi editor?

    a. 10G

    b. G10

    c. :m10

    d. M10

22. The _____ command is used to undo the last command in the Emacs editor.

    a. Ctrl+U

    b. Ctrl+X

    c. Ctrl+U, X

    d. Ctrl+X, U

23. In the Emacs editor, what command is used to paste text that you have just marked to be copied?

    a. Ctrl+Y

    b. Ctrl+P

    c. Ctrl+X, P

    d. Alt+X

24. You are working in the vi editor on the YearEnd file. What command can you use to print that file without first closing the editor?

    a. lpr

    b. Ctrl+pr

    c. :!lpr

    d. pp

25. Which vi command enables you to go back one word?

    a. j

    b. b

    c. a

    d. l

26. Which vi command copies text to the buffer?

    a. :c

    b. :y

    c. yy

    d. cc

3

27. True or False: Unlike the vi editor, in the Emacs editor the down arrow is used to repeat the last command.

28 Which of the following is an option on the Emacs Edit menu?

    a. copying and pasting text

    b. undoing a change

    c. cutting text

    d. all of the above

    e. only a and c

29 How can you go forward one screen in the vi editor?

    a. Use the Ctrl+F command.

    b. Press the up arrow twice while holding the Ctrl key.

    c. Press Ctrl+Alt

    d. Use the Alt+U command

30. What vi command enables you to exit the vi editor and save your work?

    a. Ctrl+q+s

    b. :x

    c. :w

    d. Alt+F8

DISCOVERY EXERCISES

The following exercises enable you to practice using the vi editor:

1. Using the vi editor:
   - Create a document with four lines each containing the word "today."
   - Copy the first four lines using only one command.
   - Save the file, and exit vi.
   - Reopen the document, and change "today" to "yesterday" only on the first four lines.

2. Using the vi editor:
   - Create a document called first.file, and enter a few lines of text in it. Save it.
   - Create a second document called second.file, and enter a few lines of text in it. Save it.
   - Create a third document called third.file, by merging the text from the first two files.
   - Save the third file, and exit from the editor.
   - Type vi third.file and press Enter to be sure third.file contains the text from both files.

3. Delete all text from third.file that you created using vi, and then restore it.

 Use Table 3-3 to find the correct commands for performing the following exercises for practice using the Emacs editor.

4. Using the Emacs editor, create a new file, called sonnet, that contains the first four lines of Shakespeare's 80th Sonnet:

    O, how I faint when I of you do write,

    Knowing a better spirit doth use your name,

    And in the praise thereof spends all his might,

    To make me tongue-tied, speaking of your fame!

5. Move the cursor to any letter except "b" in the word "better" on the second line.

6. Use the command that causes the current word to be transposed with the one that follows it. After executing the command, the line should read:

    Knowing a spirit better doth use your name,

7. Move the cursor to the word "doth" on the same line.

8. Use the command to delete the current word.

9. Move the cursor to the first character of the word "spirit" on the same line.

10. Use the command that capitalizes the letters of the word.

11. Move the cursor under the letter "y" in the word "your" on the same line.

12. Use the command that deletes the character above the cursor. The line should now read:

    Knowing a SPIRIT better use our name,

13. Move the cursor to the word "spends" on the third line.

14. Use the command that deletes text to the end of the line. The line should now read:

    And in the praise thereof

15. Move the cursor to the beginning of the first line.

16. Use the command that puts a mark at the cursor location.

17. Move the cursor to the end of the first line. Use the command that marks that particular cursor location.

18. Move the cursor to the first character of the first line.

19. Use the command that deletes marked text, that is, deletes the first line.

20. Move the cursor to the end of the file. Use the command that restores deleted text. The text that was the first line of the file is now at the end of the file.

Use the vi editor with the following Discovery Exercises to sharpen your editing skills.

21. Create a file with 12 lines of text. Delete the second word in the text.

22. Go to the fifth line, and insert your First and Last Name.

23. Remove the eighth line, and place it at the end of the file.

24. Use one command to go to the first line of the file.

25. Search for your last name.

26. Save the file, but do not exit vi.

27. Without exiting vi, temporarily execute the ls command to confirm that the file is saved.

28. Enter the command that causes line numbers to appear.

29. Delete lines 9 and 10.

30. Move to the line of text that contains your first and last name, cut it, and place the text on the clipboard.

31. Using the sonnet file you created in Discovery Exercise 4, practice copying and pasting text to rearrange the order of the lines.

Use the Emacs editor for these Discovery Exercises.

32. Using the practice file, practice copying and pasting the text to rearrange the order of the lines.

33. Add text to the file, and practice using the cursor movement commands.

34. Replace all occurrences of the word "the" with "a".

35. Select five words, and convert them to all uppercase.

36. Delete a line, and then undo the deletion.

37. Transpose the first two words in each line.

38. Save the file, and exit Emacs.

4

UNIX FILE PROCESSING

Your manager at Dominion Consulting, Rolfe Williamson, wants you to extract a list of names from the phone number file you created earlier, and sort the list. Then he wants you to help a Dominion client, Worldwide Hotels, design a new vendor and product report. The hotel firm wants to produce an alphabetical list of vendors and the products each offers. The vendor and product names reside in separate files: a product file and a vendor file. Both files contain vendor numbers. Rolfe asks you to use the UNIX file-processing tools to produce a vendor report using the two files.

Now that you know how to work with UNIX files and editors, you're ready to learn how to manipulate files and work with their contents. After a brief discussion of UNIX file types and file structures, Lesson A defines file processing and shows you how to use redirection operators when processing files. You also learn how to manipulate files by creating, deleting, copying, and moving them, to extract information from files, to combine fields, and to sort a file's contents, all in the context of the opening case. In Lesson B, you learn how to assemble information you extracted from files. You also create a script to automate a series of commands, link files with a common field, and use the awk command to format output. You complete these tasks to meet the goals of the opening case.

◀ LESSON A ▶

EXTRACTING INFORMATION FROM FILES

After completing this lesson, you should be able to:
- ♦ Explain the UNIX approach to file processing
- ♦ Use basic file manipulation commands
- ♦ Extract characters and fields from a file using the cut command
- ♦ Rearrange fields inside a record using the paste command
- ♦ Merge files using the sort command
- ♦ Create a new file by combining cut, paste, and sort

UNIX's Approach to File Processing

UNIX file processing is based on the idea that files should be treated as nothing more than character sequences. This concept of a file as a series of characters offers a lot of flexibility. Because you can directly access each character, you can perform a range of editing tasks, such as correcting spelling errors and organizing information as necessary.

Understanding UNIX File Types

Operating systems support several types of files. UNIX, like MS-DOS, has regular files, directories, and special files. **Regular files** contain information you create and manipulate, and include either ASCII files, such as the text files you created in Chapter 3, or binary files, such as those you create while compiling source code. You use regular files, also called **ordinary files**, in this chapter. Other file types include directories and special files, such as character files and block files. Chapter 2 explained that directories are system files for maintaining the structure of the file system. **Character special files** are related to serial input/output devices, such as printers. A character special file communicates one character at a time, providing what is called raw data. The first character in the file access permissions is "c," which represents the file type. **Block special files** are related to devices, such as disks, and send information to devices using blocks of data. The first character in these files is "b."

File Structures

Files can be structured in several ways. For example, UNIX stores data, such as letters, product records, or vendor reports, in **flat ASCII files**. A programmer structures a file depending on the kind of data it stores. Three kinds of regular files are unstructured ASCII characters, records, and trees. Figure 4-1 illustrates these three kinds of regular files.

Figure 4-1(a) shows a file that is an unstructured sequence of bytes and is a typical example of a text file. This file structure gives you the most flexibility in data entry, because you can store any kind of data in any order. However, you can only retrieve the data in the same order, which may limit its overall usefulness. For example, suppose you list Worldwide Hotel's vendors in an unstructured ASCII file. It would then be convenient to only view or print the entire list, not just the vendor names or vendor numbers.

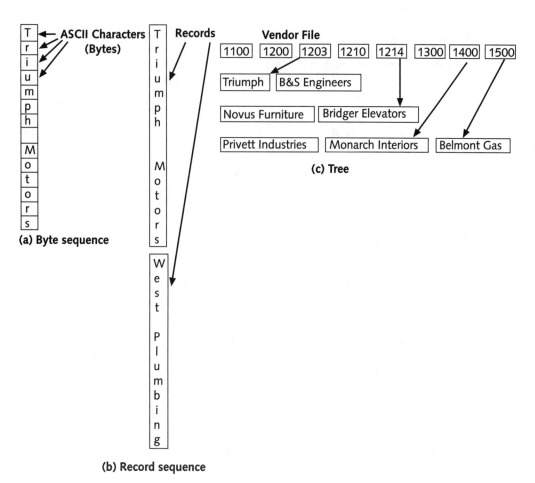

Figure 4-1   Three kinds of regular files

Figure 4-1(b) shows data as a sequence of fixed-length records, each having some internal structure. In a UNIX file, a record is a line of data, corresponding to a row. For example, in a file of names, the first line or row might contain information about a single individual, such as last name, first name, middle initial, address, and phone number. The second row would contain the same kind of data about a different person, and so on. In this structure, UNIX reads the data as fixed-length records. Although you must enter data as records, you can also manipulate and retrieve the data as records. For example, you can select only certain vendor records to retrieve from the file.

The third kind of file, illustrated in Figure 4-1(c), is structured as a tree of records that are not necessarily the same length. Each record contains a key field, such as a record number, in a fixed position in the record. The key field sorts the tree, so you can quickly search for a record with a particular key. For example, you can quickly find the record for Triumph Motors by searching for record #1203.

PROCESSING FILES

When performing commands, UNIX processes data by receiving input from the standard input device—from your keyboard, for example—and then sending it to the standard output—the monitor or console. System administrators and programmers refer to standard input as **stdin**. They refer to standard output as **stdout**. The third standard device, or file, is called **standard error**, or **stderr**. When UNIX detects errors in processing system tasks and user programs, it directs the errors to stderr—which is the screen, by default.

You can use the redirection operators to save the output of a command or program in a file, or use a file as an input to a process. The redirection operators, therefore, help you process files.

Using Input and Error Redirection

You can use redirection operators (>, >>, 2>, <, and <<) to retrieve input from something other than the standard input device and to send output to something other than the standard output device.

You already used the output redirection operators in Chapter 1 when you created a new file by redirecting the output of several commands to files. Redirect output when you want to store the output of a command or program in a file. For example, recall that you can use the ls command to list the files in a directory, such as /home. The ls command sends output to stdout, which by default is the screen. To redirect the list to a file called homedir.list, use the redirection symbol by typing ls > homedir.list.

You may also redirect the input to a program or command with the < operator. For instance, a program that accepts keyboard input may be redirected to read information from a file instead. In the following steps you create a file from which the vi editor reads its commands, instead of reading them from the keyboard.

To create a file from which the vi editor reads commands:

1. Use the vi editor, or the cat command with output redirection, to create the file testfile, containing the text:

   ```
   This is line 1.
   This is line 2.
   This is line 3.
   This is line 4.
   ```

2. Create another text file containing some vi commands as follows. Type **cat > commands** and press **Enter**. Type **dd** and press **Enter**. Type **G** and press **Enter**. Type **p** and press **Enter**. Type **:wq** and press **Enter**. Your entries should look like those in Figure 4-2. Press **Ctrl+D**.

3. Type **cat commands** and press **Enter** to verify the contents of the commands file.

4. Type **vi testfile < commands** and press **Enter**. (Because the input is from a file and not the keyboard, you may see a warning that the input is not from a terminal. Simply ignore the warning.) This loads testfile into the vi editor, and redirects vi's input to the text in the command file. The text in the command file is treated as commands typed on the keyboard.

5. Type **cat testfile** and press **Enter**. You see the contents of testfile after the vi commands execute. The contents are:

```
This is line 2.
This is line 3.
This is line 4.
This is line 1.
```

Figure 4-2   Using cat to create the commands file

You may also use the 2> operator to redirect commands or program error messages from the screen to a file.

To redirect error messages:

1. Force the ls command to display an error message by giving it an invalid argument. Assuming you have no file or directory in your home directory named jojo, type **ls jojo** and press **Enter**. You see the error message:

```
ls: jojo: No such file or directory
```

2. Redirect the error output of the ls command. Type **ls jojo 2> errfile** and press **Enter**. There is no output on the screen.

3. Type **cat errfile** and press **Enter**. You see errfile's contents:

```
ls: jojo: No such file or directory
```

MANIPULATING FILES

When you manipulate files, you work with the files themselves as well as their contents. This section explains how to complete the following tasks:

- Create files
- Delete files
- Copy files
- Move files
- Find files
- Display files
- Combine files
- Cut and paste file contents
- Sort files

Creating Files

You can create a new file by using the output redirection operator (>). You learned how to do this to redirect the cat command's output in Chapters 1-3. You can also use the redirection operator without a command to create an empty file.

To create an empty file:

1. After the $ command prompt, type > **newfile1** and press **Enter**.

   This creates an empty file called newfile1.

2. To list the new file, type **ls -l newfile1** and press **Enter**.

   You see only the information listed next, where jean is your user name.

   ```
   -rw-rw-r-- 1 jean jean    0 Nov 1 16:57 newfile1
   ```

3. To create another new file, type > **newfile2** and press **Enter**.

You may also use the touch command to create empty files. For example, the following command creates the file newfile3, if the file does not already exist.

```
touch newfile3
```

The primary purpose of the touch command is to change a file's time and date stamp. UNIX maintains the following date and time information for every file:

- *Change date and time*—the date and time the file's inode was last changed
- *Access date and time*—the date and time the file was last accessed
- *Modification date and time*—the date and time the file was last modified

4

In UNIX, an **inode (information node)** is a system for storing key information about files. Inode information includes the inode number, the owner of the file, the file group, the file size, the change date of the inode, the file creation date, the date the file was last modified and last read, the number of links to this inode, and information regarding the location of the blocks in the file system in which the file is stored.

Although the touch command cannot alter a file's inode changed date and time, it can alter the file's access and modification dates and times. By default, it uses the current date and time for the new values.

To create a file and alter its date/time stamp with the touch command:

1. Type **touch newfile3** and press **Enter**. This command creates the file newfile3.

2. Type **ls –l newfile3** and press **Enter**. You see a long listing for the newfile3 file. Note its modification date and time.

3. Wait at least one minute.

4. Type **touch newfile3** and press **Enter**. This updates the file's access and modification date and time stamps with the system date and time.

5. Type **ls –l newfile3** and press **Enter**. Look at the file's modification time. It should be different now.

Table 4–1 lists and describes the touch command's options.

Table 4-1   Touch command options

Command Option	Description
-a	Updates the access time only
-m	Updates the modification time only
-c	Prevents touch from creating the file if it does not already exist

Deleting Files

When you no longer need a file, you can delete it using the rm (remove) command. If you use rm without options, UNIX deletes the specified file without warning. Use the –i (interactive) option to have UNIX warn you before deleting the file. You can use the rm command to delete the new files you just created.

To delete a file from the current directory:

1. After the $ command prompt, type **rm newfile1** and press **Enter**.

   This permanently deletes newfile1 from the current directory.

2. Type **rm –i newfile2** and press **Enter**.

   You see the message, "rm: remove 'newfile2'?".

3. Type **y** for yes, and press **Enter**.

To delete a group of files using wildcards (see Chapter 2 for more information about wildcards):

1. You can specify multiple filenames as arguments to the touch command. Type **touch file1 file2 file3 filegood filebad** and press **Enter**. This command creates these files: file1, file2, file3, filegood, and filebad.

2. Type **ls file*** and press **Enter**. You see the listing for the files you created in Step 1.

3. Type **rm file*** and press **Enter**.

4. Type **ls** and press **Enter**. The files have been erased.

Removing Directories

When you no longer need a directory, you can use the rmdir command to remove it. The command takes the form:

Syntax **rmdir** *directoryname*

A directory must be empty before you can remove it using rmdir.

To remove a directory with the rmdir command:

1. Type **mkdir newdir** and press **Enter**. This creates a new directory named newdir.

2. Use a relative path with the touch command to create a new file in the newdir directory. Type **touch newdir/newfile** and press **Enter**. This creates the file newfile in the newdir directory.

3. Type **ls newdir** to see a listing of the newfile file.

4. To attempt to remove the directory, type **rmdir newdir** and press **Enter**. You see an error message similar to:

   ```
   rmdir: 'newdir': Directory not empty
   ```

5. Use a relative path with the rm command to delete newfile. Type **rm newdir/newfile** and press **Enter**.

6. The directory is now empty. Type **rmdir newdir** and press **Enter**.

7. Type **ls** and press **Enter**. The newdir directory is no longer there.

Copying Files

Chapter 2 introduced the cp command. Its general form is:

4

Syntax **cp** [–options] *source destination*

The command copies the file or files specified by the source path to the location specified by the destination path. You can copy files into another directory, with the copies keeping the same names as the originals. You can also copy files into another directory with the copies taking new names, or copy files into the same directory as the originals, with the copies taking new names.

For example, assume Tom is in his home directory (/home/tom). In this directory he has the file reminder. Under his home directory he has another directory, duplicates (/home/tom/duplicates). He copies the reminder file to the duplicates directory with the following command:

    cp reminder duplicates

After he executes the command, a file named reminder is in the duplicates directory. It is a duplicate of the reminder file in the /home/tom directory. Tom also has the file class_of_78 in his home directory. He copies it to a file named classmates in the duplicates directory with the following command:

    cp class_of_78 duplicates/classmates

After he executes the command, the file classmates is stored in the duplicates directory. Although it has a different name, it is a copy of the class_of_78 file. Tom also has a file named memo_to_boss in his home directory. He wants to make a copy of it, and keep the copy in his home directory. He types the following command:

    cp memo_to_boss memo.safe

After he executes this command, the file memo.safe is stored in Tom's home directory. It is a copy of his memo_to_boss file.

You may specify multiple source files as arguments to the cp command. For example, Tom wants to copy the files project1, project2, and project3 to his duplicates directory. He types the following command:

    cp project1 project2 project3 duplicates

 The last entry in a multiple copy (cp) or move (mv) is a directory, as in the previous example.

After he executes the command, copies of the three files are stored in the duplicates directory. You may also use wildcard characters with the cp command. For example, Tom has a directory named designs under his home directory (/home/tom/designs). He wants to copy all files in the designs directory to the duplicates directory. He types the following command:

```
cp designs/* duplicates
```

After he executes this command, the duplicates directory contains a copy of every file in the designs directory.

The cp command is especially useful for preventing data loss; you can use it to make back-up copies of your files. You can create three new files, and then copy them to a different directory. Then you can duplicate one file, and give it a different name. Start by creating the subdirectory source in your home directory. You can create three new files, and then copy them to the source directory.

To create three files and copy them to a directory:

1. If you do not already have a subdirectory source, make sure you're in your home directory, and then create the directory. After the $ command prompt, type **mkdir source** and then press **Enter**.

2. To create three files in your home directory, type > **file1** and press **Enter**, type > **file2** and press **Enter**, and then type > **file3** and press **Enter**.

3. Now you can copy the three files to the source directory. Type **cp file1 file2 file3 source** and press **Enter** (or to save time, you can type **cp file* source**).

   Now you can copy one of the files, and give it a different name so you can distinguish it as a back-up file.

4. After the $ command prompt, type **cp file1 file1.sav** and press **Enter**.

   Now your working directory contains two files with identical contents but different names.

Recursively Removing Directories

The rm command normally requires that a directory be empty before you can remove it. This can be inconvenient when you need to remove a directory that has several subdirectories under it. The -r option, however, tells the rm command to remove a directory and everything it contains, including subdirectories. It even removes subdirectories of subdirectories. This operation is known as recursive removal.

To recursively remove a directory with several subdirectories:

1. Create a directory with several subdirectories. Type **mkdir company** and press **Enter**. Type **mkdir company/sales** and press **Enter**. Type **mkdir company/marketing** and press **Enter**. Type **mkdir company/accounting** and press **Enter**.

2. Create three empty files in the company directory. Type **touch company/file1 company/file2 company/file3** and press **Enter**.

3. Copy the files to the other directories by doing the following:

 - Type **cp company/file1 company/file2 company/file3 company/sales** and press **Enter**.

 - Type **cp company/file1 company/file2 company/file3 company/marketing** and press **Enter**.

 - Type **cp company/file1 company/file2 company/file3 company/accounting** and press **Enter**.

The three commands you just typed are very similar. You can reduce your typing by using the up arrow key to recall the first command.

4. Use the ls command to verify that the files were copied into all three directories.

5. Remove the company directory and everything it contains. Type **rm –r company** and press **Enter**.

6. Type **ls** and press **Enter**. The company directory is removed.

Be very careful with the rm –r command. It can permanently delete massive amounts of information. Some users prefer to accompany it with the –i command—as in rm –i –r company—which interactively asks if you are certain you want to delete each file and directory.

Moving Files

Moving files is similar to copying them, except you remove them from one directory and store them in another. However, as insurance, a file is copied before it is moved. To move a file, use the mv (move) command. The command has the general form:

Syntax **mv** [–options] *source destination*

You can also use the mv command to rename a file by moving one file into another file with a different name.

To move a file from one directory to another:

1. To create the new file thisfile in your home directory, type **> thisfile** and then press **Enter**.

2. Type **mv thisfile source** and press **Enter** to move the new file to the source directory.

3. Type **ls** and press **Enter**. thisfile is not listed. Type **ls source** and press **Enter**. You see thisfile listed.

4. To move more than one file, type the filenames before the directory name. For example, type **mv file1 file1.sav source** and press **Enter**.

5. To create the new file my_file, type **> my_file** and press **Enter**.

6. To rename my_file to your_file, type **mv my_file your_file** and press **Enter**.

7. Type **ls** and press **Enter**. You see your_file listed, but my_file is not listed.

Moving and renaming a file are essentially the same operation.

You can also use the –i option with the mv command. It causes the command to prompt you before it overwrites an existing destination file.

Finding Files

The find command searches for files that have a specified name. Use the find command to locate files that have the same name or to find a file in any directory. The command has the form:

Syntax **find** *pathname* **-name** *filename*

Dissection

- *pathname* is the path name of the directory you want to search. The **find** command searches recursively; that is, it starts in the named directory and searches down through all files and subdirectories under the directory specified by pathname.

- **–name** indicates that you are searching for files with a specific *filename*. You may use wildcard characters in the filename. For example, you may use phone* to search for all filenames that begin with "phone." For other search conditions you can use with find, refer to Appendix B, "Syntax Guide to UNIX Commands."

When you are using the find command, you can only search areas where you have adequate permissions. As the search progresses, the find command may enter protected directories; you receive a "Permission denied" message each time you attempt to enter a directory for which you do not have adequate permissions.

You can use the find command to find every file named file1 in the /home directory and all its subdirectories.

To find a file:

1. After the $ command prompt, type **find /home -name file1** and press **Enter**.

4

Although Linux does not require it, some UNIX versions require the -print option after the filename to display the names of files the find command locates.

Combining Files

Now you're ready to work on the vendor report for Worldwide Hotels, Dominion's client. Two separate files, illustrated in Figure 4-3, store the data you need.

```
File Name: product1

Lobby Furniture         1201
Ballroom Specialties    1221
Poolside Carts          1320
Formal Dining Specials  1340
Reservation Logs        1410
```

```
File Name: product2

Plumbing Supplies       1423
Office Equipment        1361
Carpeting Services      1395
Auto Maintenance        1544
Pianos and Violins      1416
```

Figure 4-3 Two product descripton files

You can use the cat command to combine the two files in a new vendor products master file. Do so by redirecting the output of cat to create the product1 file in your home directory. The file contains two colon-separated fields.

To use the cat command to combine files:

1. After the $ command prompt, type **cat > product1** (but do not press Enter).

2. Type the following text, pressing **Enter** at the end of each line:

   Lobby Furniture:1201

   Ballroom Specialties:1221

   Poolside Carts:1320

   Formal Dining Specials:1340

   Reservation Logs:1410

3. Press **Ctrl+D**.

   Now you can redirect the output of cat to create the product2 file in your home directory. This file also contains two colon-separated fields.

4. After the $ command prompt, type **cat > product2** (but do not press Enter).

5. Type the following text, pressing **Enter** at the end of each line:

   Plumbing Supplies:1423

   Office Equipment:1361

   Carpeting Services:1395

   Auto Maintenance:1544

   Pianos and Violins:1416

6. Press **Ctrl+D**.

7. Now you can combine the two files in a master products file. After the $ command prompt, type **cat product1 product2 > products3** and press **Enter**.

8. To list the contents of products, type **more products3** and press **Enter**. You see the list:

   ```
   Lobby Furniture:1201
   Ballroom Specialties:1221
   Poolside Carts:1320
   Formal Dining Specials:1340
   Reservation Logs:1410
   Plumbing Supplies:1423
   Office Equipment:1361
   Carpeting Services:1395
   Auto Maintenance:1544
   Pianos and Violins:1416
   ```

The Paste Command

The paste command combines files side by side, whereas the cat command combines files end to end. When you use paste to combine two files into a third file, the first line of the third file contains the first line of the first file followed by the first line of the second file. For example, Becky has the file vegetables in her home directory. Its contents are:

```
Carrots
Spinach
Lettuce
Beans
```

She also has the file bread in her home directory. Its contents are:

```
Whole wheat
White bread
Sourdough
Pumpernickel
```

After she executes the command paste vegetables bread > food, the vegetables and bread files are combined, line by line, into the file food. The food file's contents are:

```
Carrots    Whole wheat
Spinach    White bread
Lettuce    Sourdough
Beans      Pumpernickel
```

 The paste command normally sends its output to the screen. To capture it in a file, use the redirection symbol.

As you can see, the paste command is most useful when you combine files that contain columns of information. When paste combines items into a single line, it separates them with a tab. For example, look at the first line of the food file:

```
Carrots    Whole wheat
```

When paste combined "Carrots" and "Whole wheat," it inserted a tab between them. You can use the –d option to specify another character as a delimiter. For example, to insert a comma between the output fields instead of a tab, Becky types the paste command:

```
paste -d',' vegetables bread > food
```

After Becky's command executes, the food file's contents are:

```
Carrots,Whole wheat
Spinach,White bread
Lettuce,Sourdough
Beans,Pumpernickel
```

Now you can use the paste command to combine the two product files in one. (Use paste instead of cat, because you're combining fields from two or more files into columns, and then converting all the fields into columns.)

To use the paste command to combine files:

1. After the $ command prompt, type **paste product1 product2** and press **Enter**.

   This means "combine the file called product1 with the file called product2." You see the list of product descriptions:

   ```
   Lobby Furniture:1201          Plumbing Supplies:1423
   Ballroom Specialties:1221     Office Equipment:1361
   Poolside Carts:1320           Carpeting Services:1395
   Formal Dining Specials:1340   Auto Maintenance:1544
   Reservation Logs:1410         Pianos and Violins:1416
   ```

Using the Cut Command to Extract Fields

You have learned that files can consist of records, fields, and characters. You may want to retrieve some, but not all, fields in a file. You can use the cut command to remove specific columns or fields from a file. The syntax of the cut command is:

Syntax **cut -f** *list* [**-d** *char*] *file1 file2* ... Or   **cut -c** *list file1 file2* ...

Dissection

- **-f** specifies that you are referring to fields.

- *list* is a comma-separated list or a hyphen-separated range of integers that specifies the field. For example, -f 1 indicates field 1, -f 1,14 indicates fields 1 and 14, and -f 1-14 indicates fields 1 through 14.

- **-d** indicates that a specific character separates the fields.

- *char* is the character used as the field separator (delimiter), for example, a comma. The default field delimiter is the Tab character.

- *file1, file2* are the files from which you want to cut columns or fields.

- **-c** references character positions. For example, -c 1 specifies the first character and -c 1,14 specifies characters 1 and 14.

Recall the vegetables and bread files in Becky's home directory. She also has the file meats. When she uses the command paste vegetables bread meats > food, the contents of the food file are:

```
Carrots   Whole wheat   Turkey
Spinach   White bread   Chicken
Lettuce   Sourdough     Beef
Beans     Pumpernickel  Ham
```

Becky wants to extract the second column of information (the bread list) from the file, and display it on the screen. She types the following command:

```
cut -f2 food
```

The option –f2 tells the cut command to extract the second field from each line. Tab delimiters separate the fields, so cut knows where to find the fields. She sees the following output on the screen:

```
Whole wheat
White bread
Sourdough
Pumpernickel
```

She extracts the first and third columns from the file with the command:

```
cut -f1,3 food
```

The results of the command are:

```
Carrots   Turkey
Spinach   Chicken
Lettuce   Beef
Beans     Ham
```

Now you can complete your work with the Dominion phone number files by extracting a list of names from the files. First, you create two files: corp_phones1 and corp_phones2. The corp_phones1 file includes five records of variable size, and a colon separates each field in the record. (Figure 4–1(c) illustrates this type of file structure.) The corp_phones2 file also includes five records of fixed length (the type of file structure illustrated in Figure 4–1(b)). Figure 4-4 illustrates the contents of the two files. You can use the cut command with either file to extract a list of names.

```
File Name:  corp_phones1 (Variable Size Records - Fields separated by colon :)

219:432:4567:Harrison:Joel:M:4540:Accountant:09-12-1985
219:432:4587:Mitchell:Barbara:C:4541:Admin Asst:12-14-1995
219:432:4589:Olson:Timothy:H:4544:Supervisor:06-30-1983
219:432:4591:Moore:Sarah:H:4500:Dept Manager:08-01-1978
219:432:4527:Polk:John:S:4520:Accountant:09-22-1998

Storage space = 279 bytes
```

```
File Name:  corp_phones2 (Fixed length records)

Character positions
1-3 5-7 9-12 14-25         26-35    36 38-41 43-58          59-68
================================================================
219 432 4567 Harrison     Joel      M 4540 Accountant       09-12-1985
219 432 4587 Mitchell     Barbara   C 4541 Admin Asst       12-14-1995
219 432 4589 Olson        Timothy   H 4544 Supervisor       06-30-1983
219 432 4591 Moore        Sarah     H 4500 Dept Manager     08-01-1978
219 432 4527 Polk         John      S 4520 Accountant       09-22-1998

Storage space = 345 bytes
```

Figure 4-4   Two versions of the company telephone file

To create the `corp_phones1` and `corp_phones 2` files:

1. Use the vi or Emacs editor to create the file **corp_phones1**.

2. Type the following lines of text, exactly as they appear. Press **Enter** at the end of each line:

   ```
   219:432:4567:Harrison:Joel:M:4540:Accountant:09-12-1985
   219:432:4587:Mitchell:Barbara:C:4541:Admin Asst:12-14-1995
   219:432:4589:Olson:Timothy:H:4544:Supervisor:06-30-1983
   219:432:4591:Moore:Sarah:H:4500:Dept Manager:08-01-1978
   219:432:4527:Polk:John:S:4520:Accountant:09-22-1998
   ```

3. Save the file, and create a new file named **corp_phones2**.

4. Type the following lines of text, exactly as they appear. Consult Figure 4-4 for the precise position of each character. Press Enter at the end of each line.

   ```
   219 432 4567 Harrison Joel M 4540 Accountant 09-12-1985
   219 432 4587 Mitchell Barbara C 4541 Admin Asst 12-14-1995
   219 432 4589 Olson Timothy H 4544 Supervisor 06-30-1983
   219 432 4591 Moore Sarah H 4500 Dept Manager 08-01-1978
   219 432 4527 Polk John S 4520 Accountant 09-22-1998
   ```

5. Save the file, and exit the editor.

You want to extract the first and last names from the corp_phones1 file first. This file includes variable-length records and fields separated by colon characters. You can select the fields you want to cut by specifying their positions and separator character.

To use the cut command to extract fields from variable-length records:

1. After the $ command prompt, type **cut -f4-6 -d: corp_phones1** and press **Enter**.

   This command means "cut the fields (-f) in positions four through six (4-6) that the colon character (-d:) delimits in the corp_phones1 file."

   You see the list of names:

   ```
   Harrison:Joel:M
   Mitchell:Barbara:C
   Olson:Timothy:H
   Moore:Sarah:H
   Polk:John:S
   ```

4

Now you can extract the first and last names from the corp_phones2 file. This file includes fixed-length records, so you can cut by specifying character positions.

To use the cut command to extract fields from fixed-length records:

1. After the $ command prompt, type **cut -c14-25,26-35,36 corp_phones2** and press **Enter**.

   This command means "cut the characters (-c) in positions 14 through 25, 26 through 35, and position 36 (14-25,26-35,36) in the corp_phones2 file."

   You see the list of names:

   ```
   Harrison   Joel       M
   Mitchell   Barbara    C
   Olson      Timothy    H
   Moore      Sarah      H
   Polk       John       S
   ```

Make sure not to include a space in the code sequence after the dash (-) options in the cut command. For example, the correct syntax is cut (space) -c14-25,26-35,36 (space) corp_ phones2.

Using the cut command with variable-length or fixed-length records produces similar results. Cutting from fixed-length records creates a more legible display, but requires more storage space. For example, corp_phones2 requires 345 bytes and corp_phones1 requires 279.

Using the sort Command

Use the sort command to sort a file's contents alphabetically or numerically. UNIX displays the sorted file on the screen by default, but you can specify that you want to store the sorted data in a particular file.

The sort command offers many options, which Appendix B, "Syntax Guide to UNIX Commands," describes. Here is an example of its use:

```
sort file1 > file2
```

In this example, the contents of file1 are sorted and the results stored in file2. (If the output is not redirected, sort displays its results on the screen.) Here is a more complex example:

```
sort -k 5 file1 > file2
```

This command specifies a **sorting key**. A sorting key is a field position within each line. The sort command sorts the lines based on the sorting key. The -k is the key field within the file. For instance, "-k 5" provides the instruction to sort on the basis of the fifth field, which is the key for the sort in this example.

Sorting the corp_phones1 and corp_phones2 files is relatively easy, because you can refer to field numbers. In the first two steps, you sort the corp_phones1 file by last name and first name, respectively. In the third and fourth steps, you do the same thing with corp_phones2. Notice that the output of these four steps goes to stdout (the screen). The last step uses the -o option, instead of output redirection, to write the sorted output to a new disk file, sorted_phones.

In earlier versions of UNIX, you had to specify character positions of fields to sort a fixed-length file, such as the corp_phones2 file in our exercise examples. This was done by using the +F.C option, where F is the number of the field and .C is the character position. The +F.C option is still available, but it is easier to use the -k option.

To sort the corp_phones1 file:

1. After the $ prompt, type **sort -t: -k 4 corp_phones1** and press **Enter**.

   In this example, the -t option indicates the separator character between fields, which is a colon (:). The -k option specifies sorting on the fourth field, or the last name field in this instance. You see the following on your screen:

```
219:432:4567:Harrison:Joel:M:4540:Accountant:09-12-1985
219:432:4587:Mitchell:Barbara:C:4541:Admin Asst:12-14-1995
219:432:4591:Moore:Sarah:H:4500:Dept Manager:08-01-1978
219:432:4589:Olson:Timothy:H:4544:Supervisor:06-30-1983
219:432:4567:Polk:John:S:4520:Accountant:09-22-1998
```

2. Type **sort -t: -k 5 corp_phones1** and press **Enter**.

   This sorts the variable-length records (-t: indicates the fields are delimited by a colon) starting at the First Name field (-k 5). You see the following on your screen:

   ```
   219:432:4587:Mitchell:Barbara:C:4541:Admin Asst:12-14-1995
   219:432:4567:Harrison:Joel:M:4540:Accountant:09-12-1985
   219:432:4567:Polk:John:S:4520:Accountant:09-22-1998
   219:432:4591:Moore:Sarah:H:4500:Dept Manager:08-01-1978
   219:432:4589:Olson:Timothy:H:4544:Supervisor:06-30-1983
   ```

3. Type **sort -k 4 corp_phones2** and press **Enter**.

   This sorts the fixed-length file by last name, starting at the fourth field. In this example, no separator is specified, because fixed-length files don't use a separator. You see the following on your screen:

   ```
   219 432 4567 Harrison  Joel     M 4540 Accountant    09-12-1985
   219 432 4587 Mitchell  Barbara  C 4541 Admin Asst    12-14-1995
   219 432 4591 Moore     Sarah    H 4500 Dept Manager  08-01-1978
   219 432 4589 Olson     Timothy  H 4544 Supervisor    06-30-1983
   219 432 4527 Polk      John     S 4520 Accountant    09-22-1998
   ```

4. Type **sort -k 5 corp_phones2** and press **Enter**.

   This sorts the file by first name, starting at the fifth field. You see the following on your screen:

   ```
   219 432 4587 Mitchell  Barbara  C 4541 Admin Asst    12-14-1995
   219 432 4567 Harrison  Joel     M 4540 Accountant    09-12-1985
   219 432 4527 Polk      John     S 4520 Accountant    09-22-1998
   219 432 4591 Moore     Sarah    H 4500 Dept Manager  08-01-1978
   219 432 4589 Olson     Timothy  H 4544 Supervisor    06-30-1983
   ```

5. Type **sort -t: +3 corp_ phones1** and press **Enter**.

   This sorts the variable-length records (-t:) starting at the Last Name field (+3).

6. To sort by first name and create the output file sorted_phones, type **sort -t: -k 5 -o sorted_phones corp_phones1** and press **Enter**. This sorts the corp_phones1 file by first name, and creates an output file, sorted_phones. Type **cat sorted_phones** to verify that you successfully created the sorted_phones file.

Putting It All Together

Now you can use the many file processing tools you've learned all at once. First, use the cat command to create the vendors file. The records in the vendor names file consist of two colon-separated fields: the vendor number and vendor name.

To create the vendors file:

1. After the $ command prompt, type **cat > vendors** and press **Enter**.

2. Type the following text, pressing **Enter** at the end of each line:

```
1201:Cromwell Interiors
1221:Design Extras Inc.
1320:Piedmont Plastics Inc.
1340:Morgan Catering Service Ltd.
1350:Pullman Elevators
1360:Johnson Office Products
```

3. Press **Ctrl+D**.

Figure 4-5 shows the two files that Worldwide can use to determine which product each vendor supplies.

```
File Name: vendors

Vendor   Vendor Name
Number
=================================
1201:Cromwell Interiors
1221:Design Extras Inc.
1320:Piedmont Plastics Inc.
1340:Morgan Catering Service Ltd.
1350:Pullman Elevators
1360:Johnson Office Products
```

```
File Name: products

Prod      Product      Vendor
Number   Description  Number
=================================
S0107:Lobby Furniture:1201
S0109:Ballroom Specialties:1221
S0110:Poolside Carts:1320
S0130:Formal Dining Specials:1340
S0201:Reservation Logs:1410
```

Figure 4-5   Vendors and products

In the next steps, use the cat command to create the products file. The records in the products file consist of three colon-separated fields: the product number, the product description, and the vendor number.

To create the products file:

1. After the $ command prompt, type **cat > products** and press **Enter**.

2. Type the following text, pressing **Enter** at the end of each line, including the last line:

   ```
   S0107:Lobby Furniture:1201
   S0109:Ballroom Specialties:1221
   S0110:Poolside Carts:1320
   S0130:Formal Dining Specials:1340
   S0201:Reservation Logs:1410
   ```

3. Type **Ctrl+D** to end the cat command

Now use the cut, paste, and sort commands to create a single vendor report for Worldwide Hotels. Start by using the cut command to extract product descriptions and vendor numbers from the products file and storing them in separate files, p1 and p2. Then extract vendor numbers and names from the vendors file, and store them in v1 and v2. Use the paste command to combine the two vendor files (v1 and v2) in a third file, v3. Then combine the two product files (p1 and p2) in a file, p3. Sort and merge the v3 and p3 files, and send their output to the vrep file, the vendor report.

To use the cut, paste, and sort commands to create a report:

1. After the $ command prompt, type **cut –f2 –d: products > p1** and press **Enter**.

   This means "extract the data from the second field delimited by a colon in the products file, and store it in the p1 file." It stores these product descriptions in the p1 file:

   ```
   Lobby Furniture
   Ballroom Specialties
   Poolside Carts
   Formal Dining Specials
   Reservation Logs
   ```

2. Type **cut –f3 –d: products > p2** and press **Enter**.

   This means "extract the data from the third field delimited by a colon in the products file, and store it in the p2 file." It stores these vendor numbers in the p2 file:

   ```
   1201
   1221
   1320
   1340
   1410
   ```

3. Type **cut –f1 –d: vendors > v1** and press **Enter**.

   This means "extract the data from the first field delimited by a colon in the vendors file, and store it in the v1 file." It stores these vendor numbers in the v1 file:

   ```
   1201
   1221
   1320
   1340
   1350
   1360
   ```

4. Type **cut –f2 –d: vendors > v2** and press **Enter**.

   This means "extract the data from the second field delimited by a colon in the vendors file, and store it in the v2 file." It stores these product descriptions in the v2 file:

   ```
   Cromwell Interiors
   Design Extras Inc.
   Piedmont Plastics Inc.
   Morgan Catering Service Ltd.
   Pullman Elevators
   Johnson Office Products
   ```

5. Type **paste v1 v2 > v3** and press **Enter**.

   This means "combine the data in v1 and v2, and direct it to the file v3. It stores these vendor numbers and product descriptions in the v3 file:

   ```
   1201   Cromwell Interiors
   1221   Design Extras Inc.
   1320   Piedmont Plastics Inc.
   1340   Morgan Catering Service Ltd.
   1350   Pullman Elevators
   1360   Johnson Office Products
   ```

6. Type **paste p2 p1 > p3** and press **Enter**.

   This means "combine the data in p2 and p1, and direct it to a file called p3." It stores these vendor numbers and product descriptions in the p3 file:

   ```
   1201   Lobby Furniture
   1221   Ballroom Specialties
   1320   Poolside Carts
   1340   Formal Dining Specials
   1410   Reservation Logs
   ```

7. Type **sort –o vrep –m v3 p3** and press **Enter**.

   This means "merge the data in v3 and p3, and direct the output to a file called vrep." It stores these vendor numbers and product descriptions in the vrep file:

   ```
   1201   Cromwell Interiors
   1201   Lobby Furniture
   ```

```
1221    Ballroom Specialties
1221    Design Extras Inc.
1320    Piedmont Plastics Inc.
1320    Poolside Carts
1340    Formal Dining Specials
1340    Morgan Catering Service Ltd.
1350    Pullman Elevators
1360    Johnson Office Products
1410    Reservation Logs
```

4

You used the cut, paste, and sort commands to extract information from files, combine the information, and then sort and merge the information in a new file.

◀ LESSON B ▶

ASSEMBLING EXTRACTED INFORMATION

After completing this lesson, you should be able to:
- ◆ Create a script file
- ◆ Use the join command to link files using a common field
- ◆ Use the awk command to create a professional-looking report

USING SCRIPT FILES

As you have seen, command-line entries can become long, depending on the number of options you need to use. You can use the shell's command-line history retrieval feature to recall and reexecute past commands. This feature works well for you, but others who need to execute your commands cannot access them repeatedly. MS-DOS users resolve this problem by creating batch files. UNIX users do the same: they create **shell script files** to contain command-line entries. Like MS-DOS batch files, script files contain commands that can be run sequentially as a set. A good candidate for a script file is the series of cut, paste, and sort commands that you entered in Lesson A. You can use the vi editor to create the script file, and then make the script executable using the chmod command with the x argument.

Rolfe Williamson is delighted with your vendor report, but wants a way to generate the report whenever the data changes. You can create a script that includes a series of commands for creating the file ven_report.

To use the vi editor to create a script:

1. After the $ command prompt, type **vi ven_report** and press **Enter**.

   The vi editor starts and creates a new file, ven_report.

2. Enter insert mode, and then type the following, pressing **Enter** at the end of every line:

```
cut -f2 -d: products > p1
cut -f3 -d: products > p2
cut -f1 -d: vendors > v1
cut -f2 -d: vendors > v2
paste v1 v2 > v3
paste p2 p1 > p3
sort -o vrep -m v3 p3
```

   These are the same commands you used in Lesson A to create the first vendor report. Figure 4-6 illustrates how the vi editor screen should look after you have entered the commands.

3. Press **Esc**.

4. Type **:wq** to exit the vi editor.

Figure 4-6   Creating the ven_report file using the vi editor

Now you can make the script executable with the chmod command. The chmod command sets file permissions. In the example that follows, the chmod command and its ugo+x option make the ven_report file executable by **u**sers (owners), **g**roup, and **o**thers. Run a test to make sure it works.

To make the script executable:

1. After the $ command prompt, type **chmod ugo+x ven_report** and press **Enter**.

   See "Setting File Permissions for Security" in Chapter 2 for more information on the chmod command.

2. To make sure the script works, type **./ven_report** and press **Enter**.

   The vrep file contains the same list of vendor numbers and product descriptions that you saw in Lesson A.

4

In addition to making a shell script executable, it is a good idea to specify the shell for which the script is designed to run. For example, if you have designed a script for the Bash shell, you can place #!/bin/bash as the first line in the script. You learn how to do this in Chapter 7, "Advanced Shell Programming." Also, after you change the permissions on a script, you can run it without the ./ command, if your currently defined path includes the directory in which the script resides.

USING THE JOIN COMMAND

The join command differs from the other file processing commands in this chapter, because it is used in relational database processing. **Relational databases** consider files as tables and records as rows. They also refer to fields as columns that can be joined to create new records. The join command is the UNIX method that lets you extract information from two files sharing a common field.

For example, you can use the join command to combine information in the vendor and product files, thereby producing the vendor report for Worldwide's purchasing department. Both the vendor and product reports include the vendor number. The syntax of the join command is:

Syntax **join** [options] *file1 file2*

Dissection

- *file1, file2* are two input files that must be sorted on the join field—the field you want to use to **join** the files. The join field is also called a **key**. You must sort the files before you can join them. When you issue the join command, UNIX compares the two fields. Each output line contains the common field followed by a line from file1, and then a line from file2. You can modify output using the options described next. If records with duplicate keys are in the same file, UNIX joins on all of them. You can create output records for unpaired lines, for example, to append data from one file to another without losing records.

Options

- **-j** specifies the common fields on which the join is to be made.

- **-o** specifies a list of fields to output. The list contains blank-separated field specifiers in the form m.n, where *m* is the file number and *n* is the position of the field in the file. Thus -o 1.2 means "output the second field in the first file."

- **-t** specifies the field separator character. By default this is a blank, tab, or new line character. Multiple blanks and tabs count as one field separator.

- **-a** *filename* produces a line for each unpairable line in the file *filename*.

- **-e** *str* replaces the empty fields for the unpairable line in the string specified by *str*. The string is usually a code or message to indicate the condition; for example, -e "No Vendor Record."

For an example of join logic, see Figure 4-7.

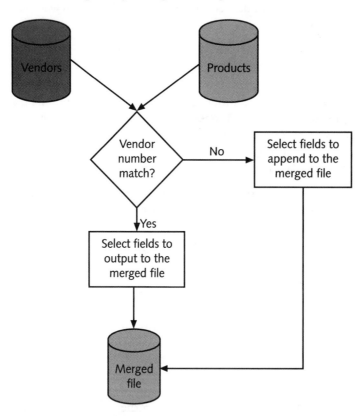

Figure 4-7   Relational join

In Figure 4-7, the join command combines fields from the vendor and product files. Then it searches for vendor numbers in the vendor file matching those in the product file. If a field does not match, UNIX selects it and later appends it to the merged file. If the field does match, UNIX sends it to the merged file.

Using the Join Command to Create the Vendor Report

You can use the join command to create a vendor report showing what products Worldwide's purchasing department has in stock.

To use the join command to create a report:

1. After the $ command prompt, type **join -a1 -e "No Products" -j1 1 -j2 3 -o 1.2 2.2 -t: vendors products > vreport; cat vreport** and press **Enter**. (Remember that if you make a typing mistake, you can use the up arrow to recall a command, press the left arrow key to correct the mistake, and then run the command again.)

   In this command, the -j option indicates the first or second specified file, such as vendors or products. Numbers following j1 and j2 specify field numbers used for the join or match. Here, UNIX uses the first field of the vendors record to join the third field of the products file.

   The -a option tells the command to print a line for each unpairable line in the file number. In this case, a line prints for each vendor record that does not match a product record.

   The -e option lets you display a message for the unmatched (-a 1) record, such as "No Products."

   The -o option sets the fields that will be output when a match is made.

   The 1.2 indicates that field two of the vendors file is to be output along with 2.2, field two of the products file.

   The -t option specifies the field separator, the colon. This join command redirects its output to a new file, vreport. The cat command displays the output on the screen.

   See Figure 4-8 to view the output of the report.

Figure 4-8   Vreport output from the join command

A BRIEF INTRODUCTION TO THE AWK PROGRAM

Awk, a pattern-scanning and processing language, helps to produce reports that look professional. Although you can use the cat and more commands to display the output file that you create with your join program, the awk command (which starts the Awk program when you type it on the command line) lets you do the same thing more quickly and easily. The syntax of the awk command is:

Syntax **awk [-Fsep]** ' *pattern {action} ..' filenames*

Dissection

- **awk** checks to see if the input records in the specified files satisfy the *pattern* and, if they do, awk executes the *action* associated with it. If no pattern is specified, the action affects every input record.

- **-F:** means the field separator is a colon.

 For more information about awk, type man awk to read the online documentation.

 To generate and format the vendor report:

1. After the $ command prompt, type **awk -F: '{printf "%-28s\t %s\n",** **$1, $2}' vreport** and then press **Enter**.

You see the vendor report, including vendor names and product descriptions, as shown in Figure 4-9.

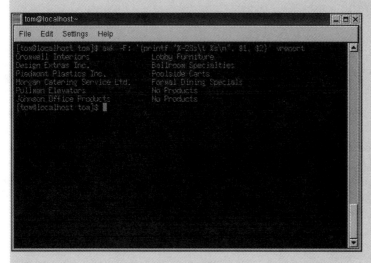

Figure 4-9   Vendor report created via awk

The parts of the awk command you typed in Step 1 are:

- **awk –F:** calls the Awk program, and identifies the field separator as a colon.

- **'{printf "%–28s\t %s\n", $1, $2}'** represents the action to take on each line that is read in. Single quotes enclose the action.

- **printf** is a print formatting function from the C language. It lets you specify an edit pattern for the output. The code inside the double quotes defines this pattern. The code immediately following the % tells how to align the field to be printed. The – sign specifies left alignment. The number that follows, 28, indicates how many characters you want to display. The trailing s means that the field consists of nonnumeric characters, also called a string. The \t inserts a tab character into the edit pattern. The %s specifies that another string field should be printed. You do not need to specify the string length in this case, because it is the last field printed (the product name). The \n specifies to skip a line after printing each output record. The $1 and $2 separated with a comma indicate that the first and second fields in the input file should be placed in the edit pattern where the two s characters appear. The first field is the vendor name, and the second is the product description. (You learn much more about printf in Chapter 10; it is presented here to provide you a brief introduction on which to build as you progress through the book.)

- **vreport** is the name of the input file.

Using the awk Command to Refine the Vendor Report

To refine and automate the vendor report, you can create a shell script, as you did at the beginning of this lesson. This new script, however, includes only the awk command, not a series of separate commands. You then call the Awk program using awk with the -f option. This option tells Awk that the code is coming from a disk file, not from the keyboard. You can present the action statements inside the Awk program file in a different way. The program file includes additional lines needed to print a heading and the current date for the report.

The next steps show what happens when you enter the Awk program in a file like this. You use the FS variable to tell the program what the field separator is, in this example, a colon. FS is one of many variables that awk uses to advise the program about the file being processed. Other codes you see here set up an initial activity that executes once when the program loads. BEGIN followed by the opening curly brace ({) indicates this opening activity. The closing curly brace (}) marks the end of actions performed when the program first loads. These actions print the headings, date, and dash lines that separate the heading from the body of the report.

To create the awk script:

1. After the $ command prompt, type **vi awrp** and press **Enter** to start the vi editor and create the file awrp. Press **i** to start the insert mode.

2. Type the code:

```
BEGIN {
  { FS = ":"}
    { print "\t\tVendors and Products\n" }
    { "date" | getline d }
    { printf "\t  %s\n",d }
    { print "Vendor Name\t\t\t Product Names\n" }
    { print"=========================================\n" }
    }
  { printf "%-28s\t%s\n",$1, $2 }
```

In the code you have typed, the getline option is used. getline is designed to read input. In this case, it reads the date and places it into the d variable, which then is printed via the printf command.

Your vi edit session should look like the one in Figure 4-10.

3. Press **Esc**.

4. Type **:wq** to exit the vi editor.

5. After the $ command prompt, type **awk -f awrp vreport > v_report** and press **Enter**.

This means "using the Awk program, combine the fields from the awrp file with the fields from the vreport file, and send them to a new file called v_report."

6. Type **cat v_report** and press **Enter**.

You see the following report:

```
                    Vendors and Products

               Sun Dec 20 21:03:41 EST 2000
Vendor Name                         Product Names


=============================================================

Cromwell Interiors              Lobby Furniture
Design Extras Inc.              Ballroom Specialties
Piedmont Plastics Inc.          Poolside Carts
Morgan Catering Service Ltd.    Formal Dining Specials
Pullman Elevators               No Products
Johnson Office Products         No Products
```

7. To print the report on the default printer, type **lpr v_report** and press **Enter**.

You produced a vendor and product name report, and then formatted and printed the report.

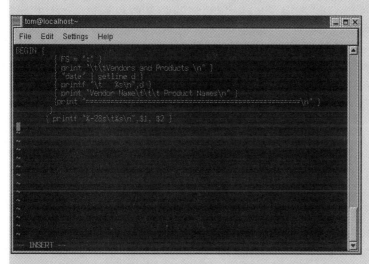

Figure 4-10   Creating the awrp file using the vi editor

CHAPTER SUMMARY

- UNIX supports regular files, directories, character special files, and block special files. Regular files contain user information. Directories are system files for maintaining the file system's structure. Character special files are related to serial input/output devices, such as printers. Block special files are related to devices, such as disks.

❐ Files can be structured in several ways. UNIX stores data, such as letters, product records, or vendor reports, in flat ASCII files. File structures depend on the kind of data being stored. Three kinds of regular files are unstructured ASCII characters, records, and trees.

❐ When performing commands, UNIX processes data—it receives input from the standard input device and then sends output to the standard output device. UNIX refers to the standard devices for input and output as stdin and stdout, respectively. By default, stdin is the keyboard and stdout is the monitor. Another standard device, stderr, refers to the error file that defaults to the monitor. Output from a command may be redirected from stdout to a disk file. Input to a command may be redirected from stdin to a disk file. The error output of a command may be redirected from stderr to a disk file.

❐ The touch command updates a file's time and date stamps and creates empty files.

❐ The rmdir command removes an empty directory.

❐ The cut command extracts specific columns or fields from a file. Select the fields you want to cut by specifying their positions and separator character, or you can cut by character positions, depending on the data's organization.

❐ To combine two or more files, use the paste command. Where cat appends data to the end of the file, the paste command combines files line by line. You can also use paste to combine fields from two or more files.

❐ Use the sort command to sort a file's contents alphabetically or numerically. UNIX displays the sorted file on the screen by default, but you can also specify that you want to store the sorted data in a particular file.

❐ To automate command processing, include commands in a script file that you can later execute as a program. Use the vi editor to create the script file, and the chmod command to make it executable.

❐ Use the join command to extract information from two files sharing a common field. You can use this common field to join the two files. You must sort the two files on the join field—the one you want to use to join the files. The join field is also called a "key." You must sort the files before you can join them.

❐ Awk is a pattern-scanning and processing language useful for creating a formatted report with a professional look. You can enter the awk language instructions in a program file using the vi editor and call it using the awk command.

COMMAND SUMMARY

Review of Chapter 4 Commands		
Command	**Purpose**	**Options Covered in This Chapter**
awk	Start the awk program to format output	**-F** identifies the field separator **-f** indicates code is coming from a disk file, not the keyboard
cp	Copy one or more files	
cut	Extract specified columns or fields from a file	**-c** refers to character positions **-d** indicates a specified character separates the fields **-f** refers to fields
find	Find files	**-name** specifies the name of the files you want to locate
join	Combine files having a common field	**-a** *n* produces a line for each unpairable line in file *n* **-e** *str* replaces the empty fields for an unpairable file with the specified string **-j** uses specified common fields when joining **-o** outputs a specified list of fields **-t** indicates a specified character separates the fields
less	Display the file's contents, pausing at the end of each screen; move up and down in the file	
lpr	Print the command output on the default printer	
more	Display the contents of a file, pausing at the end of each screen, but only allowing you to move down in the file	
mv	Move one or more files	
paste	Combine fields from two or more files	
rm	Remove one or more files	**-i** specifies that UNIX should request confirmation of file deletion before removing the files **-r** specifies that directories should be recursively removed
rmdir	Remove a directory	

Review of Chapter 4 Commands (continued)		
Command	Purpose	Options Covered in This Chapter
sort	Sort the file's contents	**-k** *n* sorts on the key field separated by *n* **+***n* sorts on the field specified by *n* **+** designates the position that follows an offset (+) as a character position, not a field position **-t** indicates that a specified character separates the fields **-m** means to merge files before sorting **-o** redirects output to the specified file **-k** sorts on a key at the position given after the -k
touch	Update an existing file's date and time stamp or creates empty new files	**-a** specifies that only the access date and time are to be updated **-m** specifies that only the modification date and time are to be updated **-c** specifies that no files are to be created

REVIEW QUESTIONS

1. What command is used to delete a directory?

   a. del

   b. dirdel

   c. rmdir

   d. kill

2. You have just used the command in Question 1 to attempt to delete a directory, but the directory is still not deleted. What might be the problem?

   a. The directory contains files, subdirectories, or both.

   b. Someone else has used the directory permission "nodel" to prevent that directory from being deleted.

   c. The directory is too large to be deleted.

   d. all of the above

   e. only a and b

3. When you join two files using a specific field common to both files, what is that field called?

   a. an operator

   b. the linker

   c. the key

   d. the executable

4. A UNIX file that contains commands that can be executed at the command prompt is called a _____.

   a. shell script file

   b. batch file

   c. running file

   d. C program file

5. Used with the awk command, the -f option specifies _____.

   a. the format of the field separator

   b. that the input data file has fixed–length records

   c. that the input data file has variable-length records

   d. that commands are coming from a disk file and not the keyboard

6. The -o parameter is used to _____ when it is specified with the join command.

   a. designate that output goes to the screen

   b. specify the number of title lines in a report

   c. run an additional command

   d. specify the fields to be output in a report

7. _____ is a C language function that is used for print formatting in the awk command.

   a. -p

   b. { format }

   c. printf

   d. procprint

8. A _____ file typically contains information needed to communicate with serial devices or printers.

   a. vendor file

   b. character special file

   c. block special file

   d. master printer file

9. Stdout usually goes to the _____.

   a. keyboard

   b. modem

   c. console

   d. network connection

4

10. True or False: In the join command –j is used to reverse fields when they are displayed.

11. You can use the touch command to _____.

    a. create a new file

    b. change the time and date stamp on a file

    c. merge sorted data to a new file

    d. all of the above

    e. only a and b

12. The command "cat accounts persons > info" is used to _____.

    a. sort the accounts file, and merge it with the info file, creating a new file called persons

    b. sort the accounts and persons files to print on a printer called info

    c. replace only the numeric data in the accounts file with the numeric data in the persons file, and write the result in the info file

    d. combine the contents of the accounts and persons files into the info file

13. The 2> operator redirects _____.

    a. standard output

    b. standard error

    c. standard input

    d. the contents of one file into two files

14. The command cp source/accounts* newaccounts is used to _____.

    a. copy all of the source directory's files that start with "accounts" to the newaccounts directory

    b. move the source code for the accounts program into the file newaccounts

    c. combine all of the files beginning with the name "accounts" into one file called newaccounts, and place that file in the source directory

    d. merge the source directory's accounts file into the main directory's newaccounts file

15. True or False: The –c option for the cut command is used to reference character positions.

16. You want to sort a file with variable-length records in which the character between fields in each record is a semi-colon (;). What parameter do you use with the sort command to specify that fields are separated by the semi-colon?

    a. –d:

    b. +d;

    c. –t;

d. all of the above

e. only b and c

17. What does the command, paste vendors1 vendors2 accomplish?

    a. It copies the contents of vendors1 over the contents of vendors2, and saves the result in the vendors2 file.

    b. It copies the contents of the vendors2 over the contents of vendors1, and saves the result in the vendors1 file.

    c. It displays the combined contents of vendors1 and vendor2 to the screen.

    d. It saves the contents of the vendors1 and vendors2 files in a buffer that can be accessed later by the vi editor.

18. What happens when you use the command sort –o vendorstemp –m office industrial?

    a. The contents of the office and industrial files are merged into the vendorstemp file.

    b. The contents of the vendorstemp file are deleted, and at the same time the contents of the office file replace the contents of the industrial file.

    c. The vendorstemp file is sorted by the last field in each record, but only if the vendorstemp file contains fields that are identical to those in the office and industrial files.

    d. You see an error message, because the –o parameter needs to be accompanied by a field-separator, such as ":".

19. When using the join command and you want to display the text "None" for an unmatched record, use the _____ option.

    a. –u "None"

    b. –e "None"

    c. –N

    d. –nomatch

20. Which of the following commands enables you to recursively remove a directory and all of its contents?

    a. rmdir –all

    b. rm –r

    c. cut –a

    d. del ignore-fail-on-non-empty

21. Which of the following commands enables you to view only the second field in the names file, in which the contents of the names file are arranged in variable-length records separated by a colon?

    a. cat –d: –t2 names

    b. list –c: –f2 names

    c. sort –o: –l2 names

    d. cut –f2 –d: names

22. True or False: The sort command only works when the separator between fields in records is a semicolon (;), a colon (:), or a hyphen (-).

23. Used with the join command, which of these displays the fourth field in the second file?

    a. –o 2.4

    b. –f 2.4

    c. –o 4.2

    d. –f 4.2

24. You've just created the report file, newreport. To print this report, you type _____ at the command line.

    a. > newreport

    b. stdout newreport

    c. lpr newreport

    d. all of the above

    e. only b and c

25. What happens when you type the command mv vendors newvendors?

    a. The vendors file is copied into the newvendors file.

    b. The vendors file is renamed to become the newvendors file.

    c. The vendors and newvendors files are merged, so that both have identical contents.

    d. The first field of the vendors file is set up to be the same as the first field used in the newvendors file.

DISCOVERY EXERCISES

1. List three ways to create a new file.

2. What can you accomplish with the paste command that you cannot with the cat command?

3. How can you change only the time that a file was last modified?

4. Write the command-line command that sorts the records in the corp_phones2 file by job position, the second-to-last field in the record. Refer to Figure 4-4.

5. Write the command-line command that displays only the last names in the corp_phones1 file.

6. What are some examples of how you might use scripts?

7. What is the difference between join and awk?

8. Suppose you have three files: sales1, sales2, and sales3. Write the paste command that combines these files and separates the fields on each line with a ! character. The command should store the results in the file sales4.

9. Write the cut command that extracts the second field from each line of the sales4 file (that you created in Discovery Exercise 8). The command should store its results in the file sales5.

10. Why is the operation performed by the join command called a "relational join?"

11. Write a command that Becky uses to search for the file johnson_account. She knows the file is somewhere in a directory under her home directory.

12. Change the awk script that you created earlier so that the title reads "Product Information for Vendors."

13. Create a join script for the products and vendors files showing which vendors do not have a matching product in the products file.

14. Add a line to the join script you wrote in Discovery Exercise 13 so that the output is sent to a printer.

15. Write a simple awk program script file to print only the contents of the first field in the vendors file.

16. Use the cut command to create the file prod_desc using the products file shown in Figure 4-5. The only field in the file should be the product description.

17. Create a file similar to the products file (Figure 4-5) named prod_desc1. The prod_desc1 file should have the same fields as the products file, but contain different data. Use the sort command with the merge option to create an output file, merged_product. Use the input files of prod_desc1 and products.

18. Use any combination of cut and paste to create a new file using the input file, corp_phones2, shown in Figure 4-4. Place the employee's last name, first name, and middle initial in fields 1, 2, and 3.

19. Use vi, Emacs, or the method of your choice to create the files cust_names, cust_ids, and cust_status. The files should have the following contents.

Contents of cust_names:

```
Smith Furniture Co.
Wells Manufacturing
Rose Department Store
Haywood Resort
```

Contents of cust_ids:

```
101
102
114
197
```

Contents of cust_status:

```
ACTIVE
ACTIVE
INACTIVE
ACTIVE
```

20. Use the paste command to create a file named cust1. Combine the cust_ids and cust_names files to create cust1. Use the colon character as the field delimiter.

21. Use the paste command to create a file called cust2. Combine the cust_ids and cust_status files to create cust2. Use the colon character as the field delimiter.

22. Use the join command to join cust1 and cust2, and create the file cust_info. The key field is the first field of cust1 and cust2 (which lists the customer ID).

23. Write an awk command that reads the cust_info file and displays the customer IDs followed by the customer names. The customer IDs should be printed in a right-justified field of 10 spaces.

5

ADVANCED FILE PROCESSING

Dominion Consulting is evaluating its programming staff and the staff's current workload. Management wants a Programmer Activity Status Report that shows programmers' names and the number of projects on which each programmer is working. Your assignment: to design and create the files necessary to obtain the data and then produce the report.

Creating the Programmer Activity Status Report challenges you to make practical use of your UNIX file-processing skills. You used many file-processing commands in previous chapters. Lesson A introduces new commands that let you complete advanced file-processing tasks. Lesson B focuses on how to design a new application. You learn to design the application, create its files and shell scripts, and produce the final report.

◀ LESSON A ▶

SELECTING, MANIPULATING, AND FORMATTING INFORMATION

After completing this lesson, you should be able to:

♦ Use the pipe operator to redirect the output of one command to another command

♦ Use the grep command to search for a specified pattern in a file

♦ Use the uniq command to remove duplicate lines from a file

♦ Use the comm and diff commands to compare two files

♦ Use the wc command to count words, characters, and lines in a file

♦ Use the manipulate and format commands, which are sed, tr, and pr

ADVANCING YOUR FILE-PROCESSING SKILLS

In Chapter 4, you learned to use several UNIX commands to extract and organize information from existing files and transform that information into a useful format. This chapter explains how to use other file-processing commands. These commands are organized into two categories: select commands, and manipulation and transformation commands. Table 5-1 lists the **select commands**, which extract information.

Table 5-1   Select commands

Command	Purpose
comm	Compare sorted files and show differences
cut	Select columns (fields)
diff	Compare and select differences in two files
grep	Select lines or rows
head	Select lines from the beginning of a file
tail	Select lines from the end of a file
uniq	Select unique lines or rows
wc	Count characters, words, or lines in a file

The **manipulation and transformation commands** alter and transform extracted information into useful and appealing formats. Table 5-2 lists these commands.

Table 5-2   Manipulation and transformation commands

Command	Purpose
awk	Invoke awk, a processing and pattern-scanning language
cat	Concatenate files
chmod	Change security mode of a file or directory
join	Join two files, matching row by row
paste	Paste multiple files, column by column
pr	Format and print
sort	Sort and merge multiple files
sed	Edit data streams
tr	Translate character by character

USING THE SELECT COMMANDS

You used the head and tail commands in Chapter 1, and the cut command in Chapter 4. Now you can work with the grep, diff, uniq, comm, and wc commands, which also let you process files.

The command usage in this chapter demonstrates how commands generally work. Appendix B, "Syntax Guide to UNIX Commands," gives additional information about these commands.

5

Using Pipes

As you have seen, most UNIX commands take their input from stdin (the standard input device) and send their output to stdout (the standard output device). You have also used the > operator to redirect a command's output from the screen to a file, and the < operator to redirect a command's input from the keyboard to a file. The pipe operator (|) redirects the output of one command to the input of another command. The pipe operator is used in the following manner:

```
first_command | second_command
```

The pipe operator connects the output of the first command with the input of the second command. For example, the output of the ls command is commonly redirected to the more command. Using this technique, you can view multiple screens of the directory listing and advance your view with the Spacebar.

To redirect the output of the ls command to the more command:

1. Type **ls –l /etc** and press **Enter**. The output of the command scrolls quickly by.

2. Type **ls –l /etc | more** (but do not press Enter).

   Notice the output fills the screen and pauses with the prompt "More" displayed on the bottom line. Each time you press the Spacebar, the output advances to the next screen. Press the Spacebar to scroll a screen at a time or press Enter to advance one line at a time until the command has finished; you also can type q to exit the display of the directory contents.

The pipe operator can connect several commands on the same command line, in the following manner:

```
first_command | second_command | third_command . . .
```

To connect several commands with the pipe operator:

1. Type **ls /etc | sort –r | more** and press **Enter**. This command redirects the directory listing of the /etc directory to the sort –r command. sort –r sorts the directory listing in reverse order. The sort command's output is redirected to the more command.

You see the directory listing of /etc in reverse order, one screen at a time, as shown in Figure 5-1.

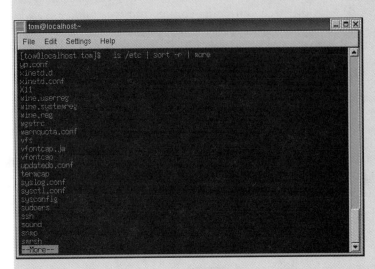

Figure 5-1 Redirecting the output of the ls command

Using the grep Command

Use the grep command to search for a specified pattern in a file, such as a particular word or phrase. UNIX finds and then displays the line containing the pattern you specified. As you recall from Chapter 1, you can use the head command to retrieve the first 10 lines of a file. You can combine the grep and head commands to retrieve only the first 10 lines containing the word or phrase. For example, use grep with head to find the first 10 lines in /etc/termcap that contain the characters "IBM."

To display lines in a file containing a particular word or phrase:

1. To see all the lines in the /etc/termcap file that contain the characters "IBM," type **grep IBM /etc/termcap** and press **Enter**. There are numerous lines, and the output scrolls by quickly.

2. Redirect the output of the grep command to the input of the more command. Type **grep IBM /etc/termcap | more** and press **Enter**.

3. Press the **Spacebar** until the command is finished.

4. Redirect the output of the grep command to the head command. Type **grep IBM /etc/termcap | head** and press **Enter**.

The code that you typed in Step 4 told grep to look for "IBM" in the /etc/termcap file, and then display the first 10 lines that are found. See Figure 5-2 for an example of the result of the command.

```
tom@localhost:~                                                    _ □ X
File  Edit  Settings  Help
[tom@localhost tom]$ grep IBM /etc/termcap | head
# The IBM PC alternate character set.  Plug this into any Intel console entry.
# Define IBM PC keypad keys for vi as per MS-Kermit while using ANSI.SYS.
# :tkh=\E[Y:.  Added IBM-PC forms characters and highlights, they match
ibmpc-|xenix|ibm|IBM PC xenix console display:\
or|ibpc3|origibmpc3|IBM PC 386BSD Console:\
oldbc3|oldibmpc3|old IBM PC BSD/386 Console:\
bsdos-pc|IBM PC BSD/OS Console:\
# with little  snowflake or star characters (IBM PC ROM character \017 = ^O)
# IBMPC Kermit 1.2:
pckermit|pckermit12|NCB IBMPC Kermit 1.2:\
[tom@localhost tom]$
```

Figure 5-2   Redirecting the output of the grep command

The grep command's options and wildcard support allow powerful search operations.

To expand the grep command's search capabilities with its options and regular expression support:

1. To see each line in the /etc/termcap file that contains the word "Linux," type **grep Linux /etc/termcap** and press **Enter**. (Make sure to capitalize the L in Linux.)

2. Some lines in the file contain the word "linux" (with a lowercase l). The search you performed in Step 1 only displayed the lines that contain "Linux." The –i option tells grep to ignore the case of the search characters. Type **grep –i linux /etc/termcap** and press **Enter**. You see the lines that contain either "Linux" or "linux."

3. The grep command supports regular expression characters in the search string. To see all the lines of the /etc/termcap file that start with "lin" followed by any set of characters, type **grep –i "^lin" /etc/termcap** and press **Enter**.

> **Note** The ^ character is a special grep expression called a metacharacter. Its purpose is to search for words that begin with the string that immediately follows it. In Step 3, the ^ character is searching for words that begin with the string "lin".

4. The grep command can process multiple files one after another. Type **grep linux /etc/*** and press **Enter**. You see the lines that contain "linux" from all the files in the /etc directory.

5. The –l (lowercase L) option instructs grep to display only the names of the files that contain the search string. Type **grep –l linux /etc/*** and press **Enter**. You see the names of the files in the /etc directory that contain "linux."

The grep command also searches files for phrases that contain spaces, as long as the phrase is specified on the command line inside quotation marks. For example, grep can search for the phrase "IBM PC," as demonstrated in the next example.

To search a file for a phrase:

1. Type **grep "IBM PC" /etc/termcap** and press **Enter**.

   You see all lines in the /etc/termcap file that contain the phrase IBM PC.

In the previous examples, grep searches the file specified on the command line. grep can also take its input from another command, through the pipe operator.

To redirect the output of a command to the grep command:

1. Type **ls /etc | grep magic** and press **Enter**. You see a list of the files whose names contain the word "magic."

The shell programming chapters that follow describe the grep file search command in more detail.

Using the uniq Command

The uniq command removes duplicate lines from a file. Because it compares only consecutive lines, the uniq command requires sorted input. The syntax of the uniq command is:

Syntax **uniq** [options] *file1* > *file2*

In its simplest form, the uniq command removes identical lines or rows from a file. The following command creates the file inventory. It contains all the lines in the parts file, with duplicate lines eliminated.

```
uniq parts > inventory
```

The –u option instructs uniq to generate as output only the lines of the source file that are not duplicated. (If a line is repeated, it is not generated as output.) Here is an example:

```
uniq -u parts > single_items
```

The –d option instructs uniq to generate as output one copy of each line that has a duplicate. Unduplicated lines are not generated as output. Here is an example:

```
uniq -d parts > multi_items
```

The next steps illustrate common uses of the uniq command. To practice the uniq command, start by using the cat command with the output redirection operator to create a new file, zoo1, in your working directory. The file lists animal names, food descriptions, pounds eaten daily, and food costs. Type the duplicate records in Step 1 as shown. Then you use the uniq command to remove the duplicate records.

To remove duplicate lines with the uniq command:

1. After the $ command prompt, type the following text, pressing **Enter** at the end of each line:

```
cat > zoo1
Monkeys:Bananas:2000:850.00
Lions:Raw Meat:4000:1245.50
Lions:Raw Meat:4000:1245.50
Camels:Vegetables:2300:564.75
Elephants:Hay:120000:1105.75
Elephants:Hay:120000:1105.75
```

2. Press **Ctrl+D**.

3. To use uniq to remove duplicate lines from the zoo1 file and use the output redirection operator to create the new file zoo2, type **uniq zoo1 > zoo2** and press **Enter**.

4. To use the cat command to display the zoo2 file, type **cat zoo2** and press **Enter**.

5. You see the contents of zoo2 as listed next. Notice that the uniq command removed the duplicate lines.

```
Monkeys:Bananas:2000:850.00
Lions:Raw Meat:4000:1245.50
Camels:Vegetables:2300:564.75
Elephants:Hay:120000:1105.75
```

Using the comm Command

Like the uniq command, the **comm** command identifies duplicate lines. Unlike the uniq command, it doesn't delete duplicates, and it works with two files rather than one. The comm command locates identical lines within two identically sorted files. It compares lines common to file1 and file2, and produces three-column output:

- The first column contains lines found only in file1.

- The second column contains lines found only in file2.

- The third column contains lines found in both file1 and file2.

The syntax of comm is:

Syntax **comm** [options] *file1 file2*

To practice using the comm command, start by creating the file my_list. Duplicate the file, and then use the comm command to compare the two files.

To use the comm command to compare files:

1. To create the file my_list, after the $ command prompt, type **cat > my_list** and press **Enter**.

2. Type the following text, pressing **Enter** at the end of each line:

   ```
   Football
   Basketball
   Skates
   ```

3. Press **Ctrl+D**.

4. To copy my_list to a second file, your_list, type **cp my_list your_list** and press **Enter**.

5. Now use the comm command to compare my_list to your_list. Type **comm my_list your_list** and press **Enter**.

6. You see the three-column output. (Note that the text in the first row was put in for your reference. This text does not appear on your screen.) Notice that the lines in the third column are those that both files contain. The files are identical.

   ```
   Column 1      Column 2      Column 3
                               Football
                               Basketball
                               Skates
   ```

7. Now add a new line to my_list. Type **cat >> my_list** and press **Enter**.

8. Type **Books** and press **Enter**.

9. Press **Ctrl+D**.

10. Use comm to compare my_list to your_list again. Type **comm my_list your_list** and press **Enter**.

11. You see the three-column output, with the unique new line in my_list in column 1.

    ```
    Column 1      Column 2      Column 3
                                Football
                                Basketball
                                Skates

    Books
    ```

Using the diff Command

The diff command attempts to determine the minimal set of changes needed to convert file1 to file2. The command's output displays the line(s) that differ. The code 3d2 displayed above the line indicates that you need to delete the third line in file1, so file1 matches file2. The d means delete, the 3 means the third line from file1, and the 2 means that file1 and file2 will be the same up to, but not including, line 2. The code 2a3 indicates you need to add a line to file1, so file1 matches file2. The a means add a line or lines to file1. The 3 means line 3 is to be added from file2 to file1. The 2 indicates that the line must be added following line 2.

To find differences between two files:

1. After the $ command prompt, type **diff zoo1 zoo2** and press **Enter**.

2. You see this information:

```
3d2
< Lions:Raw Meat:4000:1245.50
5d3
< Elephants:Hay:120000:1105.75
```

This means that you need to delete the third and fifth lines from zoo1 so the file matches zoo2.

3. To reverse the comparison order, type **diff zoo2 zoo1** and press **Enter**.

4. You see this information:

```
2a3
> Lions:Raw Meat:4000:1245.50
3a5
> Elephants:Hay:120000:1105.75
```

This means that you need to add the two lines shown to zoo2, so the file matches zoo1.

Using the wc Command

Use the wc command to count the number of lines (option –l), words (option –w), and bytes or characters (option –c) in text files. You may specify all three options in the command line, that is, –lwc. If you enter the command without options, you see counts of lines, words, and characters in that order. You can use the wc command to count the number of lines in a new file called "counters" in the next set of steps.

To create a file and count its lines:

1. After the $ command prompt, type **cat > counters** and press **Enter**.

2. Type this text, pressing **Enter** at the end of each line:

```
Linux is a full featured UNIX clone.
Linux blends the best of BSD and Sys V.
```

3. Type **Ctrl+D**.

4. To find the number of lines in counters, type **wc -l counters** and press **Enter**. UNIX reports that the file contains two lines.

5. To find the number of bytes in counters, type **wc -c counters** and press **Enter**. UNIX reports that the file contains 77 bytes.

6. To find the number of words in counters, type **wc -w counters** and press **Enter**. UNIX reports that the file contains 16 words.

7. To count words, characters, and lines in counters, type **wc -lwc counters** and press **Enter**. UNIX reports the counts for lines (2), words (16), and bytes (77). See Figure 5-3 to view the output of the wc command.

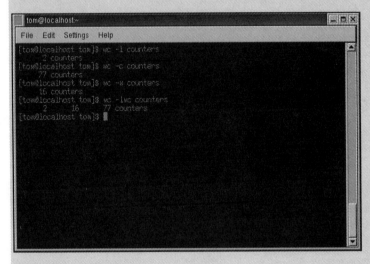

Figure 5-3   Using the wc command

USING THE MANIPULATE AND FORMAT COMMANDS

In addition to the commands that you learned about in Chapter 4 that are used to manipulate and format data, you can also use the sed, tr, and pr commands to edit and transform data's appearance before you display or print it.

Introducing sed

When you want to make global changes to large files, you need a different kind of tool than an interactive editor such as vi and Emacs. Another UNIX editor, **sed**, is designed specifically for this purpose. The minimum requirements to run sed are an input file and a command that lets sed know what actions to apply to the file. Sed commands have two general forms:

Syntax **sed** [options] *'command' file(s)*   **sed** [options] *-f scriptfile file(s)*

Dissection

- The first form lets you specify an editing command on the command line.

- The second form lets you specify a script file containing **sed** commands.

You can use sed to work with a new file, unix_stuff, to display only certain lines and to replace text.

5

To use sed to manipulate a file:

1. To create a new file, unix_stuff, in your working directory, type **cat > unix_stuff** and press **Enter**.

2. Type this text, pressing **Enter** at the end of each line:

   ```
   Although UNIX supports other database systems,
   UNIX has never abandoned the idea of working with
   flat files. Flat files are those that are based on pure
   text with standard ASCII codes. Flat files
   can be read by any operating system.
   ```

3. Press **Ctrl+D**.

4. To display only lines 3 and 4, type **sed -n 3,4p unix_stuff** and press **Enter**. (The n option prevents sed from displaying any lines except those specified with the p command.)

   This means "find lines numbered (-n) 3 and 4 in the file unix_stuff and display them (p)."

   You see lines 3 and 4:

   ```
   flat files. Flat files are those that are based on pure
   text with standard ASCII codes. Flat files
   ```

5. In sed, you can place two commands on one line. If you want to delete lines 3 and 4 and then display the file, you must use sed's -e option to specify multiple commands on the same line. To delete lines 3 and 4 from unix_stuff and display the results, type **sed -n -e 3,4d -e p unix_stuff** and press **Enter**.

   You see this text:

   ```
   Although UNIX supports other database systems,
   UNIX has never abandoned the idea of working with
   can be read by any operating system.
   ```

> Lines 3 and 4 are not actually deleted from the file, but simply filtered out so that they are not displayed.

6. To display only lines containing the word "Flat," type **sed -n /Flat/p unix_stuff** and press **Enter**.

   You see this text:

   ```
   flat files. Flat files are those that are based on pure
   text with standard ASCII codes. Flat files
   ```

7. To replace all instances of the word "Flat" with "Text," type **sed -n s/Flat/Text/p unix_stuff** and press **Enter** (make sure that you capitalize the words "Flat" and "Text"). (The s command substitutes one string of characters for another.)

   You see this text:

   ```
   flat files. Text files are those that are based on pure
   text with standard ASCII codes. Text files
   ```

To append new lines in sed, you must use the a\ command. This command appends lines after the specified line number. Like all other sed commands, it operates on all lines in the file if you do not specify a line number.

Next you can create a new script file, more_stuff. Include the append command, a\, in the file with the lines to be appended to the file unix_stuff. You must terminate each line, except for the last line of the file being added, with a backslash character. In the next steps, the $ preceding the a\ symbol tells sed to append more_stuff to unix_stuff after the last line in unix_stuff; without $, sed repeatedly adds all the lines in more_stuff after each line in unix_stuff.

To create a script file to append lines to another file:

1. To create the script file more_stuff, type **cat > more_stuff** and press **Enter**.

2. Type this text, pressing **Enter** at the end of each line:

   ```
   $a\
   Informix and Oracle, two major relational database\
   companies have installed their RDBMS packages on UNIX\
   systems for many years.
   ```

3. Press **Ctrl+D**.

4. To use the sed command to run the script file, type **sed -f more_stuff unix_stuff** and press **Enter**.

You see this text:

```
Although UNIX supports other database systems,
UNIX has never abandoned the idea of working with
flat files. Flat files are those that are based on pure
text with standard ASCII codes. Flat files
can be read by any operating system.
Informix and Oracle, two major relational database
companies have installed their RDBMS packages on UNIX
systems for many years.
```

5. Use vi to create the file stuff_replace. Insert the following sed commands into the file:

```
s/UNIX/Linux/
s/abandoned/given up/
s/standard/regular/
```

The lines in the file instruct sed to replace all occurrences of "UNIX" with "Linux," "abandoned" with "given up," and "standard" with "regular."

6. Execute sed, with the script file you created in Step 5, on the unix_stuff file. Redirect sed's output to the file unix_stuff2. Type **sed –f stuff_replace unix_stuff > unix_stuff2** and press **Enter**.

7. Type **cat unix_stuff2** and press **Enter**. You see the file with the changes specified by the stuff_replace script file, as shown in Figure 5-4.

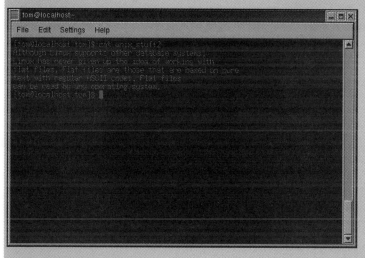

Figure 5-4   Resulting changes in the unix_stuff2 file

Translating Characters Using the tr Command

The tr command copies data from the standard input to the standard output, substituting or deleting characters specified by options and patterns. The patterns are strings and the strings are sets of characters.

Syntax **tr** [options] *string1 string2*

Dissection

- In its simplest form, **tr** translates each character in *string1* into the character in the corresponding position in *string2*. The strings may need to be "quoted" with either single or double quotes.

- Two options used most frequently are –d (delete character) and –s (substitute character).

A popular use of tr is converting lowercase characters to uppercase characters. You can translate the file counters from lowercase to uppercase characters by using [a–z] to specify the lowercase characters and [A–Z] to specify the uppercase characters.

To translate lowercase characters to uppercase characters in the file counters:

1. After the $ command prompt, type **tr [a-z] [A-Z] < counters** and press **Enter**.

    You see these lines:

    ```
    LINUX IS A FULL FEATURED UNIX CLONE.
    LINUX BLENDS THE BEST OF BSD AND SYS V.
    ```

You can also use the –d option with the tr command to delete input characters found in *string1* from the output. This is helpful when you need to remove an erroneous character from the file.

To delete specified characters from the counters file:

1. To delete the characters "full" from the output, type **tr -d "full" < counters** and press **Enter**.

    You see this text:

    ```
    Linx is a eatred UNIX cone.
    Linx bends the best o BSD and Sys V.
    ```

    Notice that the command deleted all characters in "full"—every f, u, and l from the output—rather than occurrences of the word "full".

The –s option of the tr command checks for sequences of a string1 character repeated several consecutive times. When this happens, tr replaces the sequence of repeated characters

with one occurrence of the corresponding character from string2. For example, use the
-s option when you need to change a field delimiter in a flat file from one character to
another. For instance, in the file zoo2, use tr to replace the field delimiter ":" with a space
character, " ". First, use cat to display the file.

To replace characters in the file counters:

1. After the $ command prompt, type **cat zoo2** and press **Enter**.

   You see this text:

   ```
   Monkeys:Bananas:2000:850.00
   Lions:Raw Meat:4000:1245.50
   Camels:Vegetables:2300:564.75
   Elephants:Hay:120000:1105.75
   ```

2. **Type tr -s ":"" "** < **zoo2** and press **Enter**.

   You see this text:

   ```
   Monkeys Bananas 2000 850.00
   Lions Raw Meat 4000 1245.50
   Camels Vegetables 2300 564.75
   Elephants Hay 120000 1105.75
   ```

Using the pr Command to Format Your Output

The pr command prints the specified files on the standard output in paginated form. If
you do not specify any files or you specify a filename of "-", pr reads the standard input.

By default, pr formats the specified files into single-column pages of 66 lines. Each page
has a five-line header, which, by default, contains the current file's name, its last modification date, current page, and a five-line trailer consisting of blank lines.

Syntax **pr** [options] [*file...*]

Dissection

- The three most frequently used options are –h (header format), which lets you customize your header lines; –d, which double-spaces output; and –l n, which sets the
  number of lines per page.

Use pr to format the unix_stuff file. Use the pipe operator (|) to send the output to the
more command (in other words, you would type this: | more) so that the output screen
does not flash by.

To format a file:

1. After the $ command prompt, type **pr –h "UNIX Files & Databases"** <
   unix_stuff | more, and press **Enter**. Type **q** to exit after you have viewed
   the text display. Figure 5-5 illustrates the screen that you see.

Now you can type the same command, but add the –l 23 option to limit the number of lines per page to 23. Because the standard number of lines on most monitors is 24, you do not need to send the output to the more or less commands to hold the screen.

2. Type **pr –l 23 –h "UNIX Files & Databases" < unix_stuff** and press **Enter**. See Figure 5-6 to view how the screen should look.

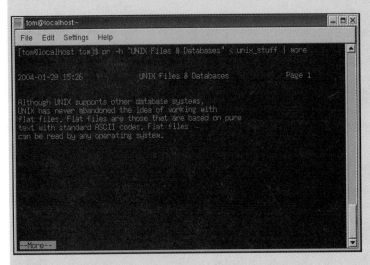

Figure 5-5   Results after piping the pr command

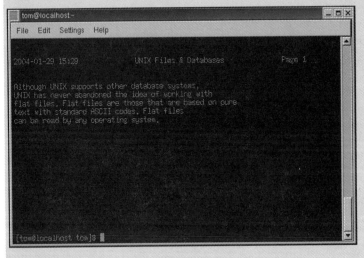

Figure 5-6   Results when not piping the pr command

◀ LESSON B ▶

USING UNIX FILE-PROCESSING TOOLS

TO CREATE AN APPLICATION

> **After completing this lesson, you should be able to:**
> ♦ Design a new file-processing application
> ♦ Design and create files to implement the application
> ♦ Use awk to generate formatted output
> ♦ Use cut, sort, and join to organize and transform selected file information
> ♦ Develop customized shell scripts to extract and combine file data
> ♦ Test individual shell scripts and combine all scripts into a final shell program

DESIGNING A NEW FILE-PROCESSING APPLICATION

The most important phase in developing a new application is creating a design. The design defines the information an application needs to produce. The design also defines how to organize this information into files, records, and fields, which are called **logical structures**, because each represents a logical entity such as a payroll file, an employee pay record, or an employee social security field. Files consist of records, and records consist of fields.

Now you're ready to create the Programmer Activity Status Report for Dominion Consulting. The report will show programmers' names and the number of projects on which each programmer is working. Start by designing and creating the files, including the records and fields, and then using advanced file processing commands to select, manipulate, and format information in the report.

Designing Records

The first task in the design phase is to define the fields in the records. These definitions take the form of a **record layout** that identifies each field by name and data type (such as numeric or nonnumeric). Design the file record to store only those fields relevant to the record's primary purpose. For example, you need two files for Dominion Consulting: one for programmer information and another for project information. Include a field for the programmer's name in the programmer file record and a field for the project description in the project file record. Do not store a programmer's name in a project file, even though the programmer may be assigned to the project. Conversely, do not store project names in the programmer files.

Allocating the space needed for only the necessary fields of the records keeps records brief and to the point. Short records, like short sentences, are easier to understand. Likewise, the simpler you make your application, the better it performs. However, make sure to include a field that uniquely identifies each record in the file. For example, the programmer file record includes a programmer number field to separate programmers who may have the same name.

The programmer number field in the programmer file record should be numeric. Numeric fields are preferable to nonnumeric fields for uniquely identifying records, because the computer interprets numbers faster than nonnumeric data in the fields. The project record can use a nonnumeric project code to uniquely identify each project record, because Dominion project codes contain letters and numbers (EA-100).

Linking Files with Keys

Multiple files are joined by a key—a common field that each of the linked files share. Another important task in the design phase is to plan a way to join files, if necessary. For example, the programmer-project application uses the programmer's number to link the programmer to the project file. Add the programmer's number field to the project record to link programmers to projects.

The flexibility to gather information from multiple files comprised of simple, short records is the essence of a relational database system. UNIX includes several file-processing commands that provide some of this relational database flexibility. You implement some of these commands in this lesson.

Before you begin to create files for the application, review the record layouts for the programmer and project files illustrated in Figure 5-7.

```
┌─────────────────────────────────────────────────────────────────────────┐
│                                                                           │
│  Programmer File – Record Layout                                          │
│                                                                           │
│  Field Name               Data Type          Example                     │
│  programmer_number        Numeric            101                          │
│  lname                    Alpha              Johnson                      │
│  fname                    Alpha              John                         │
│  midinit                  Alpha              K                            │
│  salary                   Numeric            39000                        │
│                                                                           │
│                                                                           │
│  Field Separator is a colon :                                             │
│  Sample Record:                                                           │
│  101:Johnson:John:K:39000                                                 │
│                                                                           │
└─────────────────────────────────────────────────────────────────────────┘

┌─────────────────────────────────────────────────────────────────────────┐
│                                                                           │
│  Project File – Record Layout                                             │
│                                                                           │
│  Field Name               Data Type          Example                     │
│  project_code             Alpha              EA-100                       │
│  project_status           Numeric            1 (*See Note)                │
│  project_name             Alpha              Reservation Plus             │
│  programmer_number        Numeric            110                          │
│                                                                           │
│                                                                           │
│  Field Separator is a colon :                                             │
│  Sample Record:                                                           │
│  EA-100:1:Reservation Plus:110                                            │
│  *Note: Project Status Codes 1=Unscheduled 2=Started 3=Completed 4=Cancelled │
│                                                                           │
└─────────────────────────────────────────────────────────────────────────┘
```

Figure 5-7   Programmer and project application record layouts

CREATING THE PROGRAMMER AND PROJECT FILES

Now that you have reviewed the basic elements of designing and linking records, you can begin to implement your application design. As you recall from Chapters 2 and 3, UNIX file processing predominantly uses flat files. Working with these files is easy, because you can create and manipulate them with text editors like vi and Emacs. The flowchart in Figure 5-8 provides an overview and analysis of programmer project assignments as derived from the programmer and project files.

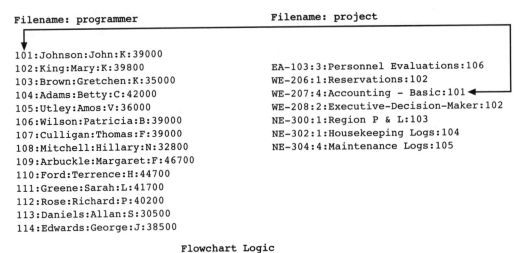

Filename: programmer

101:Johnson:John:K:39000
102:King:Mary:K:39800
103:Brown:Gretchen:K:35000
104:Adams:Betty:C:42000
105:Utley:Amos:V:36000
106:Wilson:Patricia:B:39000
107:Culligan:Thomas:F:39000
108:Mitchell:Hillary:N:32800
109:Arbuckle:Margaret:F:46700
110:Ford:Terrence:H:44700
111:Greene:Sarah:L:41700
112:Rose:Richard:P:40200
113:Daniels:Allan:S:30500
114:Edwards:George:J:38500

Filename: project

EA-103:3:Personnel Evaluations:106
WE-206:1:Reservations:102
WE-207:4:Accounting - Basic:101
WE-208:2:Executive-Decision-Maker:102
NE-300:1:Region P & L:103
NE-302:1:Housekeeping Logs:104
NE-304:4:Maintenance Logs:105

Flowchart Logic

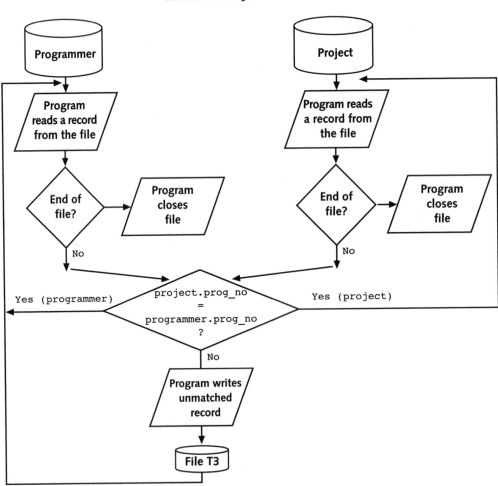

Figure 5-8   Overview and analysis of programmer assignments

Start by creating the programmer file in the vi editor.

To create the programmer file:

1. After the $ command prompt, type **vi programmer** and press **Enter**.

2. Type **i** to switch to insert mode, and then type the following text, pressing **Enter** at the end of each line except for the last line:

```
101:Johnson:John:K:39000
102:King:Mary:K:39800
103:Brown:Gretchen:K:35000
104:Adams:Betty:C:42000
105:Utley:Amos:V:36000
106:Wilson:Patricia:B:39000
107:Culligan:Thomas:F:39000
108:Mitchell:Hillary:N:32800
109:Arbuckle:Margaret:F:46700
110:Ford:Terrence:H:44700
111:Greene:Sarah:L:41700
112:Rose:Richard:P:40200
113:Daniels:Allan:S:30500
114:Edwards:George:J:38500
```

3. Press **Esc** to switch to command mode.

4. Type **:wq** to write the file and exit from vi.

To create the project file:

1. After the $ command prompt, type **vi project** and press **Enter**.

2. Type **i** to switch to insert mode, and type the following text, pressing **Enter** at the end of each line except for the last line:

```
EA-100:1:Reservation Plus:110
EA-100:1:Reservation Plus:103
EA-100:1:Reservation Plus:107
EA-100:1:Reservation Plus:109
EA-101:2:Accounting-Revenues Version 4:105
EA-101:2:Accounting-Revenues Version 4:112
EA-102:4:Purchasing System:110
EA-103:3:Personnel Evaluations:106
WE-206:1:Reservations:102
WE-207:4:Accounting - Basic:101
WE-208:2:Executive-Decision-Maker:102
NE-300:1:Region P & L:103
NE-302:1:Housekeeping Logs:104
NE-304:4:Maintenance Logs:105
```

3. Press **Esc** to switch to command mode.

4. Type **:wq** to write the file and exit from vi.

Formatting Output

Chapter 4 introduced the awk command, which simplifies preparation of formatted output. Awk is actually a full-featured programming language and requires a chapter unto itself. The limited presentation here explains only the use of the printf action within the awk command, which formats output. The printf function has the syntax:

Syntax **printf** *(format, expr1, expr2, expr3)*

Dissection

- *format* is always required. It is an expression with a string value that contains literal text and specifications of how to format expressions in the argument list. Each specification begins with a percentage character (%), which identifies the code that follows as a modifier (- to left justify; width to set size; .prec to set maximum string width or digits to the right of the decimal point; s for an array of characters (string); d for a decimal integer; f for a floating-point decimal number). Enclosed in double quotes (" "), format is often referred to as a mask that overlays the data fields going into it.

- *$expr1, $expr2, $expr3* are awk expressions that represent data fields. These expressions typically take the form $1, $2, $3, etc. In the programmer file, the expression $1 indicates the programmer number (the first field), $2 indicates the programmer's last name (the second field), and $3 indicates the programmer's first name (the third field).

You can use the awk command and printf function to print the programmer_number, programmer last name, and programmer first name, all left-justified.

To print three fields:

1. After the $ command prompt, type **awk -F:'{printf "%d %-12.12s %-10.10s\n", $1, $2, $3}' programmer** and press **Enter**. See Figure 5-9 for an example of the output.

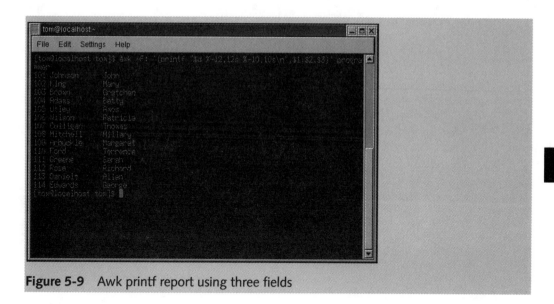

Figure 5-9   Awk printf report using three fields

Each % symbol in the format string corresponds with a $ field: The %d specifies how to display the $1 field, the %–12.12s specifies how to display the $2 field, and the %–10.10s specifies how to display the $3 field. Here is a breakdown of each specifier:

- %d indicates that field $1 is to appear in decimal digits.

- %–12.12s indicates that field $2 is to appear as a string. The minus sign (–) specifies the string is to be left-justified. The 12.12 indicates the string should appear in a field padded to 12 spaces, with a maximum size of 12 spaces.

- %–10.10s indicates that field $3 is to appear as a string. The minus sign (–) specifies the string is to be left-justified. The 10.10 indicates the string should appear in a field padded to 10 spaces, with a maximum size of 10 spaces.

The spaces that appear in the format string are printed exactly where they appear in relation to the fields (one is printed after $1, and another is printed after $2). The trailing \n tells awk to skip a line after displaying the three fields.

Awk provides a shortcut to other UNIX file-processing commands when you need to extract and format data fields for output. For example, although it takes a few lines of code, you can use the cut, paste, and cat commands to extract and display the programmers' last names and salaries. Start by using the cut command to extract the last name (field 2) from the programmer file, and store the output in temp1. Next use the cut command to extract the salary (field 5) from the programmer file, and store the output in temp2. Then use the paste command to combine temp1 and temp2, and create the file progsal. Finally, use the more command to display the output. You can also accomplish the same task with one awk command.

To extract and display information using cut, paste, and more:

1. After the $ command prompt, type **cut –f2 –d: programmer > temp1** and press **Enter**.

2. Type **cut –f5 –d: programmer > temp2** and press **Enter**.

3. Type **paste temp1 temp2 > progsal** and press **Enter**.

4. To use the more command to display the output, type **more progsal** and press **Enter**.

   You see output similar to the following excerpt:

   ```
   Johnson        39000
   King           39800
   Brown          35000
   Adams          42000
   Utley          36000
   . . .
   ```

To accomplish the same task with one awk command:

1. After the $ command prompt, type **awk –F: '{printf "%–10.10s %7.0f\n", $2, $5}' programmer** and press **Enter**.

   You see output similar to the following excerpt:

   ```
   Johnson        39000
   King           39800
   Brown          35000
   Adams          42000
   Utley          36000
   . . .
   ```

There are two important differences between using the cut and paste commands and using the awk command. First, you don't have to create three extra files when using awk. Second, the column display has a more even appearance because of the use of awk.

Cutting and Sorting

Now that you've created the programmer information file, you can select the programmer_number fields stored in the project file. These fields identify programmers who are currently assigned to projects. Refer to Figure 5-7 as you work through the next task.

Start by cutting the programmer_number fields from the project file (field 4), and piping (|) the output to the sort command to place any duplicate numbers together. Pipe the sorted output to the uniq command to remove any duplicate programmer_numbers.

Finally, redirect the output to a temporary file, t1. (The t1 file is a list of programmer numbers that identifies programmers who are assigned to projects.)

To select fields from the project file:

1. After the $ command prompt, type **cut -d: -f4 project | sort | uniq > t1** and press **Enter**.

2. To display the contents of t1, type **cat t1** and press **Enter**.

   You see the list of programmer numbers:

   ```
   101
   102
   103
   104
   105
   106
   107
   109
   110
   112
   ```

   The next step is to cut the programmer_number fields (field 1) from the programmer file, and pipe the output as you did in Step 1. Call the new temporary file t2, which is a list of programmer numbers that identifies all programmers who work for Dominion.

3. Type **cut -d: -f1 programmer | sort | uniq > t2** and press **Enter**.

4. To display the contents of t2, type **cat t2** and press **Enter**.

   You see this list of programmer numbers:

   ```
   101
   102
   103
   104
   105
   106
   107
   108
   109
   110
   111
   112
   113
   114
   ```

   Now that t1 and t2 are sorted in the same order, you can match them. Use the comm command to select the lines from t1 that do not match lines in t2, and redirect the output to another file, t3, which lists programmer numbers of all programmers who are not assigned to projects.

5

5. Type **comm –13 t1 t2 > t3** and press **Enter**.

6. To display the programmer numbers for programmers who are not working on projects, type **cat t3** and press **Enter**.

You see this list of programmer numbers:

```
108
111
113
114
```

To display the names of unassigned programmers, you can now sort the programmer file in programmer_number order, and write the output to t4.

7. Type **sort -t: +0 –1 –o t4 programmer** and press **Enter**.

Now use the join command to match programmer_numbers in t4 and t3, and redirect the output to t5, which contains the names of all programmers who are not assigned to a project.

8. Type **join -t: –1 1 –2 1 –o 1.2 –o 1.3 –o 1.4 t4 t3 > t5** and press **Enter**.

9. To display the contents of t5, type **cat t5** and press **Enter**.

You see the following list of programmer names:

```
Mitchell:Hillary:N
Greene:Sarah:L
Daniels:Allan:S
Edwards:George:J
```

Now you can transform the output using the sed editor to eliminate the colon field separators in t5.

10. Type **sed –n 's/:/ /gp' < t5** and press **Enter**.

You see this list of programmer names:

```
Mitchell Hillary N
Greene Sarah L
Daniels Allan S
Edwards George J
```

USING A SHELL SCRIPT TO IMPLEMENT THE APPLICATION

Your application for Dominion Consulting currently consists of many separate commands that must run in a certain order. As you recall from Chapter 4, you can create a script file to simplify the application. Store your commands in a script file, which in effect becomes a program. (When you develop an application, you should usually test and debug each command before you place it in your script file.) You can use the vi editor to create the script files.

Chapter 6 covers the subject of shell script programming in more detail.

A shell script should contain not only the commands to execute, but also the comments to identify and explain the shell script so that users or programmers other than the script's author can understand how it works. Comments also enable the original author to remember the logic of the script over time. Use the pound (#) character in script files to mark comments. This tells the shell that the words following # are a comment, not a UNIX command. The next set of steps show how to add comments to your shell programs. Start by using the vi editor to create the new script file, which is called pact. Notice that you begin by inserting comments to identify and explain the script.

To create a script and add comments:

1. After the $ command prompt, type **vi pact** and press **Enter**.

2. Type **a** (you can type a as well as i) to switch to insert mode, and then type the text below, pressing **Enter** at the end of each line:

```
# ===========================================================
# Script Name:  pact
# By:           Your initials
# Date:         January 2004
# Purpose:      Create temporary file, pnum, to hold the
#               count of the number of projects each
#               programmer is working on. The pnum file
#               consists of:
#               prog_num and count fields
# ===========================================================
cut -d: -f4 project | sort | uniq -c | awk '{printf "%s:
%s\n",$2,$1}' > pnum
# cut prog_num, pipe output to sort to remove duplicates
# and get count for prog/projects.
# output file with prog_number followed by count
```

3. Press **Esc** to switch to command mode.

4. Type **:wq** to write the file and exit from vi.

RUNNING A SHELL SCRIPT

You can run a shell script in virtually any shell that you have on your system. In this book, you use the Bourne Again Shell, or Bash, which is commonly used in Linux systems. As you learned earlier, a script is a text file containing commands. In different shells, there often are some incompatibilities in terms of the exact use, syntax, and options associated with commands. One advantage to using the Bash shell is that it accepts more variations in command structures than the original Bourne shell; Bash is a freeware derivative of the Bourne and Korn shells.

When you create a shell script to run in Bash, you can immediately run the script by typing sh (to call the Bash shell interpreter) and then the name of the script, as follows:

```
sh testscript
```

Another advantage of using sh is that you can accompany it with several debugging options to help you troubleshoot problems with your script (you learn more about these debugging options in Chapter 6). For your first experiences with shell scripts in this chapter, you use sh simply to run your scripts.

Another way to run a shell script, which you learn more about in Chapter 6, is to make it executable by using the x permission and then typing ./ prior to the script name when you run the script itself. In addition, when you write a script, it is advisable to specify with what shell the script is intended to be used. You do this by including a statement—such as #!/bin/bash for the Bash shell—on the first line of the script. Chapter 7 shows you how to implement this practice as your shell scripts become more advanced.

For now, you can use the sh (shell) command to run the pact script, and use the less command to display the contents of pnum.

To run the pact script that you created earlier:

1. After the $ command prompt, type **sh pact** and press **Enter**.

2. Type **less pnum** and press **Enter** to view the contents of the pnum file that is created by the pact script.

3. You see these programmer numbers and count fields:

   ```
   101:1
   102:2
   103:2
   104:1
   105:2
   106:1
   107:1
   109:1
   110:2
   112:1
   ```

4. If necessary, press **q** to exit the text display and return to the command line.

You now have a file that contains programmer numbers and the number of projects on which each programmer is working. Next, create a script file, pnumname, to extract the programmer names and numbers from the programmer file, and redirect the output to the file pnn.

To create another script file:

1. After the $ command prompt, type **vi pnumname** and press **Enter**.

2. Type **a** to switch to insert mode, and then type the text below, pressing **Enter** at the end of each line:

```
# ========================================================
# Script Name:   pnumname
# By:            Your initials
# Date:          Jan 2004
# Purpose:       Extract Programmer Numbers and Names
# ========================================================
cut -d: -f1-4 programmer | sort -t: +0 -1 | uniq > pnn
# The above cuts out fields 1 through 4.
# The output is piped to a sort by programmer number.
# The sorted output is piped to uniq to remove
# duplicates.
# Uniq redirects the output to pnn.
```

3. Press **Esc** to switch to command mode.

4. Type **:wq** to write the file and exit from vi.

5. To run the shell program and use the less command to display the contents of pnn, type **sh pnumname** and press **Enter**.

6. Type **less pnn** and press **Enter**.

7. You see the programmer names and numbers, with duplicates eliminated:

```
101:Johnson:John:K
102:King:Mary:K
103:Brown:Gretchen:K
104:Adams:Betty:C
105:Utley:Amos:V
106:Wilson:Patricia:B
107:Culligan:Thomas:F
108:Mitchell:Hillary:N
109:Arbuckle:Margaret:F
110:Ford:Terrence:H
111:Greene:Sarah:L
112:Rose:Richard:P
113:Daniels:Allan:S
114:Edwards:George:J
```

8. Press **q** to exit the text display, if necessary.

Now you can create a script file, joinall, to join the files pnn and pnumname, and redirect the output to pactrep.

To create a script file that joins two files:

1. After the $ command prompt, type **vi joinall** and press **Enter**.

2. Type a to switch to insert mode, and then type the text below, pressing **Enter** at the end of each line:

```
# =======================================================
# Script Name:   joinall
# By:            Your initials
# Date:          Jan 2004
# Purpose:       Join pnum and pnn to create a report file
# =======================================================
# Join the files including the unassigned programmers.
# You do this by placing the programmer names (pnn) file,
# first, in the join sequence.
join -t: -a1 -j1 1 -j2 1 pnn pnum  > pactrep
```

3. Press **Esc** to switch to command mode.

4. Type **:wq** to write the file and exit from vi.

5. To run joinall and use less to display the contents of pactrep, type **sh joinall** and press **Enter**.

6. Type **less pactrep** and press **Enter**.

7. You see the programmer names, including unassigned programmers' names:

```
101:Johnson:John:K: 1
102:King:Mary:K: 2
103:Brown:Gretchen:K: 2
104:Adams:Betty:C: 1
105:Utley:Amos:V: 2
106:Wilson:Patricia:B: 1
107:Culligan:Thomas:F: 1
108:Mitchell:Hillary:N
109:Arbuckle:Margaret:F: 1
110:Ford:Terrence:H: 2
111:Greene:Sarah:L
112:Rose:Richard:P: 1
113:Daniels:Allan:S
114:Edwards:George:J
```

8. Type **q** to exit, if necessary.

PUTTING IT ALL TOGETHER TO PRODUCE THE REPORT

An effective way to develop applications is to combine small scripts in a larger script file. Because you have already executed the individual scripts and tested for accuracy, you can now place each in a script file in the proper sequence to produce the final programmer and project report for Dominion.

Start by using the vi editor to create the shell script practivity. Use the :r command to retrieve the pact, pnumname, and joinall scripts, and place them in the practivity shell script. You can then use the dd command in vi to remove the lines indicated in the comments.

To create a final shell script:

1. After the $ command prompt, type **vi practivity** and press **Enter**.

2. Type **a** to switch to insert mode, and then type the text below, pressing **Enter** at the end of each line:

```
# =========================================================
# Script Name:  practivity
# By:           Your initials
# Date:         Jan 2004
# Purpose: Generate Programmer Activity Status Report
# =========================================================
```

3. Press **Esc** to switch to command mode.

4. To retrieve the three script files, type **:r pact** and press **Enter**. Move the cursor to the end of the file, type **:r pnumname** and press **Enter**. Move the cursor to the end of the file, type **:r joinall** and press **Enter**.

5. Use the **dd** command to delete the comments from the script. For example, you could move the cursor to each line that begins with a #, and then type dd. You could also move the cursor to the first line beginning with a #, and then type 9dd to delete the current line and the eight comment lines after it. Do the same for the remaining comment lines in the file.

Only these four lines should remain in the script:

```
cut -d: -f4 project | sort | uniq -c | awk '{printf "%s:
%s\n",$2, $1}' > pnum
cut -d: -f1-4 programmer | sort -t: +0 -1 | uniq > pnn
join -t: -a1 -j1 1 -j2 1 pnn pnum > pactrep
```

6. Type the following in the script:

```
# Print the report
awk '
BEGIN {
  { FS = ":"}
  { print "\tProgrammer Activity Status Report\n" }
  { "date" | getline d }
  { printf "\t    %s\n",d }
  { print "Prog#\t*—Name—*  Projects\n" }
  {print "=========================================\n"}
  }
  { printf "%-s\t%-12.12s %-12.12s %s\t%d\n",
      $1, $2, $3, $4, $5 } ' pactrep
# remove all the temporary files
  rm pnum pnn pactrep
```

7. Press **Esc** to switch to command mode. Make sure the script looks similar to the one in Figure 5-10.

8. Type **:wq** to write the file and exit from vi.

9. After the $ command prompt, type **sh practivity** and press **Enter**. Figure 5-11 illustrates the report.

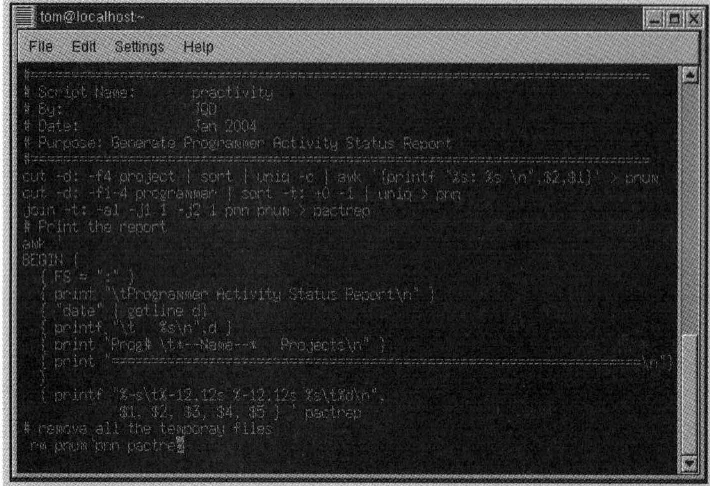

Figure 5-10   Entering the practivity script

Figure 5-11   Report produced by the shell script

CHAPTER SUMMARY

❑ The UNIX file-processing commands can be organized into two categories: select commands and manipulation and transformation commands. Select commands extract information. Manipulation and transformation commands alter and transform extracted information into useful and appealing formats.

❑ The uniq command removes duplicate lines from the file. You must sort the file, because uniq compares only consecutive lines.

❑ The comm command compares lines common to file1 and file2, and produces three-column output that reports variances between the files.

❑ The diff command attempts to determine the minimal set of changes needed to convert file1 into file2.

❑ The tr command copies data read from the standard input to the standard output, substituting or deleting the characters specified by options and patterns.

❑ The sed command is a file editor designed to make global changes to large files. Minimum requirements to run sed are an input file and a command that tells sed what actions to apply to the file.

❑ The pr command prints the standard output in pages.

❑ The design of a file-processing application reflects what the application needs to produce. The design also defines how to organize information into files, records, and fields, which are also called logical structures.

❑ Use a record layout to identify each field by name and data type (numeric or non-numeric). Design file records to store only those fields relevant to each record's primary purpose.

❑ Shell programs should contain commands to execute and comments to identify and explain the program. The pound (#) character used in script files denotes comments.

❑ Write shell scripts in stages so that you can test each part before combining them into one script. Using small shell scripts and combining them in a final shell script file is an effective way to develop applications.

COMMAND SUMMARY

Review of Lesson A Commands		
Command	**Purpose**	**Options Covered in This Chapter**
comm	Compare and output lines common to two files	
diff	Compare two files and determine which lines differ	
grep	Select lines or rows	**-i** ignores case **-l** lists only filenames
pr	Format a specified file	**-d** double-spaces the output **-h** customizes the header line **-l***n* sets the number of lines per page
sed	Specify an editing command or a script file containing sed commands	**-a ** appends text after a line **-d** deletes specified text **-e** specifies multiple commands on one line **-n** indicates line numbers **-p** displays lines **-s** substitutes specified text
tr	Translate characters	**-d** deletes input characters found in *string1* from the output **-s** checks for sequences of *string1* repeated consecutive times
uniq	Remove duplicate lines to create unique output	
wc	Count the number of lines, bytes, or words in a file	**-c** counts the number of bytes or characters **-l** counts the number of lines **-w** counts the number of words

Review of Lesson B Commands		
Command	**Purpose**	**Options Covered in This Chapter**
printf	Tell the awk program what action to take for formatting and printing information	none
sh	Execute a shell script	none

REVIEW QUESTIONS

1. Which of the following can you accomplish using select commands?

   a. include or exclude specific fields in the records of a file

   b. create script files

   c. combine the contents of two files

   d. all of the above

   e. only a and b

2. Which of the following are text manipulation and transformation commands?

   a. awk

   b. chmod

   c. sort

   d. all of the above

   e. only a and c

3. What result do you get when using this command: grep "character" /etc/termcap?

   a. The resulting display deletes the word "character" wherever it is used in the original file.

   b. The resulting display adds the word "character" at the beginning of each line.

   c. The resulting display shows all of the lines in the file that contain the word "character."

   d. The resulting action renames the /etc/termcap file to /etc/character.

4. The pr command is used to _____.

   a. merge files

   b. format and print files

   c. count the number of paragraphs in a file

   d. pair two files into one

5. When you type ls –l /bin | more, what is accomplished by the "| more" portion of the command?

   a. It causes long lines in the display to automatically wrap to the next line so that you can view them.

   b. It copies the directory listing into a permanent file called "more."

   c. It pipes the directory listing to the "more" file on a central network server.

   d. It causes the directory contents to be displayed one screen at a time, for easier reading.

5

6. You are working on a memo for your boss, who does not want the memo to be over 500 words long. After you have used one of the UNIX editors to write the memo and saved it in a file, what command-line command can you use to determine the number of words in the file?

   a. head

   b. tail

   c. wc

   d. uniq

7. Which of these commands enables you to compare the budget_taskforce file to the pay_taskforce file to immediately see which employee names are in both files?

   a. comm budget_taskforce pay_taskforce

   b. counter budget_taskforce pay_taskforce

   c. chmod budget_taskforce pay_taskforce

   d. tail budget_taskforce pay_taskforce

8. You are preparing a mailing from the customers file, but want to make sure that you remove duplicate name entries. You can use the _____ command to most easily eliminate the duplicates.

   a. cat

   b. uniq

   c. join

   d. paste

9. You are converting a spreadsheet file, salesfigs, in which the columns of numbers are separated by a space. You need to replace the spaces with colons, so that the file can be imported into a different spreadsheet program. Which of the following commands enables you to insert the colons?

   a. sed " " ":" salesfigs

   b. pr –r " " ":" > salesfigs

   c. > –f " " ":" salesfigs

   d. tr –s " " ":" < salesfigs

10. In the command sed –n 20,21p namesfile, the "–n 20,21p" portion of the command is used to _____.

    a. transpose the 20th and 21st records in the file

    b. transpose the 20th and 21st fields in the file

    c. delete the 20th and 21st lines in the file

    d. display only the 20th and 21st lines in the file

11. True or False: One limitation of the sed command is that it cannot be used with a script file.

12. In the command pr –1 15 –h "Department Names" < names, the "–l 15" portion is used to _____.

    a. search only the first 15 lines

    b. search for duplicates within only the last 15 lines

    c. display output 15 lines per page

    d. omit displaying the first 15 lines

13. You have two flat files, salaries1 and salaries 2, that are supposed to contain identical records of employee salaries. However, when these files are used to compute how much to withhold from paychecks, it is obvious that there are some differences between them. Which of the following commands enables you to identify the records that do not match?

    a. diff salaries1 salaries2

    b. sort –d salaries1 salaries2

    c. wc –d salaries1 salaries2

    d. uniq –u salaries1 salaries2

14. The _____ command enables you to convert lowercase characters to uppercase.

    a. paste

    b. $a \

    c. grep

    d. tr

15. Which of the following is true of a record layout?

    a. It must keep individual records under 56 characters in length.

    b. It identifies fields by name and data type.

    c. The entire record layout must be stored in the file /etc/key.

    d. all of the above

    e. only a and c

16. In the awk printf command, the format option "–" when used after "%" is used to _____.

    a. omit a record

    b. print a percentage

    c. left-justify text

    d. right-justify text

17. Which of the following commands enables you to format a title using awk printf?

    a. { print "\tMYTITLE\n" }

    b. { -tMYTITLE }

    c. { "title=MYTITLE" }

    d. { title "tMYTITLE" }

18. Use the _____ command to run a shell script.

    a. sh

    b. runex

    c. start

    d. cmd

19. When using awk printf formatting, "$2" represents _____.

    a. the instruction to create two lines between text

    b. an expression to extract information from the second field in a file

    c. an expression to extract the second record in a file

    d. the instruction to create a common header on each page, beginning with page 2

20. When you extract numeric information from a file using the awk printf command, use a(n) _____ to specify that the data is numeric (numbers) instead of alphanumeric (text).

    a. n

    b. a

    c. s

    d. d

21. When using the grep command, the –i option enables you to _____.

    a. suppress the first line of output

    b. ignore case

    c. indicate that code is coming from the keyboard

    d. suppress the last line of output

22. With the pr command, the –d option is used to _____.

    a. print to a disk file

    b. show line numbers

    c. double-space the output

    d. print output on a printer

23. True or False: You cannot pipe output when you use the cut command.

24. Which of the following is true of the sed command?

    a. It can be used to make global changes in a large file.

    b. You need an input file when you use sed.

    c. sed can be used with a script file to specify commands.

    d. all of the above

    e. only a and b

25. The –d option, when used with the tr command, _____.

    a. is used to delete characters or strings

    b. is used to substitute characters or strings

    c. can transpose two characters or strings

    d. can insert new characters or strings

5

DISCOVERY EXERCISES

1. Use either the vi editor or cat >> to add the following lines to the counters file that you created earlier in this chapter:

    ```
    Linux supports using X Windows.
    GNOME and KDE are two examples of X Windows desktops.
    A desktop can make your work easier and faster.
    The GNOME desktop includes software for office
    productivity.
    ```

2. Determine the total number of words in the counters file.

3. Use a command to determine which lines in the counters file contain the word "Linux."

4. Use a command to replace all references to "Linux" with "UNIX" in the counters file.

5. Make a copy of the counters file, and call it countersbak. Use the vi editor to delete the first two lines in the counters file. Use a command to display which lines are now different between the counters and countersbak files.

6. Write a script file, called salaries, using awk to print the salary, first name, last name, and programmer number fields (in that order) from the programmer file. Give the report the title "Programmers and Salaries." Use the sh command to execute salaries.

7. Write a script file, called projects, using awk to print the project name and project code fields from the project file. Give the report the title "Projects." Use the sh command to execute projects. Create the script using as few lines of code as possible.

8. Create a new file, CD_list, and enter these lines in the file:

```
country:1000:210
rock:1001:380
classical:1002:52
alternative:1003:122
light rock:1004:151
light rock:1004:151
celtic:1005:44
jazz:1006:62
soundtracks:1007:32
soundtracks:1007:32
```

Use the sed command and a script file to add these lines to the end of the CD_list file:

```
hard rock:1008:70
misc:1009:22
```

9. Use a command to find the duplicate lines (records) in the CD_list file.

10. Use the uniq command to remove the duplicate lines in the CD_list file, placing the corrected information in a file called CD_list_new.

11. In the CD_list_new file, replace the word "misc" with "other," and then compare the contents of the CD_list file with the CD_list_new file to make sure your changes are implemented.

12. Use the grep command to find all the lines that contain the word "celtic" in the CD_list_new file.

13. Use a command to make all letters uppercase in the CD_list_new file.

14. Use the sed command on the CD_list_new file to replace the words "LIGHT ROCK" with "EASY LISTENING" and the word "ALTERNATIVE" with "EXPERIMENTAL".

15. Create a file called software with these fields:

   ❏ Project Number, using the same numbers shown in the project file (which you created earlier in this chapter)

   ❏ Software Code, using any three-digit number

   ❏ Software Description, such as Excel

   Then, write a small application joining records in the software file to matching records in the project file, and use the awk program to print a report describing the software for each project you created earlier.

CHAPTER

6

INTRODUCTION TO SHELL SCRIPT PROGRAMMING

Dominion Consulting needs a program to maintain its phone records file, which contains the following information about each employee: telephone number, name, department, job title, and date of hire. This program should let users add, change, delete, locate, and display specific employee information. You can meet these needs by creating a UNIX shell script. In Lesson A of this chapter, you learn the basic tools used to create UNIX shell scripts and to debug them. In Lesson B, you create shell scripts that let users view and add records to the phone database.

◀ LESSON A ▶

USING THE UNIX SHELL AS A SCRIPTING LANGUAGE

After completing this lesson, you should be able to:

♦ Understand the program development cycle using a high-level computer language and UNIX shell scripts

♦ Compare the shells to determine the best choice for creating scripts

♦ Learn about shell variables, operators, and wildcard characters

♦ Write simple shell scripts to illustrate programming logic

PREVIEWING THE APPLICATION

The corp_phones file, which you create in this chapter, contains records with fields delimited by colons. Here is a sample record from the file:

```
219-555-4587:Mitchell:Barbara:C:4541:Admin Asst:12-14-1995
```

In Chapters 4 and 5 you learned several commands such as grep, cut, paste, and awk, which you can use to manipulate, extract, and format information stored in files. Although these commands are powerful, they can be difficult for nontechnical users. In addition, you must often use these commands together in long sequences to achieve the results you want. Repeatedly executing these command sequences can be cumbersome, even for the experienced technical user. UNIX shell scripts eliminate both of these problems. You can write shell scripts that present user-friendly screens, and that automatically issue commands like grep and awk to extract, format, and display information. This gives the nontechnical user access to powerful features of UNIX. Shell scripts also save you time by automating long command sequences that you must perform often.

The shell script application you develop in this chapter and in Chapter 7 presents a menu of operations from which the user may choose. Among other tasks, these operations automate the process of searching for, formatting, and displaying the phone number records in corp_phones. The application also provides data-entry screens to ease the task of adding new records to the file.

To accomplish this chapter's case project, you learn about these scripting and programming features of the UNIX shell:

- *Shell variables*—Your scripts often need to keep values in memory for later use. Shell variables are symbolic names that can access values stored in memory.

- *Operators*—Shell scripts support many operators, including those for performing mathematical operations.

- *Logic structures*—Shell scripts support sequential logic (for performing a series of commands), decision logic (for branching from one point in a script to a different point), looping logic (for repeating a command several times), and case logic (for choosing an action from several possible alternatives).

In addition, you learn special commands for formatting screen output and positioning the cursor.

Before you begin writing shell scripts, you should understand the program development cycle.

THE PROGRAM DEVELOPMENT CYCLE

The process of developing an application is known as the **program development cycle**. The steps involved in the cycle are the same whether you are writing shell scripts or high-level language programs.

The process begins by creating program specifications—the requirements the application must meet. The specifications determine what data the application takes as input, the processes that must be performed on the data, and the correct output.

After you determine the specifications, the design process begins. During this process, programmers create file formats, screen layouts, and algorithms (logical and mathematical procedures) that the program uses. Programmers use a variety of tools to design complex applications. In the next chapter, you study flowcharts and pseudocode, two important program design tools.

After the design process is complete, programmers begin writing the actual code, which they must then test and debug. When they find errors, they must correct them, and begin the testing process again. This procedure continues until the application performs satisfactorily.

Figure 6-1 illustrates the program development cycle.

Using High-Level Languages

Computer programs are instructions often written using a high-level language such as COBOL, C, or C++. A **high-level language** is a computer language that uses English-like expressions. For example, the following COBOL statement instructs the computer to add 1 to the variable COUNTER:

```
ADD 1 TO COUNTER.
```

Here is a similar statement, written in C++:

```
counter = counter + 1;
```

A program's high-level language statements are stored in a file called the **source file**. This is the file that the programmer creates with an editor such as vi or Emacs. The source file cannot execute, however, because the computer can only process instructions written in low-level machine language. As you recall from Chapter 3, machine-language instructions are cryptic codes expressed in binary numbers. Therefore, the high-level source file must be converted into a low-level machine language file, as described next.

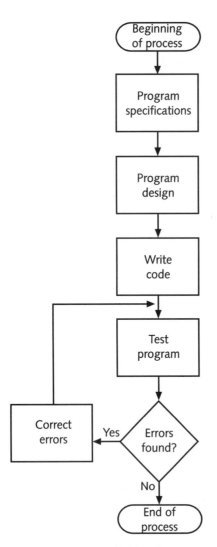

Figure 6-1   Program development cycle

The source file is converted into an executable machine-language file by a program called a **compiler**. The compiler reads the lines of code that the programmer wrote in the source file and converts them to the appropriate machine language instructions. For example, the Linux C and C++ compilers are named gcc and g++. The following command illustrates how to compile the C++ source code file, datecalc.C, so that you can run it as the program datecalc:

```
g++ datecalc.C -o datecalc
```

In this sample command, the -o option followed by datecalc instructs the compiler to create an executable file, datecalc. The source file is datecalc.C. The command causes the compiler to translate the C++ program datecalc.C into an executable machine-language program, which is stored in the file datecalc. You learn more about C and C++ programming in Chapter 10.

As you will learn in Chapter 10, there are some important differences between C and C++ source code, and therefore it is necessary to use the right compiler (gcc versus g++). Remember, when you invoke one of these compilers in Linux, the gcc compiler expects C files to end in .c, whereas the g++ compiler expects C++ files to end in .C.

If a source file contains **syntax errors** (grammatical mistakes in program language use), it cannot be converted into an executable file. The compiler locates and reports any syntax errors, which the programmer must correct.

After compiling, the executable program may still contain fatal run-time errors or logic errors. Fatal run-time errors cause the program to abort due to an invalid memory location specified in the program code, for example. Logic errors cause the program to produce invalid results because of such problems as flawed mathematical statements.

Another way to accomplish programming tasks is to develop UNIX shell scripts.

Using UNIX Shell Scripts

Introduced in Chapter 4, UNIX **shell scripts** are text files that contain sequences of UNIX commands. Like high-level source files, a programmer creates shell scripts with a text editor. Unlike high-level language programs, shell scripts do not have to be converted into machine language by a compiler. This is because the UNIX shell acts as an **interpreter** when reading script files. As an interpreter reads the statements in a script file, it immediately translates them into executable instructions, and causes them to run. No executable file is produced because the interpreter translates and executes the scripted statements in one step. If a syntax error is encountered, the execution of the shell script halts.

After you create a shell script, you simply tell the operating system that the file is a shell script that can be executed. This is accomplished by using the **chmod** ("change mode") command to change the file's mode. The mode determines how the file may be used. Recall that modes are denoted by single-letter codes, the most common being r (read), w (write), and x (execute). Further, the chmod command tells the computer who is allowed to use the file: the owner (u), the group (g), or all other users (o). For a description of the chmod command, see Appendix B, "Syntax Guide to UNIX Commands."

As you recall from Chapter 4, you can change the mode of a file so that UNIX recognizes it as an executable program (mode x) that everyone (user, group, and others) can use. In the following example, the user is the owner of the file.

```
$ chmod ugo+x filename        <Enter>
```

To make a file executable for all users, you can also use either of the following:
```
$ chmod a+x filename <Enter>
```
or
```
$ chmod 755 filename <Enter>
```

After you make the file executable you can run it in one of several ways:

- You can simply type the name of the script at the system command prompt. However, before this method can work, you must modify your default directory path to include the directory in which the script resides. The directory might be the source or bin directory under your home directory. If you use this method, before any script or program can be run it must be retrieved from a path identified in the **PATH variable**, which provides a list of directory locations where UNIX looks to find the executable scripts or programs. You learn how to temporarily modify the PATH variable in the "Variables" section later in this chapter, and how to permanently modify the PATH variable in Chapter 7.

- If the script resides in your current directory, which is not in the PATH variable, you can run the script by preceding the name with a dot slash (./) to tell UNIX to look in the current directory to find it, as follows:
```
$ ./filename      <Enter>
```

- If the script does not reside in your current directory and is not in the PATH variable, you can run it by specifying the absolute path to the script. For example, if the script is in the data directory under your home directory, you would type either of the following (using Tom's home directory as an example):
```
$ /home/tom/data/filename      <Enter>
```
or
```
$ ~/data/filename      <Enter>
```

Shell scripts run less quickly than do compiled programs, because the shell must interpret each UNIX command inside the executable script file before it is executed. Whether a programmer uses a script or a compiled program (such as a C++ program) is often related to several factors:

- If the programmer is more proficient in writing scripts than source code for a compiler

- If there is a need for the script or program to execute as quickly as possible, such as to reduce the load on the computer's resources when there are multiple users

- If the job is more or less complex; a compiled program may offer more flexible options or features

Prototyping an Application

A **prototype** is a running model of your application, which lets you review the final results before committing to the design. Using a shell script to create a prototype is often the quickest and most efficient method, because prototyping logic and design capabilities reside within UNIX.

After the working prototype is approved, the script can be rewritten to run faster using a compiled language such as C++. If the shell script performs well, however, you may not need to convert it to a compiled program.

Now that you have a glimpse of the program development cycle, you realize that it is more efficient to maintain Dominion Consulting's phone records using a shell script. Your next step is to select the programming shell that is the most efficient for your application.

6

THE PROGRAMMING SHELL

All Linux versions use the Bash shell (Bourne Again Shell) as the default shell. Table 6-1 lists the three shells that come with most Linux distributions, their derivations, and distinguishing features.

Table 6-1   Linux shells

Shell Name	Original Shell From Which It is Derived	Description
Bash	Bourne and Korn shells	Offers strong scripting and programming language features like shell variables, control structures, and logic/math expressions; combines the best features of the Bourne and Korn shells
csh/tcsh	C shell	Conforms to a scripting and programming language format; shell expressions use operators such as those found in the C programming language
ksh/zsh	Korn shell	Similar to the Bash shell in many respects, but also has syntax similar to that of C programming; useful if you are familiar with older Korn shell scripts

The Bash shell offers improved features over the older Bourne and Korn shells and is fully backward-compatible with the Bourne shell. Additionally, the Bash shell, when compared to the other shells, has a more powerful programming interface. As a result, you should use the Bash shell (as contained in Red Hat Linux 7.2) to complete your assignment.

 The manual pages in Red Hat Linux contain a generous amount of documentation about the Bash shell. Just type man bash to access the documentation.

Now that you have selected the shell, you need to learn about what the shell scripts include, such as the variables, operators, and special characters.

VARIABLES

Variables are symbolic names that represent values stored in memory. The three types of variables discussed in this section are configuration variables, environment variables, and shell variables. Use **configuration variables** to store information about the setup of the operating system, and do not change them. You can set up **environment variables** with initial values that you can change as needed. These variables, which UNIX reads when you log in, determine many characteristics of your session. For example, you have already learned about the PS1 environment variable, which determines the way your prompt appears. Additionally, UNIX uses environment variables to determine such things as where it should look for programs, which shell to use, and the path of your home directory. **Shell variables** are those you create at the command line or in a shell script. They are very useful in shell scripts for temporarily storing information.

In this chapter, you learn several commands to create, access, and manipulate variables. For example, to see a list of your environment variables, use the **printenv command**.

To see a list of your environment variables:

1. The list of environment variables probably spans more than one screen, so use the more command with printenv. Type **printenv | more** and press **Enter**.

You see a list of environment variables similar to the one shown in Figure 6-2.

Figure 6-2   Output of the printenv | more command

2. Press the **Spacebar** until the output is complete.

If you specify the name of a variable as an argument to the printenv command, it displays only the contents of that variable.

Environment and configuration variables bear standard names such as PS1, HOME, PATH, SHELL, USERNAME, and PWD. (Configuration and environment variables are capitalized to distinguish them from user variables). A script file in your home directory sets the initial values of environment variables. You can use these variables to set up and personalize your login sessions. For example, you can set your PATH variable to search for the location of commands that other users have created. Table 6-2 lists standard Bash shell variables.

6

Table 6-2   Standard Bash shell environment and configuration variables

Name	Variable Contents	Determined By
HOME	Path name for user's home directory	System
LOGNAME	Holds the account name of the user currently logged on	System
PPID	Refers to the parent ID of the shell	System
TZ	Holds the time zone set for use by the system	System
IFS	Enables the user to specify a default delimiter for use in working with files	Redefinable
LINEND	The current line number of a function or script	Redefinable
MAIL	Name of mail file checked by mail utility for received messages	Redefinable
MAILCHECK	Interval for checking for received mail (example: 60)	Redefinable
PATH	List of path names for directories searched for executable commands	Redefinable
PS1	Primary shell prompt	Redefinable
PS2	Secondary shell prompt	Redefinable
PS3 and PS4	Holds prompts used by the set and select commands	Redefinable
SHELL	Path name of program for type of shell you are using	Redefinable
BASH	Contains the absolute path to the Bash shell, such as /bin/bash	User defined
BASHVERSION	Version number of Bash	User defined
CDPATH	Path names for directories searched by cd command for subdirectories	User defined
ENV	Filename containing commands to initialize the shell, as in .bashrc or .tcshrc	User defined
EUID	Holds the user identification number (UID) of the currently logged on user	User defined
EXINIT	Initialization commands for vi editor	User defined
FCEDIT	FC is a Bash shell utility that enables you access a range of commands in the command history file; FCEDIT is the variable used to specify which editor (vi by default) is used when you invoke the FC command	User defined
FIGNORE	Specifies file name suffixes to ignore when working with certain files	User defined

Table 6-2 Standard Bash shell environment and configuration variables (continued)

Name	Variable Contents	Determined By
FUNCNAME	Contains the name of the function that is running, or is empty if there is no shell function running	User defined
GROUPS	The current user's group memberships	User defined
HISTCMD	Contains the sequence number that the currently active command is assigned in the history index of commands that already have been used	User defined
HISTFILE	File in which the history of the previously executed commands is stored	User defined
HISTFILESIZE	Sets the upward limit of command lines that can be stored in the file specified by the HISTFILE variable	User defined
HISTSIZE	Establishes the upward limit of commands that the Bash shell can recall	User defined
HOSTFILE	Holds the name of the file that provides the Bash shell with information about its network host name (such as localhost.localdomain) and IP address (such as 129.0.0.24); if the HOSTFILE variable is empty, the system uses the file/etc/hosts by default	User defined
HOSTTYPE	Contains information about the type of computer that is hosting the Bash shell, such as i386 for an Intel-based processor	User defined
INPUTRC	Filename for the Readline start-up file overriding the default of ~/.inputrc	User defined
MACHTYPE	Type of system including CPU, operating system, and desktop	User defined
MAILPATH	List of mail files to be checked by mail for received messages	User defined
MAILWARNING	When this variable is set, it enables the user to determine if he or she has already read the mail currently in the mail file	User defined
OLDPWD	Directory accessed just before the current directory	User defined
OPTIND	When a command is run using one or more option arguments, this variable shows the index number of the argument to be processed next	User defined
OPTARG	When a command is run using one or more option arguments, this variable contains the last option specified	User defined
OPTERR	If set to 1 (which is the default established each time the Bash shell is invoked), this variable enables Bash to display error messages associated with command option arguments	User defined
OSTYPE	The type of operating system on which Bash is running, such as linux-gnu	User defined
PROMPT-COMMAND	Holds the command to be executed prior to displaying a primary prompt	User defined
PWD	Holds the name of the directory that is currently accessed	User defined
RANDOM	Yields a random integer each time it is called, but you must first assign a value to the RANDOM variable to properly initialize random number generation	User defined
REPLY	Specifies the line to read as input, when there is no input argument passed to the built-in shell command, which is read	User defined

Table 6-2   Standard Bash shell environment and configuration variables (continued)

Name	Variable Contents	Determined By
SHLVL	Contains the number of times Bash is invoked plus one, such as the value 3 when there are 2 Bash (terminal) sessions currently running	User defined
TERM	Contains the name of the terminal type in use by the Bash shell	User defined
TIMEFORMAT	Timing for pipelines	User defined
TMOUT	Enables Bash to stop or close due to inactivity at the command prompt, after waiting the number of seconds specified in the TMOUT variable (TMOUT is empty by default so that Bash does not automatically stop due to inactivity)	User defined
UID	Holds the user identification number of the currently logged on user	User defined

Operators are used to define and evaluate variables. Let's take a look at the various operators that UNIX uses.

SHELL OPERATORS

The Bash shell operators are divided into three groups: defining and evaluating operators, arithmetic operators, and redirecting and piping operators.

Defining and Evaluating Operators

Use the equal sign (=) operator to set a variable, as follows:

```
NAME=Becky
```

This example sets the NAME variable to the value Becky. The variable names or values that appear to the left and right of an operator are its **operands**. The name of the variable you are setting must appear to the left of the = operator. The value of the variable you are setting must appear to the right.

Notice there are no spaces between the = operator and its operands.

To create a variable, and assign it a value:

1. Type **DOG=Poodle** and press **Enter**.

   You created the variable DOG and set its value to Poodle.

The echo command is used to display the contents of a variable.

To see the contents of a variable:

1. Type **echo DOG** and press **Enter**.

   You see the word "DOG."

2. To see the contents of the DOG variable, you must precede the name of the variable with a $ operator. Type **echo $DOG** and press **Enter**.

   You see the word "Poodle."

Enclose the value in double quotes ("") if it contains spaces. The next command is an example.

To set a variable to a string of characters containing spaces:

1. Type **MEMO="Meeting will be at noon today"** and press **Enter**.

2. Type **echo $MEMO** and press **Enter**.

   You see the contents of the MEMO variable: Meeting will be at noon today.

You may also use single quotes. However, they suppress the evaluation of a variable like $HOME, whereas double quotes do not.

To demonstrate the " and ' characters used with a variable name:

1. Type **echo '$HOME'** and press **Enter**.

   You see $HOME on the screen.

2. Type **echo "$HOME"** and press **Enter**.

   You see the path of your home directory on the screen.

Finally, the **backquote (`) operator** is used to enclose UNIX commands, the output of which becomes the contents of a variable. On some computer keyboards, the backquote is located at the upper-left corner, under the Esc key and on the same key as the tilde (~).

To demonstrate the backquote operator:

1. Type **TODAY=`date`** and press **Enter**. This command creates the variable TODAY, executes the date command, and stores the output of the date command in the variable TODAY. (No output appears on the screen.)

2. Type **echo $TODAY** and press **Enter**. You see the output of the date command that was executed in Step 1.

Exporting Shell Variables to the Environment

Shell scripts cannot automatically access variables created on the command line or by other shell scripts. To make a variable available to a shell script, you must use the export command to make it an environment variable.

To demonstrate the export command:

1. Type **cat > testscript** and press **Enter**.

2. Type **echo $MY_VAR** and press **Enter**.

3. Type **Ctrl+D**. You have created a simple shell script named testscript. Its only function is to display the value of the MY_VAR variable.

4. To make the script executable, type **chmod ugo+x testscript** and press **Enter**.

5. After the $ prompt, type **MY_VAR=2** and press **Enter**.

6. Type **echo $MY_VAR** and press **Enter** to confirm the operation above. You see 2 on the screen.

7. Next look at the list of environment variables. Type **printenv | more** and press **Enter**.

   Look carefully as you scroll through the output of the printenv command. You do not see the MY_VAR variable.

8. Execute the shell script by typing **./testscript** and pressing **Enter**. The script displays a blank line. This is because it does not have access to the shell variable MY_VAR.

9. Make the variable available to the script by typing **export MY_VAR** and pressing **Enter**.

10. Execute the script again by typing **./testscript** and pressing **Enter**. This time the value 2 appears.

11. Now look at your list of environment variables by typing **printenv | more** and pressing **Enter**. Again, look carefully as you scroll through the list. This time you see MY_VAR listed.

6

Notice that in the previous exercise you had to type the ./ characters before the name of the script file. This is because the shell looks for programs in the directories specified by the PATH variable.

To see the contents of the PATH variable:

1. Type **echo $PATH** and press **Enter**.

   You see a list of directories. Notice that the path names are separated by colons (:) as in Figure 6-3.

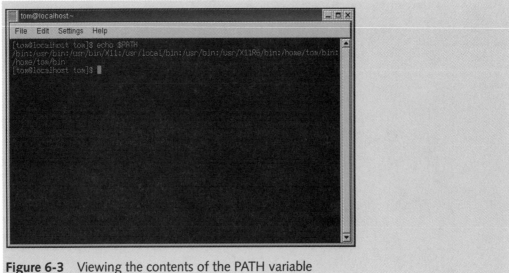

Figure 6-3   Viewing the contents of the PATH variable

Because new shell scripts are most often kept in the current directory while they are being tested, you should add the current working directory to the PATH variable. Here is an example:

```
PATH=$PATH:.
```

Remember, the shell interprets $PATH as the contents of the PATH variable. The sample command sets the PATH variable to its current contents. The colon and dot (.) add the current directory to the search path so that the shell program can locate the new program.

To add the current working directory to the PATH variable:

1. Type **PATH=$PATH:.** and press **Enter**.

2. Type **echo $PATH** and press **Enter**. The dot (.) is now appended to the list.

3. You can now run scripts in your current working directory without typing the ./ characters before their names. Test this by typing **testscript** and pressing **Enter**. You see testscript execute.

Arithmetic Operators

Arithmetic operators consist of the familiar plus (+) for addition, minus (–) for subtraction, asterisk (*) for multiplication, and slash (/) for division. Table 6-3 explains other operators.

Table 6-3   Examples of the shell's arithmetic operators

Operator	Description	Example	
-, +	Unary minus and plus	**+R**	(denotes positive R)
		-R	(denotes negative R)
!, ~	Logical and bitwise negation	**!Y**	(returns 0 if Y is nonzero, returns 1 if Y is zero)
		~X	(reverses the bits in X)
*, /,%	Multiplication, division, and remainder	**A * B**	(returns A times B)
		A / B	(returns A divided by B)
		A % B	(returns the remainder of A divided by B)
+,-	Addition, subtraction	**X + Y**	(returns X plus Y)
		X – Y	(returns X minus Y)
>,<	Greater than and less than	**M > N**	(Is M greater than N?)
		M < N	(Is M less than N?)
=,!=	Equality and inequality	**Q = R**	(Is Q equal to R?)
		Q != R	(Is Q not equal to R?)

When using arithmetic operators, the usual mathematical precedence rules apply: multiplication and division are performed before addition and subtraction. For example, the value of the expression 6 + 4 * 2 is 14, not 20. Precedence can be overridden, however, by using parentheses. For example, the value of the expression (6 + 4) * 2 is 20, not 14. Other mathematical rules also apply; for example, division by zero is treated as an error.

To store arithmetic values in a variable, use the let statement. For example, the following command stores 14 in the variable X:

```
let X=6+4*2
```

You can use shell variables as operands to arithmetic operators. Assuming the variable X has the value 14, the following command stores 18 in the variable Y:

```
let Y=X+4
```

To practice using the arithmetic operators:

1. Type **let X=10+2*7** and press **Enter**.

2. Type **echo $X** and press **Enter**. You see 24 on the screen.

3. Type **let Y=X+2*4** and press **Enter**.

4. Type **echo $Y** and press **Enter**. You see 32 on the screen.

Constants beginning with 0 are interpreted as octal numbers. An x preceding a constant denotes a hexadecimal number.

PREVENTING REDIRECTION FROM OVERWRITING FILES

Recall that the > redirection operator overwrites an existing file. If you write a shell script that uses the > operator to create a file, you may want to prevent it from overwriting important information. You can use the set command with the **-o noclobber option** to prevent a file from being overwritten, as in the following example:

```
$ set -o noclobber      <Enter>
```

However, you can choose to overwrite a file anyway by placing an exclamation point after the redirection operator:

```
$ set -o noclobber      <Enter>
$ cat new_file > old_file <Enter>
  bash: : old_file: cannot overwrite existing file
  cat: file exists
$ cat new_file >! old_file <Enter>
```

On some systems, such as Red Hat Linux, you can use a | symbol instead of ! to overwrite a file.

Avoid employing the -o noclobber option if you are using the Bash shell in the X Window interface with the KDE desktop. Using the option in this manner can unexpectedly terminate the command line session.

MORE ABOUT WILDCARD CHARACTERS

Shell scripts frequently use the asterisk (*) and other wildcard characters (such as ? and [ ]), which help to locate information containing only a portion of a matching pattern. For example, to retrieve all program files with names that contain a .c extension, use the following command:

```
ls *.c
```

Wildcard characters are also known as **glob** characters. If an unquoted argument contains one or more glob characters, the shell processes the argument for filename generation. Glob characters are part of **glob patterns,** which are intended to match filenames and words. Special constructions that may appear in glob patterns are:

- The question mark (?) matches exactly one character, except for the backslash and period.

- The asterisk (*) matches zero or more characters in a filename.

- [chars] defines a class of characters. The glob pattern matches any single character in the class. A class may contain a range of characters, as in [a-z].

For example, assume the working directory contains files chap1, chap2, and chap3. The following command displays the contents of all three files:

```
more chap[1-3]    <Enter>
```

Now that you understand some of the tools used to construct shell scripts, here are some examples of how shell scripts are written to support the four basic logic structures needed for program development.

SHELL LOGIC STRUCTURES

The four basic logic structures needed for program development are:

- sequential logic
- decision logic
- looping logic
- case logic

Each of these logic structures is discussed in the sections that follow.

Sequential Logic

Sequential logic works so that commands are executed in the order in which they appear in the script or program. The only break in this sequence comes when a branch instruction changes the flow of execution by redirecting to another location in the script or program. The following hands-on activity presents a very simple example of a shell script using sequential logic. In these steps, you create a simple shell script called seqtotal.

To demonstrate sequential logic:

1. Type **vi seqtotal** and press **Enter**.

2. Type **i** to switch to vi's insert mode.

3. Type the following lines:

```
let a=1
let b=2
let c=3
let total=a+b+c
echo $total
```

4. Press **Esc** to switch to vi's command mode.

5. Type **:wq** and press **Enter** to save the file and exit vi.

6. Next, test the new shell script, seqtotal. (To save a few keystrokes, use the sh command instead of the chmod command.) Type **sh seqtotal** and press **Enter**.

You see the output of the script, which is 6.

Many scripts are simple, straightforward command sequences. An example is the programmer activity report script you wrote in Chapter 5. The shell executes the script's commands in the order they appear in the file. You use sequential logic to write this type of application.

Decision Logic

Decision logic enables your script or program to execute a statement or series of statements only if a certain condition exists. The **if statement** is the primary decision-making control structure in this type of logic. In the steps that follow, notice that the semicolon (;) separates commands on the same line.

Throughout the sample scripts, variables are always enclosed in double quotes, as in "$choice," "$looptest," "$yesno," "$guess," and "$myfavorite," because of how the shell interprets variables. All shell variables, unless declared otherwise, are **strings**, which are arrays of alphanumeric characters. If you do not enter data in the string variables, the variables are treated as blank strings, which result in an invalid test. The enclosing double quotes therefore maintain the validity of strings, with or without data, and the test is carried out without producing an error condition.

To demonstrate decision logic:

1. Type **vi os_choice** and press **Enter**.

2. Type **i** to switch to vi's insert mode.

3. Type the following lines:

```
echo -n "What is your favorite operating system? "
read OS_NAME
if [ "$OS_NAME" = "UNIX" ]
then
    echo "You will like Linux."
else
    echo "You should give Linux a try!"
fi
```

4. Make sure your edit session looks like the one in Figure 6-4. Press **Esc** to switch to vi's command mode.

5. Type **:wq** and press **Enter** to save the file and exit vi.

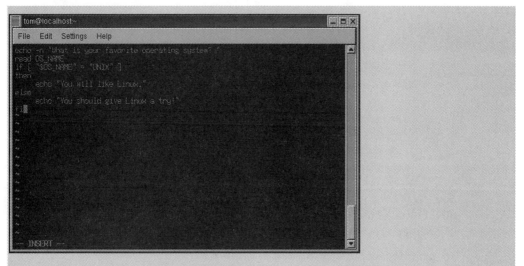

Figure 6-4   Creating a script with decision logic

6

Before you run the script, let's examine its contents. The first statement uses the echo command to display a message on the screen. The -n option suppresses the line feed that normally appears after the message. The second statement uses the read command, which waits for the user to type a line of keyboard input. The input is stored in the variable specified as the read command's argument. The line in the script reads the user's input into the OS_NAME variable.

The next line begins an if statement. The word "if" is followed by an expression inside a set of brackets ([]). (The spaces on either side that separate the [and] characters from the enclosed expression are necessary.) The expression, which is tested to determine if it is true or false, compares the contents of the OS_NAME variable with the string UNIX. (When you use the = operator in an if statement's test expression, it tests its two operands for equality. In this case, the operands are the variable $OS_NAME and the string UNIX. If the operands are equal, the expression is true—otherwise, it is false. If the contents of the OS_NAME variable is equal to UNIX, the statement that follows the word "then" is executed. In this script, it is the echo statement, "You will like Linux."

If the if statement's expression is false (if the contents of the OS_NAME variable does not equal UNIX), the statement that follows the word "else" is executed. That statement reads, "You should give Linux a try!" In this script, it is a different echo statement.

Notice the last statement, which consists of the characters "fi." fi ("if" spelled backward) always marks the end of an if or an if...else statement.

Now, test your code by executing it at least twice:

1. Make the script executable by typing **chmod ugo+x os_choice** and pressing **Enter**. Next, run the script by typing **./os_choice** and pressing **Enter**.

2. When asked to enter the name of your favorite operating system, answer **UNIX**.

3. Run the script again and respond with **MS-DOS** or some other operating system name.

Remember that you must use the chmod command first to make the script executable. Then, after the command prompt, type the path to the script plus the script's name to execute it. Another way to run the script is to use the sh command, as you did with the seqtotal script.

You can nest a control structure, such as an if statement, inside another control structure. For example, a script may have an if statement inside another if statement. The first if statement controls when the second if statement is executed.

To practice writing a nested if statement:

1. Open the os_choice file in vi or Emacs.

2. Edit the file so it contains the following lines. (Code has been added to the else part of the original if statement.)

```
echo -n "What is your favorite operating system? "
read OS_NAME
if [ "$OS_NAME" = "UNIX" ]
then
   echo "You will like Linux."
else
   if [ "$OS_NAME" = "WINDOWS" ]
   then
        echo "A great OS for applications."
   else
        echo "You should give Linux a try!"
   fi
fi
```

3. Execute the script and respond with **WINDOWS** when asked for your favorite operating system. The result should look like that in Figure 6-5.

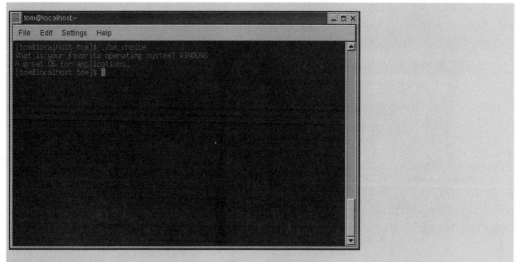

Figure 6-5   Running a script with a nested if statement

As you can see, the second if statement is located in the first if statement's else section. It is only executed when the first if statement's expression is false.

Decision logic structures, such as the if statement, are used in applications where different courses of action are required, depending on the result of a command or comparison.

Looping Logic

In **looping logic**, a control structure (or loop) repeats until some condition exists or some action occurs. You learn two looping mechanisms in this section: the for loop and the while loop.

Use the **for command** for looping through a range of values. It causes a variable to take on each value in a specified set, one at a time, and perform some action while the variable contains each individual value. The loop stops after the variable has taken on the last value in the set and has performed the specified action with that value.

To demonstrate looping logic:

1. Create the file our_users with vi or Emacs.

2. Type the following lines into the file:

```
for USERS in john ellen tom becky eli jill
do
    echo $USERS
done
```

3. Save the file, and exit the editor.

4. Give the file execute permission, and run it. Your screen appears similar to Figure 6-6.

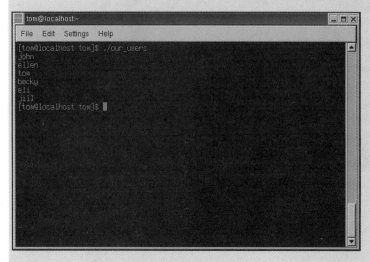

Figure 6-6 Output of the our_users script

The for statement you typed in Step 2 specifies that the variable USERS take on the values john, ellen, tom, becky, eli, and jill. Because there are six values in the set, the loop repeats six times. Each time it repeats, USERS contains a different value from the set, and the statement between the do and done statements is executed. The first value in the set is john, so the echo statement executes the first time with john stored in USERS. That is why john appears on the screen. The second time the loop executes, USERS contains ellen, so the echo statement displays ellen. This procedure repeats until no other names are left in the set.

Executing Control Structures at the Command Line

Most shell script control structures, such as the if and for statements, must be written across several lines. This does not prevent you from executing them directly on the command line, however.

To demonstrate entering program control structures at the command line:

1. Enter the following directly on the command line, and press **Enter**.

```
$ for myhobbies in tennis swimming movies travel <Enter>
> do <Enter>
> echo $myhobbies  <Enter>
> done  <Enter>
```

After you finish typing, you see results similar to Figure 6-7.

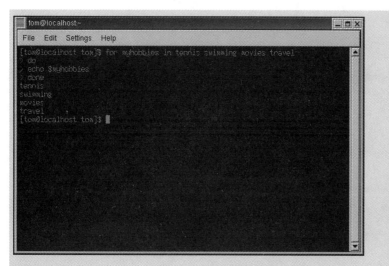

Figure 6-7   Results of the for loop typed at the command line

The shell knows more code will come after you type the first line. It displays the > prompt indicating it is ready for the control structure's continuation. The shell reads further input lines until you type the word "done," which marks the end of a for loop.

Using Wildcard Characters in a Loop

Now, see how the for statement works with wildcard characters when you want to print a few chapters of a book.

To create test data and use wildcards in a for loop:

1. Type **cat > chap1** and press **Enter**.

2. Type **This is chapter 1** and press **Enter**.

3. Type **Ctrl+D**. The file chap1 is created.

4. Type **cat > chap2** and press **Enter**.

5. Type **This is chapter 2** and press **Enter**.

6. Type **Ctrl+D**. The file chap2 is created.

7. Type **cat > chap3** and press **Enter**.

8. Type **This is chapter 3** and press **Enter**.

9. Type **Ctrl+D**. The file chap3 is created.

10. Use the vi or Emacs editor to create the shell script, chapters. The script should have these lines:

```
for file in chap[123]; do
  more $file
done
```

11. Save the file, and exit the editor.

12. Give the file execute permission, and test it. You see output similar to Figure 6-8.

Figure 6-8   Results of the chapters script

The While Loop

A different pattern for looping is created using the while statement. The while statement best illustrates how to set up a loop to test repeatedly for a matching condition.

To use the while statement:

1. Use the vi or Emacs editor to create a shell script called colors.

2. Enter the following lines of code:

```
echo -n "Try to guess my favorite color:   "
read guess
while [ "$guess" != "red" ]; do
  echo "No, not that one. Try again. "; read guess
done
```

3. Save the file, and exit the editor.

4. Give the file execute permission, and test it. You see output similar to Figure 6-9.

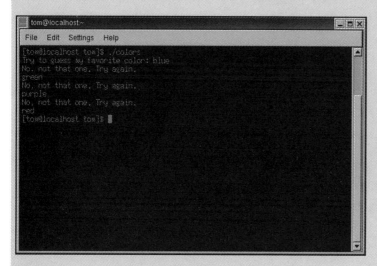

Figure 6-9   Results of the colors script

The while loop tests an expression in a manner similar to the if statement. As long as the statement inside the brackets is true, the statements inside the do and done statements repeat.

Notice the use of the != symbol, which is the not-equal operator. It tests two operands and returns true if they are not equal. Otherwise, it returns false. In the steps you just completed, the echo and read statements inside the loop repeat until the user enters red (false).

Another example of the while loop is in a data-entry form, as illustrated in the next hands-on activity.

To create a while loop that serves as a data-entry form:

1. Use vi or Emacs to create a script file, **nameaddr**.

2. Type these lines into the file:

```
looptest=y
  while [ "$looptest" = y ]
   do
    echo -n "Enter Name : "; read name
    echo -n "Enter Street : "; read street
    echo -n "Enter City  : "; read city
    echo -n "Enter State  : "; read state
    echo -n "Enter Zip Code: "; read zip
    echo -n "Continue? (y)es or (n)o: "; read looptest
   done
```

Chapter marker: **6**

3. Save the file, and exit the editor.

4. Give the file execute permission, and test it. You see output similar to Figure 6-10.

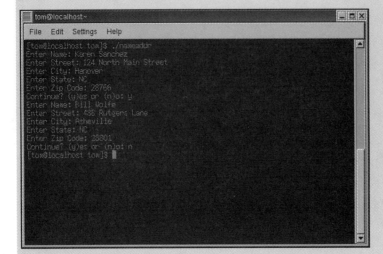

Figure 6-10   Output of the nameaddr script

As you test the script, enter several names and addresses. When you finish, answer n (for no) when the script asks you, "Continue? (y)es or (n)o."

Use looping logic in applications where code must be repeated a determined or undetermined number of times.

Case Logic

The **case logic** structure simplifies the selection of a match when you have a list of choices. It allows your script to perform one of many actions, depending upon the value of a variable. Note the use of two semicolons (;;) that terminate the action(s) taken after the case matches what is being tested.

To demonstrate case logic:

1. Use the vi or Emacs editor to create the manycolors shell script.

Type these lines into the file:

```
echo —n "Enter your favorite color: "; read color
  case "$color" in
      "blue")  echo "As in My Blue Heaven.";;
      "yellow") echo "As in the Yellow Sunset.";;
      "red")   echo "As in Red Rover, Red Rover.";;
```

```
        "orange") echo "Autumn has shades of Orange.";;
        *     ) echo "Sorry, I do not know that color.";;
esac
```

2. Save the file, and exit the editor

3. Give the file execute permission, and test it. You see output similar to that shown in Figure 6-11.

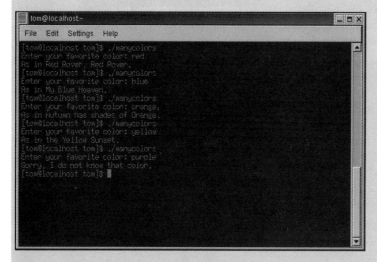

Figure 6-11   Output of the manycolors script

In the manycolors script, the case structure examines the contents of the color variable, and searches for a match among the values listed. When a match is found, the statement that immediately follows the case value is executed. For example, if the color variable contains red, the echo statement that appears after "red") is executed. If the contents of the color variable does not match any of the values listed, the statement that appears after *) is executed.

As you can see, case logic is designed to pick one course of action from a list of many, depending upon the contents of a variable. This control structure is ideal for menus, in which the user chooses one of several values. The case structure is terminated by the word "esac," which is "case" spelled backwards.

In this section, you learned about shell variables, operators, and wildcard characters. You also learned about the four logic structures.

DEBUGGING A SHELL SCRIPT

Sometimes a shell script does not execute because there is an error in one or more commands within the script. For example, maybe you have entered a colon instead of a semicolon or left out a bracket. Running a shell script using sh plus one of several options enables you to more quickly debug the problem.

Two of the most commonly used sh options are sh –v and sh –x. The sh –v option displays the lines of code in the script as they are read by the interpreter. The sh –x option shows somewhat different information by displaying the command and accompanying arguments line by line as they are run.

To compare the results of the sh –v and sh –x options to debug a script:

1. Type **sh –v colors** (remember that colors is the script you created earlier in this chapter in which the favorite color is red), and press **Enter**.

2. Type **green** and press **Enter**.

3. Type **red** and press **Enter**. Notice that the command lines are printed.

4. Type **sh –x colors** and press **Enter**.

5. Type **green** and press **Enter**.

6. Type **red** and press **Enter**. Now the command lines and arguments are displayed with a plus in front of them. Figure 6-12 illustrates the output of the sh –v and sh –x options.

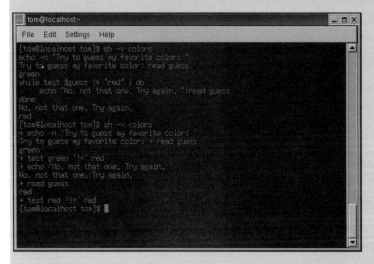

Figure 6-12   Using the sh -v and sh -x options for debugging

Using these commands, you can view the script line by line as it is running and determine the location and nature of an error on a line when a script fails.

Sometimes you want to test a script that updates a file, but you want to give the script a dry run without actually updating the file—particularly so that data in the file is not altered if the script fails at some point. Use the sh -n option for this purpose, because it reads and checks the syntax of commands in a script, but does not execute them. For example, if the script is used to add new information to a file, the script does not actually process the information or add it to the file, but if there is a syntax error, you can still quickly locate it.

◀ LESSON B ▶

CREATING AND COMPLETING THE

CORPORATE PHONES APPLICATION

6

After completing this lesson, you should be able to:

♦ Create screen-management scripts

♦ Learn how to edit the .bashrc file to customize you personal working environment

♦ Use the trap command

♦ Enter and test shell scripts to print the phone records, view the contents of the corp_phones file, and add new phone records to the file

USING SHELL SCRIPTING TO CREATE A MENU

Before creating your corporate phone script, you first create a menu, which is a good example of a shell script that employs the four basic logic structures: sequence, decision, looping, and case. A significant feature of the menu script is the screen presentation, which you want to be as appealing and user-friendly as possible. You can choose one of UNIX's lesser-known commands, tput, to make your screen place the prompt (cursor) at the user's data-entry point on the screen. The **tput command** initializes the terminal to respond to a setting that the user chooses. Some examples of this are:

- tput cup 0 0: moves the cursor to row 0, column 0, which is the upper-left corner of the screen

- tput clear: clears the screen

- tput cols: prints the number of columns for the current terminal

- bold=`tput smso` offbold=`tput rmso`: sets boldfaced type

To practice using the tput command:

1. Type the following command sequence, and press **Enter**:

```
tput clear ; tput cup 10 15 ; echo "Hello" ; tput cup
20 0
```

You see the results of the command sequence. The screen clears; the cursor is positioned at row 10, column 15, on the screen; the word "Hello" is printed; and the prompt's position is row 20, column 0. See Figure 6-13 to verify the screen output.

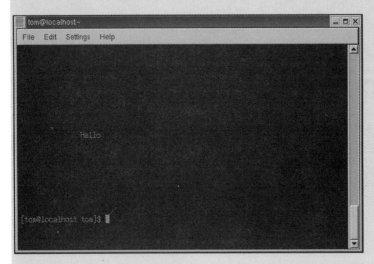

Figure 6-13   Formatting the screen output using tput

Now, use the tput command to create screen management and cursor scripts for displaying menus and data entry screens.

To use the tput command:

1. Use the vi or Emacs editor to create a screen-management script, scrmanage, containing the following lines:

```
tput cup $1 $2  # place cursor on row and col
tput clear    # clear the screen
bold=`tput smso` # set standout mode - bold
offbold=`tput rmso` # reset screen — turn bold off
echo $bold      # turn bold on
tput cup 10 20; echo "Type Last Name:" # bold caption
tput cup 12 20; echo "Type First Name:" # bold caption
echo $offbold   # turn bold off
tput cup 10 41; read lastname # enter last name
tput cup 12 41; read firstname # enter first name
```

2. Save the file, and exit the editor.

3. Give the file execute permission, and then test it. Your output should look like Figure 6-14.

The single backquotes around `tput smso` and `tput rmso` must be in the direction as shown or the bold/unbold command does not work. This single quote mark is found in the upper left corner of most keyboards, usually on the same key as the tilde (~).

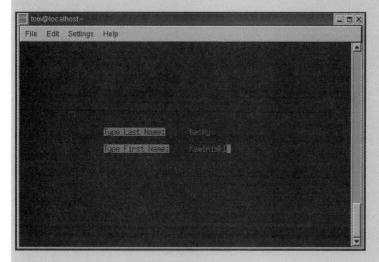

Figure 6-14   Output of the scrmanage script

You are now ready to enter the script to display the menu. (You use this script as part of your application later in this section.)

To enter the script:

1. Use the vi or Emacs editor to enter the phmenu script shown below.

```
#=============================================================
# Script Name:        phmenu
# By:                 Your initials here
# Date:               February 2004
# Purpose:            A menu for the Corporate Phone List
# Command Line:       phmenu
#=============================================================
loop=y
while [ "$loop" = y ]
```

```
  do
    clear
    tput cup 3 12; echo "Corporate Phone Reporting Menu"
    tput cup 4 12; echo "================================="
    tput cup 6 9; echo "P - Print Phone List"
    tput cup 7 9; echo "A - Add New Phones"
    tput cup 8 9; echo "S - Search for Phones"
    tput cup 10 9; echo "Q - Quit: "
    tput cup 10 19;
    read choice || continue
  done
```

2. Save the file, and exit the editor.

3. Give the file execute permission by typing **chmod a+x phmenu** and pressing **Enter**. Next, test the script by typing **./phmenu** and pressing **Enter**. The resulting screen should look similar to the one in Figure 6-15. (You have to press **Ctrl+C** to exit the script, because the Quit option has not yet been programmed.)

Figure 6-15   Running the phmenu script

Now that you have an idea of how to create a menu script, it is helpful to learn some additional shell features and commands before creating your application. You first learn how to customize your personal environment so that creating and testing a new script does not interfere with your other scripts and programs.

CUSTOMIZING YOUR PERSONAL ENVIRONMENT

When your work requirements center on computer programming and shell scripting, consider customizing your environment by modifying the initial settings in the login scripts. A **login script** is a script that runs just after you log into your account. For example, many programmers set up a personal bin directory where they can store and test their new programs without interfering with ongoing operations. (bin is the traditional UNIX name for directories that hold executable files.) You can also modify the editors to make them automatically indent the text inside their programs in accordance with programmer usage.

An **alias** is a name that represents another command. You can use aliases to simplify and automate commands you use frequently. For example, the following command sets up an alias for the rm command.

```
alias rm="rm -i"
```

This command above causes the rm –i command to execute any time the user enters the rm command. This is a commonly used alias, as it ensures users are always prompted before the rm command deletes a file. Here are two other common aliases that help safeguard files:

```
alias mv="mv -i"
alias cp="cp -i"
```

To practice creating an alias:

1. To create an alias called ll for the ls command, type **alias ll="ls -l"** and press **Enter**. Now, when you use the new ll alias, the ls –l command executes automatically.

2. Test the alias by typing **ll** and pressing **Enter**. You see a long directory listing.

The **.bashrc file** that resides in your home directory can be used to establish customizations that take effect for each login session. The .bashrc script is executed each time you generate a shell, such as when you run a shell script. Any time a subshell is created, the .bashrc is reexecuted. The following .bashrc file is commented to explain how you can make your own changes.

```
.bashrc
# Source global definitions
if [ -f /etc/bashrc ]; then
      . /etc/bashrc # if any global definitions are defined
                    # run them first
alias rm 'rm -i'  # make sure user is prompted before
                    # removing files
alias mv 'mv -i'  # make sure user is prompted before
                    # overlaying files
set -o ignoreeof  # Do not allow Ctrl-D to logout
```

```
set -o noclobber   # Force user to enter >! To write
                   # over existing files
PS1="\w \$"        # Set prompt to show working directory
```

In addition to knowing how to customize your work environment, you should also be familiar with the trap command.

THE TRAP COMMAND

The trap command is useful when you want your shell program to automatically remove any temporary files that are created when the shell script runs. The **trap command** specifies that a command, listed as the argument to trap, is read and executed when the shell receives a specified system signal. Here is an example of the command:

```
trap "rm ~/tmp/* 2> /dev/null; exit" 0
```

This command has two arguments: a command to be executed, and a signal number from the operating system. The command, rm ~/tmp/* 2> /dev/null; exit, deletes everything in the user's tmp directory, redirects the error output of the rm command to the null device (so it does not appear on the screen), and issues an exit command to terminate the shell. The signal specified is 0, which is the operating system signal generated when a program exits. So, if this sample command is part of a script file, it causes the specified rm command to execute when signal 0 is sent by the operating system.

The programmer often sets up ~/tmp (a subdirectory of the user's home directory) to store temporary files. When the script file exits, any files placed in ~/tmp can be removed. This is called "good housekeeping" on the part of the programmer.

CREATING THE CORP_PHONES FILE

The steps that follow require you to create the corp_phones file, and place it in your ~/source directory.

To create the corp_phones file:

1. Use the vi or Emacs editor to create the corp_phones file.

2. Enter the following records in the file. (Note that the second and third lines are to be typed as if they were one line.)

```
219-555-4567:Harrison:Joel:M:4540:Accountant:09-12-1985
219-555-4587:Mitchell:Barbara:C:4541:Admin Asst:12-14-
1995
219-555-4589:Olson:Timothy:H:4544:Supervisor:06-30-1983
219-555-4591:Moore:Sarah:H:4500:Dept Manager:08-01-1978
219-555-4567:Polk:John:S:4520:Accountant:09-22-2001
219-555-4501:Robinson:Albert:J:4501:Secretary:08-12-1997
```

3. Save the file, and exit the editor.

4. Use the following grep command to search the file for specific phone numbers:

grep 219-555-4591 corp_phones <Enter>

The output should look like this:

219-555-4591:Moore:Sarah:H:4500:Dept Manager:08-01-1978

5. Type **grep Accountant corp_phones** and press **Enter** to search the file for all Accountants. Your screen should look similar to Figure 6-16.

6. Make a source directory, if you do not have one already, and copy the corp_phones file into the source directory so that you have a copy to work with as you continue to develop the corporate phone list scripts. If you need to make a source directory, type **mkdir source** and press **Enter** (from your home directory). Type **cp corp_phones source** and press **Enter** to copy the corp_phones file to your source directory.

Figure 6-16   Results of the grep command

Notice that you can extract information from the corp_phones file using grep, as well as other commands you learned in previous chapters. You can use such commands in building your script application.

You now complete the menu script that you started at the beginning of this lesson.

To complete the phone menu script:

1. Use the vi or Emacs editor, and retrieve phmenu. Add the following bold-faced lines to the script.

```
#===========================================================
# Script Name:    phmenu
# By:             Your initials here
# Date:           February 2004
# Purpose:        A menu for the Corporate Phone List
# Command Line:   phmenu
#===========================================================
```

```
phonefile=~/source/corp_phones
loop=y
while [ "$loop" = y ]
do
  clear
  tput cup 3 12; echo "Corporate Phone Reporting Menu"
  tput cup 4 12; echo "================================="
  tput cup 6 9; echo "P - Print Phone List"
  tput cup 7 9; echo "A - Add New Phones"
  tput cup 8 9; echo "S - Search for Phones"
  tput cup 10 9; echo "Q - Quit: "
  tput cup 10 19;
  read choice || continue
    case $choice in
      [Aa]) ./phoneadd ;;
      [Pp]) ./phlist1 ;;
      [Ss]) ./phonefind ;;
      [Vv]) less $phonefile ;;
      [Qq]) exit ;;
      *) tput cup 14 4; echo "Invalid Code"; read choice ;;
    esac
done
```

2. Save the file, and exit the editor.

3. Test the script. (Acceptable entries are A, a, P, p, S, s, V, v, Q, and q. Any other entries cause the message "Invalid Code" to appear.) Type **Ctrl+C** to exit.

When you demonstrate your script to Dominion Consulting managers, they point out that some errors may occur when entering additional information. To locate errors quickly, you need to view unformatted records.

VIEWING UNFORMATTED RECORDS

It is often useful to have a script that displays unformatted file data, which means that the records appear exactly as they are stored on the disk. In the case of the phone records, the display shows the colon (:) characters that separate the variable-length fields. If problems develop, it is convenient to have a look at the raw data. To do this, you use the less command to display the records on the screen.

To use the less command to view unformatted records:

1. Open phmenu in the editor of your choice, and add the boldfaced line shown.

```
#===========================================================
# Script Name:    phmenu
```

```
# By:                Your initials here
# Date:              February 2004
# Purpose:           A menu for the Corporate Phone List
# Command Line:      phmenu
#===========================================================
phonefile=~/source/corp_phones
loop=y
while [ "$loop" = y ]
do
  clear
  tput cup 3 12; echo "Corporate Phone Reporting Menu"
  tput cup 4 12; echo "=============================="
  tput cup 6 9; echo "P - Print Phone List"
  tput cup 7 9; echo "A - Add New Phones"
  tput cup 8 9; echo "S - Search for Phones"
  tput cup 9 9; echo "V - View Phone List"
  tput cup 10 9; echo "Q - Quit: "
  tput cup 10 19;
  read choice || continue
    case $choice in
      [Aa]) ./phoneadd ;;
      [Pp]) ./phlist1 ;;
      [Ss]) ./phonefind ;;
      [Vv]) less $phonefile ;;
      [Qq]) exit ;;
      *) tput cup 14 4; echo "Invalid Code"; read choice ;;
    esac
done
```

  2. Save the file, and exit the editor.

  3. Test the script.

You are now ready to run a prototype of your script. To do this, you use the awk program.

USING AWK

The awk program offers a good example of how the UNIX shell programmer can quickly create an application model. Using awk accelerates development because a single awk command can select fields from many records and display them in a specified format on the screen. To run a prototype of your corporate phone script using awk, you create the phlist1 script in the next exercise.

To use the awk program:

  1. Use the editor of your choice to create the **phlist1** script. Use the following code as a guide:

```
# ========================================================
# Script Name:    phlist1
# By:             Your initials here
# Date:           February 2004
# Purpose:        Use awk to format colon-separated fields
#                 in a flat file and display to the screen
# Command Line:   phlist1
# ========================================================
clear
tput cup 2 20; echo "Corporate Phone List"
tput cup 3 20; echo "===================="
tput cup 5 0;
awk -F: '{printf "%-12s %-12s %s\t%s %s %10.10s %s\n",
$2, $3, $4, $1, $5, $6, $7}' corp_phones
```

2. Save the file, and exit the editor.

3. Give the file execute permission by typing **chmod a+x phlist1** and pressing **Enter**. Run the script by typing **./phlist1** and pressing **Enter**. Your screen should look like Figure 6-17.

Figure 6-17   Output of the phlist1 script

You realize that names are continually added to the corp_phones file, so you need to modify your shell script.

CREATING THE PHONEADD SHELL SCRIPT

The phmenu script that you created earlier offers the option to add a phone record to the corp_phones file in which the user interacts with the script to enter a new employee's phone record. However, phmenu calls another script, called phoneadd, to enable you to add a new record. In this section, you create the phoneadd script.

To create the phoneadd script to allow additions:

1. Use the editor of your choice to create the script phoneadd. Enter this code:

```
# ============================================================
# Script Name:   phoneadd
# By:            Your initials here
# Date:          February 2004
# Purpose:       A shell script that sets up a loop to add
#                new employees to the corp_phones file.
# Command Line: phoneadd
#
# ============================================================
trap "rm ~/tmp/* 2> /dev/null; exit" 0 1 2 3
phonefile=~/source/corp_phones
looptest=y
while [ $looptest = y ]
do
  clear
  tput cup 1 4; echo "Corporate Phone List Additions"
  tput cup 2 4; echo "=============================="
  tput cup 4 4; echo "Phone Number: "
  tput cup 5 4; echo "Last Name    : "
  tput cup 6 4; echo "First Name   : "
  tput cup 7 4; echo "Middle Init : "
  tput cup 8 4; echo "Dept #       : "
  tput cup 9 4; echo "Job Title    : "
  tput cup 10 4; echo "Date Hired  : "
  tput cup 12 4; echo "Add Another? (y)es or (q)uit: "
  tput cup 4 18; read phonenum
  if [ "$phonenum" = "q" ]
        then
            clear; exit
  fi
  tput cup 5 18; read lname
  tput cup 6 18; read fname
  tput cup 7 18; read midinit
  tput cup 8 18; read deptno
  tput cup 9 18; read jobtitle
  tput cup 10 18; read datehired
  # Check to see if last name is not a blank before you
  # write to disk
```

6

```
    if [ "$lname" > "            " ]
    then
    echo "$phonenum:$lname:$fname:$midinit:$deptno:$
jobtitle:$datehired" >> $phonefile
    fi
    tput cup 12 33; read looptest
    if [ "$looptest" = "q" ]
     then
        clear; exit
    fi
  done
```

2. Save the file, and exit the editor.

3. Give the file execute permission by typing **chmod a+x phoneadd** and pressing **Enter**.

4. Run the script by typing **./phoneadd** and pressing **Enter**.

5. Next, test the script by adding the following employees. (Note that the second and third lines should be typed as if they were one continuous line.)

   219-555-7175 Mullins Allen L 7527 Sales Rep 02-19-2004
   219-555-7176 Albertson Jeannette K 5547 DC Clerk 02-19-2004

6. Now run the phmenu script, and select **A** from the menu to execute the script and add new records.

   Your screen should look similar to Figure 6-18. (Note that the script shows only one person's information at a time.)

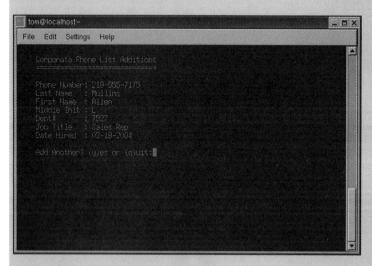

Figure 6-18   Phoneadd script screen

You created the shell script for the corporate phones application. However, you still need to address several deficiencies. For example, how can you return to a previous field as you enter the data? What happens when you enter the same employee twice? What happens if you assign a new employee a phone number that has already been assigned to someone else? Chapter 7, "Advanced Shell Programming," addresses these issues.

CHAPTER SUMMARY

- A high-level language (such as C, C++, or COBOL) is a language that uses English-like expressions. A high-level language must be converted into a low-level (machine) language before the computer can execute it.

- The shell interprets UNIX shell scripts. Shell scripts do not need to be converted to machine language because UNIX converts and executes them in one step.

- UNIX shell scripts, created with the vi or Emacs editor, contain instructions that do not need to be written from scratch, but can be selectively chosen from the operating system's inventory of executable commands.

- Linux shells are derived from the UNIX Bourne, Korn, and C shells. The three typical Linux shells are Bash, csh/tcsh, and ksh/zsh; Bash is the most commonly used Linux shell.

- UNIX employs three types of variables: configuration, environment, and shell. Configuration variables contain set-up information for the operating system. Environment variables hold information about your login session. Shell variables are created in a shell script or at the command line. The export command is used to make a shell variable an environment variable.

- The shell supports numerous operators, including many for performing arithmetic operations.

- You can use wildcard characters in shell scripts, including the bracket ([]) characters. Brackets surround a set of values that can match an individual character in a name or string.

- The logic structures supported by the shell are sequential, decision, looping, and case.

- You can use the tput command to manage cursor placement.

- You can customize the .bashrc file that resides in the user's home directory to suit the needs of programmers and system administrators.

- You can create aliases and enter them into .bashrc to simplify commonly used commands, such as ls -l and rm -i.

- Use the trap command inside a script file to remove temporary files after the script file has been run (exited).

6

❏ The grep command serves a key role in the development of shell scripts by letting you search and retrieve information from files.

❏ The awk program serves as an effective and easy-to-use tool for generating reports.

COMMAND SUMMARY

Review of Chapter 6 Commands	
Command	**Purpose**
alias	Establishes an alias
case...in...esac	A programming structure that allows one action from a set of possible actions to be performed, depending upon the value of a variable
export	Makes a variable an environment variable
for: do...done	Causes a variable to take on each value in a set of values; an action is performed for each value
if...then...else...fi	Causes one of two actions to be performed, depending on the condition
let	Stores arithmetic values in a variable
printenv	Prints a list of environment variables
set –o noclobber	Prevents files from being overwritten by the > operator
tput cup	Moves the screen cursor to a specified row and column
tput clear	Clears the screen
tput cols	Prints the number of columns on the current terminal
tput smso	Enables boldfaced output
tput rmso	Disables boldfaced output
trap	Executes a command when a specified signal is received from the operating system
while: do...done	Repeats an action while a condition exists

REVIEW QUESTIONS

1. Which of the following commands enables others to run the shell script add2 that you have just created?

    a. chmod a+x add2

    b. run ogu add2

    c. chmod 755 add2

    d. all of the above

    e. only a and c

2. _____ variables are used to store setup information about the operating system.

   a. Environment

   b. System

   c. Shell

   d. Configuration

3. You want to view what directory paths are already set up just after you log into your account. To do this, you type _____.

   a. MYPATH$

   b. echo $PATH

   c. DIR

   d. $DRI

4. What command is useful for removing temporary files that are created when a shell script is run?

   a. tempdel

   b. clear

   c. trap

   d. mv –x

5. The _____ command places the cursor on the fourth row and in the tenth column.

   a. echo 4 10

   b. tput cup 4 10

   c. tput cup 10 4

   d. echo put 10 4

6. Which of these writes the variables lname and fname into the file "names"?

   a. echo "$lname:$fname" >> names

   b. link "lname, fname" to names

   c. insert "lname:fname" < names

   d. place names "$lname:$fname"

7. The _____ operator enables you to test whether a value, such as the variable "appliance", is not equal to another value, such as the string "toaster."

   a. >=

   b. !

   c. !=

   d. <=

6

8. Why doesn't the following script work?

```
for file in page[567];
        more $file
```

   a. It is missing a do statement after the semicolon.

   b. It is missing an echo statement after the semicolon.

   c. On the second line, you must use ls with a for loop instead of more.

   d. On the first line, you must use a dollar sign in front of file, as in $file.

9. The if statement is an example of a(n) _____.

   a. arithmetic operator

   b. glob character

   c. decision–making control structure in decision logic

   d. import control for an environment variable

10. You can use the grep command to _____.

   a. search a file for a matching pattern

   b. alter the text in a file

   c. create a mathematical formula

   d. create a pattern of words enclosed with brackets [ ]

11. After you type the _____ command and press Enter, you can type lh and press Enter to view the hidden files in a directory.

   a. alt lh="ls –a"

   b. change ls –a lh

   c. master ls –s = "lh"

   d. alias lh="ls –a"

12. Many programmers create a directory in their home directory for storing executable programs. The traditional name for this directory is _____.

   a. programs

   b. executables

   c. prg

   d. bin

13. The printenv command is used to show a list of _____.

   a. script variables

   b. environment variables

   c. shell operators

   d. prototypes for a script

14. Case logic is terminated by _____.

    a. Ctrl+D

    b. end

    c. stop

    d. esac

15. What value is stored in variable Y when you use the command let Y=5+9*2/0?

    a. 0

    b. 23

    c. 28

    d. No value is stored because this command yields an error.

16. The _____ file is executed each time you log on using the Bash shell as your default.

    a. .login

    b. autoexec

    c. .welcome

    d. .bashrc

17. True or False: You can call one script from a different script.

18. The tput clear command _____.

    a. transfers the value $clear to a variable in a script

    b. changes the text displayed within the cursor

    c. clears the screen and places the cursor in the upper-left corner

    d. strips the contents of a variable so that it is empty

19. The tput smso command _____.

    a. enables boldfaced printing

    b. disables boldfaced printing

    c. positions the cursor

    d. clears the screen

20. What command enables you to place a variable from a shell script into the UNIX environment?

    a. shell

    b. estore

    c. export

    d. insert

6

21. You are designing a shell script that involves a menu. Which of the following is particularly well-suited for creating the menu?

    a. a while loop

    b. a case statement

    c. a series of cat commands

    d. a for statement

22. In a script, _____ represents the seventh field in a record.

    a. ./7

    b. $7

    c. .F8

    d. 7!

23. What is wrong with the following code in a shell script?

    ```
    while [ "$looptest" = y ]
    do
       echo -n "Type your first name: "; read fname
       echo -n "Type your last name:  "; read lname
       echo -n "Continue? (Y)es or (N)o: "; read looptest
    fi
    ```

    a. There must be a semicolon after while.

    b. There must be a semicolon after do.

    c. fi should be replaced with done.

    d. all of the above

    e. only a and b

24. What is wrong with the following awk statement?

    ```
    awk -F: 'printf "%-12s %-12s %s\t%s %s %10.10s %s\n",
    $2, $3, $4, $1, $5, $6, $7}' corp_phones
    ```

    a. There must be a double quote before printf, not a single quote.

    b. There are too many fields extracted from the corp_phones file; only six fields can be extracted using awk and printf.

    c. The backslashes before t and n should be replaced with forward slashes.

    d. There must be an open curly bracket ({) between the single quote and printf.

25. Which Bash shell variable contains the path and name of a user's file containing e-mail, which is checked by the mail utility?

    a. MAILCHECK

    b. MAIL

    c. USERMAIL

    d. CHECKMAIL

DISCOVERY EXERCISES

1. Create the file sports with the following entries:

   ◻ track

   ◻ football

   ◻ swimming

   ◻ basketball

   ◻ soccer

   ◻ rowing

2. Sort the sports file in reverse order, and place the result in a file called sports2.

3. Use the command to make sure that the sports2 file cannot be overwritten.

4. Use cat to create another file, called addition, and enter one line that is baseball. Try to overwrite the sports2 file by typing cat addition > sports2. What happens when you try to overwrite the file? How can you bypass the overwrite restriction?

5. Fix these two lines of code to make them work:

   ```
   case "$brandname"
           GM") echo "General" Motors";;
   ```

6. Create a directory called docs in your home directory. Look at the contents of the PATH variable. If it does not include the path to your docs directory, add it.

7. Create the variable NAME. Store your full name in it.

8. Use the printenv command to display a list of environment variables. Is the NAME variable listed? Execute the command that makes NAME an environment variable.

9. From the command line, issue a command that clears the screen; positions the cursor at row 8, column 20; displays your name; and positions the cursor at row 12, column 5.

10. Create the alias w that executes this command: who -Hi. Test your new alias by running it.

11. Store the alias you created in Discovery Exercise 10 in the correct file so that it takes effect each time you log in.

12. Change the phlist1 script to add a heading over the displayed fields when the file is viewed. For example, you could have it look like the following:

    ```
    Last Name First Name MI Phone Number Dept# Title Date Hired
    ===========================================================
    ```

13. Create a new menu script that has the following selections (note that the sole purpose of the menu script for this exercise is to simply display the menu selections):

    Travel Menu

    ==========

    (L)ondon Scenic Tour

    (P)aris in the Spring

    (N)ew York Shopping Fantasy

    Make your selection ... (Q) to quit

14. Enter the command to store the output of the pwd command in the variable PLACE. Display the contents of the PLACE variable on the screen.

15. Write a script named change_prompt. The script should change your prompt to display the date and the name of your working directory. Give the file execute permission, and then test it.

16. Execute each of these commands:

    ```
    let x=14+5+4*8
    let y=(14+5)+4*8
    ```

    Display the contents of each variable on the screen. Are the contents the same or different and why?

17. Write a script file that:

    a. Stores 5 in variable A.

    b. Stores 10 in variable B.

    c. Stores the sum of A plus B in variable C.

    d. Stores the difference of B minus A in variable D.

    e. Stores the product of A times B in variable E.

    f. Stores the quotient of B divided by A in variable F.

    g. Displays the contents of all the variables.

18. Write a script that asks the user to enter his or her first name. The script should include an if statement that compares the name the user entered with your name. If they are the same, the script should display the message, "That is my name, too." Otherwise it should display the message, "That is a nice name."

19. Write a script file with a for loop that displays a list of your favorite music groups.

20. Write a script file that asks users to guess your name. If they guess incorrectly, the script should ask them to guess again. Repeat this until users correctly guess your name. (*Hint*: Use the while loop.)

21. Write a script file that asks the user to choose and enter the name of a country from the following list: America, Italy, France, and Germany. The script then uses a case structure to display the name of a car made in the selected country. Use the following list of cars for reference:

Country	Car
America	Ford
Italy	Ferrari
France	Peugeot
Germany	Porsche

22. Remove the colon characters from the phoneadd script's screen, and reposition the cursor to improve the appearance of the data entry.

23. Create a small shell script to display the employee phone records showing only their names and the date hired.

24. Create a script file that clears the screen, places two highlighted (boldfaced) lines on row 5, column 10, and row 6, column 12. Display two more, nonboldfaced lines on row 8, column 10, and row 10, column 10.

25. Create a file, music, that contains information on your CD collection. Each record in the file should have these fields: Artist, CDName, PurchaseDate, and Cost. Next, create a script file with a menu that lets you view the contents of the file, search for all CDs from a particular artist, and add new records to the file.

26. Design an awk statement that formats and displays the records in the music file created in Discovery Exercise 25.

27. Describe how you would use the trap command to display the message "That's all, folks" when a script file exits.

6

7

ADVANCED SHELL PROGRAMMING

Dominion Consulting's managers are pleased with the new shell program that maintains the employee phone file. Based on the relatively small volume of transactions and file size, the programming supervisor agrees that the shell program is a permanent solution for maintaining the corporate phone file. However, you need to enhance the program and incorporate new features, such as preventing the same phone number from being assigned to more than one person, reentering data to correct errors, and sorting by employees' last names.

In the last chapter, you began developing a program to automate the maintenance of the phone records in the corp_phones file. You developed a menu that presents several options, and a data-entry screen that allows records to be added to the file.

In this chapter, you complete the program. You add code that deletes a specified record from the file, searches for a specified record, and sorts and displays all records in the file. You perform these tasks with the test, grep, sed, and tr commands. Before you begin adding this code, you learn about two standard program development tools: flowcharts and pseudocode.

◀ LESSON A ▶

DEVELOPING A FULLY FEATURED PROGRAM

After completing this lesson, you should be able to:
- Use flowcharting and pseudocode tools
- Learn to write scripts that tell the system which shell to use as an interpreter
- Use the test command to compare values and validate file existence
- Use the translate command, tr, to display a record with duplicate fields
- Use the sed command in a script to delete phone records

ANALYZING THE PROGRAM

A computer program is developed by analyzing the best way to achieve the desired results. Standard programming analysis tools help you do this. The two most popular and proven analysis tools are the program flowchart and pseudocode.

Flowcharting

The **flowchart** is a logic diagram that uses a set of standard symbols that explain the program's sequence and each action it takes. For example, look at the flowchart in Figure 7-1.

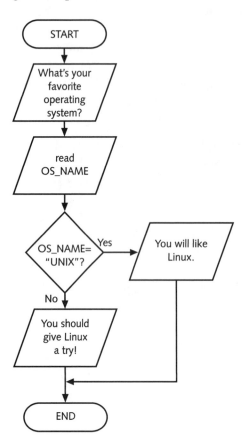

Figure 7-1   Sample flowchart

Figure 7-1 is a flowchart for the following program, which you wrote in Chapter 6.

```
echo -n "What is your favorite operating system? "
read OS_NAME
if [ "$OS_NAME" = "UNIX" ]
then
     echo "You will like Linux."
else
     echo "You should give Linux a try!"
fi
```

Each step in the program is represented by a symbol in the flowchart. The shape of the symbol indicates the type of operation being performed, such as input/output or a decision. Figure 7-2 shows standard flowcharting symbols and their meanings.

The arrows that connect the symbols represent the direction in which the program flows from one symbol to the next. In the flowchart in Figure 7-1, the arrow after the START terminator shows the program flowing to an output operation that displays the message, "What is your favorite operating system?" Next, the program flows to an input operation that reads a value into OS_NAME. A decision structure (represented by a diamond-shaped symbol) is encountered next, which compares OS_NAME to "UNIX" to determine if the two are equal. If so, the program follows the "Yes" branch. This leads to an output operation that displays the message, "You will like Linux." If OS_NAME and "UNIX" are not equal, the program follows the "No" branch. This leads to an output operation that displays the message, "You should give Linux a try!" The two paths then converge and flow to the END terminator.

You manually create a flowchart using a drawing template. Flowchart templates provide the symbols that denote logical structures, input-output operations, processing operations, and the storage media that contain the files as shown in Figure 7-2. A variety of flowcharting software packages, such as Microsoft Visio, let you create flowcharts on your computer. Popular word-processing packages, such as Microsoft Word and WordPerfect, are also equipped with flowcharting tools.

Writing Pseudocode

After creating a flowchart, the next step in designing a program is to write **pseudocode**. Pseudocode instructions are similar to actual programming statements. Use them to create a model that you can later use as a basis for a real program. For example, here are pseudocode statements for the os_choice program:

```
Display "What is your favorite operating system? " on the screen.
Enter data into OS_NAME.
If OS_NAME is equal to "UNIX"
    then
    Display "You will like Linux." on the screen.
Else
    Display "You should give Linux a try!" on the screen.
End if.
```

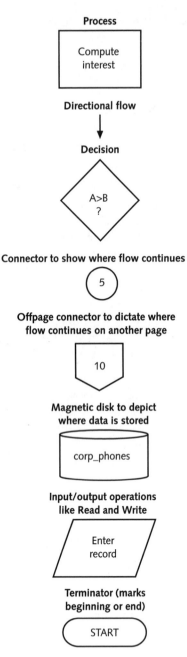

Figure 7-2   Standard flowchart symbols

Pseudocode is a design tool only, and never processed by the computer. Therefore, there are no strict rules to follow. The pseudocode should verbally match the symbolic representation of logic illustrated on the flowchart. For example, Figure 7-3 shows the flowchart and pseudocode that represent one change Dominion Consulting wants to make to its phone program (reentering data in a field).

Pseudocode:

```
While entry = minus
     do
          Reposition cursor in previous field.
          Enter the data.
          Reposition cursor in field following the field that was
             just entered (reentered data)
          Continue testing while loop.
     Done
```

Flowchart:

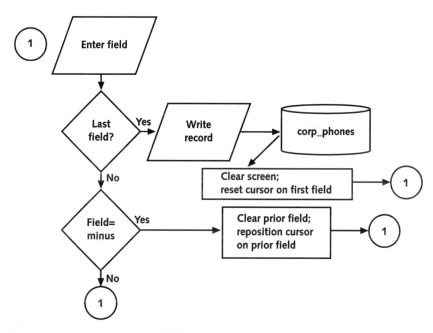

Figure 7-3   Pseudocode and flowchart for reentry of previous fields

Before you can begin to work on the program, however, you need to do some preliminary work. First, you must ensure that everyone who runs the program does so with the correct shell. To do this, modify the program so it informs the operating system which shell to use while interpreting the statements in the script.

ENSURING THE CORRECT SHELL RUNS THE SCRIPT

Each UNIX user has the freedom and capability of choosing which shell he or she prefers. When developing a shell script, you must be responsible for ensuring that the correct shell is used to interpret your script. This is because all shells do not support the same commands and programming statements.

You can instruct the system to run a script with a specific shell. You do so in the first line of the script. The line must start with the # character, followed by the ! character and the path of the shell. For example, this line tells the system to use the Bash shell:

```
#!/bin/bash
```

When the system reads this code line, it loads the Bash shell and uses it to interpret the statements in the script file. Since UNIX includes many shells, you should always begin your scripts with this statement.

Next, you need to make sure that the necessary directories and files are in place before you execute programs that depend on them. To do this, use the test command.

USING THE TEST COMMAND

The **test command** makes preliminary checks of the UNIX internal environment and other useful comparisons (beyond those that the if command alone can perform). See Appendix B, "Syntax Guide to UNIX Commands," for a description of options available for the test command. You can place the test command inside your shell script or execute it directly from the command line. In this section, you learn to use the test command at the command line. In the next section, you use it in a script file.

The test command uses operators expressed as options to perform the evaluations. The command can be used to:

- Perform relational tests with integers (such as equal, greater than, less than, etc.)
- Test strings
- Determine if a file exists and what type of file it is
- Perform Boolean tests

Each type of test operation is discussed in more detail in the following sections.

Relational Integer Tests with the test Command

The test command can determine if one integer is equal to, greater than, less than, greater than or equal to, less than or equal to, or not equal to another integer. Table 7-1 describes the integer testing options of the test command.

Table 7-1 Integer testing options of the test command

Option	Meaning	Example Command
-eq	equal to	test a -eq b
-gt	greater than	test a -gt b
-lt	less than (small L and small T)	test a -lt b
-ge	greater than or equal to	test a -ge b
-le	less than or equal to (small L and small E)	test a -le b
-ne	not equal to	test a -ne b

The test command returns a value known as an exit status. An **exit status** is a numeric value that the command returns to the operating system when it finishes. The value of the test command's exit status indicates the results of the test performed. If the exit status is 0 (zero), the test result is true. An exit status of 1 indicates the test result is false.

The exit status is normally detected in a script by the if statement or in a looping structure. You can view the last command's exit status by typing the command:

```
echo $?
```

To demonstrate the test command with integer expressions:

1. Create the variable number with the value 20 by typing the command **number=20** and pressing **Enter**.

2. Type **test $number -eq 20** and press **Enter**.

3. Type **echo $?** and press **Enter**. The result displayed on your screen is 0, as in the following example:

```
[tom@localhost tom]$ number=20
[tom@localhost tom]$ test $number -eq 20
[tom@localhost tom]$ echo $?
0
```

The echo $? command displays the exit status of the last command that was executed. In this example, the test command returns the exit status 0, indicating the expression $number -eq 20 is true. This means the variable number ($number) is equal to 20.

4. Type **value=10** and press **Enter**.

5. Type **test $number -lt $value** and press **Enter**.

6. Type **echo $?** and press **Enter**. The result of the test that appears on your screen is now 1:

```
[tom@localhost tom]$ value=10
[tom@localhost tom]$ test $number -lt $value
[tom@localhost tom]$ echo $?
1
```

In this example, the test command returns the exit status 1, indicating the expression $number –lt $value is false. This means $number is not less than $value.

In some systems, you must have the test command echo the exit code on the same line as the test command, as in the following example:
`test $name = "Bjorn" ; echo $?`

String Tests with the test Command

You can use the test command to determine if a string has a length of zero characters or a nonzero number of characters. It can also test two strings to determine if they are equal or not equal. Table 7-2 describes the string testing options of the test command.

Table 7-2   String tests with the test command

Option or Expression	Meaning	Example
-z	Tests for a zero-length string	test -z string
-n	Tests for a nonzero string length	test -n string
string1 = string2	Tests two strings for equality	test string1 = string2
string1 != string2	Tests two strings for inequality	test string1 != string2
string	Tests for a nonzero string length	test string

To demonstrate the test command's string testing capabilities:

1. Type **name="Bjorn"** and press **Enter**.

2. Type **test $name = "Bjorn"** and press **Enter**.

3. Type **echo $?** and press **Enter**. The result shown on your screen is 0:

```
[tom@localhost tom]$ name="Bjorn"
[tom@localhost tom]$ test $name = "Bjorn"
[tom@localhost tom]$ echo $?
0
```

In this example, the test command returns the exit status 0 indicating the expression $name = "Bjorn" is true. This means $name and "Bjorn" are equal.

4. Type **test $name != "Barn"** and press **Enter**.

5. Type **echo $?** and press **Enter**. Your screen looks similar to the following:

```
[tom@localhost tom]$ test $name != "Barn"
[tom@localhost tom]$ echo $?
0
```

In the example above, the test command returns the exit status 0 indicating the expression $name != "Barn" is true. This means $name and "Barn" are not equal.

6. Type **test –z $name** and press **Enter**.

7. Type **echo $?** and press **Enter**. Your screen looks similar to the following:

```
[tom@localhost tom]$ test -z $name
[tom@localhost tom]$ echo $?
1
```

The last test command in the example above returns the exit status 1 indicating the expression –z $name is false. This means the string $name is not zero length.

Testing Files with the test Command

The test command can determine if a file exists and if it has a specified permission or attribute (such as executable, readable, writeable, directory, etc.). Table 7-3 describes several of the command's file testing options.

Table 7-3   File testing options of the test command

Option	Meaning	Example
-e	True if a file exists	test -e file
-r	True if a file exists and can be read	test -r file
-w	True if a file exists and can be written to	test -w file
-x	True if a file exists and can be executed	test -x file
-d	True if a file exists and it is a directory	test -d file
-f	True if a file exists and it is a regular file	test -f file
-s	True if a file exists and its size is greater than zero	test -s file
-c	True if a file exists and is a character special file (which is a character-oriented device, such as a terminal or printer)	test -c file
-b	True if a file exists and is a block special file (which is a block-oriented device, such as a disk or tape drive)	test -b file

To demonstrate the test command's file testing capabilities:

1. Use the touch command to create an empty file named test_file.

2. Use the **ls –l test_file** command to view the file's permissions. The permissions should look similar to the following:

```
[tom@localhost tom]$ ls -l test_file
-rw-rw-r-- 1  tom     tom        0 Feb 8 12:43 test_file
```

3. Note that the file has read and write permissions for you, the owner.

4. Next, type **test –x test_file** and press **Enter**.

5. Type **echo $?** and press **Enter**. Your screen looks similar to the following:

```
[tom@localhost tom]$ test -x test_file
[tom@localhost tom]$ echo $?
1
```

The test command returns an exit status of 1, because test_file is not executable.

6. Type **test -r test_file** and press **Enter**.

7. Type **echo $?** and press **Enter**. Your screen should be similar to the following:

```
[tom@localhost tom]$ test -r test_file
[tom@localhost tom]$ echo $?
0
```

The test command returns an exit status of 0 indicating test_file is readable.

Performing Boolean Tests with the test Command

The test command's Boolean operators let you combine multiple expressions with AND and OR relationships. You can also use a Boolean negation operator. Table 7-4 describes Boolean operators.

Table 7-4   Test command's Boolean operators

Option	Meaning	Example
-a	Logical AND	test expression1 -a expression2
-o	Logical OR	test expression1 -o expression2
!	Logical negation	test !expression

The -a operator combines two expressions, and tests a logical AND relationship between them. The form of the test command with the -a option is:

```
test expression1 -a expression2
```

If both expression1 and expression2 are true, the test command returns true (with a 0 exit status). However, if either expression1 or expression2 is false, the test command returns false (with an exit status of 1).

The -o operator also combines two expressions. It tests a logical OR relationship. The form of the test command with the -o option is:

```
test expression1 -o expression2
```

If either expression1 or expression2 is true, the test command returns true (with a 0 exit status). However, if neither of the expressions is true, the test command returns false (with an exit status of 1).

The ! operator negates the value of an expression. This means that if the expression normally causes test to return true, it returns false instead. Likewise, if the expression normally causes test to return false, it returns true instead. The form of the test command with the ! operator is:

```
test !expression
```

To demonstrate the test command's Boolean operators:

1. Recall that the test_file file you created in the previous exercise has read and write permissions. Type **test -r test_file -a -w test_file** and press **Enter**.

   This command tests two expressions using an AND relationship: -r test_file and -w test_file. If both expressions are true, the test command returns true.

2. Type **echo $?** and press **Enter**. The results on your screen look similar to this:

   ```
   [tom@localhost tom]$ test -r test_file -a -w test_file
   [tom@localhost tom]$ echo $?
   0
   ```

   The test command returns an exit status of 0 indicating that test_file is readable and writeable.

3. Type **test -x test_file -o -r test_file** and press **Enter**.

   This command tests two expressions using an OR relationship: -x test_file and -r test_file. If either of these expressions is true, the test command returns true.

4. Type **echo $?** and press **Enter**. The results on your screen look similar to the following:

   ```
   [tom@localhost tom]$ test -x test_file -o -r test_file
   [tom@localhost tom]$ echo $?
   0
   ```

   The test command returns an exit status of 0 indicating that test_file is either executable OR readable.

5. Type **test ! -r test_file** and press **Enter**.

   This command negates the result of the expression -r test_file. If the expression is true, the test command returns false. Likewise, if the expression is false, the test command returns true.

6. Type **echo $?** and press **Enter**. Your screen looks similar to the following:.

   ```
   [tom@localhost tom]$ test ! -r test_file
   [tom@localhost tom]$ echo $?
   1
   ```

   The test command returns an exit status of 1 indicating the expression ! -r test_file is false.

7

You next use the test command to determine if a directory exists. This lets you set up your environment properly to run the shell scripts you complete in Lesson B. In the following exercise, you determine if you have a source directory in your home directory. If not, you create one and add it to the PATH variable. This enables you to run script files stored there without having to type **./** before their names.

To determine if a directory exists:

1. Type **test -d source ; echo $?** and press **Enter**. This command determines if source exists and if it is a directory. Because the echo $? command is included on the same line, the exit status appears immediately after you press Enter.

   If the exit status is 0, you already have a source directory. If this is so, skip to Step 3. Otherwise, continue to Step 2.

2. If the command you entered in Step 1 results in exit status 1, you must create the ~/source directory. Type **mkdir source** and press **Enter**.

3. In Chapter 6 you created the file corp_phones and the shell scripts phmenu and phoneadd. Determine if you have the corp_phones file by typing **test -e corp_phones ; echo $?** and pressing **Enter**. If you see the exit status 0, the file exists.

4. Repeat the test command for the phmenu, phoneadd, and phlist1 files. After you confirm that these files exist, copy them to the source directory.

If you do not have the files from Chapter 6, see your instructor or technical support person for assistance.

5. If you permanently add the /home/*username*/source (where *username* is your login name) directory to your PATH variable, it takes effect each time you log in. You should do this in your .bash_profile file. Load the file into the vi editor. Your screen looks similar to Figure 7-4.

6. Move the cursor to the line that reads:

   `PATH=$PATH:$HOME/bin`

7. Type **i** to switch to insert mode. Type **:$HOME/source** (include the colon) at the end of the line.

8. Press **Esc**, then type **:wq** and press **Enter** to save the file and exit the editor.

9. To make the new PATH value take effect, you must log off and then log back on. Do so now.

10. After you log back on, type **$PATH** and press **Enter**. At the end of the paths listed on the screen, you should see the path you just added.

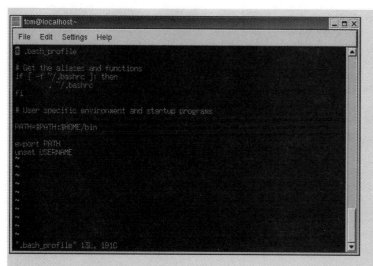

Figure 7-4   .bash_profile file

You created the source directory and added it to your PATH variable. You can store your script files there and execute them just by typing their names at the command line. In the next exercise, you validate the existence of the corp_phones file.

To validate the existence of a file:

1. Make sure you are in your source directory by typing **cd ~/source** (or you can simply type cd source because you have just logged back on and are in your home directory) and then press **Enter**.

2. Type **test -e corp_phones ; echo $?** and then press **Enter**. Your screen should show a "0," which indicates a true status.

3. To see a demonstration of a false status, repeat the test for the file phone_corp, which does not exist.

Next, you practice using the test command in a script file. Once again, recall the os_choice script you wrote and modified in Chapter 6:

```
echo -n "What is your favorite operating system? "
read OS_NAME
if [ "$OS_NAME" = "UNIX" ]
then
  echo "You will like Linux."
else
      if [ "$OS_NAME" = "WINDOWS" ]
      then
         echo "A great OS for applications."
      else
```

```
             echo "You should give Linux a try!"
    fi
fi
```

In the following exercise, you modify the if statement so it uses the test command. When done, the program runs identically as it did before.

To modify the if statement to use the test command:

1. Type **cd** to change back to your home directory. Load the os_choice file into vi or Emacs.

2. Change the line that reads:

   ```
   if [  "$OS_NAME" = "UNIX"  ]
   ```

   to this:

   ```
   if test $OS_NAME = "UNIX"
   ```

3. Save the file, and exit the editor.

4. Test the script by executing it. Type **UNIX** and press **Enter** when asked "What is your favorite operating system?" The output of the script should be similar to the following:

   ```
   [tom@localhost tom]$ ./os_choice
   What is your favorite operating system? UNIX
   You will like Linux.
   ```

In the next exercise, you modify a while loop so it uses the test command.

To modify a while loop to use the test command:

1. Recall the script in your home directory named colors, which you wrote in Chapter 6. It repeatedly asks the user to guess its favorite color, until the user guesses the color red. The code for the colors script is as follows (it uses a while loop until the guess variable contains the word red):

   ```
   echo -n "Try to guess my favorite color: "
   read guess
   while [ "$guess" != "red" ]; do
     echo "No, not that one. Try again. "; read guess
   done
   ```

2. Load the file into vi or Emacs.

3. Change the line that reads:

   ```
   while [ "$guess" != "red" ]; do
   ```

   to this:

   ```
   while test $guess != "red" ; do
   ```

4. Save the file, and exit the editor.

5. Test the script. Figure 7-5 shows sample output of the program.

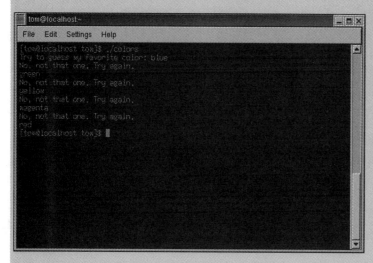

Figure 7-5 Output of the updated colors script

So far, you used the test command from both the command line and from within script files. You also configured your home directory structure and your PATH variable so you can run your script files directly from the source directory. Your next step is to begin enhancing the corp_phones program by formatting record output.

FORMATTING RECORD OUTPUT

To format record output, use the translate utility. The **translate utility (tr)**, as you recall from Chapter 5, changes the standard input (characters you type at the keyboard) character by character. The standard input can also be redirected with the < operator to come from a file rather than the keyboard. For example, the following command sends the contents of the counters file as input to the tr command. It converts lowercase characters to uppercase.

```
tr [a-z] [A-Z] < counters
```

The syntax of the tr command can vary from version to version of UNIX. For that reason, Red Hat Linux 7.2 generally accepts most variations. For example, you can run any of the following formats in Red Hat Linux 7.2:

```
tr "[a-z]" "[A-Z]" < counters
tr '[a-z]' '[A-Z]' < counters    (do not use
    back quotes)
tr a-z A-Z < counters
```

By using the | operator, the translate utility also works as a filter in cases where the input comes from the output of another UNIX command. For example, the following command sends the output of the cat command to tr:

```
cat names | tr -s ":" " "
```

This sample command sends the contents of the names file to tr. The tr utility replaces each occurrence of the : character with a space. The tr utility works like the sed command, except that sed changes the standard input string by string, not character by character.

You now use the tr utility to change lowercase characters to uppercase, as well as replace colon characters with spaces.

To format using the grep and tr commands:

1. Type **cd~/source** and press **Enter** to change to the source directory.

2. Use the grep command to retrieve a record from the corp_phones file that matches the phone number 219-555-4501, and then pipe the output to tr to replace the colon characters in the record with space characters. Type **grep 219-555-4501 corp_phones | tr ':' ' '** and then press **Enter**. The output on your screen looks similar to the following:

```
[tom@localhost tom]$ grep 219-555-4501 corp_phones
      | tr ':' ' '
219-555-4501 Robinson Albert Secretary J 4501 08-12-1997
```

3. Change lowercase characters to uppercase in the corp_phones file by typing **$ cat corp_phones | tr '[a-z]' '[A-Z]'** and then pressing **Enter**. Your screen looks similar to Figure 7-6.

Figure 7-6 Output of the cat and tr commands

To search for phone numbers in the corp_phones file, your program can use techniques similar to those you executed in the steps above.

To add record-searching capability to your program:

1. The phmenu program is already equipped to call the script phonefind when the user selects S from the menu. This command instructs the program to search for a phone number. Switch to the source directory, and use the vi or Emacs editor to create the phonefind program. Type the following:

```
#!/bin/bash
#=======================================================
# Script Name: phonefind
# By:          Your initials here
# Date         February 2004
# Purpose:     Searches for a specified record in the
#              corp_phones file
#=======================================================
phonefile=~/source/corp_phones
clear
tput cup 5 1
echo "Enter phone number to search for: "
tput cup 5 35
read number
echo
grep $number $phonefile | tr ':' ' '
echo
echo "Press ENTER to continue..."
read continue
```

2. Save the file, and exit the editor.

3. Use the **chmod** command to make the file executable, and then test the script by searching for the number 219-555-7175. Your screen should look similar to Figure 7-7

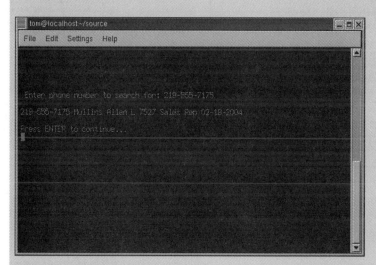

Figure 7-7   Output of the phonefind script

You formatted the record output of the program; your next task is to delete phone records.

DELETING PHONE RECORDS

In this section you review the sed command. Recall from Chapter 5 that sed takes the contents of an input file and applies actions, provided as options and arguments, to the file's contents. The results are sent to the standard output device. A simple way to delete a phone record using sed is with the d (delete) option. Here is a pseudocode representation of the necessary steps:

```
Enter phone number
Use sed -d to delete the matching phone number and output
to a temporary file, f
Confirm acceptance
If the output is accepted, copy the temporary file f back
to corp_phones (overlaying it)
```

Revise the phmenu script to include the delete option. In this revision, you use sed to create a temporary file called f. After you are finished using f, it is deleted near the end of the script by using the rm f statement. To make your script more foolproof, you also use the trap command, as you learned in Chapter 6, to be certain the f file is deleted before starting any code. Just before the phonefile=~/source/corp_phones line, you insert this statement: trap "rm ./f 2> /dev/null; exit" 0 1 3. The advantage of this technique is that it makes sure that the f file is deleted. After all, your previous run of phmenu could have aborted before deleting the f file near the end of the script.

To delete phone records by editing the phmenu program:

1. Make sure you are in the source directory. Using the vi or Emacs editor, retrieve the revised phmenu program and add the code shown in boldface.

```
#!/bin/bash
#===========================================================
# Script Name:   phmenu
# By:            Your initials here
# Date:          February 2004
# Purpose:       A menu for the Corporate Phone List
# Command Line:  phmenu
#===========================================================
trap "rm ./f 2> /dev/null; exit" 0 1 3
phonefile=~/source/corp_phones
loop=y
```

```
while test $loop = "y"
do
 clear
 tput cup 3 12; echo "Corporate Phone Reporting Menu"
 tput cup 4 12; echo "================================="
 tput cup 6 9; echo "P - Print Phone List"
 tput cup 7 9; echo "A - Add New Phones"
 tput cup 8 9; echo "S - Search for Phones"
 tput cup 9 9; echo "V - View Phone List"
 tput cup 10 9; echo "D - Delete Phone"
 tput cup 12 9; echo "Q - Quit: "
 tput cup 12 19;
 read choice || continue
   case $choice in
    [Aa]) ./phoneadd ;;
    [Pp]) ./phlist1 ;;
    [Ss]) ./phonefind ;;
    [Vv]) clear ; less $phonefile ;;
    [Dd])  tput cup 16 4; echo "Delete Phone Record"
           tput cup 17 4; echo "Phone: "
           tput cup 17 11; read number
           tput cup 18 4; echo "Accept? (y)es
           or (n)o: "
           tput cup 18 27; read Accept
           if test $Accept = "y"
                 then
                     sed /$number/d $phonefile > f
                     cp f $phonefile
                   rm f
            fi
            ;;
       [Qq]) clear ; exit ;;
          *)tput cup 14 4; echo "Invalid Code"; read
          choice ;;
       esac
   done
```

2. Save the file, and exit the editor. Later, when you test the program, the menu appears similar to Figure 7-8.

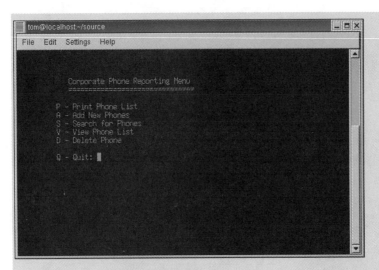

Figure 7-8   Output of the phmenu script

3. Use the more command to display the contents of the corp_phones file in the source directory before you delete a record (type **more corp_phones** and press **Enter**). Your screen should be similar to Figure 7-9.

Figure 7-9   Contents of the corp_phones file before deleting a record

4. Run the phmenu program, and test the delete option by removing the phone number, which is 219-555-4567. Figure 7-10 shows the Delete Phone Record screen.

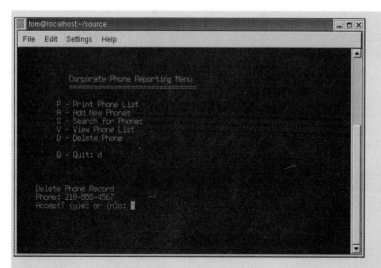

Figure 7-10   Delete Phone Record screen

5. Type **y** to confirm the deletion, and then press **Enter**.

6. On the main menu, select option **V** to view the phone file, and then press **Enter**. Your screen looks similar to Figure 7-11.

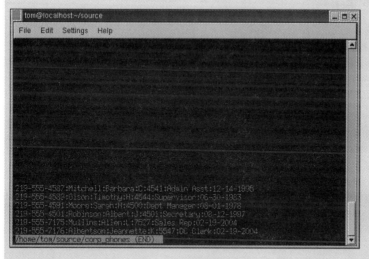

Figure 7-11   View Phone List option

Notice the record for phone number 219-555-4567 is no longer in the file (there were initially two records with this phone number and both are now removed).

7. Press **q** to return to the menu, press **q**, and then press **Enter** to exit the phmenu script.

In this section, you began to revise the shell phone program to meet Dominion Consulting's needs. You added code for the delete option to the phmenu script. In the next section you add code that prevents duplicate phone numbers from being entered in the file.

◀ LESSON B ▶

COMPLETING THE CASE PROJECT

After completing this lesson, you should be able to:
♦ Set up a quick screen-clearing technique
♦ Create a program algorithm to solve a cursor-repositioning problem
♦ Develop and test a program to reenter fields during data entry
♦ Develop and test a program to eliminate duplicate records
♦ Create shell functions and use them in a program
♦ Load shell functions automatically when you log in

CLEARING THE SCREEN

Before you begin to complete the programming tasks, you decide you want to clear screens more quickly. The clear command is a useful housekeeping utility for clearing the screen before new screens appear (which happens frequently in shell scripts), but you can use a faster method. You can store the output of the clear command in a shell variable. Recall from Chapter 6 that you can store the output of a command in a variable by enclosing the command in single backquotes (use the ` character usually found in the upper-left portion of the keyboard, along with the tilde ~). For example, this command stores the output of the date command in the variable TODAY:

```
TODAY=`date`
```

The output of the clear command is a sequence of values that erases the contents of the screen. Storing these values in a variable, and then echoing the contents of the variable on the screen accomplishes the same thing, but about ten times faster. This is because the system does not have to locate and execute the clear command, as it does when executing the clear command.

To clear screens by setting a shell variable:

1. Type **cd** and press **Enter** to change to your home directory.

2. Set a shell variable, CLEAR, to the output of the clear command, by typing the following:

```
CLEAR=`clear`
export CLEAR
```

3. Use your new variable in your shell programs for a fast clear operation by typing **echo "$CLEAR"** and pressing **Enter**.

4. To make this fast clear always available, place these two lines of code at the end of your .bashrc file (or the equivalent login initialization file for your shell):

```
CLEAR=`clear`
export CLEAR
```

5. Save the file, exit, and then log in again to activate the login script. Test your change to the login script by typing **echo "$CLEAR"** and then pressing **Enter**. Verify that the screen clears.

You are now ready to complete your first task: correcting entries. To do this, you need to manipulate the cursor.

MOVING THE CURSOR

The first task is to let the user return to a previously entered field and to correct data in that field before continuing. You want to allow users to return the cursor to a previous field on the screen when adding records to the corp_phones file. You decide that the minus character (-) can signal this. If the user enters a minus and presses Enter, the cursor is repositioned at the start of the previous field, as shown on the screen. You make this change by editing the phoneadd program (which provides the user with data-entry screens) that you already created. Your first step in editing the program is to create a program algorithm.

CREATING PROGRAM ALGORITHMS

An **algorithm** is a sequence of commands or instructions that produces a desired result. The algorithm to solve a specific problem is frequently developed by following both the logic shown in a flowchart and the expressed conditions necessary to carry out the logic described in the pseudocode.

Here is the pseudocode for repositioning the cursor at the previous field when the user enters the minus sign (-):

```
Read information into field2.
While field2 equals "-"
```

7

```
            Move cursor to position of previous field, field1.
            Clear current information displayed in field1.
            Read new information into field1.
            If field1 = "q"
            then
                Exit program.
            End if.
            Move cursor to position of field2.
            Read information into field2.
    End While.
```

One code addition to the phoneadd program uses the algorithm for reentering fields:

```
tput cup 5 18; read lname
    while test "$lname" = "-"
        do   tput cup 4 18; echo "        "
             tput cup 4 18; read phonenum
             tput cup 5 18; read lname
    done
```

This code reads the last name into the variable lname. If lname contains a minus sign (-), the cursor moves to the previous field, which contains the phone number. The value displayed for the phone number is cleared from the screen, and a new value is entered into phonenum. The cursor is then moved back to the last name field, and the last name is entered. The while statement repeats this process as long as the user types a minus sign for the last name.

Using the if statement instead of the while statement allows only one return to the prior field. Instead, you need a loop so the process repeats as long as the user enters a minus sign for the field.

Look at this while statement:

```
while test "$lname" = "-"
```

The argument "$lname" is enclosed in quotation marks to prevent the command from producing an error, in the event the user presses just Enter or more than one word for the last name. For example, if the user enters Smith Williams for the last name, the statement above is interpreted as:

```
while test "Smith Williams" = "-"
```

However, if the statement is written without the quotation marks around $lname, the statement is interpreted as:

```
while test Smith Williams = "-"
```

This statement causes an error message, because it passes too many arguments to the test command.

You are now ready to edit the phoneadd program. You add the field reentering algorithm to each part of the program that reads a value into a field.

To allow reentry of data:

1. Make sure you are in the source directory. Load the phoneadd program into the vi or Emacs editor.

2. Add the boldfaced code shown below to the program. Notice that the revised code also includes your new, faster, screen clear feature. It also changes the existing if statements, so they use the test command.

```bash
#!/bin/bash
#=============================================================
# Script Name:  phoneadd
# By:           Your initials here
# Date:         February 2004
# Purpose:      A shell script that sets up a loop to add
#               new employees to the corp_phones file.
#               The code also prevents duplicate phone
#               numbers from being assigned.
# Command Line: phoneadd
#
#=============================================================
trap "rm ~/tmp/* 2> /dev/null; exit" 0 1 2 3
phonefile=~/source/corp_phones
looptest=y
while test "$looptest" = "y"
do
      clear
      tput cup 1 4; echo "Corporate Phone List Additions"
      tput cup 2 4; echo "=============================="
      tput cup 4 4; echo "Phone Number: "
      tput cup 5 4; echo "Last Name    :"
      tput cup 6 4; echo "First Name   :"
      tput cup 7 4; echo "Middle Init :"
      tput cup 8 4; echo "Dept #       :"
      tput cup 9 4; echo "Job Title   :"
      tput cup 10 4; echo "Date Hired :"
      tput cup 12 4; echo "Add another? (y)es or (q)uit: "
      tput cup 4 18; read phonenum
      if  test $phonenum = "q"
      then
          clear ; exit
      fi
      tput cup 5 18 ; read lname
      while test "$lname" = "-"
      do
```

7

```
                    tput cup 4 18 ; echo "        "
                    tput cup 4 18 ; read phonenum
                    if test "$phonenum" = "q"
                    then
                        clear ; exit
                    fi
                    tput cup 5 18 ; read lname
          done
          tput cup 6 18 ; read fname
          while test "$fname" = "-"
          do
                    tput cup 5 18 ; echo "        "
                    tput cup 5 18 ; read lname
                    if test "$lname" = "q"
                    then
                        clear ; exit
                    fi
                    tput cup 6 18 ; read fname
          done
          tput cup 7 18 ; read midinit
          while test "$midinit" = "-"
          do
                tput cup 6 18 ; echo "        "
                    tput cup 6 18 ; read fname
                    if test "$fname" = "q"
                    then
                        clear ; exit
                    fi
                    tput cup 7 18 ; read midinit
          done
          tput cup 8 18 ; read deptno
          while test "$deptno" = "-"
          do
                    tput cup 7 18 ; echo "        "
                    tput cup 7 18 ; read midinit
                    if test "$midinit" = "q"
                    then
                        clear ; exit
                    fi
                    tput cup 8 18 ; read deptno
          done
          tput cup 9 18 ; read jobtitle
          while test "$jobtitle" = "-"
          do
                    tput cup 8 18 ; echo "        "
                    tput cup 8 18 ; read deptno
                    if test "$deptno" = "q"
                    then
                        clear ; exit
                    fi
```

```
                tput cup 9 18 ; read jobtitle
        done
        tput cup 10 18; read datehired
        while test "$datehired" = "-"
        do
                tput cup 9 18 ; echo"                "
                tput cup 9 18 ; read jobtitle
                if test "$jobtitle" = "q"
                then
                   clear ; exit
                fi
                tput cup 10 18 ; read datehired
        done
        #Check to see if last name is not blank before you
        #write to disk
        if  test "$lname" != ""
        then
                echo "$phonenum:$lname:$fname:$midinit:$deptno:
        $jobtitle:$datehired" >> $phonefile
        fi
        tput cup 12 33 ; read looptest
        if  test "$looptest" = "q"
        then
           clear ; exit
        fi
done
```

Tip For each echo statement in the code in Step 2, make sure that you have placed 12 blank spaces between the opening double quote and the closing double quote.

3. Save the file, and exit the editor.

4. Execute the phoneadd script. For the phone number, enter **219-555-4523** and press **Enter**. Your screen appears similar to Figure 7-12

5. In the Last Name field, type the **minus sign** (-) and press **Enter**. Your cursor moves back to the Phone Number field. Your screen looks like Figure 7-13.

6. Reenter the phone number as **219-555-4511** and press **Enter**.

7. Complete the remaining fields with the information shown below. As the cursor moves to each field, test the program by typing the **minus sign**(-) and pressing **Enter**. The cursor should move to the previous field each time.

Last name: **Brooks**   Department Number: **4540**

First name: **Sally**   Job Title: **Programmer**

Middle initial: **H**   Date Hired: **02-20-2004**

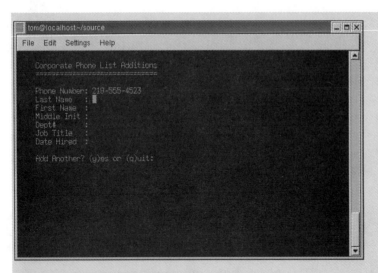

Figure 7-12 The phoneadd script screen

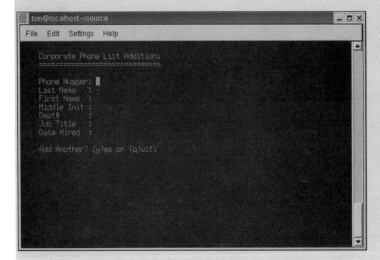

Figure 7-13 The phoneadd screen ready for reentry

8. After you enter all the information, quit the program. Use the cat command to display the contents of the corp_phones file. The new record should appear.

You completed the first task. You are now ready to work on the second task: protecting against duplicate phone numbers.

PROTECTING AGAINST ENTERING DUPLICATE PHONE NUMBERS

Because users do not always enter valid data, a program should always check its input to ensure the user has entered acceptable information. This is known as **input validation**. Your next task is to create an input validation algorithm that prevents the user from adding a phone number that has already been assigned. The pseudocode and flowchart to accomplish this are shown in Figure 7-14.

Pseudocode:

```
If phone number is already on file
     then
         display message on the screen "This number has already been assigned to:"
         display the person's record who has the duplicate number.
         Clear the screen and prepare for another entry
End if
```

Flowchart:

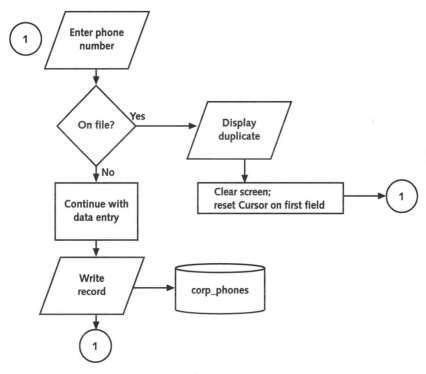

Figure 7-14   Second revision to the phoneadd program script

In the following steps, you add input validation code to the phoneadd script.

To prevent phone number duplications:

1. Make sure you are in the source directory. Load the phoneadd script into vi or Emacs.

2. Add the boldfaced section of code to complete the revised script.

```
#!/bin/bash
# ===========================================================
# Script Name:   phoneadd
# By:            Your initials here
# Date:          February 2004
# Purpose:       A shell script that sets up a loop to add
#                new employees to the corp_phones file.
#                The code also prevents duplicate phone
#                numbers from being assigned.
# Command Line: phoneadd
#
# ===========================================================
trap "rm ~/tmp/* 2> /dev/null; exit" 0 1 2 3
phonefile=~/source/corp_phones
looptest=y
while test "$looptest" = "y"
do
   clear
      tput cup 1 4; echo "Corporate Phone List Additions"
      tput cup 2 4; echo "=============================="
      tput cup 4 4; echo "Phone Number:"
      tput cup 5 4; echo "Last Name    :"
      tput cup 6 4; echo "First Name   :"
      tput cup 7 4; echo "Middle Init :"
      tput cup 8 4; echo "Dept #       :"
      tput cup 9 4; echo "Job Title    :"
      tput cup 10 4; echo "Date Hired :"
      tput cup 12 4; echo "Add another? (y)es or (q)uit "
      tput cup 4 18; read phonenum
      if  test $phonenum = "q"
      then
            clear ; exit
      fi
      # Check to see if the phone number already exists
      while grep "$phonenum" $phonefile > ~/tmp/temp
      do
            tput cup 19 1 ; echo "This number has already
            been assigned to: "
            tput cup 20 1 ; tr ':' ' ' < ~/tmp/temp
```

```
                  tput cup 21 1 ; echo "Press ENTER to
                   continue... "
                  read prompt
                  tput cup 4 18 ; echo "          "
                  tput cup 4 18 ; read phonenum
                  if test $phonenum = "q"
                  then
                          clear ; exit
                  fi
          done
          tput cup 5 18 ; read lname
             ... The remainder of the program is unchanged
```

3. Save the file, and exit the editor.

4. If you have not already created a tmp directory under your home directory, do so now.

5. Run the program. Test it by entering a phone number that already exists in the file, such as **219-555-4587** and then press **Enter**. Your screen should look like Figure 7-15.

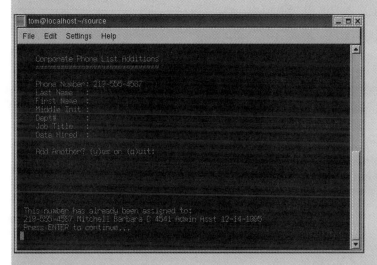

Figure 7-15   Revised phoneadd program

6. Complete the data-entry screen by entering a valid phone number.

Looking at the phoneadd program, you realize that it contains code that you may want to reuse for other programs. To reuse code, you use shell functions.

USING SHELL FUNCTIONS

A **shell function** is a group of commands that is stored in memory and assigned a name. Shell scripts can use the function name to execute the commands. You can use shell functions to isolate reusable code sections, so that you do not have to duplicate algorithms throughout your program. For example, the phlist1 script can use several functions to sort the phone list in a variety of ways.

A function name differs from a variable name, because a function name is followed by a set of parentheses, and the commands that make up the function are enclosed in curly braces. For example, look at the code for a function:

```
datenow()
{
date
}
```

The name of the function is "datenow." It has only one command inside its braces: the date command. When the datenow function is executed, it calls the date command.

Functions are usually stored in script files and loaded into memory when you log in. However, you can also enter them at the command line.

To declare the simple datenow function:

1. Type **cd** and press **Enter** to change to your home directory.

2. At the command line, type **datenow()** and press **Enter**. Notice the prompt changes to the **>** symbol. This indicates the shell is waiting for you to type more information to complete the command you started.

3. At the > prompt, type **{** and press **Enter**.

4. At the > prompt, type **date** and press **Enter**.

5. At the > prompt type **}** and press **Enter**. The normal prompt returns.

6. You created the datenow function and stored it in the shell's memory. Call it by typing **datenow** and pressing **Enter**. Your screen looks similar to the following:

   ```
   [tom@localhost tom]$ datenow
   ```

   Mon Feb 9 21:41:08 MST 2004

Arguments are passed to functions in the same manner as any other shell procedure. The function accesses the arguments using the positional variables $1 ... $9. Simply type the arguments following the command name, placing a space between each argument. Now, redefine the datenow function so it accepts an argument.

To redefine the datenow function to accept an argument:

1. At the command line, type **datenow()** and press **Enter**. The commands you are about to type replace those currently stored in the datenow function.

2. At the > prompt, type **{** and press **Enter**.

3. At the > prompt, type **echo "$1"** and press **Enter**. When the function runs, this command displays the information passed to the function in the first argument.

4. At the > prompt, type **date** and press **Enter**.

5. At the > prompt type **}** and press **Enter**. The normal prompt returns.

6. Test the function by typing **datenow "Today is"** and pressing **Enter**. Your screen looks similar to the following:

```
[tom@localhost tom]$ datenow "Today is"
Today is
Mon Feb 9 21:49:45 MST 2004
```

The exercises you just completed demonstrate how functions work in general. Typing functions at the command line is hardly productive, however, because they must be reentered each time you log in. You now learn how to use shell functions to reuse code and to make functions available each time you log in.

REUSING CODE

To improve your programming productivity, you should learn to reuse your code. This means that the functions and programs you develop should be shared with other programs and functions as much as possible, thereby helping to prevent duplications, save time, and reduce errors. A good illustration of this potential use of reusable functions can be demonstrated in the current phonelist program. You can create several different sort functions and store them in memory. The phlist1 script can then call these functions to display the list of phone numbers sorted in a variety of ways. (You may want to review the syntax of the sort command by referring to the section "Using the sort Command" in Chapter 4.)

You can place multiple functions inside a shell script such as .myfuncs, and execute them from your .bash_profile login script, or simply run .myfuncs from the command line. This loads all your functions into memory just as you load environment variables.

When you name a file with a period in the front, it is stored as a hidden file. Remember to use ls -a to view hidden files.

To place several functions inside a shell script:

1. Make sure you are in the source directory.

2. Use the vi or Emacs editor to create the .myfuncs file inside your source directory.

3. Enter the following functions:

```
sort_name()
  {
  sort +1 -t: corp_phones
  }
 sort_date()
  {
  sort +6 -t: corp_phones
  }
 sort_dept()
  {
  sort +4 -t: corp_phones
  }
```

4. Save the file, and exit the editor.

Your next task is to load the .myfuncs file into memory so its functions may be executed. To do this, type a period (.) followed by a space, followed by the name of the file containing the functions.

To load the .myfuncs file:

1. At the command line, type **. .myfuncs** (that is, type a period, press the **Spacebar**, type a period, and type myfuncs) and press **Enter**. Nothing appears, but the functions are loaded into memory. Test some functions. Type **sort_name** and press **Enter**. You see the phone records sorted by individuals' names.

2. Type **sort_dept** and press **Enter**. You see the phone records sorted by department number.

You can load functions automatically using your .bash_profile or .bashrc files when you log in. This way, the functions are always available to any shell script that needs them.

To modify your .bashrc file to load the .myfuncs script:

1. Type **cd** to make sure you are in your home directory. Load your .bashrc file into the vi or Emacs editor.

2. At the end of the file, add the following command (make sure that you put a space between the period (.) and the tilde (~):

. ~/source/.myfuncs

3. Save the file, and exit the editor.

4. Log out and log back on to load the functions.

5. Test the sort_name, sort_dept, and other functions.

Your last task is to display the phone listing in sorted order by employees' last names. You can do this by using your sort_name function, as stored in the .myfuncs file.

SORTING THE PHONE LIST

To sort the phone list, make a minor revision to phlist1 to load the functions, and then call sort_name to redirect the sorted output to a temporary file. The sorted temporary file serves as input to the awk program that displays the records. The revised code also uses the CLEAR variable and the cursor script.

To sort the phone listing:

1. Switch to the source directory, if you are not already in it. Use the vi or Emacs editor to add the code to the phlist1 script. The additions and revisions are in boldface.

```
#!/bin/bash
# ========================================================
# Script Name:    phlist1
# By:             Your initials here
# Date:           February 2004
# Purpose:        Use awk to format colon-separated
#                 fields
#                 in a flat file and display to the
#                 screen
# Command Line:   phlist1
# ========================================================
echo "$CLEAR"
tput cup 2 20; echo "Corporate Phone List"
tput cup 3 20; echo "===================="
tput cup 5 0;
. .myfuncs
sort_name > sorted_phones
awk -F: ' { printf "%-12s %-12s %s\t%s %s %10.10s %s\n",
$2, $3, $4, $1, $5, $6, $7 } ' sorted_phones
tput cup 23 1; echo "Review"
tput cup 22 8; read prompt
```

2. This code includes the .myfuncs shell script, which contains sort functions. Thus, the code works regardless of whether the .myfuncs shell script is already loaded in memory via the .bashrc file. Save the file, and exit the editor.

3. Test the file by typing **phlist1** and pressing **Enter**. Your screen looks similar to Figure 7-16. Press **Enter** when you finish observing the screen.

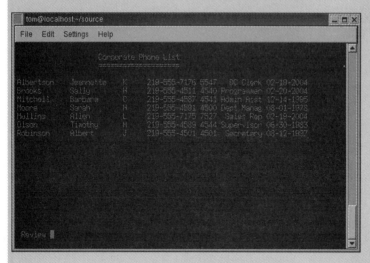

Figure 7-16   Output of the revised phlist1 script

You add code to call the other sort functions as a Discovery Exercise at the end of this chapter.

In this chapter, you have learned to plan algorithms and programs using flowcharts and pseudocode. You have also learned to create complex decision expressions with the test command. You have expanded your use of the grep, tr, and sed commands to format output. In addition, you have learned advanced programming techniques, such as repositioning the cursor at a previous field in a data-entry screen, and creating shell functions.

CHAPTER SUMMARY

- The two most popular and proven analysis tools are the program flowchart and pseudocode. The flowchart is a logic diagram drawn using a set of standard symbols that explain the flow and the action to be taken by the program.

- Pseudocode is a model of a program. It is written in statements similar to your natural language.

- You can use the first line in a script file to tell the operating system which shell to use when interpreting the script.

- You can use the test command to validate the existence of directories and files as well as compare numeric and string values. You can place it inside your shell script or execute it directly from the command line.

❏ The translate utility (tr) changes the characters typed at the keyboard, character by character, and also works as a filter when the input comes from the output of another UNIX command. Standard input can also be redirected to come from a file rather than the keyboard.

❏ The sed command reads a file as its input and outputs the file's modified contents. You specify options and pass arguments to sed to control how the file's contents are modified.

❏ To speed clearing the screen, assign the clear command sequence to the shell variable CLEAR that can be set inside your login script, which is .bashrc. This clears your screen faster because it does not require a look-up sequence in a file every time it executes.

❏ An algorithm is a sequence of instructions or commands that produce a desired result. The logic flow expressed in a flowchart and pseudocode is the basis of an algorithm.

❏ Shell functions can simplify program code by isolating code that can be reused throughout one or many programs.

7

COMMAND SUMMARY

Review of the test Command		
Option	Meaning	Example Command
-eq	equal to	test a -eq b
-gt	greater than	test a -gt b
-lt	less than	test a -lt b
-ge	greater than or equal to	test a -ge b
-le	less than or equal to	test a -le b
-ne	not equal to	test a -ne b
-z	Tests for a zero-length string	test -z string
-n	Tests for a nonzero string length	test -n string
string1 = string2	Tests two strings for equality	test string1 = string2
string1 != string2	Tests two strings for inequality	test string1 != string2
string	Tests for a nonzero string length	test string
-e	True if a file exists	test -e file
-r	True if a file exists and is readable	test -r file
-w	True if a file exists and is writeable	test -w file
-x	True if a file exists and is executable	test -x file
-d	True if a file exists and is a directory	test -d file
-f	Tests if a file exists and is a regular file	test -f file
-s	True if a file exists and has a size greater than zero	test -s file

Review of test Command (continued)		
Option	Meaning	Example Command
-c	Tests if a file exists and is a character special file (which is a character-oriented device, such as a terminal or printer)	test -c file
-b	Tests if a file exists and is a block special file (which is a block-oriented device, such as a disk or tape drive)	test -b file
-a	Logical AND	test expression1 -a expression2
-o	Logical OR	test expression1 -o expression2
!	Logical negation	test !expression

REVIEW QUESTIONS

1. Which of the following is true about using a flowchart?
   a. It uses a standard set of symbols.
   b. It should be pasted into the comments section of a script for documentation.
   c. It demonstrates the sequence and logic that a program follows.
   d. all of the above
   e. only a and c

2. Which of the following is true of pseudocode?
   a. It should not include logic statements or tests.
   b. It should only include the arithmetic operators used in a program.
   c. It is used as a model on which to base the writing of a program.
   d. all of the above
   e. only b and c

3. The test _____ command compares two numeric values to see if they are equal to one another.
   a. –eq
   b. string
   c. –ne
   d. equal

4. Which of the following syntax formats is valid for creating a function called timeplace?
   a. timeplace()
   b. timeplace.
   c. timeplace{}
   d. ...timeplace

5. The test command's return value appears when you type _____ at the command line.

   a. echo $$

   b. echo $?

   c. echo $–

   d. echo $.

6. When you use the test command, along with the command that is the correct answer for Question 5, to show the outcome of the test command, a return value of _____ means false.

   a. nil

   b. none

   c. 0

   d. 1

7. The test command's –a option is the _____ operator.

   a. absolute value

   b. logical AND

   c. test for hidden files

   d. logical OR

8. After you store the clear command in a variable, you can clear the screen by typing _____ .

   a. !c

   b. a variable named #CLEAR

   c. echo "$CLEAR"

   d. ??

9. Which of the following determines if the value stored in the menu variable is greater than 5?

   a. find $menu < 5

   b. test menu > 5

   c. cacl menu –g 5

   d. test $menu –gt 5

10. An algorithm is _____ .

    a. a name that replaces the standard UNIX command name

    b. a derived formula made up of a sequence of commands that produce a desired result

    c. always entered into the system–wide initialization file, /etc/profile

    d. an alternate name for a UNIX command

11. True or False: After you load into memory a shell script that contains functions, you must type + and the function name, such as +calcdate, as the shorthand for running the script's functions from the command line.

12. The tr command translates _____.
    a. only what is typed at the keyboard
    b. on a line basis, like sed
    c. on a character-by-character basis
    d. characters originating from within files only

13. You want to set up your account so that the path automatically includes the data directory that is in your home directory. To do this, you append _____ to the PATH= line in the .bash_profile file, when Bash is your default shell.
    a. :$HOME/data
    b. $HOME\data:
    c. /data:
    d. /data!

14. The code for a function is surrounded by:
    a. { }
    b. [ ]
    c. ; ;
    d. < >

15. To load a shell containing functions into memory, you type _____.
    a. Ctrl+m
    b. a backward slash and a period, as in \.
    c. a forward slash and a period, as in /.
    d. a period and a space

16. How do you pass arguments to a shell function?
    a. Use the < character.
    b. Use forward quote marks.
    c. Use the positional variables, $1, $2, $3 ... $9.
    d. Use the characters $#.

17. Which of the following writes to the screen records in the names file so that all alpha characters are lowercase?
    a. cat names | tr '[A–Z]' '[a–z]'
    b. cat names | tr –lc
    c. cat names > tr –lc
    d. cat names < tr [a–z]

18. True or False: You can use the .bashrc or .bash_profile files to load a script of functions so that the functions are available every time you log in.

19. Creating shell functions _____.
    a. makes your scripts execute more slowly, so that they are easier for the user to read on the screen
    b. enables you to reuse lines of code so that you do not have to keep rewriting the same lines of code in multiple scripts
    c. requires that you first load the shell function generator
    d. all of the above
    e. only b and c

20. What does the command, test -d bin, accomplish?
    a. It deletes the bin directory.
    b. It deletes the hidden files in the bin directory.
    c. It tests for the existence of the bin directory.
    d. It creates the bin directory.

21. Which of the following determines if the value in the lname variable is not equal to Lincoln?
    a. echo $lname neq "Lincoln"
    b. string lname eq! "Lincoln"
    c. test lname >! "Lincoln"
    d. test $lname != "Lincoln"

22. True or False: You can use the grep command to retrieve a specific record from a file.

23. You can use the _____ option with the sed command to delete a record in a file.
    a. d
    b. e
    c. :
    d. s

24. Providing code to check and make sure a user cannot enter the same record (information) twice is an example of _____.
    a. shell system organization
    b. input validation
    c. record regeneration
    d. shell redirection

25. True or False: One limitation of the test command is that it cannot be used to determine the permissions associated with a file.

DISCOVERY EXERCISES

1. Use the tr command to translate the phone records file to contain a hyphen as the field separator instead of a colon (:). (Be sure to save the translated records to a different file.)

2. Set an environment variable, RHL, to the value "Red_Hat_Linux," and use the test and echo $? commands to determine if it matches "Red_Hat_Linux" and "RED_HAT_LINUX." How can you tell which one matches?

3. Set an environment variable called NUMVAL to 2000, and use the test and echo $? commands to determine if it matches the value 2000. What about 2020? How can you tell which one matches?

4. Write a flowchart for a program that tests your ability to perform simple arithmetic. The program should display two numbers that are to be added. The program should ask the user to enter the sum. If the correct answer is given, the program should congratulate the user. If an incorrect answer is given, the program should show the user the correct answer.

5. Write pseudocode for the flowchart program you created in Discovery Exercise 4.

6. Write the actual code for the math testing program you put in a flowchart in Discovery Exercise 4 and for which you developed pseudocode in Discovery Exercise 5. Figure 7-17 shows an example of the program's screen output.

Figure 7-17   Math testing program

7. From the command line, create the function dir to execute this: ls -lq | more.

8. From the command line, create the function simple_date to execute this: date +%D.

9. Create the executable script file .mystuff to contain the two functions created in Discovery Exercises 7 and 8. Have it call each function from the command line.

10. Use vi or Emacs to create the file my_old_cars. The file should contain these records:

```
1948:Ford:sedan
1952:Chevrolet:coupe
1960:Ford:Mustang
1972:Chevrolet:Corvette
1977:Plymouth:Roadrunner
```

Next, write a shell script that displays a data-entry screen. The script should allow additional records to be entered into the file. Note that you also use the my_old_cars file for Discovery Exercises 11 through 15.

11. Write a shell script that displays all records in the my_old_cars file that you created in Discovery Exercise 10. The colons should be converted to spaces before the output appears.

12. Again using the my_old_cars file that you created in Discovery Exercise 10, write a shell script that allows the user to enter a search string and display all records in the file that contain a string matching the search string. For example, if the user enters "Ford," the script displays all records that contain the word "Ford."

13. Write a shell script that allows the user to enter a search string and delete all records in the my_old_cars file that contain a string matching the search string. For example, if the user enters "1948," the script deletes all records containing "1948."

14. Create shell functions that sort the records in the file my_old_cars. Your functions should sort the records by year (the first field), by make (the second field), and by car model (the third field). Write a menu program that calls each sort function.

15. Write a Main menu program for the my_old_cars file and all the script files you have created so far. Here is a list of the script files you should have:

   ◻ Data-entry screen

   ◻ Script that displays all records in the file

   ◻ Script that searches for and displays records containing a string

   ◻ Script that deletes specified records from the file

   ◻ Script that displays the records sorted in various ways

16. Sort the corp_phones file by last name, and pipe the output to a tr command to convert all characters to uppercase and to store output in a new file, phoneupper.

17. Create a directory called scripts in your source directory, and use the test command to validate that the directory exists.

18. Make a copy of the corp_phones file and call it corp_phones_convert. Use your choice of the sed or tr command to convert all occurrences of the word "Supervisor" to "Manager" in the corp_phones_convert file.

19. UNIX keeps users' login names stored in an environment variable named USER. Design a flowchart for a User Authentication program that asks users who they are. Their response should be compared against the contents of the USER variable. If the two strings do not match, users should be asked again. This process should repeat until the correct user name is entered.

20. Write the pseudocode for the flowchart you designed in Discovery Exercise 19.

21. Write the actual code for the program you put in a flowchart in Discovery Exercise 19 and for which you wrote pseudocode in Discovery Exercise 20. Figure 7-18 shows a sample of the program's output.

22. Place the screen display from the phoneadd program in a function, called phscreen. Using the vi editor, type the function into .mystuff (from Discovery Exercise 9), and test the function by calling it from the command line.

23. Add menu items to phmenu that call the sort_date and sort_dept functions you created in the .myfuncs file. Test the program.

24. Create a shell function named average. Store it in a file named avgfunc. The function should accept three arguments. Assume the arguments are numbers. The function should calculate and output the average of the three numbers.

25. Create a script file named minmax. In the file, create a shell script named min. It should accept two arguments, assumed to be numbers. The function is to generate the output that is the lesser of the two arguments. For example, if 5 and 10 are passed to the function, it should write 5.

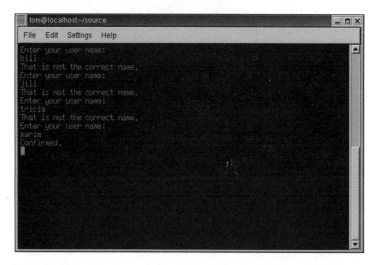

Figure 7-18   Output of the User Authentication program

26. Edit the minmax file you created in Discovery Exercise 25. Add a shell function named max. It should accept two arguments, assumed to be numbers. The function is to generate the output that is the greater of the two arguments. For example, if 8 and 4 are passed to the function, it should write 8.

8

EXPLORING THE UNIX UTILITIES

Your supervisor at Dominion Consulting asks you to accomplish several computer tasks, including creating a bootable floppy disk, making backups on floppy disks, auditing system performance, analyzing hard disk storage, and removing unnecessary files. Further, you have been asked to create a man page to describe the phmenu program that you wrote in Chapter 7.

In this chapter, you continue to explore UNIX utilities. Utilities are designed to provide basic services to UNIX users, just like your local utility companies provide basic services (such as electricity and running water) to your community. This chapter lets you practice using UNIX commands and utilities, such as using the man command with UNIX's text formatting utilities.

◀ LESSON A ▶

USING THE UNIX UTILITIES

After completing this lesson, you should be able to:

♦ Understand what UNIX utilities are available and the classifications of utilities

♦ Make a bootable floppy disk to boot the system in case of an emergency

♦ Duplicate files on a floppy disk

♦ Determine hard disk usage and available free space

♦ Locate and remove unnecessary files from the hard disk

♦ Display the CPU status and internal memory usage

UNDERSTANDING UNIX UTILITIES

UNIX utilities let you create and manage files, run programs, produce reports, and generally interact with the system. Beyond these basics, the utility programs offer a full range of services that let you monitor and maintain the system and recover from a wide range of errors. UNIX utilities are classified into seven major function areas dictated by user needs: file processing, system status, networking, communications, programming, source code management, and miscellaneous.

 UNIX utilities are programs, but they are often referred to as commands in the documentation. In this chapter, you will see both "utility" and "command," depending on the information that is being conveyed to you.

 For the sake of completeness, this chapter contains some references and commentary about utilities in general, but it concentrates on those utilities that relate to file processing, system status, and miscellaneous tasks.

Utility programs are vital for working through an operating system. You have already worked with dozens of utilities, many of which are reviewed for your convenience in the tables included with this chapter. For example, you have already worked with many of the file-processing utilities, some of the system status utilities, and some of the miscellaneous utilities.

In this and later chapters, you work with more system status, programming, and miscellaneous utilities. There are many, many UNIX utilities, and there is not room in this book to cover them all. However, you can come back to the tables in this chapter for a quick reference to utilities you have used or to find a utility for a specific task. You can learn more about these utilities using the man and info documentation options (such as man mesg or info mesg).

New utility programs are continually being added as developers find better and faster ways to make UNIX run more efficiently. One thing that many utilities have in common is that they are small programs that frequently consist of only one command.

CLASSIFYING UNIX UTILITIES

Utilities can be classified in several categories, as some work exclusively with UNIX files, others handle network tasks, and still others are designed to help programmers. File-processing utilities, listed in Table 8-1, make up the largest category. These utilities display and manipulate files.

Table 8-1   File-processing utilities

Command	Brief Description of Function
afio	Creates an archive or restores files from archives
awk	Processes files
cat	Displays files (and is used with other tools to concatenate files)
cmp	Compares two files
comm	Compares sorted files, and shows differences
cp	Copies files
cpio	Copies and backs up files to an archive
cut	Selects characters or fields from input lines
dd	Copies and converts input records
diff	Compares two text files, and shows differences
dump	Backs up files
fdformat	Formats a floppy disk at a low level
find	Finds files within file tree
fmt	Formats text very simply
grep	Matches patterns in a file
groff	Processes embedded text formatting codes
gzip	Compresses or decompresses files
head	Displays the first part of a file (first 10 lines by default)
ispell	Checks one or more files for spelling errors
less	Displays files allowing for scrolling forward and backward (pauses when screen is full)
ln	Creates a link to a file
lpr	Prints file (hard copy)
ls	Lists file and directory names and attributes
man	Displays documentation for commands
mkdir	Creates a new directory
mkfs	Builds a UNIX file system
mv	Renames and moves files and directories
od	Formats and displays data from a file in octal, hexadecimal, and ASCII formats
paste	Concatenates files horizontally

8

Table 8-1 File-processing utilities (continued)

Command	Brief Description of Function
pr	Formats text files for printing and displays them
pwd	Shows the directory you are in
rdev	Queries or sets the root image device
restore	Restores files (from a dump)
rm	Removes files
rmdir	Removes directory
sed	Edits streams (noninteractive)
sort	Sorts or merges files
tail	Displays the last lines of files (last 10 lines by default)
tar	Copies and backs up files to a tape archive
touch	Changes file modification dates
uniq	Displays unique lines of sorted file
wc	Counts lines, words, and bytes

System status utilities, listed in Table 8-2, is the second largest category. It includes utilities that display and alter the status of files, disks, and the overall system. These utilities let you know who is online, the names and status of running processes, the amount of hard disk space available, and where to find other commands you need to run.

Table 8-2 System status utilities

Command	Brief Description of Function
chgrp	Changes the group associated with a file or the file's group ownership
chmod	Changes the access permissions of a file or directory
chown	Changes the owner of a file
date	Sets and displays date and time
df	Displays the amount of free space remaining on disk
du	Summarizes file space usage
file	Determines file type (e.g., shell script, executable, ASCII text, and others)
finger	Displays detailed information about users who are logged on
free	Displays amount of free and used memory in the system
edquota	Displays user disk quotas and enables them to be changed
kill	Terminates a running process
ps	Displays process status by process identification number and name
sleep	Suspends execution for a specified time
top	Dynamically displays the status of processes in real time, focusing on those processes that are using the most CPU resources
w	Displays detailed information about the users who are logged on
who	Displays brief information about the users who are logged on

Network utilities, listed in Table 8-3, consist of the essential commands for communicating and sharing information on a network, as well as for viewing information about network connection status.

Table 8-3   Network utilities

Command	Brief Description of Function
ftp	Transfers files over a network
ifconfig	Used to set up a network interface
netstat	Shows network connection information
ping	Used to poll another network station (using the TCP/IP protocol); great for a fast determination about whether your network connection is working
rcp	Remotely copies a file from a network computer
rlogin	Logs on to a remote computer
rsh	Executes commands on a remote computer
rwho	Displays the names of users attached to a network
showmount	Lists clients that have mounted volumes on a server
telnet	Connects to a remote computer on a network
wvdial	Controls a modem dialer for dial-up connections over a phone line

The communication utilities, listed in Table 8-4, handle the mail and messaging tasks. These programs include some recent advanced features such as **Multipurpose Internet Mail Extensions (MIME)** support for sending and receiving binary files in mail messages.

Table 8-4   Communications utilities

Command	Brief Description of Function
mail	Sends electronic mail messages
mesg	Denies (mesg n) or accepts (mesg y) messages
pine	Sends and receives electronic mail and news
talk	Lets users simultaneously type messages to each other
wall	Sends a message to all logged-on users (who have permissions set to receive messages)
write	Sends a message to another user

Programming utilities, listed in Table 8-5, are designed to help users develop software projects written in C and C++ programs.

8

Table 8-5   Programming utilities

Command	Brief Description of Function
configure	Configures program source code automatically
gcc	Compiles C and C++ programs
make	Maintains program source code
patch	Updates source code

The use of the source code management utilities, which are listed in Table 8-6, is vital in a programming and development environment. When there are several applications developers working on a project, there needs to be ways to track programming changes. If these changes are not tracked, then the changes made by one programmer may inadvertently be undone or changed by another, with unanticipated outcomes. For financial auditing requirements, there also must be ways to track programming changes to meet the demands of audit reviews. This protects programmers who work on applications that affect how money is handled, and it protects organizations. These UNIX utilities have a proven track record in managing teamwork programming, and are vital tools for scheduling and managing large-scale applications.

Table 8-6   Source code management utilities

Command	Brief Description of Function
ci	Creates changes in Revision Control Systems (RCS)
co	Retrieves an unencoded revision of an RCS file
cvs	Manages concurrent access to files in a hierarchy
rcs	Creates or changes the attributes of an RCS file
rlog	Prints a summary of the history of an RCS file

Finally, miscellaneous utilities include unique programs that perform very specific and special functions. As you can see from the descriptions in Table 8-7, these commands include providing a system calendar, scheduling events, and identifying terminals attached to the system.

Table 8-7   Miscellaneous utilities

Command	Brief Description of Function
at	Executes a command or script at a specified time
atq	Shows the jobs (commands or scripts) already scheduled to run
atrm	Enables you to remove a job (command or script) that is scheduled to run
batch	Runs a command or script, and is really a subset of the at command that takes you to the at> prompt, if you type only batch (in Red Hat Linux, a command or script is run when the system load is at an acceptable level)

Table 8-7   Miscellaneous utilities (continued)

Command	Brief Description of Function
cal	Displays a calendar for a month or year
crontab	Schedules a command to run at a preset time
expr	Evaluates expressions (used for arithmetic and string manipulations)
fsck	Checks and fixes problems on a file system (repairs damages)
tee	Clones output stream to one or more files
tr	Replaces specified characters (a translation filter)
tty	Displays terminal path name
xargs	Converts standard output of one command into arguments for another

Now that you understand that many diverse utilities are available, you are ready to use several of them to complete your tasks for Dominion Consulting.

USING THE FILE-PROCESSING UTILITIES

Recall that the file-processing utilities help you display and manipulate files. You can use several of these utilities to complete your tasks. First, you use the dd command to copy a file and change the format of the destination file at the same time.

Using the dd Command

Files not only store information, but they also store it in a particular format. For example, most computers store text using ASCII codes. (IBM mainframes, however, use EBCDIC codes to store text.) In addition to the internal codes that computers use to store information, some files store text in all uppercase letters. Likewise, other files store text in all lowercase letters. Some files include only records, where each record consists of several fields. A special character, such as a colon, separates the fields, and each record ends with a character denoting a line break. Different files have different internal formats, depending upon how the file is used.

Whereas the standard UNIX copy utility, cp, duplicates a file, it cannot alter the format of the destination copy. Therefore, when you need to copy a file and change the format of the destination copy, use the dd command instead. Possessing a rich set of options that allow it to handle copies when other methods are inappropriate, the dd command can handle conversions to and from IBM's Extended Binary Coded Decimal Interchange Code (EBCDIC) character types to American Standard Code for Information Interchange (ASCII) characters. The dd command is frequently used for devices such as tapes, which have discrete record sizes, or for fast multisector reads from disks.

For information about the options available for this command and others in this chapter, refer to Appendix B, "Syntax Guide to UNIX Commands."

The dd command has the general form:

Syntax **dd** [options]

Options include if=*filename* and of=*filename,* which specify the input files and output files, respectively. Another frequently used option is bs=*n,* which specifies the block size, *n,* as an integer. You also have options to specify the input block size *(*ibs=*n)* and output block size (obs=*n*). Specifying block size, an optional requirement, speeds copying, especially when copying backups to tape.

Another advantage that the dd command has over cp is that all users, not just the system administrator, can copy files to and from the floppy drive. With cp, you must mount a floppy disk if you need to copy to or from the floppy disk. Usually, only the system administrator, who must be logged on as root, can issue the mount command. With the dd command there is no need to mount the floppy device to access it.

By duplicating a file with dd, you can learn the command's basic usage.

To make a backup of a file using the dd command:

1. Use the cat command, or the editor of your choice, to create a file, datafile. The file should contain the following text:

   ```
   This is my data file.
   ```

2. Make a copy of the file by typing **dd if=datafile of=datafile.bak** and press **Enter**. Your screen looks similar to the following:

   ```
   [tom@localhost tom]$ dd if=datafile of=datafile.bak
   0+1 records in
   0+1 records out
   ```

MAKING A BOOTABLE FLOPPY DISK

It is a good idea to make a bootable floppy disk, because a computer problem (such as a crashed hard disk) may prevent you from starting UNIX from the system. To make a bootable floppy (in this case, for Red Hat Linux), you use four utility programs: the rdev, mkfs, fdformat, and dd commands. The rdev command queries and sets the **root device**, which is the hard disk partition that houses UNIX's root file system. The root file system, in turn, houses the UNIX kernel (core operating system), which is required to boot UNIX. (Under Red Hat Linux, the kernel is stored in a file with a name that starts with vmlinuz. The file is usually stored in the /boot directory.) You can use the rdev command to set the root device with two arguments, where *image* is the name of the file holding the kernel and *root device* is the name of the UNIX partition that holds the root file system:

Syntax **rdev** [*image*] [*root device*]

Use the mkfs command to build a UNIX or Linux file system on a device such as a floppy disk or a hard disk partition. The command is usually issued as follows, where *-t option* identifies the file system type and *filesystem* identifies the device name:

Syntax **mkfs** [*-t option*] [*filesystem*]

The file system type, which determines how UNIX reads and writes information from or onto the device, is stored in the file /etc/fstab (file system table), as shown in Figure 8-1.

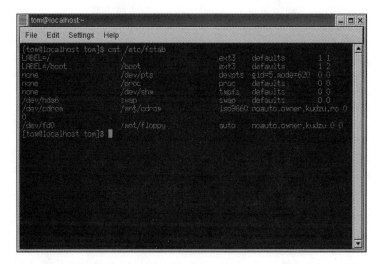

Figure 8-1   File system types as shown in /etc/fstab

The fdformat command formats a floppy at low levels to ensure that the media is clear of defects and is writeable. Unlike a high-level format that checks and verifies the disk's recording surface and sets up the file allocation tables (file system), as done on a Microsoft operating system, the low-level format prepares the recording surface, but does not set up a file system. (The latter is the function of the mkfs utility, so the two programs, fdformat and mkfs, must work in tandem to prepare the floppy disk for use.) The low-level format checks the recording surface more thoroughly than the high-level format does. The command-line entry to format a floppy follows this usage, where the -n option disables the verification performed after the format. The file system is usually indicated as /dev/fd0 for drive A (the first floppy drive) and /dev/fd1 for drive B (the second floppy drive):

Syntax **fdformat** [*-n*] [*filesystem*]

> The default format type is for 1.44 megabyte (high-density) floppies. The file system may also be indicated as /dev/fd0H1440 for a high-density floppy on drive A and /dev/fd1H1440 for a high-density floppy on drive B.

You are now ready to make a bootable disk.

The next steps make the following assumptions:

- You have system-level privileges. That is, you are logged in using the root account; check with your instructor for information about how to access this account.
- You are logged in to the host console. You cannot perform the steps if you are accessing a computer running Linux via a telnet session.

To make a bootable disk:

1. Determine where vmlinuz, the file holding the Linux kernel, is located (most likely in /boot).

If you have trouble locating the file, use the find command: type find / -name vmlinuz* and press Enter.

2. Verify the /boot partition's location by typing **rdev** and then pressing **Enter**. Your screen should look similar to the following:

```
[root@localhost root]# rdev
/dev/hda5
```

3. Insert a blank floppy disk in drive A.

4. Make a Linux file system on disk by typing **mkfs -t ext2 /dev/fd0 1440** and then pressing **Enter**. (Note that even though your system my be formatted for the Linux ext3 file system, which supports journaling, you need to use ext2 to format a floppy disk.) Your screen should now look similar to Figure 8-2.

5. Low-level format the disk by typing **fdformat /dev/fd0** and then pressing **Enter**. The utility displays its progress as it performs its operation. When the format is complete, your screen should look similar to:

```
[root@localhost root]# fdformat /dev/fd0
Double-sided, 80 tracks, 18 sec/track. Total
 capacity 1400 kB.
Formatting ... done
Verifying ... done
```

Figure 8-2 Results of the mkfs command

6. Make the floppy disk bootable by typing **dd if=/boot/vmlinuz-2.4.7-10 of=/dev/fd0** and then pressing **Enter**. (Use /boot/vmlinuz-2.4.7-10 for Red Hat Linux 7.2. If you are using an earlier or later version of Linux, type ls /boot to determine the exact name for the vmlinuz-*x.x.x-xx* file, or use the technique described in Step 1.) The results of the dd command should be displayed on your screen as follows:

```
[root@localhost root]# dd if=/boot/vmlinuz-2.4.
7-10 of=/dev/fd0
1566+1 records in
1566+1 records out
```

After you create a bootable disk, you can use it to start the system. Place the bootable disk in drive A, and turn on the system. Linux then boots from the floppy disk instead of the hard drive.

You can also use the dd command to make a back-up copy of a floppy disk. You can copy the entire contents of a floppy to a single file on your hard drive. You can then copy the file onto a second floppy disk, thus making a back-up copy of the original disk. In the next exercise, you make a back-up copy of the bootable floppy disk you created in the previous exercise. You need a second blank disk that has already been formatted.

To format a second floppy disk, follow Steps 3 through 5 in the previous exercise. Remember that you can recall previously entered commands by using the up arrow.

Like the steps in the previous exercise, the following steps can only be performed while you are logged on to the host console. The steps cannot be performed if you are accessing a Linux computer via a telnet session.

To make a back-up copy of the bootable floppy disk:

1. Insert the bootable floppy disk that you made earlier in the computer's floppy disk drive (commonly known as drive A).

2. Copy the disk's contents into your current directory on the hard drive by typing **dd if=/dev/fd0 > duplicate.floppy** and then pressing **Enter**.

3. Remove the floppy from drive A.

4. Insert a formatted floppy disk in drive A.

5. Copy the duplicate floppy disk image, duplicate.floppy, to the floppy by typing **dd if=./duplicate.floppy of=/dev/fd0** and then pressing **Enter**. Make sure to use the dot (.) reference to the input file (if=./duplicate.floppy) to indicate that the input file is located in the current directory.

You have learned some useful utilities for preparing floppy disks and copying information to them. Next, you learn to monitor the hard disk usage of your system.

CHECKING HARD DISK USAGE

UNIX system users, as well as the system itself, create and enlarge files. Eventually, unless files are removed, even the largest disk runs out of free space. To maintain adequate free space, you should use these basic strategies:

- Be vigilant against running dangerously low on free space by using the df command.
- Watch for conspicuous consumption by using the du command.
- Follow a routine schedule for "garbage" collection and removal by using the rm command.

Now, use each of these techniques to check hard disk usage.

Using the df Utility

The df utility reports the number of 1024-byte blocks that are allocated, used, and available; the percentage used; and the mount point. The reports displayed are based on the command options entered. You can be in either your account or the root account to use df and the other utilities described in this section, but it is recommended that you use your account for most practice exercises.

To use the df command to check hard disk usage:

1. Type **df** and then press **Enter**. (Note that you can enter the df utility without options.) Your screen looks similar to Figure 8-3.

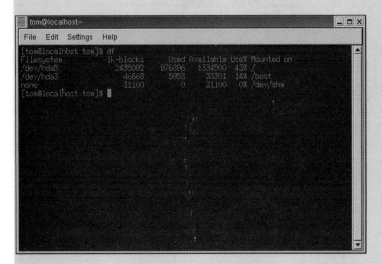

Figure 8-3   Output of the df command

Of course, your file systems and their statistics are different from those shown in Figure 8-3. In Figure 8-3, the df command reports that the /dev/hda5 file system has 2,435,092 blocks of 1 kilobyte each. There are 976,896 blocks in use, and 1,334,500 blocks available. Forty-three percent of the blocks are in use, and the file system is mounted on /.

2. You may specify a file system as an argument. The statistics for that file system alone appear on the screen. Type **df /dev/hda1** (or another partitioned disk) and press **Enter**. You see the disk statistics for that volume only.

3. The -h option causes the numbers to print in human-readable form. Instead of displaying raw numbers for size, amount of disk space used, and amount of space available, the statistics are printed in kilobyte, megabyte, or gigabyte format. Type **df -h** and press **Enter**. Figure 8-4 shows an example of the command's output.

8

Figure 8-4   Output of the df –h command

Using the du Utility

The du utility summarizes disk usage. If you enter the command without options, you receive a report based on all file usage, starting at your current directory and progressing down through all subdirectories. File usage is expressed in the number of 512-byte blocks (default) or by the number of bytes (the –b option).

To report on disk usage:

1. If you are still logged on as root, log out and then log in under your account.

2. To receive a report on disk usage starting at your home directory, type **du |
   more** and then press **Enter**. (The results of the du command can be
   lengthy, so pipe its output to the more command.) Figure 8-5 shows an
   example of the command's output.

3. The output shows the number of 512-byte blocks used in each subdirectory
   (including hidden subdirectories). Type **q** to exit the more command.

4. To view a similar report on disk usage by the number of bytes instead of by
   512-byte blocks, start at your home directory, type **du –b | more** and then
   press **Enter**.

5. Type **q** to exit the more command.

6. Like the df command, the du command supports the –h option to display
   statistics in human-readable format. Type **du –h | more** and press **Enter**.
   Figure 8-6 shows an example of the command's output.

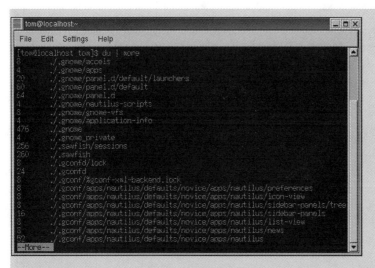

Figure 8-5   Output of the du I more command

8

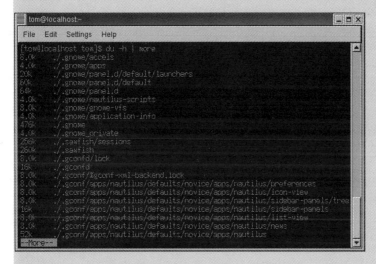

Figure 8-6   Output of the du –h I more command

 Besides the -h option, the du command supports the -x option, which enables you to omit directories in file systems other than the one in which you are working, when more than one file system is mounted.

Removing Garbage Files

An easy way to free space in your file systems is to remove garbage files. **Garbage files** are temporary files, such as a core file, that lose their usefulness after several days. A **core file** is created when an executing program attempts to do something illegal, like accessing another user's memory. The UNIX operating system detects the attempt and sends a signal to the program. The signal halts the offending program, and creates a copy of the program and its environment in a file named core in the current directory. The programmer who wrote the program that "dumps core" (slang for this event) might be interested in dissecting the core file with a debugging tool. However, all too often the core file simply languishes unused in some branch of the directory hierarchy. All files created this way have the same name: core.

Another file with a generic name is a.out, the default for the output of program compilation procedures. Like core files, the true identity of these generically named files often gets lost over time. You can use the find command to retrieve these wasteful files, and execute the rm command to remove them. You can also use the find command to search through the directory hierarchy and remove such files. You can write a find command so that it locates all files named core and a.out, and then remove each one. Here is such a command:

```
find . "(" –name a.out -o -name core ")" -exec rm {} \;
```

You have used the find command before to locate files. The command above locates every occurrence of the a.out and core files, and then deletes them with the rm command. The first argument, dot (.), tells find to start looking in the current directory. The argument "(" -name a.out -o -name core ")" uses the -o (OR) operator. It tells find to search for files named a.out OR core. The -exec rm option instructs find to execute the rm command each time it locates a file with the name being searched for. The {} characters are replaced with the matching file name. For example, when the command locates an a.out file, the {} characters are replaced with a.out, so the command rm a.out is executed. The \; terminates the command.

Now, use the find command to search for and delete all occurrences of a.out and core.

The steps that follow assume you have a source directory in your home directory. The test files, a.out and core, are quickly created using the touch command, which, when followed by the filenames, creates empty files. The tilde (~) ensures that these files go into your home and source directories.

To remove garbage files:

1. Create some garbage files, core and a.out, and place them in your home directory and in the source subdirectory under your home directory by typing **touch ~/core** and pressing **Enter**, typing **touch ~/a.out** and pressing **Enter**, typing **touch ~/source/core** and pressing **Enter**, typing **touch ~/source/a.out** and then pressing **Enter**.

2. Make sure you are in your home directory, then type **find . "(" –name a.out -o -name core ")"** and press **Enter**. The results on your screen should resemble the following:

```
[tom@localhost tom]$ find . "(" -name a.out -o -name
core ")"
./source/core
./source/a.out
./core
./a.out
```

The results of the find command in Step 2 show the core and a.out files are in the current directory and in the source directory.

3. Remove the garbage files by typing **find . "(" -name a.out -o -name core ")" -exec rm {} \;** and then pressing **Enter**.

4. Check that the files have been removed by repeating the find command you entered in Step 2. If the files have been removed correctly, there is no output. If the files still exist, you didn't enter the find command in Step 3 correctly. Retype the command exactly as it appears in Step 3, and then repeat this step (4).

8

You can locate several other garbage files with the find command. For example, users often name files test, temp, or tmp to indicate temporary files that may be forgotten over time and should be removed.

You have now had an opportunity to use several file-processing utilities. Next, you use some system status utilities.

APPLYING SYSTEM STATUS UTILITIES

As you see from the list of command descriptions in Table 8-2, the system status commands reflect the system's performance. Although system engineers who assess the CPU's performance primarily use this data, you should at least know how to obtain this information. You can redirect the output of these commands to a file that you can then print or forward to the system administrator and system tune-up specialists.

One of the most effective utilities for auditing system performance is the top command. The top command displays a listing of the most CPU-intensive tasks, such as the processor state, in real time (the display is updated every five seconds by default). This means that you can actually see what is happening inside the computer as it progresses. The top command works with these options:

Syntax   **top [-] [d delay] [q] [S] [s] [i] [c]**

Dissection

- The **d** option specifies the delay between screen updates. The **q** option causes the top utility to refresh without delay. The **S** option specifies cumulative mode, where each process is listed with the CPU time that it has spent. The **s** option allows the top utility to run in secure mode, which disables the interactive commands (a good option for those not in charge of tuning the system). The **i** option causes the top utility to ignore any idle processes. Finally, the **c** option displays the command line instead of the command name only. While running, the top command supports interactive commands, such as k, which kills a running process. The top utility continues to produce output until you press q to terminate the execution of the program.

The simplest way for most users to run the top utility is to issue the command without options.

To use the top utility:

1. Display the CPU activity by typing **top** and then pressing **Enter**. Your screen should look similar to Figure 8-7. (Don't forget this display changes while on screen.)

2. The processes are shown in the order of the amount of CPU time they use. After looking at the display for a short time, press **q** to exit from the top utility.

3. Run the top command again. Notice the far-left column of information, labeled PID. This column lists the process ID of each process shown. Notice the PID of the top command. (In Figure 8-7, the top command's PID is 3112. Yours is probably different.)

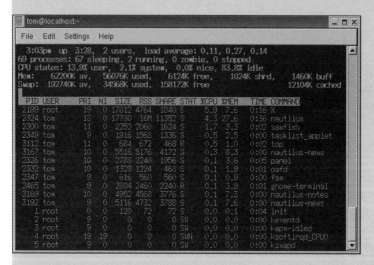

Figure 8-7   Output of the top command

4. Press **k** to initiate the kill command. The top program asks you to enter the PID to kill. Enter the PID of the top command. Your screen should resemble Figure 8-8. Press **Enter** to kill the process. (You may have to press Enter

a second time to return to a command prompt. Type **clear** to clear the lines from the screen, if necessary.) The top command is no longer running.

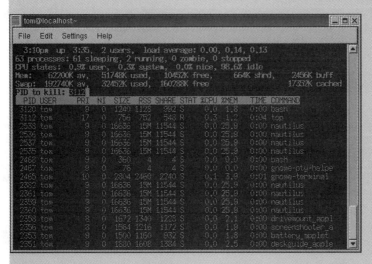

Figure 8-8   The k command

5. Run the top utility in secure mode by typing **top -s** and pressing **Enter**.

6. Press **k** to initiate the kill command. Because top is running in secure mode, it displays the message "Can't kill in secure mode," as shown in Figure 8-9.

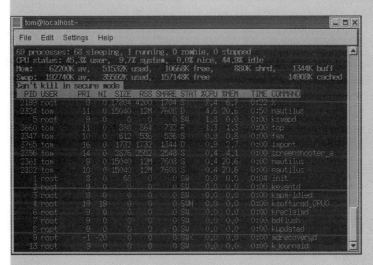

Figure 8-9   top utility in secure mode

7. Press **q** to exit the top utility.

8

Table 8-8 summarizes several of the top command's options.

Table 8-8 Options for the top command

Option	Description
-d	Determines how long top waits between updates of the information
-q	Causes the top command to display its output continually, with no delay between outputs
-s	Causes the top command to run in secure mode, disabling its interactive commands, such as k (for kill)
-S	Runs top in cumulative mode; this mode displays the cumulative CPU time used by a process instead of the current CPU time used
-i	Causes top to ignore any idle processes
-c	Causes top to display the command line that initiated each process, instead of only displaying the program name
-n	Specifies how many times to update the display
-b	Enables you to run in batch mode so that you can send the output to a file for later study (you must use the -n command with the -b option)

Another useful, though static, display of memory usage is generated by the free command. The free command displays the amount of free and used memory in the system. Unlike top, the free utility runs, and then automatically exits.

To demonstrate the free command:

1. Type **free** and press **Enter**. Your screen looks similar to Figure 8-10.

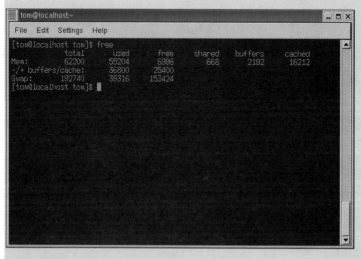

Figure 8-10 Output of the free command

2. The command displays the amount of total, used, and free memory. It also displays the amount of shared memory, buffer memory, and cached memory. In addition, the amount of total, used, and free swap memory is shown. By default, all amounts are shown in kilobytes.

3. Type **free -m** and press **Enter** to see the free command's output in megabytes.

4. Type **free -b** and press **Enter** to see the free command's output in bytes.

As mentioned earlier, you may want to forward these displays to the system administrator and tune-up specialists. You do this next.

To forward displays generated by the top and free utilities:

1. Redirect the output of the top utility to a file in your current directory by typing **top > top_out** and then pressing **Enter**.

2. Wait about 10 seconds, and then press **q** to exit the top utility.

3. Redirect the output of the free utility to a file in your current directory by typing **free > free_out** and then pressing **Enter**.

4. Print the report for the system administrator and tune-up specialists by typing **lpr top_out**, pressing **Enter**, typing **lpr free_out**, and then pressing **Enter** again. (Of course, you can always use the cat command to view the contents of these files before printing them.)

Because UNIX is a multitasking operating system, it allows you to run programs in the background while you continue to work with other programs. For example, if you have a program that prints a lengthy report, you can run it in the background and continue working with other programs while the report is printing. To run a program in the background, append the & character to the end of the command line.

To run a program in the background:

1. Experiment by running the top utility in the background. Type **top &** and press **Enter**.

   After you type the command, the system reports the PID of the program that you started in the background. In the following example, the PID is 4309:

   ```
   [tom@localhost tom]$ top &
   [1] 4309
   ```

   The top utility is running, but because it runs in the background, you see no other output.

2. Continue to run the top utility in the background. This process is the subject of the next two exercises.

8

The ps command shows you a list of the processes currently running. When you use the command with no options, it shows a list of the processes associated with the current login session. When used with the –A option, it shows a very long list of all processes running on the system.

To use the ps command:

1. Type **ps** and press **Enter**. Your screen looks similar to Figure 8-11.

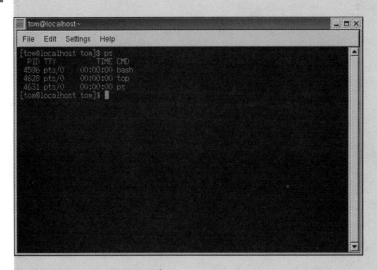

Figure 8-11   ps command

The output of the ps utility includes this information about each process:

- PID
- Name of the terminal where the process started
- Amount of time the process has been running
- Name of the process

Notice the top utility still runs in the background.

2. To see a list of all processes running on the system, type **ps –A | more** and press **Enter**. Figure 8-12 shows an example of the command's output.

Figure 8-12 ps –A command

3. Press the **Spacebar** until the command finishes its output.

To force a process to terminate, use the kill command. Its two formats are:

Syntax **kill** [*process ID*]   or   **kill** %[*process name*]

When the kill command successfully executes, it terminates the process with the PID or name that is passed as an argument.

To use the kill command:

1. In this exercise, you terminate the top utility that is still running in the background (if you received a message that it stopped, type **top &** and press **Enter**). Type **ps** and press **Enter**. Look at the list of process to find the top utility's PID.

2. Type one of these commands (both perform the same operation):

   kill *<process id>* and press **Enter**, or **kill %top** and press **Enter**

3. Type **ps r** and press **Enter** to see a list of the processes that are still running. The top utility is no longer running.

Be very careful when using the kill command. If you kill a process that the operating system needs, you can cause disastrous results!

In this section, you learned about several utilities to monitor and maintain the system. You learned to use the dd command to copy files and duplicate floppy disks. You used the mkfs command to create a file system on a floppy disk, and used the fdformat command to perform a low-level format on a floppy disk. You learned to query the partition containing the root device with the rdev command. Also, you learned to monitor disk, memory, and CPU usage with the df, du, top, and free commands. Finally, you learned to run programs in the background with the & operator, to list all running processes with the ps command, and to terminate processes no longer needed with the kill command. In the next section, you learn about utilities that format text files.

◀ LESSON B ▶

WORKING WITH THE TEXT-FORMATTING FILE UTILITIES

After completing this lesson, you should be able to:
- ◆ Check the spelling of text in a document
- ◆ Use the cmp command to compare the contents of two files
- ◆ Format text to create a man page
- ◆ Use the groff utility to test a man page you have created
- ◆ Use the man utility to view a man page you have created

CHECKING THE SPELLING OF A DOCUMENT

Sometimes, the simplest commands are the most useful. This is the case with the ispell utility. The ispell utility scans a text document, displays errors on the screen, and suggests other words with similar spellings as replacements for unrecognized words. A menu that appears on the bottom line of the screen shows corrective options and exit codes.

To become more familiar with the ispell utility, type a sample document.

To see how the ispell utility works:

1. Use the vi or Emacs editor to create a file, and name it **document1**.

2. Enter the following text, with misspellings:

   **This is a document that describes our newest
   and fastest machineery. Take the time to lern
   how to use each piece of equipment.**

3. Save the file, and exit the editor.

4. Scan the file for spelling errors by typing **ispell document1** and then pressing **Enter**. Your screen should look similar to Figure 8-13.

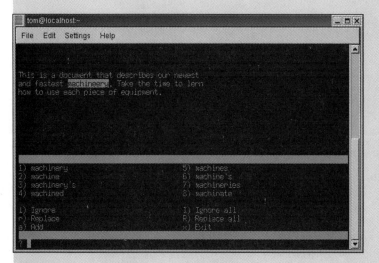

Figure 8-13   ispell utility

5. To correct the word "machineery," look at the options at the bottom of the screen, and find the one that says "machinery," which is number 1 in Figure 8-13. Type the number of that option to correct the misspelling (or you can retype the word after the question mark at the bottom of the screen). Notice that the word is then corrected in the text.

6. On the next screen, the next misspelled word, "lern," is highlighted. Find the correct spelling in the list at the bottom of the screen, and enter the number that represents the correctly spelled word.

7. The program exits and returns you to the command line. Type **cat document1** and press **Enter**.

8. The misspelled words have been corrected.

Now you learn about the cmp utility, which compares files and determines the first difference between them.

COMPARING FILES

Suppose you have a file that you work with regularly. You make a back-up copy of the file for safekeeping. Later, you want to see if the original file has changed since you made the back-up copy. You can use the cmp utility to compare the contents of two files, and report the first difference between them.

The general form of the cmp command is:

Syntax **cmp** *file1 file2*

The cmp command displays the character position and line number of the first difference between the two files.

To compare two files with the cmp command:

1. Use the vi or Emacs editor to create the file file1, containing this text:

   ```
   This is file 1.
   I made it myself.
   It belongs to me.
   ```

2. Save the file.

3. Use the editor to create the file file2, containing the text:

   ```
   This is file 2.
   I made it myself.
   It belongs to you.
   ```

4. Save the file, and exit the editor.

5. At the command line, type **cmp file1 file2** and press **Enter**. Your screen looks similar to the following:

   ```
   [tom@localhost tom]$ cmp file1 file2
   file 1 file2 differ: char 14, line 1
   ```

The cmp command displays nothing if the two files are identical.

FORMATTING TEXT IN UNIX

Text formatting in UNIX involves preparing a text file with embedded typesetting commands and then processing the marked-up text file with a computer program. This program generates commands for the output device, such as a printer, a monitor, or some other typesetter. UNIX's nroff and troff commands are often used to process the embedded typesetting commands to format the output.

UNIX users have long used the nroff and troff commands to produce manuals, corporate reports, books, and newspapers. These programs evolved from an earlier program, RUNOFF (a utility created in the late 1970s), which read pure text with embedded codes to format and print a text-enriched report. An embedded code is a special sequence of characters that is included with the regular text in the file. The special codes are not printed, but interpreted as commands to perform text formatting operations. For example, there are codes to produce boldface print, center text, and underline certain lines.

Using embedded codes in text to produce enriched output provides the advantage of not needing additional word-processing programs to produce documents. You can use any editor that works with flat files, like vi or Notepad. In addition, you can use added features, such as hyperlinks to cross-reference other documents from within your document. You do need, however, an HTML browser program like Netscape, or UNIX utilities such as nroff and troff, to translate and execute the embedded hyperlink codes.

Linux introduced groff, which implements the features of both nroff and troff. Table 8-9 lists some embedded codes supported by groff.

Table 8-9 Some groff embedded commands

Embedded Command	Meaning
.ce *n*	Center next *n* lines
.ds C	Center
.ds R	Right justify
.p *n*	Start a new paragraph indented *n* characters
.sa 0	Turn off justification
.sa 1	Turn on justification
.ul *n*	Underline the next *n* lines

The groff command's usage follows this format:

Syntax **groff** [**-T***dev*]

Dissection

- The **–T** designates a device type, which specifies an output device such as ASCII to tell **groff** that the device is a typewriter-like device. In the format example, the device type (***dev***) is for the man pages. Some other device types include *ps* for postscript printers, *dvi* for TeX dvi format, and *lj4* for an HP LaserJet4-compatible printer.

Your task for Dominion Consulting is to produce a man page that contains the standard man page sections. You are to use groff to produce the man page. The format codes consist of tags and font-change commands that control the formatting, which you type into your man page document. The tags and font-change commands consist of:

- The .TH tag indicates the man page title, as well as the date and a version number string. In the formatted man page, the version and date strings appear at the bottom of each page.

- The .SH tag indicates a section. (Section names usually appear in all upper-case characters on a man page.) Six common sections of a man page are:

  - NAME: the name of the command or program

  - SYNOPSIS: a brief description of the command or program

  - DESCRIPTION: a detailed description of the command or program

  - FILES: a list of files used by the command or program

  - SEE ALSO: a list of other commands or programs that are related to this one

  - BUGS: a list of known bugs

- The .SS tag indicates the beginning of a subsection. For example, Options is a subsection of the DESCRIPTION section.

- The .TP tag indicates each item in the Options subsection.

- The \fB command changes the font to boldface, the \fI command changes the font to italic, the \fR command changes the font to roman, and the \fP command changes the font to its former setting.

Now, write a man page for the application, phmenu, that you completed in Chapter 7.

To write and format a man page:

1. Make sure you are in your ~/source directory. Recall that the ~ indicates your home directory.

2. Use the vi or Emacs editor to create the file phmenu.1. Type the following text into the file.

```
.TH PHMENU 1 "February 27, 2004" "phmenu Version 1.01"
.SH NAME
phmenu \- Menu for Dominion Employee Telephone Listings
.SH SYNOPSIS
\fB phmenu\fP
.SH DESCRIPTION
\fP Menu for maintaining employees' phones and job titles
\fP.
\fP Record includes phone number, name, dept, and
date-hired\fP.
.SS Options
.TP
\fB -v \fIView Phone List\fR
Display unformatted phone records.
.TP
\fB -p \fIPrint Phone List\fR
 Corporate Phones report sorted by Employee Name.
```

```
.TP
\fB -a \fIAdd Phone to List\fR
Add new phone record.
.TP
\fB -s \fISearch for Employee Phones\fR
Enter Name to search and retrieve phone record.
.TP
\fB -d \fIDelete Phone\fR
Remove phone record.
.SH FILES
.TP
\fC/home/source/corp_phones\fR
```

3. Save the file, and exit the editor.

4. Test the man page by typing **groff –Tascii –man phmenu.1 | more** and then pressing **Enter**. Your screen should appear similar to Figure 8-14.

8

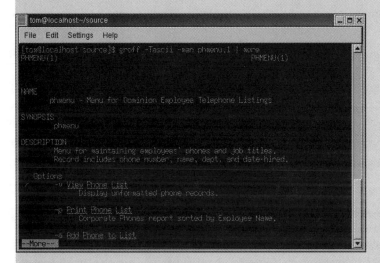

Figure 8-14   phmenu man page

 If you find any formatting discrepancies, check the dot commands and any embedded font changes against the code you typed in Step 2.

5. Press **q** to exit the more command, and then test your new man page by typing **man ./phmenu.1** and then pressing **Enter**. Your screen should be similar to Figure 8-15.

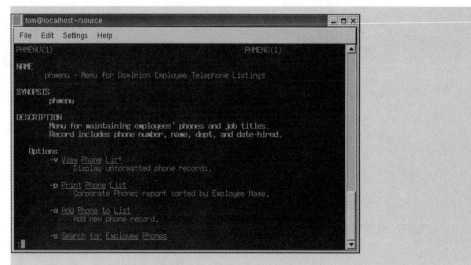

Figure 8-15   phmenu man page viewed with the man program

When you are satisfied with the man page format, you can make it available to others by copying it (while logged on as root) to one of the man page directories. All man pages are stored in subdirectories of the /usr/share/man directory (in Red Hat Linux 7.2). These subdirectories have names such as man1, man2, man3, and man4. All man pages in man1 are identified with a common suffix, .1, so phmenu.1 is copied to /usr/share/man/man1. The suffix number represents the section number of the man page.

When you request a man page using the man program, you specify the section number you want to see by placing the number after the name. (If you type only the name, man looks recursively for the page through all the subdirectories, starting with /usr/man/man1, and then displays the first match.) For example, if you want man to print the second version of the break command, follow the man command with break 2.

You need superuser privileges to copy phmenu.1 into the "root-owned" directory, /usr/man/man1. If you are not logged on to the root account, use the su command instead.

To copy the man page into a man page directory:

1. Type **su** and then press **Enter**.

2. Enter the root password, and then press **Enter**.

3. Type **cp phmenu.1 /usr/share/man/man1** to copy the man page to the man directory, and then press **Enter**. (Check with your instructor if your system uses a different location in which to store the manual pages.)

4. To exit from superuser mode, type **exit** and then press **Enter**.

5. Test that this file has been correctly copied by typing **man phmenu** and then pressing **Enter**.

In this lesson, you learned to check the spelling of a document using the ispell utility. You learned to use the cmp command to check two files that seem similar, to determine any differences between them. Finally, you learned to create your own man page with the groff utility, and test it with the man program.

CHAPTER SUMMARY

- UNIX utilities are classified into seven major functional areas dictated by user needs: file processing, networking, communications, system status, programming, source code management, and miscellaneous tasks.

- Utility programs are distinguished from other operating system programs, because they are add-ons and not a part of the UNIX shells, nor are they a component of the kernel.

- Because utility programs are executed by entering their names on the command line, these programs are commonly referred to as commands.

- The dd command possesses a rich set of options that allow it to handle copies when other copying methods fail.

- To make a bootable floppy disk, you use four utility programs: rdev, mkfs, fdformat, and the dd commands.

- The rdev command queries and sets the root device. The root device is the hard disk partition that houses the root file system for UNIX.

- The fdformat command performs a low-level format on a floppy disk to ensure that the medium is without defect and is writeable to set up a file system.

- The mkfs utility sets up a file system and works in tandem with fdformat to prepare the floppy disk for use.

- The df utility checks and reports on free disk space.

- The du command checks for disk usage (consumption).

- You can use the find command to retrieve wasteful files, and then execute the rm command to remove them from the hard disk.

- The top and free utilities provide detailed views of the "internals" of the system that are invisible to the naked eye but directly related to the CPU's performance.

- You can redirect the output of the top and free commands to a disk file to use as input for a report to the system administrator and system tune-up specialists.

8

❑ You run a program in the background by appending the & operator to the end of the command line.

❑ The ps command displays all processes currently running.

❑ The kill command terminates a specific process.

❑ The utility that checks spelling, ispell, scans a text document for typing errors.

❑ Text formatting in UNIX involves preparing a text file with embedded typesetting commands, and then processing the marked–up text file with a computer program that generates commands for the output device.

❑ The text containing the embedded typesetting commands is processed (read) by a program like UNIX's nroff or troff utility programs that formats the output.

❑ Linux introduced groff, which implements the features of both nrofff and troff.

❑ Those who have superuser (root) privileges, such as the system administrator, most often create man pages.

COMMAND SUMMARY

Please refer to the tables within the chapter for a command review.

REVIEW QUESTIONS

1. Which of the following can you accomplish using UNIX utilities?

   a. clean up garbage files

   b. view processes that are running

   c. determine used and available space on a hard disk

   d. all of the above

   e. only a and c (you must have root privileges to do b)

2. What is accomplished when you run the command, dd if=/boot/vmlinuz-2.4.7-10 of=/dev/fd0?

   a. You display the amount of disk space on a floppy disk.

   b. You delete all files on a floppy disk.

   c. You mount a floppy disk.

   d. You make a floppy disk bootable.

3. The mkfs command _____.

   a. sets the root device

   b. creates a file system type

c. initializes a modem

d. deletes a directory

4. Use the _____ command to make sure you are not running out of free space on the disk.

   a. df

   b. du

   c. dd

   d. rdev

5. The _____ utility enables you to check the spelling of words in a UNIX text document.

   a. spellchk

   b. spchk

   c. ispell

   d. edspell

6. When you use the command cmp document1 document2, you _____.

   a. perform a grammar check of the two documents

   b. count the number of letters in the two documents

   c. change document2 to match document1

   d. locate the first instance of a difference between the two documents

7. In Linux, the groff utility implements features in _____.

   a. nroff and troff

   b. mruff and fruff

   c. http and ftp

   d. man and whatis

8. Use the _____ command to determine how file space is being used by a specific set of files.

   a. df

   b. du

   c. dd

   d. rdev

9. Which of the following enables you to low-level format a floppy disk?

   a. format a:

   b. fdformat /dev/fd0

   c. init /mnt/floppy

   d. size a:

8

10. What command enables you to log into the root account from your own account?

    a. logroot

    b. su

    c. admin

    d. user

11. After you have used the command that is the correct answer for Question 10 to log into root, how do you log off of the root account and return to your own account?

    a. press Alt+F

    b. type exit and press Enter

    c. type bye and press Enter

    d. press Ctrl+Alt

12. What does the top command enable you to determine?

    a. PID of a process

    b. CPU activity of a process

    c. user who is running a process

    d. all of the above

    e. only b and c

13. The _____ command locates and displays the a.out and core files recursively starting at the current directory.

    a. find / –name "a.out" –o –name "core"

    b. find / a.out –o –name core

    c. find . "(" –name a.out –o –name core ")"

    d. find ~/ –name "a.out" –o –name "core"

14. Which of the following commands enables you to view a page, called payroll.1, that you have formatted for man, before you copy that page to an online manual?

    a. groff –Tascii –man payroll.1 | more

    b. runoff –man payroll.1 | more

    c. man ./payroll.1

    d. all of the above

    e. only a and c

15. What utility enables you to kill a program that you have determined is using too much of the CPU's resources?

    a. abort

    b. terminate

c. dd

d. top

16. Typing top & and then pressing Enter enables you to _____.

    a. view the disk space used by a process

    b. view the swap space used by a process

    c. run the top program in the background

    d. view the processes that have just been terminated

17. Which of the following commands enables you to stop a currently running process?

    a. kill

    b. remove

    c. rmprocess

    d. run –

18. On a formatted man page, the embedded command .TH is used to signify _____.

    a. bold print

    b. underlining

    c. the title of the man page

    d. the beginning of a command

19. To remove files by using the find command, type _____ at the end of the command, after specifying which files to find.

    a. !rm

    b. –exec rm {} \;

    c. –d/

    d. remove()

20. The \fI embedded command in a man page causes the _____.

    a. font to change to bold

    b. text to appear in brackets

    c. line to appear at the bottom of the screen

    d. font to change to italics

21. The .SS tag in a man page signifies the _____.

    a. beginning of a subsection

    b. end of the man page

    c. start of the man page

    d. start of a new, connecting man page

22. What type of file is left behind after a program has attempted to do something illegal?

    a. core file

    b. fix file

    c. retrieve file

    d. fail file

23. Typing dd if=accountfile of=acctfile.bak enables you to _____.

    a. delete the contents of the accountfile

    b. increase the size of the accountfile

    c. make a copy of the accountfile

    d. display the contents of the accountfile and compare them to the acctfile.bak file

24. A brief description of a command or program in a man page is signaled by _____.

    a. .SH SYNOPSIS

    b. .SH BRIEF

    c. .SH DESCRIP

    d. .SH SUMMARY

25. The rdev command displays the _____.

    a. root device

    b. root directory

    c. swap directory

    d. user's home directory

DISCOVERY EXERCISES

1. Use the cat command or the editor of your choice to create a file, my_info. The file should contain your name and address. Use the dd command to copy the file to my_info.dup.

2. Insert a blank disk in the floppy drive of your computer. Use the mkfs command to create an ext2 file system on the disk. (Hint: Log on as root to use the mkfs command.)

3. Use the fdformat command to low-level format the disk in the floppy disk drive.

4. Use the dd command to copy the file my_info (the one you created in Discovery Exercise 1) to the floppy disk.

5. Use the dd command to make a duplicate of the floppy disk. Store the duplicate in a file dup.floppy in your home directory.

6. Use the dd command to copy the dup.floppy file (the one you created in Discovery Exercise 5) onto a second blank disk.

7. Use the redirection operator (>) to create test files test1, test2, and test3 in your home directory, and copy them into the source directory. Use the find command to display all of the files.

8. Use the free command to determine the amount of free system memory.

9. Run the top program in the background.

10. Use the free command to check the amount of free system memory again. Has it changed because you are now running a program in the background?

11. Use the ps command to determine the top program's PID.

12. Use the kill command to terminate the top program, which is still running in the background.

13. Use vi to create the document Spellcheck, and then type the following four lines, with spelling errors:

```
Rosus are red,
Vilets are blu,
I luv Linux,
and So should Yu.
```

Next do the following:

❑ Make a copy of the file called Spellcheck.bak. Run ispell and correct the original document, Spellcheck.

❑ After you correct the Spellcheck file, compare it to the Spellcheck.bak file with the cmp command.

14. Create a simple man page called Movies.1 to describe a fictitious program, Movies, that searches a movie-rental database for movies using optional search-argument codes. The search-argument codes are S (enter star's name), M (enter movie name), and D (enter director's name).

 Remember to enter a suffix (.1) to the man page document name when you run man. As an ordinary user, you must enter the name plus the suffix.

Next, do the following:

❑ View the Movies man page from your current directory by typing **groff –T ascii ./Movies.1 | more** and then pressing **Enter**. What happened? Explain why this happened.

❑ Now, view the Movies man page from your current directory by typing **groff –T ascii –man ./Movies.1** and then pressing **Enter**. What happened? Explain why this happened. How would you fix the problem?

15. Use the df command with the correct option to display the number of gigabytes of disk space that are available on your system.

16. Use the du command to determine which subdirectory under your home directory holds the most information.

17. Use the du command again, but cause it to display its output in bytes rather than blocks.

18. Use the du command and specify the root directory (/) as its starting point. How many blocks does the /dev directory use?

19. In the "Removing Garbage Files" section of this chapter, you entered a find command that located and removed all files named a.out and core. Reenter the same find command, but this time, make it locate and remove the test1, test2, and test3 files you created in Discovery Exercise 7.

20. Run the man program with the argument du in the background.

21. Run the top program. Is the man program, which is currently running in the background, listed? Why or why not?

22. Use the ps command to see the currently running processes. What is the PID of the man command that is still running?

23. Use the kill command to terminate the man program.

24. Use the ispell utility on the phmenu.1 man page you created in this chapter. Why must you be careful not to change all the words the utility highlights?

25. Edit the phmenu.1 file, and add a new section named SEE ALSO. Under this section, list the following files:

    ```
    phoneadd
    phlist1
    ```

26. Save and test the revised phmenu.1 file using the groff and man programs.

27. Edit the phmenu.1 file, and add a new section named BUGS. Under this section, list a line that reads:

    ```
    None Known
    ```

28. Save and test the revised phmenu.1 file using the groff and man programs.

29. Edit the phmenu.1 file, and add a new section named AUTHOR. Under this section, list your name. Save and test the revised file using the groff and man programs.

9

PERL AND CGI PROGRAMMING

Dominion Consulting is offering a special promotion of software products. To give potential customers another method of responding to the promotion, the company's Sales Department asks you to create an interactive Web page. You can do so by creating scripts in Perl, a programming language similar to C that uses features from the Awk program (see Chapter 4) and shell scripts (see Chapters 6 and 7).

In this chapter, you learn how to use Perl to create effective, interactive Web pages. **Perl** (which stands for Practical Extraction and Report Language) was created in 1986 by Larry Wall as a simple report generator. Since then, the author and others have enhanced it to the point that it has become a powerful programming language. One of the most popular uses of Perl scripts today is to make interactive Web pages.

This chapter also expands on your previous knowledge of the awk and sed commands. You learn more options and features of both by writing awk and sed command scripts as problem-solving programs, not just as isolated commands within other programs. Before you can begin to create your Web page, however, you first need to learn more about the structure and syntax of a Perl program.

◀ LESSON A ▶

LEARNING TO USE PERL

After completing this lesson, you should be able to:

- ♦ Understand the basics of the Perl language
- ♦ Identify and use data types in Perl scripts
- ♦ Understand the difference between the Awk program and Perl programming
- ♦ Create simple Perl scripts with variables and logic structures
- ♦ Create simple Perl scripts to read and sort data files

INTRODUCTION TO PERL

Perl contains a blend of features found in other languages. It is very similar to the C language, but also contains features found in Awk and shell programs. You begin learning Perl by examining a few simple programs, such as this one:

```
#!/usr/bin/perl
# Program name: example1.pl
print("This is a simple\n");
print("Perl program.\n");
```

The first line in the program tells the operating system to use Perl to interpret the file. Recall from Chapter 7 that when the first line of a program begins with #!, the remainder of the line is assumed to give the path of the interpreter.

The second line in the sample program is a comment that lists the name of the file. Like shell scripts, Perl programs use the # character to mark the beginning of a comment. The third and fourth lines of the program display text on the screen. The program output is shown in Figure 9-1.

If you decide to reproduce this script or others in the next group of examples, make sure that you give the script files execute permissions prior to running them.

The print statements each have a single argument, which is displayed on the screen. The first print statement displays the string "This is a simple". The \n characters display a new-line, which advances the cursor to the beginning of the next line. The second print statement is similar to the first. It displays the string "Perl program." and then advances the cursor to the beginning of the next line. Notice that the two print statements end with a semicolon. All complete statements in Perl end with a semicolon.

Figure 9-1   Output of example1.pl

The parentheses surrounding the print statement's argument are optional. For example, these two statements perform the same operation:

```
print ("Hello");
print "Hello";
```

Look at the next program, which uses a variable.

```
#!/usr/bin/perl
# Program name: example2.pl
$name = "Charlie";
print ("Greetings $name\n");
```

The example2.pl program uses the variable $name. The variable is initialized with the string "Charlie." Notice that when $name is inserted in the print statement's argument, it displays the contents of the variable, with the output displayed as follows:

```
[tom@localhost tom]$ ./example2.pl
Greetings Charlie
```

Perl can also read input from the keyboard. The next program is an example.

```
#!/usr/bin/perl
# Program name: example3.pl
print ("Enter a number: ");
$number = <STDIN>;
print ("You entered $number\n");
```

The program's output is shown in Figure 9-2.

Figure 9-2   Output of example3.pl

In Perl, <STDIN> reads input from the keyboard (remember that stdin is the standard input device). The program uses this line to assign keyboard input to the variable $number:

```
$number = <STDIN>
```

Like other languages, Perl offers the if-else statement as a decision structure. Here is an example:

```
#!/usr/bin/perl
# Program name: example4.pl
print ("Enter a number: ");
$number = <STDIN>;
if ($number == 10)
{
    print ("That is the number I was thinking of.\n");
}
else
{
    print ("You entered $number\n");
}
```

The == operator tests two numeric values for equality. The if statement uses the == operator to determine if $number is equal to 10. If it is, the block (which consists of lines of code enclosed inside a set of curly braces) immediately following the if statement is executed. Otherwise, the block that follows the else statement is executed. The output that you see when you run the example4.pl script and enter 10 for the number is as follows:

```
[tom@localhost tom]$ ./example4.pl
Enter a number: 10
That is the number I was thinking of.
```

When you run example4.pl, but enter a number other than 10 you instead see the following:

```
[tom@localhost tom]$ ./example4.pl
Enter a number: 2
You entered 2
```

Perl also has operators that test for less than, greater than, less than or equal to, and greater than or equal to relationships. Table 9-1 shows Perl's numeric relational operators and Table 9-2 lists the string relational operators.

Table 9-1 Perl's numeric relational operators

Operator	Meaning
==	Equality
<	Less than
>	Greater than
<=	Less than or equal to
>=	Greater than or equal to
!=	Not equal to

Table 9-2 Perl's string relational operators

Operator	Meaning
eq	Equality
lt	Less than
gt	Greater than
le	Less than or equal to
ge	Greater than or equal to
ne	Not equal to

Notice that the numeric relational operators are symbolic, such as <= for less than or equal to, as typically is used in numeric formulas. The string relational operators are character based, such as le for less than or equal to. The next program demonstrates how two strings stored in two variables—$my_name and $your_name—are compared for equality using the eq string relational operator.

```perl
#!/usr/bin/perl
# Program name: example5.pl
$my_name = "Ellen";
$your_name = "Charlie";
if ($my_name eq $your_name)
{
        print ("Your name is the same as mine.\n");
}
else
{
        print ("Hello. My name is $my_name\n");
}
```

The output of example5.pl is as follows:

```
[tom@localhost tom]$ ./example5.pl
Hello. My name is Ellen
```

Perl also provides standard arithmetic operators: + performs addition, − performs subtraction, * performs multiplication, and / performs division. The next program, example6.pl, demonstrates a simple arithmetic operation.

```perl
#!/usr/bin/perl
# Program name: example6.pl
$num1 = 10;
$num2 = 50;
$num3 = 12;
$average = ($num1 + $num2 + $num3) / 3;
print ("The average is $average\n");
```

When you run example6.pl, you see the following on your screen:

```
[tom@localhost tom]$ ./example6.pl
The average is 24
```

9

As you can see from the program above, Perl also lets you group operations within parentheses. Now that you have a general understanding of Perl, let's study its data types.

IDENTIFYING DATA TYPES

The computer programmer must understand not only what is contained in files, records, and fields, but also the format in which it is stored. Are the fields of information numeric or alphabetic? Are the fields made up of a combination of numbers and letters? How do you treat control characters such as tab and new-line? Although it may seem obvious that a data item such as a person's name cannot be added or multiplied, the programmer must write code that properly handles any and all data items that appear in a program. Otherwise, misidentified data generates processing errors. To successfully write code, programmers need to identify data types.

Data may be represented in a Perl program in a variety of ways. In this chapter, you learn about these types of data:

- Variables and constants
- Scalars
- Numbers
- Strings
- Arrays
- Hashes

Variables and Constants

Variables are symbolic names that represent values stored in memory. For example, the variable $x might hold the value 100, and $name might hold the sequence of characters Charlie. The value of a variable can change while the program runs. **Constants**, however, do not change value as the program runs. They are written into the program code itself. For example, this statement assigns the value of the constant 127.89 to the variable $num:

```
$NUM = 127.89
```

Scalars

In the broadest sense, data is perceived as being either numeric or nonnumeric. A nonnumeric field of information is treated simply as a string of characters (hence the term string). Programmers associate strings with such items as a person's name, address, or license plate number. Numbers can also be used for logical analysis as well as for mathematical computations. A **scalar** is a simple variable that holds a number or a string. Scalar variable names begin with a dollar sign ($).

Numbers

Numbers are stored inside the computer as either signed integers (as in 14321) or double-precision, floating-point values (as in 23456.85). Numeric literals (constant values versus variable values) can be either integers or floating-point values. These numeric representations are consistent with all languages, but Perl also uses an additional convention with numeric literals to improve legibility: the underscore character, as in 5_456_678_901. (Perl uses the comma as a list separator.) The underscore only works within literal numbers specified in a program, not in strings functioning as numbers or in data read from elsewhere. Similarly, hexadecimal constants are expressed with the leading 0x prefix (as in 0xfff), and octal constants are expressed with the leading 0 prefix (as in 0256).

All of these are examples of statements that assign numeric or string values to scalar variables:

```
$x = 12;
$name = "Jill";
$pay = 12456.89;
```

Strings

Strings are often used for logical analysis, sorts, or searches. Strings are sequences of any types of characters (including numbers that are treated as characters rather than digits). String literals are usually delimited by either single quotes (' ') or double quotes (" "). Single-quoted strings are not subject to interpolation (except for \' and \\, used to put single quotes and backslashes into a single-quoted string).

Within double quotes, variables are interpolated; a backslash (\) preceding a variable name is used to ensure it is not interpolated. In addition, the backslash is used to ensure a control or escape character is not interpolated. Table 9-3 lists the code and meaning for several control or escape character sequences used within double quotes.

Table 9-3   Double-quoted string, control, and escape characters

Code	Meaning
\n	New-line
\r	Carriage return
\t	Horizontal tab
\f	Form feed
\b	Backspace
\a	Bell (alarm)
\033	ESC in octal
\x7f	Del in hexadecimal
\cC	Ctrl+C

Table 9-3   Double-quoted string, control, and escape characters (continued)

Prefix	Type
\\	Backslash
\"	Double quote
\u	Force next character to uppercase
\l	Force next character to lowercase
\U	Force all following characters to uppercase until \E is encountered
\L	Force all following characters to lowercase until \E is encountered
\Q	Backslash—quote all following nonalphanumeric characters until \E is encountered
\E	End \U, \L, \Q

For example, compare the use of special codes in the next program, example7.pl, with those shown in Table 9-3.

```
#!/usr/bin/perl
# Program name: example7.pl
print ("\\words\\separated\\by\\slashes\n");
print ("This is a \"quote\"\n");
print ("\Uupper case\n");
print ("\LLOWER CASE\n");
```

The program output is shown in Figure 9-3.

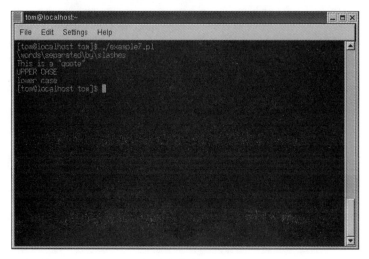

Figure 9-3   Output of example7.pl

Arrays

Arrays are variables that store an ordered list of scalar values that are accessed with numeric subscripts, starting at zero. An at sign (@) precedes the name of an array when assigning it values. When processing the individual elements of an array, however, use the $ character. For example, the following program, example8.pl, creates the array pets.

```perl
#!/usr/bin/perl
# Program name: example8.pl
@pets = ("dog", "cat", "parrot", "hamster" );
print ("My pets are:\n");
print ("$pets[0]\n");
print ("$pets[1]\n");
print ("$pets[2]\n");
print ("$pets[3]\n");
```

The output that you see when you run example8.pl is:

```
[tom@localhost tom]$ ./example8.pl
My pets are:
dog
cat
parrot
hamster
```

Hashes

A **hash** is a variable that represents a set of key/value pairs. Hash variables are preceded by a percent sign (%) when they are assigned values. To refer to a single element of a hash, use the $ character before the variable name followed by the key associated with the value in curly braces. For example:

```perl
%animals = ('Tigers', 10, 'Lions', 20, 'Bears', 30);
$animals{'Bears'}
```

returns the value 30. Another, more readable way to define this is to use the ==> operator (also called the arrow operator) to define the key/value pairs:

```perl
%animals = (Tigers ==> 10, Lions ==> 20, Bears ==> 30);
```

The following program, example9.pl, demonstrates the use of a hash variable.

```perl
#!/usr/bin/perl
# Program name: example9.pl
%animals = ('Tigers', 10, 'Lions', 20, 'Bears', 30);
print ("The animal values are:\n");
print ("$animals{'Tigers'}\n");
print ("$animals{'Lions'}\n");
print ("$animals{'Bears'}\n");
```

The program's output is as follows:

```
[tom@localhost tom]$ ./example9.pl
The animal values are:
10
20
30
```

Now that you understand about data types, you are ready to learn more about programming using Perl. Perl's similarities and differences with other programming languages can be illustrated by comparing how the same program appears in the Awk format and in Perl.

PERL VERSUS THE AWK PROGRAM

The Awk program does not require the programmer to explicitly set up looping structures as does Perl. Perl's while loop, on the other hand, is almost identical to the one found in the C and C++ programming languages. The Awk program, therefore, uses fewer lines of code to resolve pattern-matching extractions than does Perl. For example, look at the following Awk program, awkcom.a, and its output. The program counts the number of comment lines that appear in the file specified on the command line. (This assumes we are skipping the path line, which, for example, is #!/usr/bin/awk -f in the awkcom.a file.) Figure 9-4 illustrates the output of the awkcom.a program.

```
#!/usr/bin/awk -f
# program name: awkcom.a
# purpose: Count the comment lines in a file.
#            Enter the filename on the command line.

END {
  print "The file has ", line_count, " comment lines."
}
/^#/ && !/^#!/  { ++line_count }  # This occurs for
  every line.
```

Now compare and contrast the awkcom.a program with this Perl program:

```
#!/usr/bin/perl
# program name: perlcom.pl
# purpose: count the source file's comment lines
# ================================================
$filein = $ARGV[0];
while (<>)
{
    if (/^#/ && !/^#!/)
    {
    ++$line_count
    }
}
print ("File \"$filein\" has $line_count comment lines.
    \n");
```

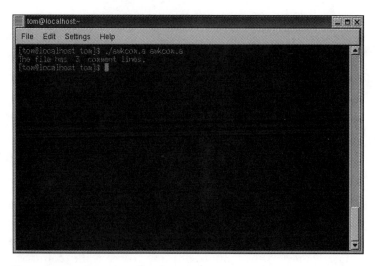

Figure 9-4   Output of awkcom.a

Although the end results of both programs are very similar, you can see where the two programs differ. The Awk program uses an implicit while loop that automatically sends the entire contents of the file named on the command line to the pattern matching and action part of the program. However, note that for the Perl program you need to build the while loop explicitly. The output of the perlcom.pl script looks like the following:

```
[tom@localhost tom]$ ./perlcom.pl perlcom.pl
File "perlcom.pl" has 3 comment lines.
```

The first line of each program tells the shell program to run either the Awk program or the Perl program, and pass the statements in the file to the program for execution. Both programs also use the pound sign (#) to specify a comment line. Further, the pattern-matching code is the same in both programs. That is where the similarities end.

The –f option in the Awk program tells the shell that the program is being called with a script file that contains the awk commands. Note that if the –f option is not included, the Awk program uses the first command line argument as its program. Recall that an Awk program contains more built-in commands to read lines from the file. All an Awk program needs is the pattern-matching conditions to select the lines. The reading of the file is implied as shown in this code:

```
/^#/&& !/^#!/   { ++line_count }
```

An Awk program also uses BEGIN and END to control when commands execute. All statements in a BEGIN block execute before the input file is read. All statements in an END block execute after all the contents of the input file have been read. This program only needs the END pattern.

In the Perl program, the code:

```
$filein = $ARGV[0];
```

takes the name of the file on the command line (ARGV[0]) and places it in a variable so it can be referenced later. The file name originally stored in ARGV[0] from the command line is destroyed during the while loop.

```
while (<>)
```

The <> symbol is called the **diamond operator**. Once the file is opened, you can access its data using the diamond operator. Each time it is called, it returns the next line from the file.

Curly braces open and close a block where you can place multiple statements:

```
if (/^#/ && !/^#!/)
{
    ++$line_count
}
```

This block tests to see if the line begins with the # character, but not with the #! characters. If true, the statement ++$line_count adds one to the $line_count variable and then closes the if block.

Whether the Awk program or Perl is a good choice for you is a personal decision, but either one or both should be part of your tool kit. There is no substitute for the kinds of work that either can quickly perform with minimal code preparation. For example, you probably would not want to write a C program for a task like scanning files for a matching pattern. However, both Perl and the Awk program are excellent when you are looking for a "needle in the haystack."

Both Perl and the Awk program (particularly the GNU Project's implementation of POSIX 1003.2 compliant awk) are portable across many UNIX systems—which is an advantage because the effort to develop code on one system is not lost if you convert to another system. Also, Perl is popular as a CGI tool for Web-based applications, as you discover later in this chapter.

How Perl Accesses Disk Files

Like most high-level programming languages, Perl uses filehandles to reference files. A **filehandle** is the name for an I/O connection between your Perl program and the operating system, and it can be used inside your program to open, read, write, and close the file. The convention is to use all uppercase letters for filehandles. In most instances, you must issue an open statement to open the file before you can access it. The exception to this occurs when you use the ARGV[0] variable to pass the filename to the program through the command line. In effect, you open it on the command line. As with other languages, every Perl program has three filehandles that are automatically opened: STDIN (the keyboard), STDOUT (the screen, to which the print and write functions are written by default), and STDERR (the screen, used to display error messages).

Here are some common methods for opening and processing external files. The first program, perlread1.pl, passes the filename on the command line, using the standard array variable that is reserved to do just that, ARGV[0]. This Perl program displays the contents of a file. (Recall that you can also use cat, less, and more for doing this.)

To use Perl to display the contents of a file:

1. Use the **cat** command (or the editor of your choice) to create the test file **students**, containing the names Joseph, Alice, Mary, Zona, Aaron, Barbara, and Larry, all on a separate line.(Do not press Enter after Larry or you will have a blank line in the file.)

2. Save the file.

3. Use the editor of your choice to create the Perl program **perlread1.pl**:

```
#!/usr/bin/perl
# program name: perlread1.pl
# purpose: Display records in a file and count lines.
$filein = $ARGV[0];
while (<>)
{
        print "$_";
        ++$line_count;
}
print ("File \"$filein\" has $line_count lines. \n");
```

4. Save the file, and quit the editor.

5. Give the file execute permission (type **chmod ugo+x perlread1.pl**).

6. Test the program by typing **./perlread1.pl students** and then pressing **Enter**. Your screen should now display the contents of the students file, shown in Figure 9-5.

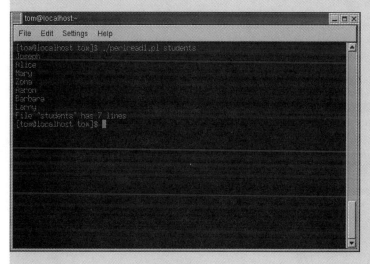

Figure 9-5   Output of perlread1.pl

The first instruction ($filein = $ARGV[0];) saves the name of the file that is passed to the program and stores it in ARGV[0]. The while loop triggers the diamond operator (<>) that sequentially reads records from the file and places the value stored in ARGV[0] in the next record. This continues until the loop reaches the end of the file. When that happens, ARGV[0] contains a null (end-of-file character), so you cannot use ARGV[0] to reference the filename when the while loop terminates. Two commands inside the while loop are enclosed within curly braces: print "$_" displays each record that is read and ++$line_count increments (counts) the records in the file. The last command, print ("File \"$filein\", has $line_count lines. \n") prints the name of the file (saved in $filein) and the number of lines in the file.

> The Perl programming language defines a set of special variables. Among these is the $_ variable, which is the default input, output, and pattern-searching space. In the perlread1.pl program, you are using it as the default input variable. However, in the perlread1.pl program, print "$_"; could also be written as print; because the $_ variable is assumed by default.

Next, you learn how to open the file from within your program, as opposed to passing it on the command line. All files opened inside programs must be closed before the program terminates.

To use Perl to open a file from within a program:

1. Use the editor of your choice to create the file **perlread2.pl**.

2. Enter this Perl program:

```
#!/usr/bin/perl
# program name: perlread2.pl
# purpose: Open disk file. Read and display the records
#           in the file. Count the number of records in
#           the file.
open (FILEIN, "students") || warn "Could not open
  students file\n";
while (<FILEIN>)
{
        print "$_";
        ++$line_count;
}
print ("File \"students\" has $line_count lines. \n");
close (FILEIN);
```

3. Save the file, and quit the editor.

4 Give the file execute permission.

5. Test the program by typing **./perlread2.pl** and then pressing **Enter**. Your output should look similar to that for the perlread1.pl script.

In the perlread2.pl program, the open function appears on the first line after the comment section:

```
open (FILEIN, "students") || warn "Could not open
students file\n";
```

Nearly all program functions are written to return a value that indicates whether the function was carried out successfully. The values returned are considered true or false. A **true value** is usually represented with a 1, and sometimes any value greater than zero. A **false value** is represented with a 0 (zero). The open function returns true if the file is opened successfully, and false if it failed to open. Opening a file can fail because the file is not found or because the file's permissions for reading and/or writing are not set. However, in Perl, a filehandle that has not been successfully opened can still be read, but you will get an immediate EOF (end-of-file signal), with no other noticeable effects. An EOF results in your program not letting you read from or write to the file, because the file is not available.

The two vertical bar characters "| |" are the logical OR operator. When an expression on the left of a logical OR operator returns false, the expression on the right of the operator executes. The warn operator, on the right of the OR operator, displays an error message indicating the file did not open. Although displaying error conditions is not absolutely necessary in your programs, you should display them when it is obvious that the errors can cause subsequent problems if the program continues to run. This additional coding is especially essential in open statements.

After the file is open, access to the data is made through the diamond operator (<FILEIN>). When the while loop reaches the end of a file, it terminates. Except for the open and close statements and the use of the diamond operator, the perlread2.pl program is identical to perlread1.pl.

USING PERL TO SORT

One of the most important tasks in managing data is organizing it into a useable format. Perl provides a powerful and flexible sort operator. It can sort string or numeric data in ascending or descending order. It even allows advanced sorting operations where you define your own sorting routine.

Using Perl to Sort Alphanumeric Fields

Now, sort words in a Perl program into alphabetical order using the sort function.

To use Perl's sort function:

1. Use the editor of your choice to create the program **perlsort1.pl**. Enter the code:

```
#!/usr/bin/perl
# program name: perlsort1.pl
```

```
# purpose: Sort a list of names contained inside an array
# Syntax: perlsort1.pl <Enter>
#============================================================
@somelist = ("Oranges", "Apples", "Tangerines", "Pears",
"Bananas", "Pineapples");
@sortedlist = sort @somelist;
print "@sortedlist";
print"\n";
```

2. Save the file, and exit the editor.

3. Use the chmod command to gant the file execute permission.

4. Run **perlsort1.pl**. Your screen should look similar to Figure 9-6.

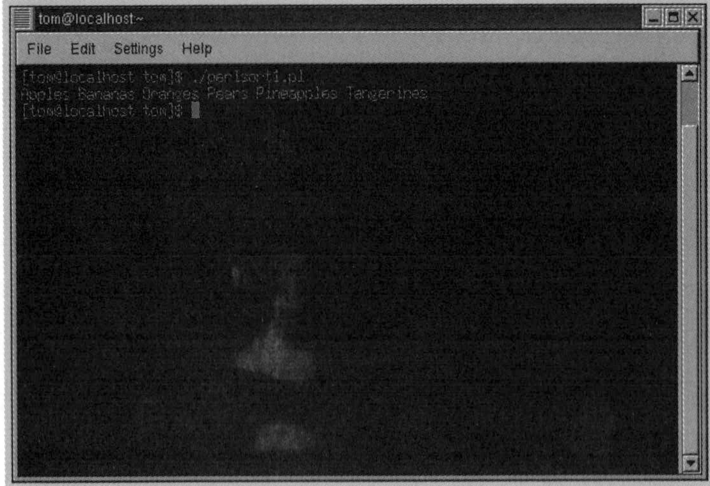

Figure 9-6   Output of perlsort1.pl

Looking at the program, the statement:

```
@somelist = ("Oranges", "Apples", "Tangerines", "Pears",
"Bananas", "Pineapples");
```

puts the value of (Oranges, Apples, Tangerines, Pears, Bananas, Pineapples) into @somelist. The statement:

```
@sortedlist = sort @somelist;
```

calls the Perl sort function and returns the sorted output to the array variable, @sortedlist. The last two statements in the program print the sorted results and skip a line before the program terminates and returns to the command line.

Data is not always coded as part of the program or entered at the keyboard. Often, programs must read information from files. The next example demonstrates how Perl accesses a file by passing the filename on the command line.

To use Perl to access a file by passing the filename on the command line:

1. Use the editor of your choice to create the program perlsort2.pl. Enter the code:

```
#!/usr/bin/perl
# program name: perlsort2.pl
# purpose: Sorts a text file alphabetically. Filename is
#              entered on the command line.
# Syntax: perlsort2.pl filename <Enter>
#=========================================================
$x = 0;
while (<>)
{
        $somelist[$x] = $_;
        $x++;
}
@sortedlist = sort @somelist;
print @sortedlist;
```

2. Save the file, and exit the editor.

3. Give the perlsort2.pl file execute permissions.

4. Run perlsort2.pl, using students as the test file, by typing **./perlsort2.pl students** and then pressing **Enter**. Your screen should now display the list of student names, shown in Figure 9-7.

9

Figure 9-7   Output of perlsort2.pl

The perlsort2.pl program uses the statement:

```
$x = 0;
```

to initialize a variable, $x, to contain an index to the array. The first element of every array is zero (0). In the while loop,

```
while (<>)
{
        $somelist[$x] = $_;
        $x++;
}
```

the next line in the file is automatically copied into the $_ variable. The assignment statement:

```
$somelist[$x] = $_;
```

copies the contents of the $_ variable into an element of the array. The element is determined by the variable $x, which is used as a subscript. After the assignment operation occurs, the following statement executes:

```
$x++;
```

The ++ operator adds one to its argument, so the statement increments the variable $x. As a result, the first name, Aaron, is placed in $somelist[0], Alice is placed in $somelist[1], and so on.

The statement:

```
@sortedlist = sort @somelist;
```

sorts the array, @somelist, placing the alphabetized names into @sortedlist, and the final instruction prints the alphabetized list of students' names.

Using Perl to Sort Numeric Fields

Sorting numeric fields requires using a subroutine where you can define comparison conditions (e.g., greater than, less then, or equal to) between the data you are sorting. The sort routine is then called repeatedly, passing two elements to be compared on each call. The scalar variables $a and $b store the two values that are compared to select the larger value. Using the comparison operation, a return code of −1, 0, or +1 is returned, depending on whether $a is less than, equal to, or greater than $b, as in the demonstrated code:

```
sub numbers
{
  if ($a < $b)    { -1; }
  elsif ($a == $b)   { 0; }
  else   { +1; }
}
```

When sorting numbers, you need to instruct Perl to use this sort subroutine as the comparison function, rather than the built-in ASCII ascending sort (the default). To do this, place the name of the subroutine between the keyword "sort" and the list of items to be sorted:

```
$sortednumbers = sort numbers 101, 87, 34, 12, 1, 76;
```

The statement instructs Perl to sort the values in the list by using the numbers subroutine to determine their order. The output is in numeric order, not ASCII order.

The numeric comparison of $a and $b is performed so frequently that Larry Wall, Perl's creator, developed a special Perl operator for numeric sorts, <=>. This sort operator, known as the **spaceship operator**, reduces coding requirements. To illustrate the code savings, compare the next sort subroutine using the spaceship operator with the previous one:

```
sub numbers
{
      $a <=> $b;
}
```

This numbers subroutine produces the same result as the first example, which uses an if-else statement. Perl allows an even more compact notation: the **inline sort block**, which looks like this:

```
@sortednumbers = sort { $a <=> $b; } @numberlist;
```

This statement uses the block { $a <=> $b; } as the sort routine. It eliminates the need for a separate subroutine. Let's examine how a Perl program sorts numeric data.

To use Perl for numeric sorting:

1. Create the file numberlist, containing the data **130, 100, 121, 101, 120,** and **122**. Press **Enter** after typing each number so that each one is on a separate line (do not press Enter after typing 122 or you will have an extra blank line).

2. Use the editor of your choice to create the perlsort3.pl program. Enter this code:

```
#!/usr/bin/perl
# program name: perlsort3.pl
# purpose: Sorts numerically using a subroutine. Filename
#          is entered on the command line.
# Syntax: perlsort3.pl filename <Enter>
#=========================================================
$x = 0;
while (<>)
{
   $somelist[$x] = $_;
   $x++;
}
@sortedlist = sort numbers @somelist;
print @sortedlist;
```

9

```
sub numbers
{
        if ($a < $b)
                { -1; }
        elsif ($a == $b)
                { 0; }
        else
                { +1; }
}
```

3. Save the file, and exit the editor.

4. Use the chmod command to grant the file execute permission.

5. Test the program by typing **./perlsort3.pl numberlist** and then press **Enter**. Your screen should appear similar to Figure 9-8.

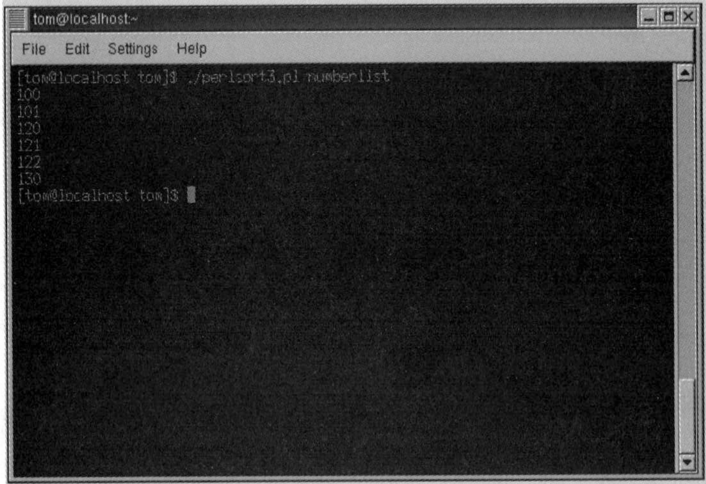

Figure 9-8   Output of perlsort3.pl

The perlsort3.pl program uses a sort subroutine that compares $a and $b numerically rather than textually. The program also initializes the array element index to start with the first element, 0. The while loop,

```
while (<>)
{
  $somelist[$x] = $_;
  $x++;
}
```

works the same as previously described, in that it reads records from a file and stores the lines inside an array.

The sort subroutine,

```
sub numbers
{
    if ($a < $b)   { -1; }
    elsif ($a == $b) { 0; }
    else { +1; }
}
```

compares the two numbers that are sequentially passed to it from the while loop. If the value in $a is less than the value in $b, the subroutine returns −1. If $a is equal to $b, the subroutine returns 0. Otherwise, the subroutine returns +1.

Now see how using the spaceship operator can save you coding time.

To use Perl's spaceship operator:

1. Use the editor of your choice to create the program perlsort4.pl. Enter this code.

```
#!/usr/bin/perl
# program name: perlsort4.pl
# purpose: Sort numerically using spaceship operator
# (<=>)
# syntax: perlsort4.pl filename <Enter>
#=========================================================
$x = 0;
while (<>)
{
    $somelist[$x] = $_;
    $x++;
}
@sortedlist = sort numbers @somelist;
print @sortedlist;
sub numbers
{
    $a <=> $b;
}
```

2. Save the file, and exit the editor.

3. Use the chmod command to grant the file execute permission.

4. Test the program by typing **./perlsort4.pl numberlist** and then press **Enter**. Again, your screen should display the list of numbers sorted in ascending order, similar to the result of perlsort3.pl:

```
[tom@localhost tom]$ ./perlsort4.pl numberlist
100
101
120
121
122
130
```

In the perlsort4.pl program, notice that the only code changes to the perlsort3.pl program are those found in the shortened subroutine.

Now that you are more familiar with Perl, you can learn how to create a Web page. Then you can begin creating the Web page for Dominion Consulting.

◀ LESSON B ▶

CREATING AN INTERACTIVE WEB PAGE

After completing this lesson, you should be able to:
- ◆ Set up an HTML Web page
- ◆ Use Perl and CGI scripts to make your Web pages interactive
- ◆ Use X Window and Netscape to retrieve Web pages

SETTING UP A WEB PAGE

In this lesson, you get a small taste of creating Web documents and Perl-based CGI programs. Both types of programming experiences are just a beginning, because there are entire books written about each of these areas. The purpose of this chapter is to help you experience them, get a glimpse of their uses, and entice you to seek additional experiences to learn more

You can create a Web page using **HTML (Hypertext Markup Language)**. HTML is a format for creating documents with embedded codes known as **tags**. When the document is viewed in a Web browser, such as Netscape Navigator or Internet Explorer, the tags give the document special properties. Examples of properties include foreground and background colors, font size and color, and the placement of graphic images. In addition, HTML tags let you place **hyperlinks** in a document. A hyperlink is text or an object that, when clicked, loads another document and displays it in the browser.

After you use HTML to create a Web page, you then publish the page on a Web server. A **Web server** is a system running Web server software, such as Apache that is connected to the Internet. The Web server software lets other users access the HTML document via the Internet.

You may experiment with and test HTML documents using your Linux system's loopback networking feature. The **loopback** feature allows your UNIX or Linux system to access its own internal network configuration instead of an external network. To use the loopback, you do not need to be connected to any network. More importantly, the loopback can emulate a real-world Web site, so you can carry out the testing and development of your new Web pages. Stand-alone testing of new Web pages is recommended: after fully testing your work, you can then transfer your documents to any Web server, knowing that they are ready to perform.

> To run the Web pages and CGI programs in this lesson, you should have access to a computer running the GNOME interface and that has an installed GUI web browser, such as Netscape Communicator or Mozilla. Also you must have the Apache Web Server program installed on your Linux computer. (See Appendix C for instructions on installing Apache.)

CREATING WEB PAGES

You may use a visual HTML editor, such as Netscape Composer or Microsoft FrontPage, to create Web pages. These programs let you graphically construct a Web page in a "what you see is what you get" fashion. If you have no visual HTML editor, all you need is a text editor. You create the HTML document by typing its text and the desired embedded tags. Here is a sample HTML file.

```
<HTML>
<HEAD><TITLE>My Simple Web Page</TITLE></HEAD>
<BODY>
<H1>Just a Simple Web Page</H1>
This is a Web page with no frills!
</BODY>
</HTML>
```

All special codes contained inside angled brackets <> are tags. The first tag, <HTML>, identifies the file as an HTML document. Notice the corresponding </HTML> tag at the end of the file. Everything between the <HTML> and </HTML> tags are considered text with HTML tags. In general, most tags are used this way. One tag marks the beginning of a section, while a corresponding tag marks the end of the section.

Note that there are two parts to the code: a head and a body. The **head** contains the title, which appears on the top bar of your browser window. The **body** defines what appears within the browser window. All other tags refine the Web page's appearance. Figure 9-9 shows the Web page's appearance in the Netscape Web browser.

You can use tags to set background and foreground colors and to manipulate text with such tags as <FONT SIZE=n>(*insert text here*). You can change text sizes with the heading tags, where <H1> is the largest and <H6> is the smallest. (However, note that users' browsers may also automatically change the actual text size.)

Because standard HTML ignores multiple spaces, tabs, and carriage returns, you can enclose text within <PRE></PRE>(preformatted text) tag pairs. Otherwise, any consecutive spaces, tabs, carriage returns, or combinations produce a single space. You can also use the <P> tag, which creates two line breaks, or the <BR> tag, which creates one line break. Neither tag requires a closing tag.

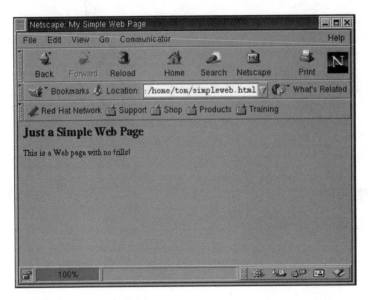

Figure 9-9   Simple Web page

Browsers automatically wrap text so you don't need to worry about page widths. To center text, however, use <CENTER>*(text here)*</CENTER>. To indent from both margins, use <BLOCKQUOTE>*(text here)*</BLOCKQUOTE>. To change color, use <FONT COLOR="RGB"*(text here)*</FONT>, where RGB is the RGB color code. An **RGB color code** is a set of three numbers that specify a color's red, green, and blue components. For example, the code 512218 specifies a red component of 51, a green component of 22, and a blue component of 18. The higher the number, the more intense the color component.

Here is another example of an HTML file.

```
<HTML>
<HEAD><TITLE>UNIX Programming Tools</TITLE></HEAD>
<BODY>
<H1><CENTER>My UNIX Programming Tools</CENTER></H1>
<H2>Languages</H2>
<P>Perl</P>
<P>Shell Scripts</P>
<P>C and C++</P>
<H2>Editors</H2>
<P>vi</P>
<P>Emacs</P>
<H2>Other Tools</H2>
<P>awk</P>
<P>sed</P>
</BODY>
</HTML>
```

Figure 9-10 shows the file as it appears in a Web browser.

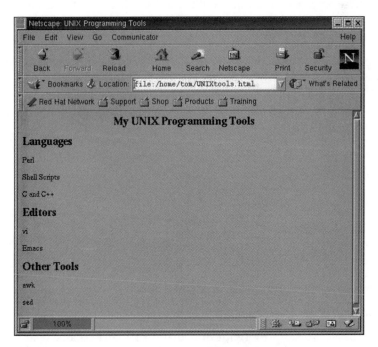

Figure 9-10   UNIX programming tools Web page

Now that you have some general knowledge of creating Web pages, you need to learn how to use Perl and CGI to make them interactive.

CGI OVERVIEW

Perl is the most commonly used language for **CGI (Common Gateway Interface) programming**. CGI is a protocol, or set of rules, governing how browsers and servers communicate. Any script that sends or receives information from a server needs to follow the standards specified by CGI. Thus, scripts written in Perl follow the CGI protocol. CGI Perl scripts are specifically written to get, process, and return information through your Web pages, that is, they make your Web pages interactive.

To allow your HTML document to accept input, especially where CGI rules apply, precede the input area with a description of what you want users to enter. For example, if you want users to enter cost, you would use this code:

```
Total Cost? <INPUT TYPE=text NAME=cost SIZE=10>
```

In addition, consistent with transmitting information to and from Web sites, you can use the special code INPUT TYPE=submit, which sends the data out when a user clicks the Submit button. The destination that you wish to receive the submitted information is coded into the FORM tag. The **FORM tag** specifies how to obtain the information to be transferred. There are two methods, GET and POST. The **GET** method transfers the data within the URL itself. **POST** uses the body portion of the HTTP request to pass parameters. (You use the POST method in this chapter.)

Various Web sites offer hundreds of prepared scripts that you can use with your own Web page applications. Some of these scripts, such as subparseform.lib, are free. We use subparseform.lib in this chapter. You can download it from *www.cookwood.com/perl*. At the site, select the Examples hyperlink (look for the downloads from the first edition, to find the subparseform.lib file).

Other sources for free Perl CGI scripts are:

- *www.worldwidemart.com/scripts*
- *www.extropia.com*
- *www.awsd.com/scripts*

The following sites provide useful Perl information and answers to FAQs (frequently asked questions):

- *www.perl.com* (a huge site that is home to a vast collection of information)
- *http://language.perl.com/faq/index.html*
- *www.redhat.com/devnet/perl/* (with information about Perl and CGI scripts)

Before creating the Web page for Dominion Consulting, you first see how a sample Web page works in UNIX.

 For the examples in the remaining portion of this chapter, you need access to a computer that is running Red Hat Linux and that has the X Window interface with the GNOME desktop already installed.

To see a sample Web page:

1. Open a Terminal emulation program window (if it is not already open) by clicking the **Terminal emulation program** icon on the Panel at the bottom of the screen (previously described in Chapter 1). The Terminal emulation window icon resembles a small monitor screen with a foot on top.

2. In the Terminal window, create a subdirectory in which to store your HTML, CGI scripts, and Perl scripts. Ask your instructor where to create the subdirectory; to create it from your home directory, type **mkdir cgi-bin** and press **Enter**. Make sure that your cgi-bin directory provides sufficient access permissions. You can ensure this by typing **chmod 755 cgi-bin** and pressing **Enter**.

3. Change to your working directory, such as the cgi-bin directory you created in Step 2.

4. See your instructor or technical support person for instructions for copying the following programs and scripts to the new directory:

```
projest.html
projest.cgi
subparseform.lib
```

5. Next, edit the projest.html file that you copied to your working directory in Step 4. In the Terminal window, load the file projest.html into the vi or Emacs editor. The contents of the file are:

```
<!- Program Name: projest.html ->
<HTML><HEAD><TITLE>Dominion Project Analysis</TITLE></
HEAD>
<BODY>
<H2>Average Profit per Project Calculation</H2>
<FORM METHOD=POST ACTION="http://localhost/home/tom/
cgi-bin/projest.cgi">
Total cost of projects last year? <INPUT TYPE=text NAME=
projcost SIZE=10>
Number of Projects? <INPUT TYPE=text NAME=projects
SIZE=10>
Project revenue received? <INPUT TYPE=text NAME=revenue
SIZE=10>
<HR><INPUT TYPE=submit NAME=submit VALUE=Submit>
<INPUT TYPE=reset NAME=reset VALUE="Start over">
</FORM></BODY></HTML>
```

6. Find the following line of code in your file:

```
<FORM METHOD=POST ACTION="http://localhost/home/tom/
cgi-bin/projest.cgi">
```

Change the code so that it includes the specific path to where you are storing your HTML and CGI files, as shown:

```
<FORM METHOD=POST ACTION="http://path to where you are
storing your HTML and CGI files/projest.cgi">
```

7. Save the file, and exit the editor.

8. From the GNOME desktop (you can use a different desktop as long as it has a network browser such as Netscape Communicator or Mozilla—but the steps are different than those described here), click the **foot** (Main Menu) icon in the Panel at the bottom of the screen, point to **Programs**, point to **Internet**, and click **Netscape Communicator** as shown in Figure 9–11. Your initial Netscape Communicator screen should look similar to the one in Figure 9–12.

9

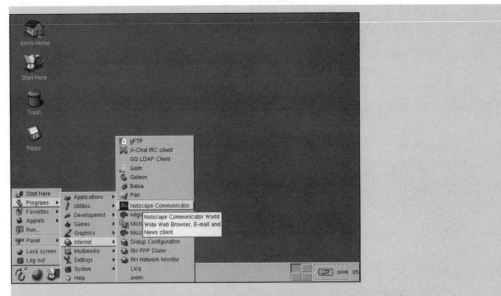

Figure 9-11   Starting Netscape Communicator from the GNOME desktop

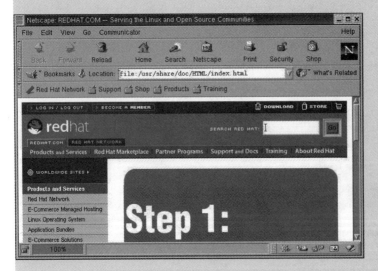

Figure 9-12   Netscape Communicator

Note

If this is the first time that you have accessed Netscape, you may have to click the Accept button to accept the licensing agreement and the OK button to acknowledge the creation of a directory in which to store Web-based files.

9. Click the **File** menu in the top left portion of the screen. Click **Open Page**, type the location of the projest.html file, such as **/home/tom/cgi-bin/projest.html**, and click **Open in Navigator**. Type **10000** in the Total cost of projects last year? text box and press **Tab** to advance to the next field. Next, type **10** in the Number of Projects? text box and press **Tab**. Finally, type **12000** in the Project Revenue received? text box. The result that you see should look similar to Figure 9-13.

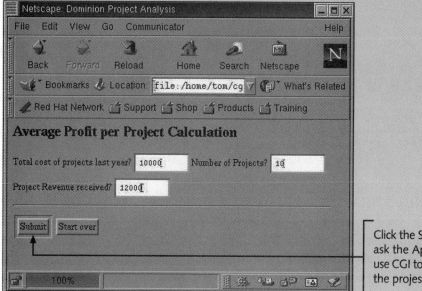

Click the Submit button to ask the Apache server to use CGI to retrieve and run the projest.cgi script

Figure 9-13   Web page generated by projest.html

10. To confirm that you want to use the Common Gateway Interface connection, click the **Submit** button. In the Confirmation screen, click **Continue Submission**. (You can avoid this confirmation screen in the future if you click the Show the Alert Next Time button to turn off this option before you click Continue Submission.) Perl executes the program, and the Apache server then passes the Web page response back to the Netscape browser for display. Your screen, which is the final screen that is part of the Perl/cgi script response, should now look similar to Figure 9-14.

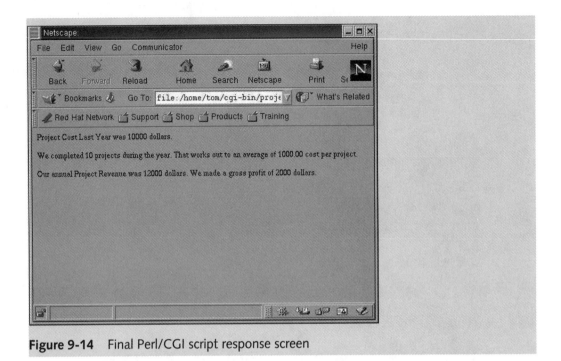

Figure 9-14   Final Perl/CGI script response screen

The source code used to generate the Web page in the previous set of steps looks similar to the following.

```perl
#!/usr/bin/perl
# Program name: projest.cgi

require "subparseform.lib";

&Parse_Form;
$projcost = $formdata{'projcost'};
$projects = $formdata{'projects'};
$revenue = $formdata{'revenue'};

$average = $projcost / $projects;
$average = sprintf("%.2f", $average);
$grossprofit = $revenue - $projcost;

print "Content-type: text/html\n\n";
print "<P>Project Cost Last Year was $projcost dollars.";
print "<P>We completed $projects projects during the year.
That works out to an average of $average cost per
    project.";
print "<P>Our annual Project Revenue was $revenue dollars.
We made a gross profit of $grossprofit dollars";
```

Now that you have seen a demonstration of how Web pages work using UNIX, you are ready to create your own Web page.

CREATING THE DOMINION CONSULTING WEB PAGE

Dominion Consulting is currently offering all its hotel management customers a special promotional price for three customized applications. The company wants to present a Web page that offers customers an opportunity to order the promotional items over the Internet. The planned Web page is shown in Figure 9-15. You now create that page.

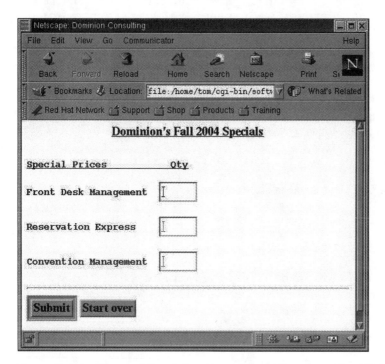

Figure 9-15 Planned Dominion Consulting sales promotion Web page

To create a Web page:

1. Use the editor of your choice to create the HTML document software.html. Enter this HTML code:

```
<!- Program Name: software.html->
<HTML><HEAD><TITLE>Dominion Consulting</TITLE></HEAD>
<BODY BGCOLOR=WHITE>
<CENTER><H1><U>Dominion's Fall 2004 Specials</H1>
</CENTER>
<FORM METHOD=POST ACTION="http://localhost/your cgi-bin
directory path/software.cgi">
<BR>
<H2><U><PRE>Special Prices        Qty</PRE></U></H2>
<FONT SIZE=5>
```

```
<PRE>Front Desk Management <INPUT TYPE=text NAME=frontdk
Size=5></PRE>
<PRE>Reservation Express   <INPUT TYPE=text NAME=reserve
SIZE=5></PRE>
<PRE>Convention Management <INPUT TYPE=text NAME=convmgt
SIZE=5></PRE>
<HR><INPUT TYPE=submit NAME=submit VALUE=Submit>
<INPUT TYPE=reset NAME=reset VALUE="Start over">
</FORM></BODY></HTML>
```

2. Save the file in your working directory, such as your cgi-bin directory, and exit the editor.

3. Now use the editor to create the CGI Perl script software.cgi. Enter this code:

```perl
#!/usr/bin/perl
# Program name: software.cgi

require "subparseform.lib";&Parse_Form;

$frontdk = $formdata{'frontdk'};

$reserve = $formdata{'reserve'};

$convmgt = $formdata{'convmgt'};

$qtotal = $frontdk+$reserve+$convmgt;

$tfrontdk = $frontdk*200;

$treserve = $reserve*150;

$tconvmgt = $convmgt*180;

$total = $tfrontdk+$treserve+$tconvmgt;

print "Content-type: text/html\n\n";
print "";
print "</FONT><FONT  SIZE=6 PTSIZE=20>
</P><P ALIGN=CENTER><B><CENTER>Dominion Special</CENTER>
</P><P ALIGN=LEFT></FONT><FONT  SIZE=3 PTSIZE=10>
";
print "<CENTER></FONT><FONT  SIZE=5 PTSIZE=16>
<U>
Thank you for your order.</U>
</FONT><FONT  SIZE=3 PTSIZE=10></CENTER>";
print "
";
print "<TABLE BORDER=1 BGCOLOR=CYAN ALIGN=CENTER WIDTH=
300 CELLSPACING=5>";
```

```
print "<TR><TH ALIGN=CENTER>Qty</TH>";
print "<TH ALIGN=CENTER>Software</TH>";
print "<TH ALIGN=CENTER>Total</TH></TR>";
print "<TR><TD ALIGN=CENTER>$frontdk</TD>";
print "<TD ALIGN=CENTER>Front Desk Management</TD>";
print "<TD ALIGN=CENTER>\$$tfrontdk</TD></TR>";
print "<TR><TD ALIGN=CENTER>$reserve</TD>";
print "<TD ALIGN=CENTER>Reservation Express</TD>";
print "<TD ALIGN=CENTER>\$$treserve</TD></TR>";
print "<TR><TD ALIGN=CENTER>$convmgt</TD>";
print "<TD ALIGN=CENTER>Convention Management</TD>";
print "<TD ALIGN=CENTER>\$$tconvmgt</TD></TR>";
print "<TR><TD ALIGN=CENTER>$qtotal</TD>";
print "<TD ALIGN=CENTER>Total:</TD>";
print "<TD ALIGN=CENTER>\$$total</TD></TR></TABLE>";
```

4. Save the file in your cgi-bin directory, and exit the editor.

5. Use the chmod command to grant the file execute permission.

9

Now that you have entered both the code for the Web page and CGI script, you should test your work.

To test a Web page:

1. Open Netscape Communicator by clicking the **foot icon** on the **Panel**, pointing to **Programs**, pointing to **Internet**, and clicking **Netscape Communicator**.

2. In the location box, type the location of your software.html file, such as **http://localhosthome/tom/cgi-bin/software.html**. Press **Enter**. (As an alternative, after you start Netscape Communicator, click the **File** menu, click **Open Page**, type the location of your software.html file, and click **Open in Navigator**.)

3. Enter quantities of **10, 15,** and **20** for the products, and then click the **Submit** button. Your screen should now look similar to Figure 9-16.

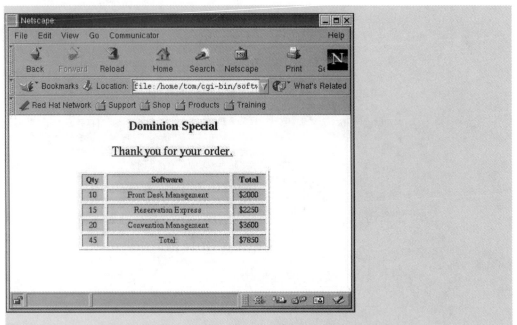

Figure 9-16   Web page returned to the browser from software.cgi

You have successfully created the Web page for Dominion Consulting by using your knowledge of Perl programming.

CHAPTER SUMMARY

- Perl is used as a powerful text-manipulation tool similar to the Awk program.

- Perl is written in scripts that are translated and executed by the Perl program.

- The Perl programmer has to write process-handling instructions for data items to prevent misidentification of data types and subsequent processing errors.

- Perl has three basic data types: scalars, arrays, and hashes. A scalar is a simple variable, such as a number or a name. Scalar variable names begin with $. Arrays are ordered lists of scalars that are accessed with numeric subscripts, starting at zero [0]. Array variable names are preceded with @, the at sign. Hashes are unordered sets of key/value pairs that you can access using the keys as subscripts. Hash variables begin with %, the percent sign.

- A list is an ordered group of simple variables or literals, separated by commas. For example, (101, 102, 103, 104) is an array of four values, 101 through 104.

◻ Anything besides a textual sort must be handled with a sort subroutine for which you can provide your own comparison function to determine greater-than, less-than, or equal-to conditions between the elements being sorted.

◻ An HTML document contains two parts: a head and a body. The head contains the title, which appears on the top bar of your browser window. The body defines what appears within the browser window.

◻ CGI (Common Gateway Interface) is a protocol or set of rules governing how browsers and servers communicate. Any script that sends or receives information from a server needs to follow the standards specified by CGI.

◻ To run your Web pages, you need to be in X Window and have access to a Web browser such as Netscape Communicator and a Web server such as Apache. Using UNIX, you can also test your Web pages using the localhost feature.

COMMAND SUMMARY

Please refer to the tables within the chapter for a command review.

9

REVIEW QUESTIONS

1. Perl contains features of _____.
   a. the Awk program
   b. C
   c. the shell scripting language
   d. all of the above
   e. none of the above

2. Which of the following formats can you use in Perl to print Good Morning! to the screen?
   a. echo (`Good Morning!`)
   b print "Good Morning!"
   c. print ("Good Morning!")
   d. all of the above
   e. only b and c

3. True or False: HTML tags are special codes enclosed in greater than/less than brackets, <>.

4. True or False: Most tags are used in pairs: one marks the beginning of a section and a corresponding tag marks the end of a section.

5. Perl uses _____ to reference a file.

   a. the Awk command

   b. a read loop

   c. a filehandle

   d. the delta statement

6. Perl scripts _____.

   a. begin with a line indicating that /usr/bin/perl is the interpreter

   b. are not made executable

   c. do not support the use of if statements

   d. do not support the use of while loops

7. Which section of an HTML document contains the title?

   a. HEAD

   b. BODY

   c. PARAGRAPH

   d. BLOCKQUOTE

8. Text between the _____ tags appears underlined.

   a. [U] and [/U]

   b. <U> and </U>

   c. <ALIGN=underline> and </ALIGN>

   d. <JUSTIFY=underline> and </JUSTIFY>

9. The spaceship operator refers to _____.

   a. CGI programming

   b. a shortcut for sorting names in Perl

   c. a shortcut for sorting numbers in Perl

   d. a Perl in-line sort

10. What does the statement $x = <STDIN>; perform?

    a. It displays the contents of $x.

    b. It copies the string "STDIN" to $x.

    c. It copies the contents of the variable STDIN to $x.

    d. It reads keyboard input into $x.

11. In Perl, the == operator _____.

    a. tests two numbers for equality

    b. tests two strings for equality

    c. tests either numbers or strings for equality

    d. performs an assignment

12. The eq operator in Perl _____.

    a. tests two numbers for equality

    b. tests two strings for equality

    c. tests either numbers or strings for equality

    d. performs an assignment

13. True or False: In Linux, you can start Netscape Communicator from the GNOME foot icon on the Panel.

14. In Perl, a scalar is a _____.

    a. for loop

    b. complex form of an if loop

    c. test for inequalities

    d. variable that holds either a number or a string

15. A hash is _____.

    a. a set of key/value pairs

    b. another name for a complicated string

    c. a string that has over 255 characters

    d. all of the above

    e. only b and c

16. In an HTML document, the H1 tag is _____.

    a. used to put text into bold

    b. signifies the largest heading size

    c. signifies the smallest heading size

    d. signifies that there is only one text heading

17. The _____ button in an HTML script is used to transfer the data to a Web server, which then passes it to a CGI script.

    a. Transfer

    b. Accept

    c. Go

    d. Submit

18. Which of the following would you find at the end of an HTML file?

    a. <END>

    b. [STOP]

    c. </HTML>

    d. {/FINAL}

9

19. In Perl, the _____ character precedes an array variable name.

    a. @

    b. $

    c. %

    d. #

20. The % character precedes _____.

    a. array names

    b. hash names

    c. scalar names

    d. constants

21. Assume that a program contains this code:

    ```
    @food = ("fruit", "steak", "bread", "vegetables" );
    ```

    The next line contains this code:

    ```
    print ("$food[2]");
    ```

    What will the second line of code print?

    a. fruit

    b. steak

    c. bread

    d. vegetables

22. Assume that this code exists in a program:

    ```
    %food = ("fruit", 5, "steak", 10, "bread", 15,
    "vegetables", 20 );
    ```

    The next line contains this code:

    ```
    print ("$food{'bread'}");
    ```

    What will the second line of code print?

    a. 5

    b. 15

    c. steak

    d. bread

23. In a Perl script, _____ is the string relational operator for "not equal to."

    a. <->

    b. ><

    c. ne

    d. not

24. The HTML tag _____ changes the background color to white.

    a. "Color=White"

    b. <BODY BGCOLOR=WHITE>

    c. [/BACK=WHITE]

    d. {Color = White}

25. True or False: The symbol <=> is also known as the spaceship operator in Perl.

DISCOVERY EXERCISES

1. Write a Perl script to print "Hello Perl".

2. Write a Perl script to sort the numbers 1, 8, 15, 1000, and 12, which are located in a memory array.

3. Create the file Ex2numbers using the numbers from Discovery Exercise 2. Write a Perl script using the spaceship operator to sort and display Ex2numbers.

4. Write a Perl script with a hash variable. The hash variable should contain these names and telephone numbers:

```
Jean James    555-9898
Rhonda Smith  555-0982
Joe Milner    555-8944
Greg Jones    555-0716
```

The program should display the phone numbers of each individual.

5. Create a personal Web page with your name, address, telephone number, and a brief paragraph describing your hobbies and interests. Your name should be centered in a large heading.

6. Modify the script perlcom.pl (developed earlier in this chapter) so that it counts all lines in the file that are not comments.

7. Write a Perl program to count the number of records in the students file (created earlier in this chapter) that begin with the letter A.

8. Write a Perl program that converts a value in inches to a value in centimeters and displays the result. (1 inch = 2.54 centimeters.)

9. Write a Perl program that uses a while loop to display the values 1 through 12 and their squares.

10. Write a Perl program that asks the user to enter two numeric values. Store the values in $x and $y. If $y is not zero, divide $x by $y and display the result. If $y is zero, display an error message indicating that division by zero is not possible.

11. Create an HTML and CGI Perl script to create an interactive Web page to accept your first and last name in the HTML file and pass it to the CGI Perl script, where it displays "Hello", followed by your first and last name.

9

12. Design a Web page that allows the user to enter his or her age. The page should have a Submit button that, when clicked, invokes a CGI script. The script should display the user's age in days. (Don't worry about leap years.)

13. Design a Web page that allows the user to enter the width and length of a rectangle. The page should have a Submit button that, when clicked, invokes a CGI script. The script should display the area of the rectangle (width * length).

14. Create a Perl program to read both the students file and the numberlist file. Display the students' names in alphabetical order. Display the numbers in the order in which they were read.

15. Design a Web page that is a simple addition calculator. It should allow the user to enter two values. When the user clicks a Submit button, a CGI script returns the sum of the two numbers.

10

DEVELOPING UNIX APPLICATIONS IN C AND C++

Dominion Consulting's customers are becoming more conscious of computer security. The programming staff is answering an increasing number of questions about data privacy and protection. Your supervisor asks you to write a simple program that can demonstrate how file encryption and decryption work. **File encryption** is an operation that scrambles a file's contents into a secret code. A **decryption operation** restores the file to its original state.

In this chapter, you learn not only how to write C programs, but also how to use other software development tools, such as the make utility. The **make utility** is a UNIX program that controls compilation as you make changes and additions to the programs during their development phase. Finally, you also write simple C++ programs so that you can understand how C++ programming differs from C programming. The programming that you learn is offered to give you an introduction to the C and C++ programming capabilities in UNIX.

◀ LESSON A ▶

C LANGUAGE PROGRAMMING

After completing this lesson, you should be able to:
- ♦ Create simple C programs
- ♦ Debug C programs
- ♦ Use the make utility to revise and maintain source files
- ♦ Identify program errors and fix them
- ♦ Create a complete C programming application

INTRODUCING C PROGRAMMING

C is the language in which UNIX was developed and refined. The original UNIX operating system was written in assembly language. **Assembly language** is a low-level language that provides maximum access to all the computer's devices, both internal and external. However, assembly language requires more coding and a greater in-depth treatment of all internal control items. The C language was partly developed to resolve the more lengthy requirements of assembly language. It has significantly reduced those requirements to a high-level set of easy-to-understand instructions. Dennis Ritchie and Brian Kernighan, two Bell Lab employees, rewrote most of UNIX using C in the early 1970s.

Ken Thompson, another Bell Lab employee, also deserves credit for his influence on the development of C. He wrote a forerunner of C, called B, in 1970 for the first UNIX system to run on the DEC PDP-7 minicomputer.

Since its inception, the C language has evolved from its original design as an operating system language to its current status as a major tool in the development of any high-performance application for general use. Since C is native to UNIX, it works best as a UNIX application development tool, where the operating system views the application as an extension of its core functionality. For example, daemons (specialized system processes that run in the background) are written in C. They access the UNIX system code just as any other part of the operating system.

C programming may be described, in a nutshell, as a language that uses relatively short, isolated functions to break down large complex tasks into small and easily resolved subtasks. This function-oriented design allows programmers to create their own program functions to interact with the predefined system functions to create powerful and comprehensive solutions to the largest of applications.

Using C to write a program for Dominion's security demonstration is a good choice. Because C is a compiled language, the program source code cannot be viewed. Before you begin to write this program, however, you first need to learn the basics of C programming.

For this chapter, you need the C and C++ compilers installed in your workstation or server setup. In Red Hat Linux, typically they are installed in a server installation by the server administrator. If the compilers are not already installed in Red Hat Linux and you have access to the root account, you can install them by running the Update Agent in the GNOME interface. To start the Update Agent, click the foot icon (Main Menu), point to Programs, point to System, and click Update Agent. Install the packages for gcc (which is the C compiler that is integrated with options for C++). Install any dependencies that the Update Agent finds are necessary for the C compiler packages.

Creating a C Program

A C program consists of separate bodies of code, known as **functions**. In other languages, bodies of code have different names, such as subroutines or procedures. Each of these bodies of code is designed so it contributes to the execution of a single task. You put together a collection of these functions, and they become a program. Within the program the functions call each other as needed and work to solve the problem for which the program was originally designed.

Creating a program is never done in a single step. As a programmer, you complete many phases before the program is ready to run. The first phase is to create the source code of the program. As with shell scripts and Perl programs, you use a text editor, such as vi or Emacs, to create C programs. The source code is stored in a file with the .c (lowercase c) extension. An example of such a file is simpleprogram.c.

The next phase is to execute the preprocessor and compiler. The **preprocessor** makes modifications to your program, such as including the contents of other files and creating constant values. After the preprocessor prepares your program, the compiler executes. The compiler is a program that translates the source code into **object code**, which consists of binary instructions. If you made errors, the compiler locates many of them. When this happens, you use the text editor to correct the errors and recompile the program. After the source code is compiled, it is stored by default into an executable file called a.out. Note, however, that at the time you compile the source code, you can override the default to a file name of your choice.

Many compilers translate source code into assembly code. This requires that an **assembler** be called up to translate the assembly code into object code. The compiler usually starts the assembler automatically, so you do not need to enter additional commands. Some compilers translate directly from source code into object code, skipping the assembly step. Whatever type of compiler you use, the outcome of this phase is the creation of a file that contains object code.

The final phase requires the use of another tool called a **linker**. This program links all the object files that belong to the program, along with any library functions the program may use. The result is an **executable file**. The entire process is depicted in Figure 10-1.

10

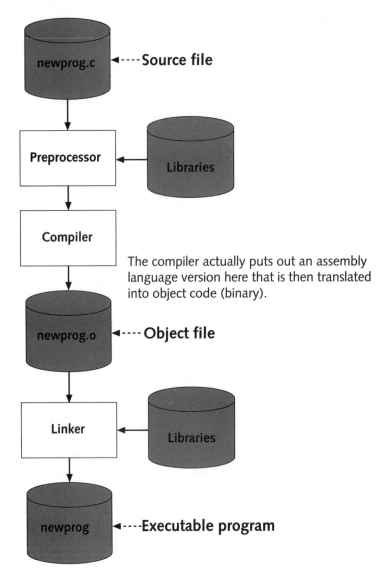

The compiler actually puts out an assembly language version here that is then translated into object code (binary).

Figure 10-1   C program compilation process

C Key Words

The C language, like all programming languages, includes **key words**. These key words have special meanings, so you cannot use them as names for variables or functions. Table 10–1 lists the C key words.

Table 10-1   C language key words

auto	double	int	struct
break	else	long	switch
case	enum	register	typedef
char	extern	return	union
const	float	short	unsigned
continue	for	signed	void
default	goto	sizeof	volatile
do	if	static	while

The C Library

As you can see from Table 10-1, the C language is very small. It has no input or output facilities as part of the language. All I/O is performed through the C library. The **C library** consists of functions that perform file, screen, and keyboard operations, as well as many other tasks. For example, certain functions perform string operations, memory allocation and control, math operations, and much more. When you need to perform one of these operations in your program, you place a **function call** at the desired point. The linker joins the code of the library function with your program's object code to create the executable file.

10

Program Format

As mentioned earlier, C programs are made up of one or more functions. Every function must have a name, and every C program must have a function called **main**. Here is a very simple C program:

```
int main()
{
}
```

This program does absolutely nothing, yet it contains all the elements necessary for a valid C program. The next two paragraphs examine the bare essentials.

Note the word "main" followed by a set of parentheses. (A following section, "Specifying Data Types," defines the first item—int.) This is the name of a function. As mentioned earlier, all C programs must have a function called main. The parentheses denote that this is a function name.

On the next line is an opening brace. In a C program this denotes the beginning of a block of code. The closing brace on the next line denotes the end of the block of code. All functions must have an opening and a closing brace. The statements that normally make up the function appear between the two braces. In the sample program there are no statements; therefore, the function does nothing. The braces are still required.

Including Comments

The /* symbol denotes the beginning of a comment, and the */ symbol denotes the end of a comment. The compiler ignores everything in between. This example shows a C program comment:

```
/* Here is a program that does nothing. */
int main()
{
}
```

In the example, the comment "Here is a program that does nothing" appears at the top of the program. The beginning of the comment is marked with /* and the end with */. The compiler sees this program as being no different than the earlier version that had no comment.

Using the Preprocessor #include Directive

Here is a sample program that creates output:

```
/* A simple C program */
#include <stdio.h>
int main()
{
        printf("Hello from the Linux World!\n");
}
```

Figure 10-2 shows the program's output.

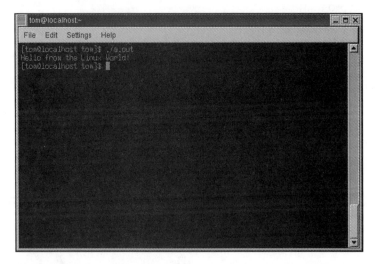

Figure 10-2   C program output

In the program above, you see the statement:

```
#include <stdio.h>
```

This is called a **preprocessor directive**. As mentioned earlier, the preprocessor processes your program before the compiler translates it into object code. It reads your program, looking for statements that begin with the # symbol. These statements are considered preprocessor directives and cause the preprocessor to modify your source code in some way. For example, the #include directive causes the preprocessor to include another file in your program at the point where the #include directive appears.

The file **stdio.h** is called a **header file** and is part of your C development system. This file contains information the compiler needs to process standard input or output statements. Any program that performs standard input or output must include the stdio header file. Because the sample program uses the printf statement (which performs standard output), it must include stdio.h.

The C development system includes a number of header files. All library functions require that you include a particular header file.

Specifying Data Types

10

Variables and constants represent data used in a C program. You must declare variables and state the type of data that the variable can hold. A variable's data type determines the upper and lower limits of its range of values. Data types with wider ranges of values occupy more memory than those with narrower ranges. The exact limits of the ranges vary among compilers and hardware platforms.

Table 10-2 shows a list of the basic data types that may be used in a C program.

Table 10-2 C data types

Data Type	Description
char	Occupies a single byte; designed to hold one character from the character set used by the running machine
int	Holds integer values; the size of an int variable should be the default size of an integer on the running machine, but this is not always the case
float	A single-precision, floating-point value
double	A double-precision, floating-point value

As mentioned earlier, the exact upper and lower limits of each of the range of values for data types depends on the compiler and hardware platform being used. You can use three modifiers with int data types: short, long, and unsigned. The short and long modifiers make an integer variable smaller or larger than its default size. Typically, a long int occupies twice as many bits as an int. On some machines a short int occupies half the number of bits as an int, but in many cases there is no difference between a short int and an int.

Table 10-3 shows typical limits and memory requirements of C data types.

Table 10-3   Typical C data type limits and bytes occupied in memory

Data Type	Bytes	Minimum Value	Maximum Value
char	1	–128	127
unsigned char	1	0	255
short int	2	–32,768	32,767
unsigned short	2	0	65,535
int	4	–2,147,483,648	2,147,483,647
long int	4	–2,147,483,648	2,147,483,647
unsigned long	4	0	4,294,967,295
float	4	–3.4028E+38	3.4028E+38
double	8	–1.79769E+308	1.79769E+308

Character Constants

Characters are represented internally in a single byte of the computer's memory. When a character is stored in the byte, it is set to the character's code in the host character set. For example, if the machine uses ASCII codes, the letter A is stored in memory as the number 65. This is because the ASCII code for A is 65.

When you represent character data in a program as a character constant, you enclose the character in single quote marks. Here are some examples:

```
'A'
'C'
'a'
'z'
```

Using Strings

A string is a group of characters, like a name. Strings are stored in memory in consecutive memory locations. When you use string constants in your C program, they must be enclosed in double quote marks. Here are some examples:

```
"Linux is a great operating system."
"Good Morning!"
"Enter your name and age."
```

Unlike higher-level languages, C does not provide a specific data type for character strings. C requires that you view strings the same way the computer does, as an array of characters. Here is how you might declare a character array to store a string:

```
char name[20];
```

This is just like declaring a char variable, except for the [20] appended to the variable name. It indicates that name should be an array of 20 characters. It is large enough to hold a string of up to 19 characters. This is because in C all strings are terminated with a null character. A **null character** is a single byte where all bits are set to zero.

Including Identifiers

Identifiers are names given to variables and functions. When naming variables and functions, resist the temptation to use short names that do not convey the meaning of the item. Using meaningful identifiers greatly enhances the style of your program. There are only a few rules to remember:

- The first character must be a letter or an underscore (the _ character).

- After the first character you may use letters, underscores, or digits.

- Variable names may be limited to 31 characters, and some compilers require the first 8 characters of variable names to be unique.

- Uppercase and lowercase characters are distinct.

These are all examples of legal identifiers:

- radius

- customer_name

- earnings_for_2000

- _my_name

10

Declaring Variables

You must declare all variables before you use them in a program. A declaration begins with a data type and is followed by one or more variable names. Here is an example:

```
int days;
```

This example declares a variable named days. Its data type is int, so days is large enough to hold any value that fits within the range of an int. Notice that the declaration ends with a semicolon, as do all complete C statements.

You can declare multiple variables of the same type on the same line. Here is an example:

```
int days, months, years;
```

This example declares three variables, each of type int, named days, months, and years. Notice that commas separate the names.

You can initialize variables with values at the time they are declared by placing an equal sign after the variable name followed by a constant value. Here is an example:

```
int days = 5, months = 2, years = 10;
```

Understanding the Scope of Variables

The **scope** of a variable is the part of the program in which the variable is defined and therefore accessible. You can declare a variable either inside a function or any place that is not inside a function.

Variables that are declared inside a function are called **automatic variables**. These variables are local to the function in which they are declared. Here is an example:

```
/* This program declares a local variable
    in function main. The program does nothing
    else.  */
int main()
{
int days;
}
```

Here, the variable days is an automatic variable and is local to the function main.

You can also declare a variable outside of any function, as in the following example:

```
/* This program declares a global variable
    The program does nothing else.  */

int days;
int main()
{
}
```

In the program above, the variable is external, or global. The scope of a global variable is the entire program, beginning at the point where the declaration was made. The scope of an automatic, or local, variable is the body of the function in which it is declared.

The only place inside a function where local variables may be declared is at the beginning of the body of the function—after the opening brace and before any statement. You can declare global variables anywhere in a program except inside a function.

Using Math Operators

Arithmetic operators perform standard math activities such as adding, subtracting, multiplying, and dividing the values held in variables or numbers. Table 10-4 lists the C arithmetic operators.

You can use these operators to create regular math expressions, as in the following examples:

```
x = y + 3;
num = num * 3;
days = months * 30;
```

These examples introduce the assignment operator (the equal sign). It works by assigning the value of the expression on its right to the variable whose name is on its left. In the example days = months * 30, the value in the variable months is multiplied by 30 and the product is stored in the variable days.

Table 10-4 C arithmetic operators

Operator	Meaning
+	addition
–	subtraction
*	multiplication
/	division
%	modulus
++	increment
––	decrement

The last two operators shown in Table 10-4 are the **increment** (++) and **decrement** (--) **operators**. These are unary operators, which means that they work with one operand. The following example shows the variable count being incremented:

```
count++;
```

Likewise, this variable can be decremented by using the following statement:

```
count--;
```

The first two examples of the count variable show these operators in their postfix form, which means they come after the variable. You can also use them as prefix operators:

```
++count;
--count;
```

The operators behave differently depending on which form is used. For example, assume the variable j is set to 4. In this statement,

```
x = j++;
```

the ++ operator is used in postfix form. This means the assignment operator (=) uses the value of j before it is incremented. In effect, it says "set x equal to j, then increment j." After the operation, x will be equal to 4 and j will be equal to 5.

If the prefix form of the operator is used, you get different results:

```
x = ++j;
```

This statement says "increment j, then set x equal to j." Both x and j will be equal to 5 after the statement executes.

10

Generating Formatted Output with printf

One of the most commonly used screen output library functions is printf. The f stands for "formatted," as the function allows you to format and print several arguments of differing data types. The printf function is used in the following manner:

Syntax **printf (*control string, expression, expression,...*)**

The first argument is called the **control string**. It specifies the way formatting should occur. Following the control string may be a varying number of arguments. Each of these is an expression with a value to be printed. Here is perhaps the most simple example of a printf statement:

```
printf("Hello");
```

The example uses only a control string. The word Hello is printed as is on the screen. Here is another example.

```
printf("Your age is %d", 30);
```

The %d that appears in the control string is called a format specifier. It is not printed as part of the message, but tells printf to substitute a decimal integer in its place. The decimal integer is the very next argument, the number 30. This printf statement prints the following message on the screen:

```
Your age is 30
```

Although this example illustrates the usage of the %d format specifier, it is not very realistic. You are more likely to use it in the following manner:

```
printf("Your age is %d", age);
```

Here, printf substitutes the value in the integer variable age for the %d. The next example prints the values of three int variables:

```
printf("The values are %d %d %d", num1, num2, num3);
```

This message contains the values of num1, num2, and num3, in that order. You can also pass arithmetic expressions to printf:

```
printf("You have worked %d minutes", hours*60);
```

In fact, you can pass any valid C expression to printf. However, be sure you use an appropriate format specifier. A format specifier is used to indicate the format of the data—one character, a string, or a decimal integer, for example. Table 10-5 shows a list of valid format specifiers.

Table 10-5 Format specifiers

Format Specifier	Meaning
%c	Single character
%d	Signed decimal integer
%e	Floating-point number, e notation
%E	Floating-point number, E notation
%f	Floating-point number, decimal notation
%g	Causes %f or %e to be used, whichever is shorter
%G	Causes %f or %E to be used, whichever is shorter
%i	Signed decimal integer
%o	Unsigned octal integer
%p	Pointer
%s	Character string
%u	Unsigned decimal integer
%x	Unsigned hex integer using digits 0-f
%X	Unsigned hex integer using digits 0-F
%%	Print a percent sign

10

At this point, you have learned enough C programming basics to write a simple program.

To write a simple C program:

1. Use the vi or Emacs editor to create the file **inches.c**. (Note that the C compiler identifies by the .c extension a file containing C code.) Enter this code:

```
/* This program converts 10 feet to inches. */

#include <stdio.h>

int main()
{
    int inches, feet;
    feet = 10;
    inches = feet * 12;
    printf("There are %d inches in %d feet.\n", inches,
      feet);
}
```

2. Save the program, and exit the editor.

3. The C compiler is executed by the gcc command in Linux. Type **gcc inches.c** and press **Enter**. If you typed the program correctly, you see no messages. If you see error messages, load the program into the editor, and correct the mistake.

4. By default, the compiler stores the executable program in a file named a.out. Execute a.out by typing **./a.out** and pressing **Enter**. Your screen looks similar to Figure 10-3.

5. You can specify the name of the executable file with the -o option. Type **gcc -o inches inches.c** and press **Enter**. The command compiles the inches.c file and stores the executable code in a file named inches.

6. Run the inches program by typing **./inches** and pressing **Enter**.

Figure 10-3   Output of a.out

 The Linux command to use the C compiler is gcc, but in some other versions of UNIX, the C compiler is invoked by using the **cc** command.

Using the if Statement

The if statement allows your program to make decisions depending upon whether a condition is true or false. The general form of the if statement is:

Syntax **if** *(condition) statement;*

If the condition is true, the statement is performed. Here is an example:

```
if (weight > 1000) printf("You have exceeded the limit.");
```

If the variable weight contains a value greater than 1000, the printf statement executes.

Sometimes you may need to execute more than one line of code if a condition is true. C allows you to substitute a block of code for the single statement, when necessary. Here is an example:

```
if (weight > 1000)
{
        printf("Warning!\n");
        printf("You have exceeded the limit.\n");
        printf("Just thought you\'d like to know.");
}
```

The program segment above causes the three printf statements to execute if weight is greater than 1000.

The if-else construct allows your program to do one thing if a condition is true and another if it is false. Here is an example:

```
if (hours > 40)
     printf("You can go home now.");
else printf("Keep working.");
```

The "Keep working" message prints only when the condition (hours > 40) is false. Here is an example using blocks of code:

```
if(hours>40)
{
    printf("Go home.\n");
    printf("You deserve it.");
}
else
{
    printf("Keep working.\n");
    printf("Stop playing with the computer.");
}
```

To practice the C if-else statement:

1. Create the file **radius.c** with your choice of editor. Enter the following C code:

```
/* This program calculates the area of a circle */
#include <stdio.h>
int main()
{
    float radius = 50, area;
    area = 3.14159 * radius * radius;
    if (area > 100)
        printf("The area, %f,  is too large.\n", area);
    else
        printf("The area, %f, is within limits.\n", area)
        ;
}
```

2. Save the file, and exit the editor.

3. Compile the program by typing **gcc -o radius radius.c** and pressing **Enter**. If you see error messages, edit the file, and correct your mistakes.

4. Execute the program by typing **./radius** and pressing **Enter**.

Using C Loops

Loops in C are similar to those you have used in shell scripts and Perl programs. C provides three looping mechanisms: the for loop, the while loop, and the do-while loop. Using the for loop is best when you know the number of times that the loop is to perform. If it is unclear how many times the loop should perform, then use the while or do-while loop.

Here is an example of the for loop:

```
for (count = 0; count < 100; count++)
    printf("Hello\n");
```

This loop means the message "Hello" will print 100 times. Following the word "for" is a set of parentheses containing three arguments. The arguments are separated by semicolons.

The first argument is the initialization. The variable count is being used to track the number of times the loop has run. The initialization is a statement that is executed before the first time through. In the example above, the initialization stores the number 0 in count.

The second argument is the test condition. The for loop executes as long as the test condition is true. It is evaluated before each iteration of the loop. If the condition is true, the iteration is performed. Otherwise, the loop terminates. In the example, the loop performs as long as count is less than 100.

The third argument is the update. It is performed at the end of each iteration. In the example, the loop increments the variable count.

This program segment shows an example of the while loop:

```
x=0;
while (x++ < 100)
    printf("x is equal to %d\n", x);
```

This loop repeats while x is less than 100. The next example illustrates a do-while loop, which is very similar to the while loop.

```
x=0;
do
        printf("x is equal to %d\n", x);
while (x++ < 100);
```

The difference between the while loop and the do-while loop is that the while loop tests its condition before each iteration, and the do-while loop tests after each iteration.

To practice using a C loop:

1. Use the editor of your choice to create the file **rain.c**. Enter this C code:.

```c
/* rain.c  */
#include <stdio.h>
int main()
{
    int rain, total_rain = 0;
    for (rain = 0; rain < 10; rain++)
    {
        printf("We have had %d inches of rain.\n", rain);
        total_rain = total_rain + rain;
    }
    printf("We have had a total ");
    printf("of %d inches of rain.\n", total_rain);
}
```

2. Save the file, and exit the editor.

3. Compile the program, and store the executable code in a file named **rain**.

4. Run the program. Your screen should look similar to Figure 10-4.

10

Figure 10-4   Output of rain

Defining Functions

When you define a function, you declare the function's name and create the lines of code that make up the function's block of code. You also state what data type is returned from the function (if any). Here is an example.

```c
void message()
{
```

```
        printf("Greetings from the function message.");
        printf("Have a nice day.");
}
```

The word "void" indicates that this function does not return a value. The name of the function is message. A set of parentheses follows the name. There are only two statements in this function, both printfs. The function might appear in a complete program as:

```
#include <stdio.h>
void message();
int main()
{
        message();
}
void message()
{
        printf("Greetings from the function message.\n");
        printf("Have a nice day.\n");
}
```

The line under the include statement that reads,

```
void message();
```

is called a function prototype. It tells the compiler about the function before the code for the function is fully defined. The word "void" means that this function returns no data. Void functions in C are like subroutines in Fortran or procedures in Pascal. They are merely modules of code that perform some task.

After the function prototype comes the function main. Main includes only one line, which reads:

```
message();
```

This is a function call. You call functions by placing their name, followed by a set of parentheses and a semicolon, at the desired place in the program. This causes the program's control to pass to the function. When the program returns from the function, it resumes execution at the next statement after the function call.

After main is the definition of the function message. The output of the program is:

```
[tom@localhost tom]$ ./func1
Greetings from the function message.
Have a nice day.
```

Using Function Arguments

Sometimes it is necessary to pass information to a function. A value passed to a function is called an argument. Arguments are stored in special automatic variables. Here is an example.

```
void print_square(int val)
{
```

```
   printf("\nThe square is %d", val*val);
}
```

This function takes an int argument. When it receives the argument, the function stores the argument in the variable val. The printf statement causes the value of the expression val*val to print. Here is a complete program that uses the function:

```
#include <stdio.h>
   void print_square(int val)
main()
{
  int num = 5;
  print_square(num);
}

   void print_square(int val)
{
   printf("\nThe square is %d\n", val*val);
}
```

The output of the program is:

```
[tom@localhost tom]$ ./func2

The square is 25
```

Using Function Return Values

In addition to accepting arguments, functions may also return a value. This means you can make function calls part of arithmetic operations and assignments. For example, suppose you have a function called triple. It is designed to take an int argument and return that value multiplied by three. You could use the function call in a manner such as:

```
y = triple(x);
```

The function receives the value in x, triples it, and then returns this value. The statement above stores the return value in a variable called y. Here is what the triple function might look like:

```
int triple(int num)
{
   return(num * 3);
}
```

The function is defined as an int function. This means that it returns an int value. You may place a call to this function anywhere in your program where an int is expected. The function takes a single argument, which is also an int. In the function the argument is stored in the variable num. There is only one line in the function's block of code:

```
return(num * 3);
```

This is the return statement. It is used to return a value back to the calling part of the program. In this example the value of num * 3 is returned. The next sample program demonstrates the function:

```
#include <stdio.h>
int triple(int num);
int main()
{
    int x = 6, y;
    y = triple(x);
    printf("%d tripled is %d\n.", x, y);
}
int triple(int num)
{
    return (num * 3);
}
```

The program's output is:

```
[tom@localhost tom]$ ./func3
6 tripled is 18
```

To practice writing functions that accept arguments and return a value:

1. Use the editor of your choice to create the file **absolute.c**. Enter the following code:

```
#include <stdio.h>
int absolute(int num);
int main()
{
    int x = -12, y;
    y = absolute(x);
    printf("The absolute value of %d is %d\n", x, y);
}
int absolute(int num)
{
    if (num < 0)
        return (-num);
    else
        return (num);
}
```

2. Save the file, and exit the editor.

3. Compile the program, and save the executable code in a file named absolute.

4. Run the program. Your screen should look similar to Figure 10-5.

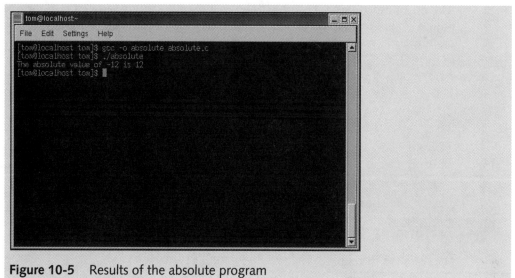

Figure 10-5   Results of the absolute program

Working with Files in C

Files are continuous streams of data. They are typically stored on disk. Many file operations are sequential, meaning they work from the beginning of the file to the end. When the file is opened, you are working with the beginning of the file. Every time a byte is read from or written to the file, your current position in the file is moved forward by one byte.

File Pointers

C file input/output is designed to use file pointers, which point to a predefined structure that contains information about the file. The structure template is found in stdio.h. You must declare a file pointer in order to use the I/O package. Here is an example:

```
FILE *fp;
```

This declares fp as a FILE pointer. It is used with various file access functions.

Opening and Closing Files

Before you can use a file, it must be opened. The library function for opening a file is fopen, as in the following example:

```
fp = fopen("myfile.dat", "r");
```

The fopen function takes two arguments: the filename and the access mode. This example opens a file named myfile.dat. The "r" means that the file is opened for reading. The following statement uses the "w" access mode for writing:

```
fp = fopen("myfile.dat", "w");
```

The fopen function returns a file pointer. If the file cannot be opened, it returns a NULL pointer (a pointer to address zero). The following code block is one way you can test to see if the file was opened:

```
if ((fp = fopen("myfile.dat", "r")) ==NULL)
{
        printf("Error opening myfile.dat\n");
        exit(0);
}
```

The opposite of opening a file is closing it. When a file is closed, its buffers are flushed, ensuring that all data was properly written to it. The fclose function is used to close files that were opened by fopen. Here is an example:

```
fclose(fp);
```

Performing File Input/Output

C provides many functions for reading and writing files. For the case project, you concentrate on two: fgetc and fputc. The two functions, fgetc and fputc, perform character input/output on files. The following is an example of fgetc:

```
ch = fgetc(fp);
```

fgetc reads a single character from the file and points to it. The character is read from the current position. Character output is performed with fputc as in the following example:

```
fputc(ch, fp);
```

In this example, the character stored in ch is written to the current position of the file referenced by fp.

Testing for the End of File

Use the feof function to determine if the end-of-file marker has been encountered during an input operation, as illustrated in the next example:

```
if (feof(fp))
    fclose(fp);
```

The feof function returns a nonzero value if the end-of-file marker was encountered. Otherwise, it returns 0.

Now that you have a basic understanding of file operations in C, you are ready to practice writing a program that performs file input/output:

To perform file input/output:

1. Use the editor of your choice to create the file **buildfile.c**. Enter this code in the file:

```
#include <stdio.h>
int main()
```

```
    {
        FILE *out_file;
        int count = 0;
        char msg[] = "This was created by a C program.\n";
        if ((out_file = fopen("testfile", "w")) == NULL)
        {
            printf("Error opening file.\n");
            exit(1);
        }
        while (count < 33)
        {
            fputc(msg[count], out_file);
            count++;
        }
        fclose(out_file);
    }
```

2. Save the program, and exit the editor.

3. Compile the program, and save the executable in a file named buildfile.

4. Run the buildfile program. The program creates another file, testfile.

5. To see the contents of testfile, use the **cat** command as shown here:

```
[tom@localhost tom]$ cat testfile
This was created by a C program.
```

10

Using the Make Utility to Maintain Program Source Files

You may often work with a program that has many files of source code. For example, the absolute program you created in a previous exercise can be divided into two files: one that holds the function main and another that holds the function absolute. The two files are then compiled and linked together, as demonstrated in the following steps.

To compile and link two files:

1. Use the editor of your choice to create the file **abs_func.c**. Enter this code:

```
int absolute(int num)
{
    if (num < 0)
        return (-num);
    else
        return (num);
}
```

2. Save the file.

3. Create the file **abs_main.c**. Enter this code:

```
#include <stdio.h>
int absolute(int num);
int main()
{
    int x = -12, y;
    y = absolute(x);
    printf("The absolute value of %d is %d\n", x, y);
}
```

4. Save the file, and exit the editor.

5. Compile and link the two programs by typing **gcc abs_main.c abs_func.c -o abs** and pressing **Enter**. The compiler separately compiles abs_main.c and abs_func.c. Their object files are linked together, and the executable code is stored in the file abs.

6. Run the abs program. Your screen should look similar to Figure 10-6.

Figure 10-6   Results of the abs program

As you develop multimodule programs and make changes, you must compile the program repeatedly. However, with multimodule source files, you only need to compile those source files in which you made changes. The linker then links the newly generated object-code files with previously compiled object code, thereby creating a new executable file. However, keeping track of what needs to be recompiled and what does not can become an overwhelming task when the program involves dozens of files of source code. This is where the make utility helps.

The make utility tracks what needs to be recompiled by using the time stamp field for each source file. All you have to do is create a control file, called the makefile (which is actually a file named makefile), for the make utility to use. The control file lists all your source files and their relationships to each other. These relationships are expressed in the form of targets and dependencies. A target file depends on another file to determine if any action needs to be taken to rebuild the target file. (The ultimate target file is, of course, the executable file that results from linking all the object files together.) The dependent files are source files, such as the .c source files, or .h files that serve as headers to be included within the source files.

The makefile must exist in the current directory. It feeds the make utility all it needs to know to recompile any changed modules and then relink the objects to produce a new executable program. You can also give the makefile another name, such as make_abs. To do this, you need to enter the −f option followed by the name of the makefile. This is useful when you are developing more than one application from within the same directory.

The contents of make_abs, an example of a makefile, are:

```
abs_main.o: abs_main.c
   gcc -c abs_main.c
abs_func.o: abs_func.c
   gcc -c abs_func.c
abs2: abs_main.o abs_func.o
   gcc abs_main.o abs_func.o -o abs2
```

Two types of lines are shown in the file: dependencies and commands. The first line is a dependency, and the second line is a command:

```
abs_main.o: abs_main.c
   gcc -c abs_main.c
```

The first line establishes a dependency between abs_main.o and abs_main.c. If abs_main.c is newer than abs_main.o, the command on the second line executes (rebuilding abs_main.o).

The third and fourth lines, as well as the fifth and sixth lines, establish similar dependencies and commands.

The command line entry to build the abs2 program using the makefile is:

```
make -f make_abs abs2
```

The -f option instructs make to read the file make_abs instead of makefile. After executing the command, you can run the abs2 program. Figure 10-7 shows the output of the make command and the abs2 program.

If you forget whether you have made changes since the last time you ran the program, you can use make to check the source files' time stamps, and rebuild the program if necessary. The make utility does not recompile if the program is current, and displays a message that the make file is up to date, as shown in the following code:

```
[tom@localhost tom]$ make -f make_abs abs2
make: 'abs2' is up to date.
```

10

Figure 10-7   Making and running the abs2 program

The make utility follows a set of rules, both defaults and user defined. In general, a make rule has:

- A target, the name of the file you want to make (in the example above, the target is abs2)
- One or more dependencies, the files upon which the target depends
- An action, a shell command that creates the target.

Now that you have learned the structure of a makefile, you can create a simple multi-module C project.

To create a simple multimodule C project:

1. Use the editor of your choice to create the file **square_func.c**. Enter this code in the file:

```c
int square(int number)
{
    return (number * number);
}
```

2. Save the file.

3. Next create the file **square_main.c**. Enter this code:

```c
#include <stdio.h>
int square(int number);
int main()
{
    int count, sq;
    for (count = 1; count < 11; count++)
    {
```

```
            sq = square(count);
            printf("The square of %d is %d\n", count, sq);
        }
    }
```

4. Save the file.

5. Next, create a makefile named **make_square**. Enter the following text:

> In many UNIX versions of the make command, such as in later versions of Red Hat Linux, you must place a tab character before each command line that calls the gcc compiler. If you do not, the make command returns an error.

```
square_func.o: square_func.c
(press Tab)gcc -c square_func.c
square_main.o: square_main.c
   (press Tab)gcc -c square_main.c
square: square_func.o square_main.o
   (press Tab)gcc square_func.o square_main.o -o
   square
```

6. Save the file, and exit the editor.

7. Build the program by typing **make -f make_square square** and pressing **Enter**. (If you have errors, load the incorrect module into the editor and correct your mistakes.)

8. Run the program. Your screen should look similar to Figure 10-8.

Figure 10-8 Building and running the square program

Now that you understand the basics of writing a program in C, you learn how to debug a program.

DEBUGGING YOUR PROGRAM

Typical errors for new C programmers include using incorrect syntax, such as forgetting to terminate a statement with a semicolon. Or, because almost everything you type into a C program is in lowercase, your program may have a case-sensitive error. Here is an example of what you might see on the screen if you omit a closing quote inside a printf command:

```
simple.c:10: unterminated string or character constant
simple.c:10: possible real start of unterminated constant
```

The compiler generally produces more error lines than the number of mistakes it finds in the code. The compiler reports the error lines and any surrounding lines affected by the mistake(s).

 Remember that every time you modify (correct or add text to) your program source file, you must recompile the program to create a new executable program.

To correct syntax errors within your programs, you must therefore perform the following steps:

1. Write down the line number of each error and a brief description.

2. Edit your source file, moving your cursor to the first line number the compiler reports.

3. Within the source file, correct the error, and then move the cursor to the next line number. Most editors display the current line number to help you locate specific lines within the file.

4. After correcting all the errors, save and recompile the file.

Now that you understand how to write and debug simple C programs, you are ready to create interactive programs that read input from the keyboard.

CREATING A C PROGRAM TO ACCEPT INPUT

You can draw from many standard library functions to accept input; that is, enter characters using the keyboard. Some, such as getchar(), are character oriented, while others, such as scanf(), are field oriented. This section concentrates on scanf().

Unlike many other library input functions, scanf can be used to input values of a variety of data types. You use it like this:

Syntax **scanf** (*control string, address, address,...*);

The scanf() function uses a control string with format specifiers in a manner similar to printf. The arguments that follow the control string are the addresses of variables where the input is to be stored. Consider the following example.

```
scanf("%d", &age);
```

The %d format specifier works just like it does for printf. Here it indicates that scanf() should interpret the input value as a decimal integer.

The &age argument tells scanf to store the input value in the variable age. The & is the address operator. When used with a general variable, it returns the memory address where this variable is located. The scanf() function needs the address of a variable to store an input value there. The next example shows how scanf() can be used to input a string.

```
scanf("%s", city);
```

Notice that this example does not use the & operator. Anytime you use the name of an array, it resolves to the address of the first element. It would be an error to use the & operator with the name of an array.

The format specifiers for scanf() are generally the same as those used with printf(). Table 10-6 shows the format specifiers for scanf().

Table 10-6   scanf() format specifiers

Format Specifier	Interpretation
%c	Single character
%d	Signed decimal integer
%e, %f, %g	Floating-point number
%E, %G	Floating-point number
%I	Signed decimal integer
%o	Signed octal integer
%p	Pointer
%s	String; ignores leading white-space characters, then reads until it encounters another white-space character
%u	Unsigned decimal integer
%x, %X	Signed hex integer

Table 10-7 shows a list of modifiers you can use with scanf format specifiers.

Table 10-7   Modifiers for scanf() format specifiers

Modifier	Meaning
h	Used to indicate a short int or short unsigned int, e.g., "%hd"
l	Used to indicate a long int or long unsigned int, e.g., "%ld" Also used to indicate a double, e.g., "%lf"
L	Used to indicate a long double, e.g., "%Lf"

Although it rarely contributes to a program's user-friendliness, the scanf statement can accept multiple inputs. Here is an example:

```
scanf("%d %f %d", &x, &y, &z);
```

The statement above accepts values in the variables x, y, and z which are int, float, and int, respectively. While typing values, the user must separate the three values with white-space characters. White-space characters are spaces, tabs, and new-lines.

You now write a C program to accept input from a keyboard.

To use C to accept keyboard input:

1. Use the editor of your choice to create a file named **keyboard.c** by entering the following lines of code:

```
/*==========================================================
Program Name: keyboard.c
Purpose:        Enter data using the keyboard
=========================================================== */
#include <stdio.h> /* the standard input/output library */
int main()
  {
   char string[50]; /* a string field */
   float my_money; /* a floating decimal field */
   int weight; /* an integer field */
   printf("\nEnter your First Name: ");
   scanf("%s", string);
   printf("\nEnter your Desired Monthly Income: ");
   scanf("%f",&my_money);
   printf("\nEnter your friend's weight: ");
   scanf("%d",&weight);
   printf("\n\n Recap\n");
   printf("I am %s and I wish to have %8.2f per month",
     string, my_money);
   printf("\nI never would have guessed you weigh %d",
     weight);
   printf("\n\n");
  }
```

2. Save the file, and exit the editor.

3. Compile the program by typing **gcc keyboard.c -o keyboard** and then pressing **Enter**.

4. Execute the program by typing **./keyboard** and then pressing **Enter**. Your screen should now look similar to Figure 10-9. Note that your screen appears differently depending on your input.

Figure 10-9   Output of the keyboard program

Now that you have created C programs that perform keyboard and file I/O, you are ready to write the security demonstration programs.

10

ENCODING AND DECODING PROGRAMS

If a file contains sensitive information, you may wish to encrypt it so others cannot read its contents. When a file is encrypted, its contents are encoded or modified in such a way that the original contents are not distinguishable. A formula is used to perform the encryption so that a complementary decryption algorithm can restore the file to its original contents.

The program you have been asked to write for Dominion Consulting's programming staff is simple in design. It opens a file, reads a character from the file, adds 10 to the character's ASCII value, and then writes the character to a second file. This procedure repeats until all characters in the file have been read, modified, and written to the second file. The second file is an encoded version of the first file.

The decoding program works opposite of the way the encoding program works. It reads a character from the encrypted file, subtracts 10 from its ASCII code, and writes the character out to another file. This procedure repeats until all encrypted characters have been converted to their original state and stored in the second file.

To create the encoding program:

1. Use the editor of your choice to create the file **encode.c**. Enter the following code in the file:

```
#include <stdio.h>
```

```
void encode(FILE *, FILE *);
int main()
{
    FILE *in_file, *out_file;
    char infile_name[81], outfile_name[81], input;
    printf("Enter the name of the file to encode: ");
    scanf("%s", infile_name);
    if ((in_file = fopen(infile_name, "r") ) == NULL)
    {
            printf("Error opening %s\n", infile_name);
            exit(0);
    }
    printf("Enter the output file name: ");
    scanf("%s", outfile_name);
    if ((out_file = fopen(outfile_name, "w") ) == NULL)
    {
            printf("Error opening %s\n", outfile_name);
            exit(0);
    }
    encode_file(in_file, out_file);
    printf("The file has been encoded.\n");
    fclose(in_file);
    fclose(out_file);
}
```

2. Save the file.

3. Create the file **encode_file.c** and enter this code:

```
#include <stdio.h>
void encode_file(FILE *in_file, FILE *out_file)
{
  char input;
  while (!feof(in_file))
  {
   input = fgetc(in_file);
      input += 10;
         fputc(input, out_file);
  }
}
```

4. Save the file.

5. Create the file **decode.c**. Enter this code:

```
#include <stdio.h>
void decode_file(FILE *, FILE *);
int main()
{
  FILE *in_file, *out_file;
  char infile_name[81], outfile_name[81], input;
```

```
        printf("Enter the name of the file to decode: ");
        scanf("%s", infile_name);
        if ((in_file = fopen(infile_name, "r") ) == NULL)
        {
                printf("Error opening %s\n", infile_name);
                exit(0);
        }
        printf("Enter the output file name: ");
        scanf("%s", outfile_name);
        if ((out_file = fopen(outfile_name, "w") ) == NULL)
        {
                printf("Error opening %s\n", outfile_name);
                exit(0);
        }
        decode_file(in_file, out_file);
        printf("The file has been decoded.\n");
        fclose(in_file);
        fclose(out_file);
    }
```

6. Save the file.

7. Create the file **decode_file.c**. Enter the following code:

```
#include <stdio.h>
void decode_file(FILE *in_file, FILE *out_file)
{
  while (!feof(in_file))
  {
   char input;
   input = fgetc(in_file);
   input -= 10;
     fputc(input, out_file);
  }
}
```

8. Save the file. You are now ready to create the makefiles for both the encode and decode programs.

9. Enter the following code in the editor, and save it in the file **encode_make**:

```
encode: encode.o encode_file.o
     gcc encode.o encode_file.o -o encode
encode.o: encode.c
     gcc -c encode.c
encode_file.o: encode_file.c
     gcc -c encode_file.c
```

10. Create a file named **decode_make**, and enter this code:

```
decode: decode.o decode_file.o
   gcc decode.o decode_file.o -o decode
```

```
decode.o: decode.c
   gcc -c decode.c
decode_file.o: decode_file.c
   gcc -c decode_file.c
```

11. Save the file. You are ready to build the programs.

12. Type **make -f encode_make** and press **Enter**.

13. Type **make -f decode_make** and press **Enter**. Your screen should resemble Figure 10-10.

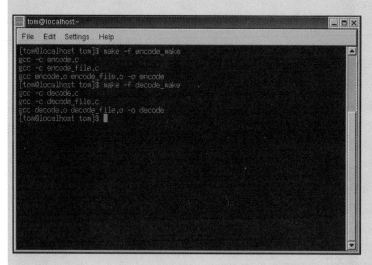

Figure 10-10   Output of the two make commands

You test the encode program by encrypting the testfile that you created in the file I/O exercise. The file contains the string "This was created by a C program."

14. Type **./encode** and press **Enter**. Your screen appears similar to Figure 10-11.

15. In response to the prompt, type **testfile** and press **Enter**.

16. The program now asks for the name of the output file.

17. Type **secret_file** and press **Enter**. The contents of testfile have been encoded and stored in secret_file.

18. Use the **cat** command to look at the contents of secret_file. Your screen looks similar to Figure 10-12.

19. Run the decode program by typing **./decode** and pressing **Enter**. The program asks you to enter the name of the file to decode.

20. Type **secret_file** and press **Enter**. Next the program asks you to enter the output file name.

Figure 10-11   Running the encode program

Figure 10-12   Results of the encode program

21. Type **normal_file** and press **Enter**. The contents of secret_file have been decoded and stored in normal_file.

22. Use the **cat** command to look at the contents of normal_file. Your screen should look similar to Figure 10-13. In some cases, you may see a couple of residual encoded characters, which display before the prompt and represent the end of file marker from the encoded file. You need not be concerned with their appearance.

Figure 10-13   Contents of the decoded normal_file

You have now learned some fundamentals of programming in C, including working with files, using the make utility to maintain program source files, debugging your program, and using the encoding and decoding programs. For summary information about using the C compiler, type man gcc at the command prompt; in Red Hat Linux, type info gcc for more extensive documentation. Also, you can find documentation about creating makefiles by typing man make or info make.

◄ LESSON B ►

C++ PROGRAMMING IN A

UNIX ENVIRONMENT

After completing this lesson, you should be able to:
- ◆ Create a C++ program that displays information on the screen
- ◆ Create a C++ program to read a textfile
- ◆ Create a C++ program with overload functions
- ◆ Create a C++ program that creates a new class object

INTRODUCING C++ PROGRAMMING

C++ is a programming language developed by Bjarne Stroustrup at AT&T Bell Labs. It builds on the C language to add object-oriented capabilities. As a result, C++ is best learned after you have been programming in C for a while. With C++ you can do "more with less" after you learn its nuances. Functions, the building blocks of C programming, are incorporated in C++ with added dimensions such as **function overloading**, which makes the functions respond to more than one set of criteria and conditions.

C and C++ are similar in many ways. For example, programs in both languages start with the main() function and call other functions that include blocks of instructions enclosed within curly braces. Both languages also have similar source files. The C++ compiler readily accepts C language syntax and coding structures. For example, you can take the file encryption and decryption programs you created in Lesson A and fully compile them using the C++ compiler. Both languages fully support compiler directives such as #include and #define. The C++ compiler's name is **CC** for most UNIX versions and **g++** for Linux versions.

One important distinction should be made about C++ programs. You can place your variable declarations anywhere inside the program, before or after the instructions. This is not true of C programs, in which program variables must precede all the instructions.

10

The major differences between the two languages become evident when you start using the C++ enhancements and class structures, which depart dramatically from standard C procedures. C follows procedural principles, whereas C++ primarily follows **object-oriented programming** principles while still allowing procedural programming methods. Procedural programming follows long-standing traditions that separate the data to be processed from the procedures that process. Procedural techniques require that the data fields be named and defined by data types (integers, characters, strings, floating decimals, and a variety of structures and arrays) before any processing begins. Object-oriented programming, on the other hand, uses objects for handling data—allowing the data to be described by name and type anywhere in the program. More significantly, C++ programs introduce objects as a new data class. An **object** is a collection of data and a set of operations, called **methods**, which manipulate the data. Unlike standard C functions, C++ methods are part of the object to which they belong, not the program.

Other more minor differences between C and C++ concern the name of the compiler (Linux calls the C++ compiler g++) and the suffix attached to a C++ source file, often .C or .cpp.

CREATING A SIMPLE C++ PROGRAM

To illustrate the similarity between C and C++, create a short program, simple.C, which displays a message on the screen exactly as the program simple.c does. The differences between the two languages start with the #include <iostream.h> instead of #include

<stdio.h> statement. The only other difference is the use of the cout I/O stream object instead of printf.

To write a C++ program:

1. Use the editor of your choice to create **simple.C**. Enter the following code:

```
//==========================================================
// Program Name: simple.C
// By:           Your initials here
// Purpose:      First program in C++ showing how to
//               produce output.
//==========================================================
#include <iostream.h>
void main(void)
{
   cout << "Welcome to C++ Programming\n";
}
```

2. Save the simple.C file and exit the editor.

3. Use the C++ compiler to create a program called sim_plus by typing **g++ simple.C -o sim_plus** and pressing **Enter**.

4. Run sim_plus. Your screen looks similar to Figure 10-14.

Figure 10-14   Output of the sim_plus program

Looking at the program, notice that C++ uses // to denote a comment line. (You can also use C's /* and */ to enclose comments in your C++ program.) Recall that comments help to identify and describe the program for all who need to review the program. Comments are ignored by the compiler and do not cause the computer to perform any action when the program runs.

Furthermore, note that the standard library functions for I/O are found in iostream.h instead of stdio.h, as in the C program. The only other difference between the C and C++ programs is the use of cout in the C++ program.

To continue the comparison between C and C++, you next see how a C++ program reads and displays the information in a file.

CREATING A C++ PROGRAM THAT READS A TEXT FILE

You learn further differences between C and C++ by entering the next C++ program, which reads a text file.

To create a C++ program that reads a text file:

1. Use the editor of your choice to create the file **fileread.C**. Enter this code:

```cpp
// A C++ file that reads the contents of a file.
#include <fstream.h>
void main(void)
{
    ifstream file("testfile");
    char record_in[256];
    if (file.fail())
        cout << "Error opening file.\n";
    else
    {
        while (!file.eof())
        {
            file.getline(record_in, sizeof(record_in));
            if (file.good())
                cout << record_in << endl;
        }
    }
}
```

2. Save the file, and exit the editor.

3. Compile the program, and save the executable code in fileread.

4. Test the fileread program. Your screen should appear similar to Figure 10-15.

10

There are several differences in the way C and C++ handle file operations. For example, the code:

```cpp
ifstream file ("testfile");
```

tells the compiler to use the ifstream class (object) to perform file input and output operations. The identifier file follows the class name. This statement is similar to the following C statement:

```cpp
FILE *file;
```

Figure 10-15   Results of the fileread program

Further, the file.fail() function is a part of the ifstream class and reports an invalid condition with the file access. The endl stream manipulator causes the screen output to skip a line.

The file.getline() function reads in a line from the file and stores it in the buffer record_in for subsequent processing. The file.good flag is a component of ifstream class and is used to determine if the record accessed contains data.

Now that you have an understanding of how C++ is similar to C, next you see how C++ provides additional enhancements.

How C++ Enhances C Functions

C++ creates a way to define a function so that it can handle multiple sets of criteria; this feature is called function overloading. Whereas C functions are quite flexible, function overloading adds considerably to the overall functions' use by expanding the function definition to accept varying kinds and numbers of parameters. During compilation, the C++ compiler determines which function to call based on the number and types of parameters the calling statement passes to the function. For example, in the next exercise you overload a function to access the system date in two different ways.

To use function overloading:

1. Use the editor of your choice to type the contents of **datestuf.C** (when you enter the statement **cout << "1. It is now " << asctime(tim);** make sure that you enter the number one after the first double quote and not the letter l):

```
// Program name: datestuf.C
// Purpose: shows you two ways to access the system date.
```

```
#include <iostream.h>
#include <time.h>
void display_time(const struct tm *tim)
{
    cout << "1. It is now " << asctime(tim);
}
void display_time(const time_t *tim)
{
    cout << "2. It is now " << ctime(tim);
}
void main(void)
{
    time_t tim = time(NULL);
    struct tm *ltim = localtime(&tim);
    display_time(ltim);
    display_time(&tim);
}
```

2. Save the file, and then exit the editor.

3. Compile datestuff.C by typing **g++ datestuf.C -o datestuf** and pressing **Enter**.

4. Test the program. Your screen should be similar to Figure 10-16.

10

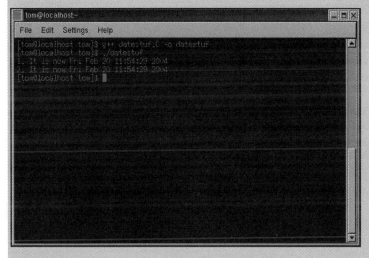

Figure 10-16   Results of the datestuf program

The #include <time.h> statement calls the C++ <time.h> library that consists of date types, structures, and functions for manipulating the time and date. Notice how the same function name is used for the different calls to the different date types that are contained in <time.h>. One is a structure (struct tm); the other is a date type for storing calendar time (time_t).

```
void display_time (const struct tm *tim)
void display_time (const time_t *tim)
```

In the line cout << "1. It is now " << asctime(tim); you see that asctime() is a function included in <time.h> that is used with struct tm to yield the local time and date. In the line cout << "2. It is now " << ctime(tim); you see that ctime() is a function in <time.h> that is used with time_t to yield the local time and date.

The program is able to distinguish which function to use based on the date type being passed to it.

```
Display_time(ltim);    Uses the structure type
Display_time(&tim);    Uses the time_t type
```

Now that you have learned the basic structure of a C++ program, you learn to create object-oriented programs with the C++ class construct.

SETTING UP A CLASS

One of the more difficult concepts to grasp is the use of the C++ class data structure. A data structure lets you create abstract data types. An abstract data type is one defined by the programmer for a specific programming task.

You might begin by thinking of the class as made up of members that interrelate to make the class perform like an object rather than just a normal structure. Its methods (which are like C functions) are part of the class and considered behaviors of the class. The similarity between a class and a structure is that both store related data. You can use structures in C++ just as you do in C. However, in C++ you can and should use a class when your program performs specific operations on the data. In the next activity, you create a class for an object called Cube when you want to compute the volume of any size cube.

To compute the volume of any size cube:

1. Use an editor to create the file, **cube.C**, and enter the code as follows:

```
//=========================================================
// Program Name: cube.C
// Purpose:      Show how to set up a class. The class is
//               called cube, and computes the volume
//               of a cube.
//=========================================================
#include <iostream.h>
//---- cube class
class Cube
{
    int height, width, depth; // private data members
public:
    // ---- constructor
    Cube(int ht, int wd, int dp)
```

```
        { height = ht; width = wd; depth = dp; }
    // ---- member function
    int volume()
      { return height * width * depth; }
};
void main(void)
{
    Cube thiscube(7, 8, 9);   // declare a Cube
    cout << thiscube.volume() << "\n";   // Compute &
    display volume
}
```

2. Save the cube.C file, and exit the editor.

3. Compile cube.C, and store the executable code in the file cube.

4. Test the cube program. Your screen should look similar to Figure 10-17.

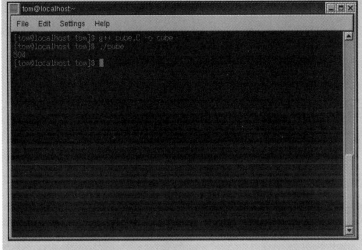

Figure 10-17   Output of the cube program

10

In looking at the program, the line "class Cube" tells the compiler that you are declaring a new class called Cube. The variables within the class are called private data members and can only be accessed by members of this class. If you create objects in your program of type Cube, then they can access Cube's private data members: height, width, and depth variables.

Constructors and other member functions can be defined outside, as well as inside, of a class definition. Unlike a structure, with all members accessible to a program, a class can have members that the program can directly access using the dot (.) operator (public members) and other members that the program cannot access directly (private members). To access the private data and methods, the program must call the public methods.

In this lesson you have learned the basic differences between C and C++ programs. You have written C++ programs that perform screen and keyboard I/O, as well as file operations. In addition, you have created a simple program with a class object. For summary information about using the C++ compiler, type man g++ at the command prompt; for more extensive documentation type info g++.

CHAPTER SUMMARY

- ◻ The C language concentrates on how best to create commands and expressions that can be elegantly formed from operators and operands.

- ◻ C programs often consist of separate source files called program modules that are compiled separately into object code and linked to the other object codes that make up the program.

- ◻ The C program structure begins with the execution of instructions located inside a main function that calls other functions that contain more instructions.

- ◻ The make utility is used to maintain the application's source files. The default make control file is called makefile.

- ◻ The major difference between C and C++ is that C follows procedural principles and C++ primarily follows object-oriented programming.

- ◻ The standard stream library used by C++ is iostream.h.

- ◻ C++ provides two statements for standard input and standard output: cin and cout, respectively. These are defined in the class libraries contained in <iostream.h>.

- ◻ C++ offers a way to define a function so that it can handle multiple sets of criteria. This function is called overloading.

- ◻ endl skips a line like "\n" does in the C language.

- ◻ You should use a class in C++ when your program performs specific operations on the data.

COMMAND SUMMARY

Please refer to the tables within the chapter for a command review.

REVIEW QUESTIONS

1. A file named averages.C contains _____.

   a. source code that can be compiled by the C++ compiler

   b. source code for a Perl script that is processed by the C++ compiler

   c. the compiled executable code for a C or C++ program

   d. only an external function that is linked to a C program

2. True or False: A compiler translates source code into object code.

3. In general, a make rule has a _____.

   a. header, a body, and a footer

   b. source, an object, and an executable

   c. target, dependencies, and an action

   d. target and an action

4. Which of the following are arithmetic operators in the C programming language?

   a. +

   b. <>

   c. *

   d. all of the above

   e. only a and c

5. In C, the statement #include <stdio.h> is an example of a _____.

   a. data type descriptor

   b. preprocessor directive

   c. modulus operator

   d. global variable declaration for a string

6. The name of a C function can be recognized because it is followed by _____.

   a. < >

   b. ( )

   c. ( );

   d. }

7. In C, a block of instructions is enclosed inside _____.

   a. < >

   b. ( )

   c. [ ]

   d. {}

10

8. True or False: One limitation of C++ is that it cannot handle function overloading, unlike C, which can.

9. In the C language statement FILE *account_file, account_file is declared as a
   _____.

   a. file consisting of integers

   b. file consisting of strings

   c. protected file

   d. file pointer

10. C++ has a stream object for displaying output, which is called _____.

    a. cout

    b. cin

    c. cerr

    d. printf

11. C++'s stream object that interacts between the user and computer to handle keyboard input is _____.

    a. cin

    b. cout

    c. cerr

    d. getchar

12. The library function for opening a file in C is _____.

    a. openl

    b. op

    c. fopen

    d. ofile

13. Up to how much memory is required for the int data type in C?

    a. 10 bytes

    b. 10 kilobytes

    c. 4 bytes

    d. 8 kilobytes

14. In a C program, character constants are enclosed in _____.

    a. #

    b. ''

    c. ()

    d. []

15. In C++, what do you call the structure that consists of a collection of data members and a set of methods?

    a. class

    b. array

    c. stream

    d. object

16. In C++, the _____ function can be used to test if there is an invalid condition in accessing a file, such as the file not being opened because it does not exist.

    a. fileget[]

    b. testfile<>

    c. file.fail()

    d. void.file()

17. The ampersand (&) that precedes a variable name is called the _____ operator.

    a. declarative-pointer

    b. address-of

    c. reference

    d. fixed-pointer

18. In C++ source code, comments are entered by _____.

    a. using two slashes "//" preceding the comment

    b. using the C /* and */ enclosures

    c. preceding the comment with ##

    d. all of the above

    e. only a and b

19. A makefile contains this line: abs_main.o : abs_main.c. The abs_main.o part of the line is the _____.

    a. option

    b. source

    c. command

    d. target

20. For what is the command, g++ used?

    a. It decrements the variable g.

    b. It increments the variable g.

    c. It calls the C++ compiler in Linux.

    d. It stores a string in C++.

21. Which statement would you find at the very beginning of a C++ program, just after the comment line(s)?

    a. #include <iostream.h>

    b. a do loop

    c. display_time[ltime]

    d. { return }

22. The C programming development tool used to facilitate compiling and maintaining the source code is the _____.

    a. precompiler

    b. make utility

    c. preprocessor

    d. memory manager

23. True or False: The notation ++ is an arithmetic operator in C.

24. The _____ statement closes the numbers_file in a C program.

    a. close("numbers_file")

    b. cl{numbers_file}_

    c. fclose(numbers_file)

    d. cfile[numbers_file}

25. What does the class Add C++ statement accomplish?

    a. It defines the class of printer on which to print.

    b. It tells the compiler that the program is declaring a new class called Add.

    c. It adds an alternate loop, similar to an else statement.

    d. It declares a variable type.

DISCOVERY EXERCISES

1. Write a C program named myname.c that displays your name on the screen.

2. Write a C program named calc.c that allows you to enter seven numbers. The program should calculate and display the sum and average of the numbers.

3. Write a program named condays.c that asks you to enter a number of days. The program should convert the number of days to a number of weeks and a number of months. Display the values.

4. Write a program named num_table.c that displays a table of the numbers 1 through 20, with the squares and cubes of the numbers.

5. Rewrite the program you created in Discovery Exercise 4 so that a function named display_table() displays the table of numbers. Next, again rewrite your solution, but enable the display_table() function to accept an argument. The argument is the starting value of the table. For example, if 5 is passed to the function as an argument, the function displays the values 5–25, along with their squares and cubes.

6. Further rewrite your solution to Discovery Exercise 5 so the display_table() function is in a separate file from function main. Compile and link the files.

7. Create a makefile to compile and create a program for the calc.c program you created in Discovery Exercise 2.

8. Write a small C++ program called nameaddr.C to display your name and address.

9. Refer to the C program, keyboard.c, presented in Lesson A, and write the equivalent program, called keyboard.C, in C++. Compile and test it.

10. Write a C++ program that does the following:

    ◻ Asks the user for values to be stored in the variables E and R.

    ◻ Multiplies E times R and stores the result in the variable I.

    ◻ If I is greater than 10, prints the message, "Value exceeds upper limit."

    ◻ If I is less than 1, prints the message, "Value does not meet the lower limit."

11. Create a C++ version of the num_table.c program you created in Discovery Exercise 4. Next, modify the new C++ num_table program so that it uses a different type of loop. For example, if the program now uses a for loop, rewrite it so it uses a while loop.

12. Create a C++ program with a class named circle. The class should have the following member variables: radius, diameter, and area. The constructor should accept one argument: the circle's radius. The constructor should calculate the diameter of the circle as radius * 2, and the area as 3.1416 * radius * radius. These values should be stored in the class's member variables. In addition, the class should have a member function that returns the circle's radius, a member function that returns the circle's diameter, and a member function that returns the circle's area. Demonstrate the class in a simple program.

10

11

THE X WINDOW SYSTEM

Traditionally, the programmers and staff at Dominion Consulting have used the UNIX Bash shell as their sole interface with the systems they operate. Management has now decided to use the X Window system, in addition to the Bash shell, on all in-house systems. Your supervisor asks you to instruct each staff member to:

- Configure a computer to launch the X Window system upon startup and implement the configuration
- Interact with the X Window system
- Personalize the desktop environment, and set up a password-protected screen saver
- Add a program to the X Window menu, and add an icon that invokes a program to the X Window desktop
- Use the Nautilus, Spreadsheet, Calendar, and gedit applications

◀ LESSON A ▶

STARTING AND NAVIGATING AN

X WINDOW SESSION

After completing this lesson, you should be able to:

- ♦ Describe the X Window system and its client/server model
- ♦ Understand the role of the Window Manager
- ♦ Start the X Window system
- ♦ Interact with the X Window system and use its components

WHAT IS THE X WINDOW SYSTEM?

The X Window system is a GUI that runs on Linux and many UNIX operating systems. Like Windows and the Macintosh operating systems, it provides an easy-to-use, graphical method of operating the computer. Programmers may also develop applications that run on the X Window system and support GUI components, such as windows, dialog boxes, buttons, and pull-down menus. Figure 11-1 shows a typical X Window screen with two windows open at the same time.

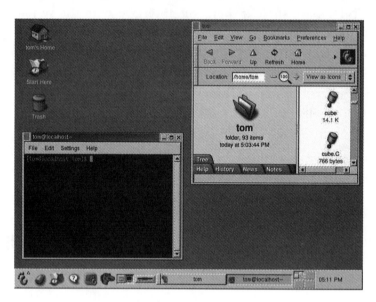

Figure 11-1 Typical X Window screen

The X Window system was originally developed at the Massachusetts Institute of Technology (MIT). It was created so different brands of hardware, running different variations of UNIX, would all look and feel the same to the user. It was also designed to run applications across a network consisting of different types of computers. The system developed at MIT, currently in its eleventh version, is appropriately called **X11**. At this writing there are six releases of X11, with the current release called R6 (X11R6). **XFree86** is a free version of X11 that was ported from non-PC-based UNIX computers to run on PCs. XFree86 is compatible with Linux, which is commonly used on PCs.

When you **port** software, you are adapting it from one type of computer or operating system to run on a different computer or operating system. A significant advantage of UNIX systems is that the operating systems and the associated software are generally adapted to work in nearly the same way when moved from less powerful (Intel-based) computers to more powerful computers (RISC-based), and vice versa. This characteristic is called **scalability**—the ability to port software to more or less powerful machines. See Appendix D for information about the types of computer hardware used with different versions of UNIX.

X WINDOW CLIENTS AND SERVERS

Although you can easily use the X Window system to run programs stored on your local computer, you can also run applications over a network. X Window uses a client/server model in which a program can run on one computer but display its output on another. For example, suppose you have a network with two computers: system A and system B. On system A, you can start and run a program that resides on system B. Although you see the program running in a window on your computer, it might actually be executing on system B. This interaction is transparent to you on system A; you may not know the program is actually running on a different computer. Additionally, systems A and B can be different types of computers, each running a different variation of UNIX.

In X Window network terminology, the desktop system from which you run a program is called the **X server**. The system that hosts and executes the program is called the **X client**.

In normal network terminology, the server is the system that hosts a program, and the client is the system run by the user. In X Window jargon, the terms client and server mean the opposite. The terms are reversed because the X Window server (on the desktop) performs operations requested by the client (on the host system). For example, the client might request that the server display a window or ask the server to move a window to a different position on the screen.

11

WINDOW MANAGERS

Like the UNIX operating system itself, the X Window system is layered and built from components. At the top layer is the **Window Manager**. The Window Manager controls how windows appear and how users control them. In many regards, the Window Manager is to the X Window system as the shell is to UNIX: each provides the user an interface to the underlying components.

Many Window Managers have been developed, and most of them are available for free. Linux supports over 50 different ones. Table 11-1 presents some common Window Managers currently in use.

Table 11-1 Common window managers

Window Manager	Description
AnotherLevel	Based on the fvwm Window Manager and commonly used with Red Hat Linux
CDE	Common Desktop Environment
Enlightenment	Popular Window Manager sometimes called E; also commonly used with Red Hat Linux

Table 11-1 Common window managers (continued)

Window Manager	Description
fvwm	Virtual Window Manager
fvwm95	Version of fvwm with a Windows 95 look and feel
gwm	Generic Window Manager (based on the Window Object Oriented Language—WOOL)
IceWM	Window Manager developed in C++
kwm	Window Manager used by KDE
olwm	Open Look Window Manager
mwm	Motif Window Manager
Oroborus	Theme-based Window Manager
sawfish	Compatible with the LISP programming language, and provides a desktop that has little clutter from icons
twm	Tab Window Manager or Tom's Window Manager
Window Maker	Provides support for the GNUstep Desktop Environment

Many of the Window Managers shown in Table 11-1 are compatible with the X Window GNOME desktop discussed in the next section. These Window Managers include Enlightenment, IceWM, fvwm, fvwm95, Oroborus, sawfish, and Window Maker.

Using GNOME

The **GNU Network Object Model Environment (GNOME)**, a product of the GNU project, is not a Window Manager, but a desktop environment that is used along with a Window Manager. Red Hat 7.2 installs the Enlightenment Window Manager when the GNOME (pronounced "guh-nome") interface is selected. GNOME is one of the packages that is checked by default when you install Red Hat 7.2. All examples in this chapter use Enlightenment and GNOME.

The GNU project is an organization that focuses on developing a free, UNIX-like, operating system named GNU. The Linux kernel is used in many GNU distributions. The project's Web site is *www.gnu.org*.

Using KDE

KDE is another popular desktop that is an alternative to GNOME or that can be installed along with GNOME. There is not room in this chapter to describe both desktops, but it is valuable for you to be aware of KDE.

Like GNOME, KDE is intended to provide UNIX users with a graphical point-and-click experience that is similar to Microsoft Windows and Mac OS. Both KDE and GNOME are compatible with X11 and with a variety of Window Managers—taking advantage of navigating UNIX through icons, windows, and other graphical features.

You can learn more about KDE by going to the KDE organization's Web site at *www.kde.com*. To learn about using KDE in the Red Hat Linux 7.2 environment, access Red Hat's Web site at *www.redhat.com* and search for the Red Hat 7.2 *Getting Started Guide*. See "Chapter 3: The KDE Desktop Environment."

STARTING THE X WINDOW SYSTEM

If your system does not start the X Window system automatically, you can start it by using the startx command.

To start the X Window System (if your system does not automatically start it):

1. Type **startx** and press **Enter**.

Your desktop should look similar to Figure 11-1, but with a Start Here window open instead of the two windows shown.

Configuring Linux to Automatically Start the X Window System

11

If your system does not automatically start the X Window system, you may configure it to do so. This is accomplished by modifying a line in the file /etc/inittab.

To view the contents of /etc/inittab:

1. Type **more /etc/inittab** and press **Enter**. Your screen looks similar to Figure 11-2.

2. Look for the line that reads:

   `id:3:initdefault`

3. Type **q** to exit the more command.

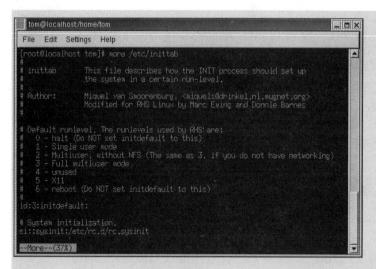

Figure 11-2   The/etc/inittab file

In Figure 11-2, the code establishes the operating system's default **run level**, or mode of operation, at 3. Run level 3 is full multi–user mode. In the next set of steps, you raise the run level to 5, (id:5:initdefault). Doing so causes the system to start in X11 mode, which automatically starts the X Window system.

Configuring your system requires superuser privileges. You must be able to log on as root to complete the following exercise.

You should be very careful any time you log on as root. The root user has privileges to alter any part of the system configuration and delete any file; you could accidentally corrupt the operating system.

The next exercise is optional and assumes you have been given permission to log on as root. Root access is required to modify the inittab file as described in the exercise.

To configure your system to start the X Window system automatically:

1. Log out of the system, and log back on as root (for this exercise you should not log into root using su from another account because you cannot use the init q command in that other account). Enter the root password, and press **Enter**.

2. Change your current working directory to /etc by typing **cd /etc** and pressing **Enter**.

3. Make a back-up copy of the inittab file by typing **cp inittab inittab.safe** and pressing **Enter**. With a backup of the file, you can restore the inittab.safe file to inittab, if you accidentally corrupt the inittab file.

4. Open the inittab file in vi or Emacs.

5. Change the line:

   `id:3:initdefault`

   `to`

   `id:5:initdefault`

6. Save the file, and exit the editor.

7. Verify your change by typing **more /etc/inittab** and pressing **Enter**.

8. Force the init program to reread its configuration file (inittab) and switch into run level 5 by typing **init q** and pressing **Enter**

9. After a few moments, you see the X Window System graphical login screen. Log on with your normal user name and password.

Now that you know how to start the X Window system, you are ready to learn to navigate it and control its common components.

INTERACTING WITH THE X WINDOW SYSTEM

11

You interact with the X Window environment through its many components. Figure 11-3 shows the opening GNOME screen, with its major components labeled.

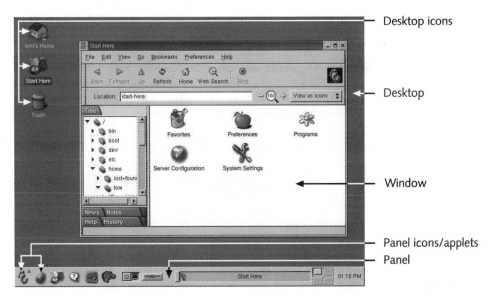

Figure 11-3   Major GNOME components

Here is a description of the components in Figure 11-3.

- *Icons*—There are a number of **icons**, or small images, on the screen. Each causes an action to take place when activated. You activate an icon by positioning the mouse pointer over it and clicking the left mouse button.

- *GNOME Panel*—This component is a strip that runs across the bottom of the screen, and includes a number of icons. Each icon invokes an **applet** when activated. An applet is a small application written specifically to be placed on the Panel.

- *Windows*—Every program, application, or applet that runs under the X Window system runs in a window. Windows have many of their own components, which you learn about in this chapter.

- *Desktop area*—This is the background area that holds the windows and icons you are working with during your X Window session.

Now that you can identify the major components of the GNOME screen, you learn to interact with each one.

Interacting with Windows

Windows have their own components, as shown in Figure 11-4.

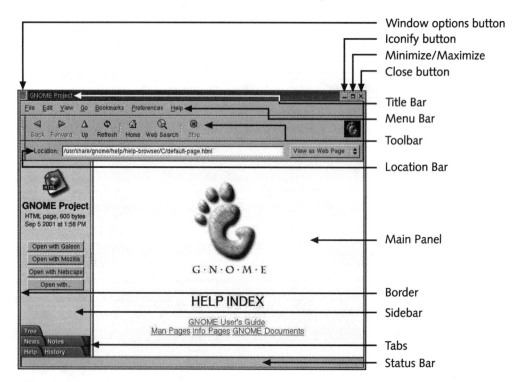

Figure 11-4   Window components

Here is a description of the window components.

- *Border*—Each window is outlined with a border.

- *Title Bar*—At the top of the window border is a Title Bar. The Title Bar lists the name of the window or the application running in the window.

- *Window options button*—Click this button to see a menu offering several useful window operations.

- *Iconify button*—Click this button to collapse the window into a small icon. The icon appears in a section of the Panel known as the Pager. The program in the window is still running, but is hidden from sight.

- *Minimize/Maximize button*—Click this button to alternately expand the window to fill the screen and reduce the window to its original size.

- *Close button*—Click this button to close the window and terminate the application running in it.

- *Sidebar*—Contains tabs that enable you to display information in the left portion of the window, such as a table of contents about help topics when you select the Help tab.

- *Tabs*—Click a tab to view information in the Sidebar—a view of the directory tree or the help contents, for example (the window for the Nautilus application discussed later in this chapter is the primary window that offers the sidebar and tabs).

- *Menu Bar*—Under the Title Bar you find menu items that are appropriate to the purpose of the window, such as a File menu from which you can open a new window or close the current one.

- *Toolbar*—Under the Menu Bar is the Toolbar, which contains buttons for activities appropriate to the window, such as a Back button to go back to the previous window display. In some cases, buttons are deactivated because they do not currently apply. For example, the Back and Forward buttons are deactivated in Figure 11-4 because this window has just been opened and thus there are no recent windows to go back or forward to.

- *Location Bar*—Enables you to access a particular location, such as a directory or a URL (address) for a Web site.

- *Scroll Bar*—If a window contains more information than it can display, you see a scroll bar (not displayed in Figure 11-4 because all of the information fits in the window). The scroll bar, which is similar to scroll bars in Microsoft Windows operating systems, lets you scroll through all the window's content.

- *Status Bar*—Shows status information related to your current actions, such the name and size of a file on which you have selected to work.

- *Main Panel*—Shows the main display information. For example, if the window is used to view files, you see the actual files in the Main Panel.

11

Many GNOME window components appear and function exactly like their counterparts in a Windows-based system, such as Windows 2000 or XP. If you are already comfortable with one of these systems, you should be comfortable with most window operations in GNOME.

You can configure a window to display or not display any of the following: SideBar, Toolbar, Location Bar, or Status Bar. To hide any or a combination of these bars, click the View menu in the Menu Bar, and select to hide the appropriate bar. Repeat this process until you have made all of your selections.

One of the basic window operations is resizing.

To practice resizing a window:

1. If you do not see a window titled "GNOME Project" on your screen, bring it up by clicking the large question mark icon on the Panel. If you do see the GNOME Project window, skip to Step 2.

2. Move the mouse pointer to the right edge of the window border. The pointer becomes a horizontal arrow with a bar. Click and hold the left mouse button while dragging the mouse pointer to the right. You see the window expand horizontally. Drag the mouse pointer back to the left, and the window shrinks horizontally. Release the mouse pointer to stop resizing the window.

3. Move the mouse pointer to the bottom edge of the screen. The pointer becomes a vertical arrow with a bar. Click and hold the left mouse button as you move the pointer, first up and then down. The window shrinks and expands vertically.

4. Move the mouse pointer to the lower-right corner of the window. The pointer becomes a slanted arrow surrounded by two bars. Click and hold the left mouse button while dragging the mouse pointer toward the lower-right corner of the screen. The window expands both horizontally and vertically. Drag the pointer back toward the upper-left corner of the screen, and the window shrinks horizontally and vertically.

5. Release the mouse pointer to stop resizing the window.

The GNOME Project window contains useful information on using GNOME. Its contents are hyperlinked in a manner similar to a Web page.

Other basic window operations are moving, shading, and unshading a window.

To practice moving, shading, and unshading a window:

1. Move the mouse pointer to the window's Title Bar.

2. Click and hold the left mouse button as you drag the mouse pointer across the screen. The window moves to follow the mouse pointer.

3. Release the mouse button to stop moving the window.

4. Shading a window means to collapse it, or "draw it up" into its Title Bar. Double-click the Title Bar to shade the window.

5. Double-click the Title Bar again to unshade the window.

Some window components offer context-sensitive, pop–up Help boxes. These are useful for discovering the purpose of a button or another component.

To practice using the pop-up Help boxes:

1. Position the mouse pointer on the window's Toolbar.

2. Move the pointer to a button that is activated (has regular print instead of lighter print), such as the Refresh or Home button.

After a brief moment, a box describing the purpose of that button pops up.

3. Perform this action with other active buttons on the window, and discover their use.

By now you have probably realized that pointing to an object on the screen and clicking the left button carries out most mouse operations. From this point forward, this action is called "clicking." Actions that require you to click the right mouse button are called "right-clicking."

The Iconify, Minimize/Maximize, and Close buttons are at the top right corner of the window. Use these to adjust the window's size and to terminate the window's application.

Refer to Figure 11-4 to review each button's location.

To practice using the Minimize, Maximize, and Close buttons:

1. Click the **Iconify** button. The window shrinks to an icon.

2. The GNOME Project is still running, however. Look at the Panel (located at the bottom of the screen). In a section known as the Pager, illustrated in Figure 11-5, you see a button for the GNOME Project.

Figure 11-5   The Pager in the GNOME Panel

3. Click the **GNOME Project** button in the Pager. You see the window reappear.

4. Click the **Minimize/Maximize** button. The window expands to fill the entire screen.

5. Click the **Minimize/Maximize** button again. The window shrinks back to its previous size.

6. Click the **Close** button. The application terminates, and its window disappears from the screen.

Finally, the Window Options button displays a menu of basic and advanced window operations. Some of the most useful are the following:

- The Minimize option makes the screen disappear into the Pager.

- The Maximize/Unmaximize option causes the window to expand to the full size of the screen or shrink back to its original size.

- The Close option terminates the application and closes the window.

- The Toggle option enables you to go between different display modes and options, such as between shading or unshading the window.

- The In group option is used to specify how to set up the contents in the window, such as in the Panel or in a different group of options (for a customized display).

- The Send window to option copies the window to a different workspace or location.

- The Stacking option is used to stack the window along with other open windows in the desktop.

- The Frame type option is used to determine how the window is framed in, such as having only a border at the top of the window.

- The Frame style option is used to give the window different types of appearances.

- The History option is used so that the window system can call up previously used positions, dimensions, or attributes.

You can customize the items in the Window Options menu, which may be different on your system.

To practice using the Window Options menu:

1. Click the **large question mark** icon on the Panel to open the GNOME Project, if it is not already open.

2. Click the **Window Option** button in the upper-left corner of the window.

3. Experiment with several options on the menu, particularly with Minimize, Maximize, Frame type, and Frame style.

4. When finished, close the **GNOME Project** window and any other open windows.

Interacting with the Panel

The Panel, which appears at the bottom of the GNOME screen, features the Pager (which you used in the previous section), a clock, and several icons. The icon at the left end of the Panel, shown in Figure 11-5, is the foot icon, or Main Menu.

Clicking the foot icon reveals the Main Menu, which offers several submenus.

To practice using the Main Menu:

1. Click the **foot** icon (Main Menu). You see the Main Menu, illustrated in Figure 11-6.

Figure 11-6   The Main Menu

2. Items followed by an arrow contain submenus. Position the mouse pointer over each of these to see the submenu appear.

3. Click the **Start Here** item. You see the Start Here window open.

4. Click the **Close** button on the Start Here window to close the application. (Note that depending on your computer's configuration, a Start Here window may open automatically when you launch the X Window GNOME desktop.)

To the right of the foot icon another set of icons appear. The icons that appear by default are:

- A lock for locking the screen so that no one can access the account without supplying the account's password

- A compass and map to launch the Start Here window

- The question mark to start the GNOME Project window

- A monitor screen with a foot over it to launch the Terminal emulation program for a terminal window from which to enter command-line commands

- A red lizard head to start Mozilla, which is an open systems browser that you can use for Internet access, for example

- Other icons for applications you have installed, such as an icon of a floppy drive for mounting and unmounting the floppy drive

- The Pager

- A clock (portable computers may also have a battery monitor before the clock)

You can determine the nature of any of icon on the Panel by pointing to it and reading the brief explanation.

To practice locking your screen and launching the Terminal emulation program:

1. Click the **lock** icon on the Panel. The system is now locked so that no one can access the console until entering an account name and password.

2. Enter your password and press **Enter**.

3. Click the **monitor and foot** icon to open the Terminal emulation program. A terminal window appears with a command prompt.

4. You cannot use the window unless it is active. If the Title Bar is blue, the window is active, and if it is grey, the window is not active. If necessary, click anywhere in the window to make it active. You see the Title Bar change to blue, if the window was not active.

5. Practice shell commands such as ls -l, date, and who in the window. Leave the window open.

   Notice the Pager on the Panel, which includes buttons for the currently started windows. On the right side of the Pager, next to the time display, there are two rows of blank buttons. On some systems, you see two buttons on two different rows. In other system, you see three or more buttons per row.

The GNOME Pager is an applet, which is a small application designed to run on the Panel. The right section of buttons in the Pager is the Desktop View. The Desktop View is typically divided into four areas. These are virtual desktops that you may switch to at any time. Currently, you are using the first desktop area, which is represented by the upper-left quadrant of the Desktop View.

To practice using the Desktop View:

1. Make sure the Terminal emulation program is running on your current desktop.

2. Your current desktop is represented by the upper-left square of the Desktop View. Click each of the other quadrants of the Desktop View. Notice that each appears as a clear desktop, with no windows open.

3. Click the **lower-right quadrant** of the Desktop View.

4. Click the **large question mark** icon on the Panel to open the GNOME Project window. Notice a small square in the lower-right quadrant of the Desktop View, approximating the position of the GNOME Project window.

5. Click the **upper-left quadrant** of the Desktop View to return to your original desktop. You see the Terminal window. Now, click the **lower-right square** to view the GNOME Project window instead of the Terminal window.

The far-left area of the Pager is the Applications View. It holds a button with an icon for each application that is running in the current desktop area. As you have already learned, an application that is represented by an icon may be restored to the desktop by clicking its icon in the Applications View.

Near the right edge of the Panel is the Clock applet. By default, the clock displays the date and time. You can modify its properties, however, by right-clicking it.

11

To modify the Clock applet properties:

1. Position the mouse pointer over the Clock applet's display, and click the right mouse button. You see a small shortcut menu.

2. Click **Properties**. You see the Clock properties window, shown in Figure 11-7.

3. The Time Format buttons allow you to choose between a 12- or 24-hour display. The Show date check box toggles the date display, or applet, on or off. The GMT time check box shows the GMT time. The UNIX time check box toggles the time display between hours and minutes, and the internal UNIX time format. The Internet time check box shows the time in Internet time format. Click the **24 hour** option button, and make sure that the checkmark is removed from both the **Show data in applet** and **Show date in tooltip** check boxes.

4. Click **OK**. The date no longer appears, and the time appears in 24-hour format.

5. Repeat the procedure in Steps 1 and 2 to open the Clock Properties window again.

6. Reset the Clock applet to display the time in a 12-hour format and show the date.

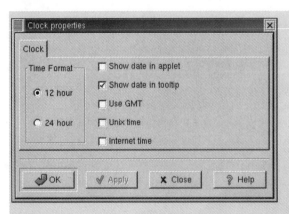

Figure 11-7   Clock properties window

If an application's window is very large or if you are using a low-resolution display, you may want to set the Panel to Auto hide.

Set the Panel to Auto hide:

1. Click the **foot** icon, point to **Panel**, point to **Properties**, point to **Hiding policy**, and click **Auto hide**.

2. Move the cursor above the Panel and it automatically hides. Now move the cursor to the bottom of the screen so that the Panel automatically appears.

3. Turn off Auto hide by clicking the **foot** icon, pointing to **Panel**, pointing to **Properties**, pointing to **Hiding policy**, and clicking **Explicit hide**.

Now that you have learned the basic techniques of interacting with the X Window system, and the GNOME desktop in particular, you are ready for more advanced operations. In the next lesson, you learn to run built-in X Window applications and configure your desktop.

◀ LESSON B ▶

RUNNING APPLICATIONS AND
CUSTOMIZING THE DESKTOP

After completing this lesson, you should be able to:

♦ Run built-in applications
♦ Use the Calendar application to keep appointments and a to-do list
♦ Start the Spreadsheet application and the gedit application
♦ Configure your desktop

RUNNING BUILT-IN APPLICATIONS

The staff at Dominion Consulting frequently needs programs for calendar, text editing, and spreadsheet operations. They could also benefit from a graphical file management utility. Your next task is to find built-in applications for all these needs.

For one of the demonstrations later in this lesson, you need to have available the encode program that you created in Chapter 10 and the ability to run the program.

Management has asked you to instruct the other staff members how to locate and execute programs that can help them do their jobs more productively. They also ask you to investigate using a graphical file management tool. You decide to consult the GNOME Project window and find references to a program called Nautilus that is used for file management. You also find out about a calendar program. Both programs are executed from the Main Menu.

To run the File Manager program:

1. Click the **foot** icon (**Main Menu**), point to **Programs**, point to **Applications**, and click **Nautilus**.

2. Click the **Tree** tab in the Sidebar of the window to view the file system as shown in Figure 11-8.

11

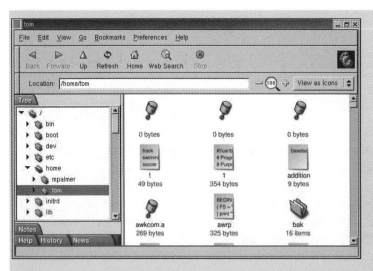

Figure 11-8   Nautilus application with the Tree tab selected

In Figure 11-8, the directories and file system tree appear in the left portion of the screen with folder icons. Notice that some directories have a dark arrow pointing to the right and others may have an arrow pointing down. The arrow pointing to the right shows that the directory's contents are not displayed in the left portion of the screen, while the arrow pointing down means that subdirectories under a particular directory are displayed.

3. Click the **right-pointing arrow** in front of the /etc directory. The tree in the left portion of the screen display expands to show all subdirectories that are immediately below the /etc directory. Use the scroll bar to move up the tree to view the beginning of the display of subdirectories under the /etc directory. Notice that the arrow in front of the /etc directory is now pointing down to indicate that you can now view the subdirectories under it.

4. Click the **down arrow** in front of the /etc directory. The view of the etc subdirectories collapses, and the down arrow turns into a right arrow.

5. The current working directory—which is likely to be your home directory when you first start Nautilus—appears highlighted in the directory tree diagram. The right area of the window, as shown in Figure 11-8, shows the files and subdirectories in the current working directory.

6. In the left portion of the screen, use the scroll bar to move up so you can view the /dev directory. Click the entry for **dev**. (Click the name dev, or click the folder icon next to the name.) Because there are so many entries in this directory, you may see a Too Many Files caution box that informs you there are too many files for Nautilus to handle at one time and thus some may not be displayed. If you see this box, click **OK**.

7. /dev is now your current working directory. You see the files and subdirectories in dev in the right window. Use the scroll bar on the right window to view more of the files and directories in /dev. Experiment by clicking several directories shown in the tree diagram. Notice that Nautilus does not allow you to enter a directory you do not have permission to enter. The toolbar, just below the Menu Bar, appears similar to Figure 11-9.

Figure 11-9   Nautilus toolbar

8. Click the **Home** button. Nautilus returns you to your home directory.

9. Click the **Back** button, and Nautilus takes you back to the last directory you opened, which is /dev, in this case (click OK if you see a caution box). If you were to click the Forward button at this point, you would return to your home directory.

10. Click the **Up** button to move up to the parent directory, which is the /home directory in this instance. Click **Home** to return to your home directory.

11. Click the **Refresh** button to redisplay the directory to which you are currently pointing. This button is particularly useful when you are using Nautilus to access a Web site and you need to refresh the screen because it is not displaying correctly. In addition, notice that you can use the Web Search button to search for information on a Web site and you can specify a Web site, such as *www.redhat.com*, in the Location Bar under the toolbar. Finally, the Stop button enables you to discontinue a Web search or activity.

12. By default, file listings appear in Icon view, as shown in Figure 11-8. You may also display them in a list. Click the **View** menu under the Title Bar, and click **View as List**. You now see a list of the directory contents in the right side of the window, with the items appearing smaller and listed up and down the screen.

13. Click the **Preferences** menu under the Title Bar, and click **Edit Preferences**. The Preferences window, similar to Figure 11-10, appears. One at a time, select each of the preference categories listed on the left side of the window, and notice the corresponding preferences that you can set in the right side of the window. Click **OK** when you are finished examining the preferences that you can set.

11

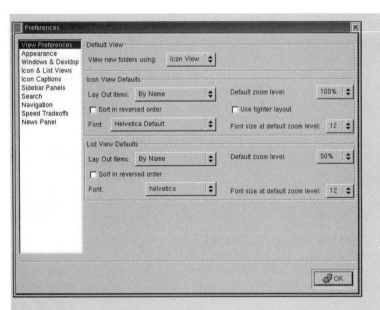

Figure 11-10   Preferences window

Nautilus also provides convenient methods for copying, renaming, and deleting files. These procedures must be part of your instruction to the other staff members at Dominion Consulting.

To copy, rename, and delete files:

1. Make sure Nautilus is still running. Before experimenting with file operations, create a set of empty files. Click the **Terminal emulation program** icon on the Panel to open a Terminal window and access the command prompt.

2. A terminal window appears with a command prompt. Click the window to activate it, if necessary, and make sure you are in your home directory.

3. Create the files test1, test2, and test3 by typing **touch test1 ; touch test2 ; touch test3** and pressing **Enter**.

4. Type **exit** and press **Enter** to close the Terminal window.

5. Use the Pager to redisplay the Nautilus window, if necessary. The Nautilus display should be updated because new files were created. Use the right side scroll bar to find the new files (if they are not displayed, click the **Refresh** button). Listings for the test1, test2, and test3 files appear in the right side of the window.

6. Select **test1** and right-click it. You see the shortcut menu. Notice all of the options on the menu that apply to working with this file, as shown in Figure 11-11.

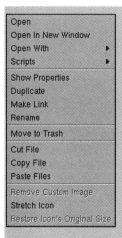

Figure 11-11   Shortcut menu

7. On the shortcut menu, click **Copy File**.

8. In the tree, click the **right arrow** in front of your home directory to open it, if it is not already opened. Click the **source** directory that you created earlier in this book.

9. Move the cursor to a blank spot in the file listing on the right side of the window. Right-click the blank spot, and click **Paste Files**. You should see the test1 file copied to the source directory. Now there is the original test1 file in your home directory and a copy of it in your source directory.

10. Find and right-click the **test1** file in the source directory. Delete the file by clicking **Move to Trash**.

11. Click the **Home** button to return to your home directory.

12. Use the scroll bar to find test2 and then click it. Click **Cut File**.

13. Click the **source** directory in the tree to open it (or click the Back button). Move the cursor to a blank spot in the File view on the right side of the screen, right-click the blank spot, and click **Paste Files**. Now the test2 file is moved from your home directory to your source directory. Verify this by finding the test2 file in your source directory via the scroll bar. Next, click the **Back** button to go to your home directory, and make sure that test2 is not there.

14. Find the test3 file in your home directory. Now you can rename it by right-clicking **test3** and clicking **Rename**.

15. Notice that the file name is now highlighted with a box around it. Type the name **test4** and press **Enter**. Notice that the name is now changed to test4.

11

16. Use the scroll bar, if necessary, to find the test1 and test4 files in your home directory. Press and hold **Ctrl** and click test1 and then click test4 so that both files are highlighted. Press the **Del** key to delete both files.

17. Open your source directory and delete the test2 file that you moved from your home directory.

When you are in the View as Icons mode (click the View menu and click View as Icons) you can select multiple files by holding down the Shift or Ctrl keys and then clicking each file you want to select. If you are in the View as List mode (click the View menu and click View as List), when you select a file and then hold down the Shift key while selecting another file, you also select all the files whose names appear between the two selected files. Also, while in the View as List mode, you can hold down the Ctrl key while selecting files to add them to your selection one at a time.

Nautilus also allows you to create new directories.

To create a directory using Nautilus:

1. Click your home directory in the tree. With Nautilus running, click **File** on the Menu Bar. The File menu appears.

2. Click **New Folder** on the File menu.

3. A new folder is created in the file listing in the window, with a highlighted box underneath that containing the text "untitled folder." Type **new-dir** and press **Enter**.

4. Move the scroll bar in the sidebar, if necessary, to locate your new directory. Notice also that the tree is updated to show your new directory under your home directory (make sure you have the home directory open to view its subdirectories).

In this section, you have learned the basic operations of Nautilus, which prove very helpful to the staff at Dominion Consulting as they learn to use the X Window system. In the next section, you explore the Calendar application.

Using the Calendar Application

The GNOME calendar application is easy to use and offers several helpful features. It allows you to set up appointments, create to-do lists, and view your calendar by the day, week, month, or year. This is a useful program for the rest of the staff at Dominion Consulting.

To use the Calendar application:

1. Click the **foot** icon in the Panel, point to **Programs**, point to **Applications**, and click **Calendar**. The Calendar window appears, as shown in Figure 11-12.

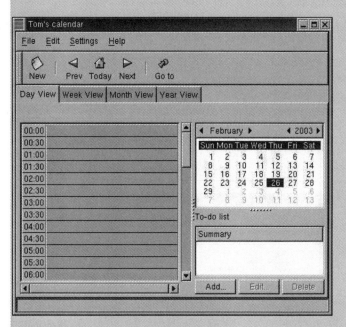

Figure 11-12   Calendar application

2. By default, the calendar appears in Day View. On the left, the day's hours appear in 30-minute increments. On the right, a calendar for the month appears, with today's date highlighted. Beneath the month's calendar is an empty to-do list. Click the **Week View** tab to see the display change to a weekly view. You see each day of the current week. The days of the month are shown in a box in the lower-left corner of the window.

3. Next, click the **Month View** tab. Now you see each day of the month with a box for every day, similar to a calendar you might hang on your wall.

4. Next, click the **Year View** tab. This displays shows small monthly calendars for every month in the current year.

5. Click the **Day View** tab to return to the Day View.

6. Before entering appointments in the calendar, you notice the times appear in 24-hour format. You need to change them to regular 12-hour format. Click **Settings** on the Menu Bar, and then click **Preferences**.

7. Notice that the 24-hour radio button is selected by default. Click the **12-hour (AM/PM)** option button.

11

8. Click **OK**. The times now appear in 12-hour format.

9. You need to enter an appointment you have with Carmen Scott later today. Click the **New** button on the Toolbar.

10. In the Summary: text box, type **Meeting with Carmen Scott to discuss projected staff development needs.**

11. You need to specify a starting time, which is 2:00 PM. Click the **up and down arrow** button across from the start time. A menu pops up. Position the mouse pointer over 2:00 PM, and then click **2:00 PM** on the submenu.

12. The meeting is scheduled to last until 3:30 PM. Click the **up and down arrow** button across from the end time. A menu pops up. Position the mouse pointer over 3:00 PM, and then click **3:30 PM** on the submenu. Your window should look similar to Figure 11-13.

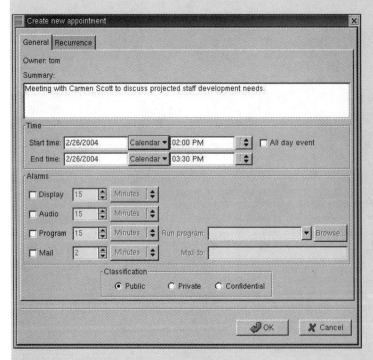

Figure 11-13   Creating a new appointment

13. Click **OK**. If a window appears informing you that the file has changed since it was loaded and asks if you want to continue, click **Yes**.

14. At 4:00 PM today, the sales team is scheduled to make a presentation. Click the **New** button on the Toolbar. The Create new appointment window appears. Type **Sales Team Presentation** in the Summary: text box.

15. Schedule the presentation to last from **4:00 PM** until **5:00 PM** (review Steps 11 and 12 for guidance on this task). Click **OK**.

16. Scroll the Day View to see the afternoon appointments. A window appears showing the two appointments that you have scheduled.

17. Click the **Week View** and then click the **Month View** tabs to see how the appointments appear in each of those views. (No appointments are visible in the Year View.)

18. You remember that Jean asked you to help her troubleshoot a printer problem. Add that to the to-do list by clicking the **Day View** tab and then clicking the **Add** button at the bottom of the window. The Create to-do item window appears.

19. In the Summary: text box, type **Troubleshoot printer**.

20. In the Due Date: text box, type tomorrow's date. Click the **up and down arrow** in the time box to set the time at 9:00. When you see the time menu, move the cursor to 9:00 AM and then click **9:00 AM** on the submenu. In the Priority box, use the down arrow to set the priority to **2**.

21. In the Item Comments: text box, type **Help Jean with her printer.** Your entries in the Create to-do item window box should look similar to Figure 11-14.

11

Figure 11-14   Creating a to-do list item

22. Click **OK**.

23. In the calendar window, notice that the item is added to the to-do list. Double-click **Troubleshoot printer** in the To-do list Summary box to review your note. Click **OK**.

24. Click the **Close** button to close the Calendar window.

When you started the Calendar application, you noticed an entry on the Applications menu named Gnumeric spreadsheet. You know the staff at Dominion Consulting need a spreadsheet program, so you decide to experiment briefly with it.

USING THE SPREADSHEET AND GEDIT APPLICATIONS

The Gnumeric spreadsheet application offers many functions that anyone with spreadsheet experience can find familiar. It supports a large set of math functions and comes with extensive online documentation. You decide to test a simple sum function to see if the spreadsheet works like other well-known spreadsheets.

To become familiar with the Gnumeric spreadsheet:

1. Click the **foot** icon to open the Main Menu, point to **Programs**, point to **Applications**, and click **Gnumeric**.

2. Enter the following values in the indicated cells, as illustrated in Figure 11-15:

    ```
    Cell A1: 147.90
    Cell A2: 459.20
    Cell A3: 712.35
    Cell A4: 923.88
    ```

    Notice that when you enter 147.90, Gnumeric displays 147.9 by default, omitting the trailing 0 in the hundredths position. However, when you enter 712.35, Gnumeric shows the full .35 in the hundredth position.

3. In cell A5, enter the function **=sum(a1:a4)** and press **Enter**. After you press Enter the sum, 2243.33 is displayed in cell A5.

4. Next, you decide to test the program's numeric formatting capabilities. Place the mouse pointer in cell A1.

5. Hold down the left mouse button, and drag the cursor to cell A5.

6. Release the mouse pointer. Cells A1 through A5 are now selected.

7. Click **Format** on the Menu Bar. A menu appears.

8. Click **Cells**. Make sure that the Number tab is selected. Notice the different number formats that you can select, such as General, Number, Currency, Accounting, Date, and so on.

9. Click the radio button in front of **Currency**.

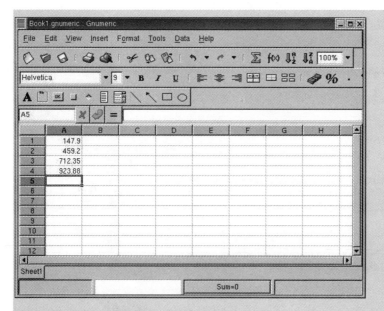

Figure 11-15   Gnumeric spreadsheet cell entries

10. Various currency format selections now appear in the bottom right portion of the window. Click the second listing that is in red, **$3210.21**.

11. Click the **OK** button. Notice that dollar signs now appear in front of each of the numbers in the spreadsheet.

You have determined that the Gnumeric spreadsheet application can be useful to the staff at Dominion, and you plan to include it in your training. Before you close the application, you decide to test the X Window system's ability to cut and paste text and objects. You recall seeing an editor named gedit, listed under the Applications menu. You decide to perform a simple cut and paste operation between the editor and the spreadsheet.

To demonstrate cut and paste:

1. Click the **foot** icon, point to **Programs**, point to **Applications**, and click **gedit**.

2. In the editor, type **Daily Revenue Figures**.

3. Press the **Home** key to move the cursor to the beginning of the line of text you just entered.

4. Press **Shift+End** to highlight the entire line of text. The gedit window should look similar to Figure 11-16.

5. Click the **Copy** button on the gedit Toolbar. The text is now copied into the Clipboard, which is a storage area for copied information.

11

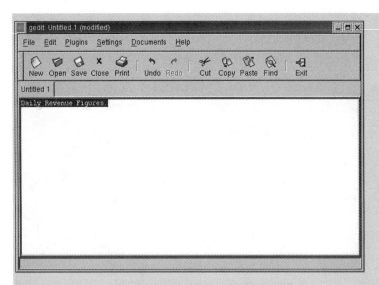

Figure 11-16   gedit editor with highlighted text

6. Activate the spreadsheet application by clicking any visible part of its window or clicking its icon in the Pager.

7. Before you paste in the text, move the cursor to cell A1. Click the **Insert** menu in Gnumeric and click **Rows** to add a blank row above the column of numbers.

8. Click cell **A1**, which is now empty.

9. Click **Edit** on the Menu Bar, and then click **Paste**. Your spreadsheet now looks similar to Figure 11-17.

10. Click the **File** menu, and click **Save As**. In the Selection box at the bottom of the window, type **Revenue** and press **OK** to save the spreadsheet in your home directory as the file Revenue.

11. Close the Gnumeric application, and then close the gedit application.

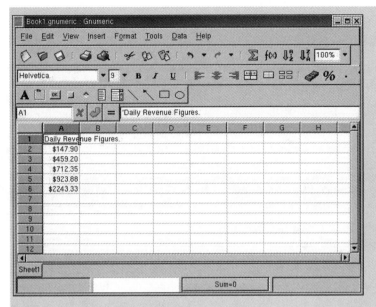

Figure 11-17   Spreadsheet with pasted text

One benefit the X Window system offers is the ability to work in multiple windows at the same time. For example, in the previous exercise you worked with the gedit application in one window while using the spreadsheet application in another window. You can also work in multiple terminal windows at once. For example, you can edit a C program in one window, compile it in another window, and execute it in third window.

To use multiple terminal windows in a production environment:

1. Click the **Terminal emulation program** icon on the Panel. A Terminal window opens. Click in the **Terminal window** to activate it, if is it not already activated.

2. Use the vi editor to open the **encode.c** source file you created in Chapter 10.

3. Click the **Terminal emulation program** icon on the Panel again. A second terminal window opens. Click in the new terminal window to activate it. Type **./encode** and press **Enter** to execute the encode program.

4. Viewing a program's source code while it is executing is a helpful debugging technique. Click the first Terminal window again to activate it, if necessary, and then move the window to a position on the screen so both terminal windows are visible. (You may need to move both windows to see them adequately.) By viewing both the program source code and the running program's output, you can see that the encode program is currently executing a scanf statement.

5. The encode program, which is running in the second Terminal window, asks you to enter a filename. To determine which file to encode, you want to open a third Terminal window, and view a directory listing. Click the **Terminal emulation program** icon on the Panel to open the third terminal window. Click in the new **Terminal window** to activate it, if necessary.

6. Type **ls** and press **Enter**.

7. Look at the list of files in the window, and decide which one to encrypt with the encode program. Click in the window in which the encode program is running, and type the filename.

8. The program next asks you to enter an output filename. Type **scrambled** and press **Enter**. The program ends, and returns to a command line.

9. Close the three terminal windows.

You have learned the primary operations of Nautilus and the Calendar application, and confirmed that the X Window system has spreadsheet and editor applications. You have also learned how to work in multiple windows at once. Now, you are ready to conduct your first training session with the staff at Dominion consulting.

CONFIGURING THE DESKTOP

You may customize many aspects of the X Window system. In this section, you learn to personalize your desktop environment by changing the background image and specifying a screen saver. Then you learn to configure the items on the Panel and add new applets to it. Finally, you learn to add your own items to the Main Menu.

Changing the Background

The background is the desktop area behind all windows and icons. You can change the color of the desktop or specify a graphic image (known as **wallpaper**) to be used as a background. You change the background by using the Main Menu.

To change the background:

1. Click the **foot** icon, point to **Programs**, point to **Settings**, point to **Desktop**, and click **Background**. You see the Background window, as shown in Figure 11–18.

2. You can choose a solid color, a gradient color, or an image to fill the background. First, set your background to a solid color. Make sure that **Solid** appears in the bar under Color. If it does not, click the **up and down arrow** button and click **Solid**. Next, click the **Primary Color** button just under the up and down arrows. You see the Pick a color window.

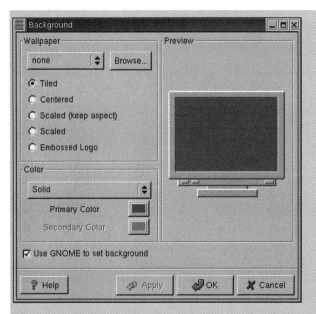

Figure 11-18   Background window

3. Look at the color wheel, and find a color you would like for your background. Click the area containing that color.

4. Click **OK**. You return to the Background window.

5. Next, try a gradient color. A gradient color gradually fades, or blends, from one color to another. Click the **up and down arrows** under Color and click **Vertical Gradient**.

6. Click the **Secondary Color** button. You see the Pick a Color window again.

7. Click another color in the color wheel, and click **OK**.

8. On the Background window, notice the example screen, which shows how your selections look.

9. Next, try a wallpaper image. Click the **Browse** button under the Wallpaper section. You see the Wallpaper Selection window. The directories and selections available to you depend on how Linux was installed on your system.

10. Double-click one of the directories listed in the Wallpaper Selection window, such as patterns. You see a list of filenames in the Files pane.

11. Click one of the listed filenames. A preview of the image appears in the preview pane. Each time you click a filename, you see a preview of the file.

12. Click an image you like, and click **OK**.

13. On the Background window, view the wallpaper image in the example screen.

14. Repeat Steps 2–13 until you find a color, gradient color, or wallpaper image you like. In the Background window click **OK**.

Changing the Screen Saver

You can use the X Window screen saver to deter unauthorized use of a server or workstation by requiring a password. When the screen saver is active, it does not deactivate until the user enters his or her login password. You use the Main Menu to configure the screen saver.

To select and configure a screen saver:

1. Click the **foot** icon, point to **Programs**, point to **Settings**, point to **Desktop**, and click **Screensaver**. You see the Screensaver window shown in Figure 11-19.

Figure 11-19   Screensaver window

2. From the Screen Saver list, click a screen saver, such as **3D Clock**. You see a preview of the screen saver in the Screen Saver Demo area.

3. In the Screen Saver Settings area, you can set the number of minutes that must elapse before the screen saver activates. Click in the **Start After** text box, and type **1**.

4. Click the **Require Password** button.

5. Click **OK** on the Screensaver window.

6. Do not type or move the mouse for one minute. When the screen saver activates, deactivate it by pressing a key or moving the mouse. A window appears requesting your password. Type your password, and press **Enter**.

7. Open the Screensaver window again (see Step 1), and adjust the screen saver time to **10** minutes (see Step 3).

8. Click **OK** to save your changes, and exit the Screensaver window.

Configuring the Panel

You may configure almost every aspect of the GNOME Panel. In this section, you learn to adjust the position of icons on the Panel, add new applets to the Panel, and add your own icon that launches a program.

To adjust the position of icons on the Panel:

1. Right-click an applet icon on the Panel, such as the question mark icon.

2. On the shortcut menu, click **Move**. The mouse pointer becomes a four-way arrow.

3. Drag the mouse pointer to the left or right. As you do, the icon moves along the Panel.

4. When you decide where you would like to move the icon, click the mouse. The icon stays in its current position.

11

You can use several other applets in addition to those that appear on the Panel by default. Management at Dominion Consulting has asked you to instruct the other staff how to add these applets to their Panels:

- The CPULoad applet displays an animated bar graph that indicates the usage of your machine's CPU.

- The Disk Usage applet displays a pie chart indicating the system's used and free disk space.

To add the CPULoad and Disk Usage applets to the Panel:

1. Position the mouse pointer over any part of the Panel not occupied by an icon, and right-click.

2. On the shortcut menu, point to **Panel**, point to **Add to Panel**, point to **Applet**, point to **Monitors**, and click **CPULoad**. (Alternatively you could click the **foot** icon, point to **Applets**, point to **Monitors**, and click **CPULoad**.)

A small square appears on the Panel, typically in the far-left position next to the foot icon. This is where the CPULoad animated bar graph appears when you use your system.

3. Use the alternate method for adding an applet to the Panel by clicking the **foot** icon, pointing to **Applets**, pointing to **Monitors**, and clicking **Disk Usage**.

A rectangular area appears on the Panel. This is where the disk usage pie chart appears, showing the system's used and free space.

4. To determine which color indicates used space and which indicates free space, right-click the area containing the pie chart.

5. On the shortcut menu, click **Properties**.

The Diskusage Settings window appears, as shown in Figure 11-20.

Figure 11-20   Diskusage Settings window

6. This window shows which colors indicate used and free disk space. Change the color settings by first clicking the **Used Diskspace** color button, selecting a new color from the color wheel, and clicking **OK**. Next click the **Free Diskspace** color button, select a new color from the color wheel, and click **OK**. When you're finished, click the **OK** button.

In addition to the available applets, you may also add your own programs as applets to the Panel. Management at Dominion Consulting has asked you to add the phoneadd script to the Panel. (You developed the phoneadd script in Chapters 6 and 7.)

To add the phoneadd script to the Panel as an applet:

1. You need to add a launcher applet to the Panel. A launcher executes another program when you click its icon. Click the **foot** icon, point to **Panel**, point to **Add to Panel**, and click **Launcher**. (Alternatively you can position the mouse pointer over an unoccupied area of the Panel, right-click, point to **Panel**, point to **Add to Panel**, and click **Launcher**.) You see the Create launcher applet window.

2. In the Name: text box, type **phoneadd Script**.

3. In the Comment: text box, type **Adds a phone number to the corp_phones file.**.

4. In the Command: text box, type **./phoneadd**.

5. Leave the Type: text box set to **Application**.

6. Click the **Run in Terminal** box. Your window should now look similar to Figure 11-21.

Figure 11-21 Create launcher applet window

7. Click the **Icon** button. The Choose an icon window appears.

8. Scroll through the set of icons. When you see one you would like to use for the phoneadd script, click it. Then click **OK**.

9. On the Create launcher applet window, click **OK**. The icon you selected appears on the Panel.

10. Position the mouse pointer over the phoneadd icon, but do not click it yet. After a moment, a Help box appears with the text you entered in the Create launcher applet Comment box.

11. Click the icon. The script file executes in a Terminal window. The window looks similar to Figure 11-22.

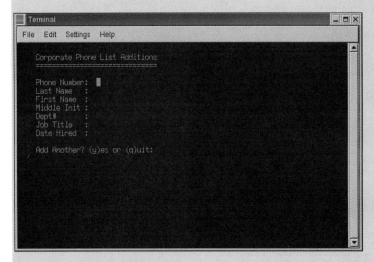

Figure 11-22   phoneadd script window

12. Test the application by entering your own name and false information for department number, job title, and date hired.

13. Finally, type **q** to quit the program. The terminal window closes.

In this section, you learned to customize the Panel by moving icons and adding applets and icons for your own programs. This makes your work easier, because the Panel displays frequently needed information (such as the amount of free disk space) and automates the execution of programs you run often. Next, you learn to further customize the desktop environment by adding your own programs to the Main Menu.

Adding Programs to the Main Menu

Management at Dominion Consulting is pleased that you have learned to add applications to the Panel. Now they ask you to instruct the staff to add applications to the Main Menu, as well. You decide to show them how to add the phoneadd script, so that it is accessible from both the Panel and the Main Menu.

To add the phoneadd script to the Main Menu:

1. Click the **foot** icon (Main Menu), point to **Programs**, point to **Settings**, and click **Menu editor.** You may see a temporary information box to show that the system is locating all of the current menus. The GNOME menu editor window appears.

2. Make sure that **Favorites (user menus)** is selected in the left area of the window, and then click the **New Item** button near the top of the window.

3. In the Name: text box, type **Add a Phone Number**.

4. In the Comment: text box, type **Adds a phone number to the corp_phones file.**

5. In the Command: text box, type **./phoneadd**.

6. Leave the Type: text box set to **Application**.

7. Check the **Run in Terminal** check box.

8. Click the **Icon** button. The Choose an icon window appears.

9. Select the same icon you selected when adding the phoneadd script to the Panel. Click **OK** to return to the GNOME menu editor window. Your screen should look similar to the one in Figure 11-23.

11

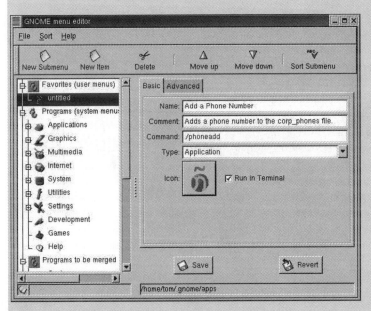

Figure 11-23   GNOME menu editor window

10. Click the **Save** button.

11. Close the GNOME menu editor window.

12. Click the **foot** icon and the Main Menu appears. Point to **Favorites** and click **Add a Phone Number**.

13. The phoneadd script executes in a Terminal window (refer to Figure 11-22). Close the terminal window (or type Ctrl+C).

The staff and management at Dominion Consulting are delighted to know how to customize their X Window system environment and add programs to the Panel and Main Menu. Executing frequently used applications from menu entries or icons is usually faster than using long commands. It also eliminates typing errors, such as misspelling a command or program name. These benefits can certainly increase productivity and make the staff's daily work easier.

SHUTTING DOWN FROM THE GNOME DESKTOP

Before you end the training, you want to show users how to properly shut down a system from the GNOME desktop. Proper shutdown is important to ensure that all files are closed and to protect the integrity of file systems. You teach users how to shutdown from the Main Menu.

To logoff and shutdown a system:

1. Click the **foot** icon, and click **Log out**.

2. In the Really log out? screen, notice that there are three options:

   - Logout, which does not shut down the system and enables you or another user to log back on.
   - Shut Down, which logs out and properly shuts down the system.
   - Reboot, which logs out, shuts down, and reboots the system.

3. When you are ready to shut down, you simply click the option button for **Shut Down**. To return to your work session, click **No**. To complete the shutdown, click **Yes**. After that, wait for the system to complete all of its shutdown steps through "power off" before you turn off the computer (many computers are automatically turned off by the system at this point).

CHAPTER SUMMARY

❑ The X Window system is a graphical user interface, or GUI, that runs on many UNIX and Linux systems. It allows users to run applications transparently across a network.

❐ The X Window system is built in layers. The top layer, with which the user interacts, is called the Window Manager. By default, Red Hat Linux 7.2 uses the Enlightenment Window Manager with the GNOME desktop environment.

❐ Use the startx command at the command line to start the X Window system. A line in the /etc/inittab file directs Linux to start the X Window system automatically.

❐ The GNOME environment consists of icons, a Panel, windows, and the desktop area.

❐ You resize, move, minimize, maximize, and close a window by interacting with its border, Title Bar, and buttons.

❐ The GNOME Panel provides access to the Main Menu and icons for applets. One applet is the Pager, which shows the virtual desktops and buttons for all the running applications. The Panel provides a button for hiding and displaying the Panel.

❐ You can configure the Clock applet to display the date and the time in 12-hour, 24-hour, or other formats.

❐ The Nautilus is a graphical application for managing your directories and files and for navigating the file system.

❐ In addition to Nautilus, the X Window system has several other built-in applications. Examples are a calendar program, a spreadsheet, and an editor.

❐ You can copy text from one window and paste it into another.

❐ You can customize the background of your display with a color or with a graphic image known as wallpaper.

❐ You may choose from a number of screen savers, which activate when there has been no keyboard or mouse activity after a specified period of time. The screen saver may be password protected, requiring the user to enter his or her password to deactivate it.

❐ You can customize the Panel by adding and moving applet icons. You can even add icons that launch your own programs.

❐ You can customize the Main Menu by adding entries that execute your own programs.

11

COMMAND SUMMARY

Review of the Chapter 11 Command	
Command	Purpose
startx	Starts the X Window System

REVIEW QUESTIONS

1. Which of the following is a free version of X11 that was ported to the PC and that runs on Linux?

   a. XFree86

   b. Windows X

   c. XClient

   d. Thin Client

2. In network terminology, the desktop system from which the user runs a program is called the _____.

   a. Y client

   b. X server

   c. Y server

   d. X client

3. How do you shut down the operating system from the GNOME desktop?

   a. Press Ctrl+X.

   b. Click the shutdown icon on the desktop.

   c. Click the foot icon, click Log out, click Shut Down, and click Yes.

   d. Click the foot icon and click Shutdown.

4. The _____ file directs UNIX to automatically start the X Window system.

   a. /usr/xwindow

   b. /etc/xwindow

   c. /root/inittab

   d. /etc/inittab

5. How do you view the directories on a system via Nautilus, after you start this application window?

   a. Click the Tools menu and click Tree.

   b. Click the Tree tab.

   c. Click the Tree button in the Toolbar.

   d. Click the History tab.

6. The Minimize/Maximize button on a window causes the window to

   _____.

   a. alternately expand to fill the screen and shrink to its original size

   b. close

   c. shrink to a smaller size

   d. collapse into a small icon in the Pager

7. True or False: The Window Manager provides the user an interface to the underlying components.

8. Which of the following views are available in the Calendar application?

    a. Week View

    b. Year View

    c. Month View

    d. all of the above

    e. none of the above because this application only hosts a Day View

9. What tool enables you to establish the background color of the desktop?

    a. resolution tool

    b. color wheel

    c. rainbow generator

    d. display icon

10. A(n) _____ is a small application written to be placed on the Panel.

    a. smallapp

    b. GNOME box

    c. applet

    d. script

11. True or False: GNU Network Object Model Environment (GNOME) is a third-generation Window Manager.

12. Run level _____ is full multi-user mode in the system initialization file.

    a. 6

    b. 5

    c. 4

    d. 3

13. What tool enables you to choose the wallpaper for your desktop?

    a. Display icon

    b. Desktop icon

    c. Background window

    d. Settings dialog box

14. The Pager's Application View shows _____.

    a. button icons for all applications currently running

    b. a history of recently run applications that have been closed

    c. a list of all available applications on the system disk

    d. how to execute an application

11

15. True or False: In UNIX, Windows can have many of their own components.

16. You can invoke a window titled "GNOME Project" on your screen by clicking the large _____ icon on the Panel.

    a. exclamation point

    b. question mark

    c. stop icon

    d. green traffic light

17. The _____ enables you to place your own application onto a menu.

    a. menu editor

    b. menu installer

    c. favorites tool

    d. initialization file

18. True or False: Most window components offer context-sensitive pop-up Help boxes.

19. You are working with a user who believes he has broken a window because he only sees the Title Bar for it. How can he most easily fix it?

    a. Close the Title Bar, and reopen the window.

    b. Press Ctrl+Atl.

    c. Double-click the Title Bar.

    d. Reboot the operating system because this is a sign that it is corrupted.

20. In Nautilus, when you are in the View as List mode, you can select a file and then hold down the _____ key while selecting another file, so that all the files between the two selected files are also selected.

    a. F1

    b. Ctrl

    c. Alt

    d. Shift

21. In Gnumeric, what formula enables you to sum the numbers in the B column that start on row 2 and end at row 40?

    a. total b:2,40

    b. add B:2,40

    c. =sum(b2:b40)

    d. +total(b2,b40)

22. How can you create a reminder to purchase paper supplies first thing in the morning?

    a. Add the reminder to the Scheduled Tasks application.

    b. Add the reminder to the to-do list in the Calendar application.

    c. Use the Launcher to create a pop-up window.

    d. Use the scheduler feature in the gedit application.

23. How can you adjust the position of icons that are on the Panel?

    a. Right-click an icon, and click Move.

    b. Left-click an icon and drag it.

    c. Right-click an icon, click Properties, and specify the location on the Panel.

    d. Delete an icon and specify its Panel location when you recreate it.

24. Which of the following can you accomplish using Nautilus?

    a. copy a file

    b. delete a file

    c. rename a file

    d. all of the above

    e. only a and b

25. Which of the following enables you to constantly monitor how much free space is left on your hard disk?

    a. DiskLoad

    b. Monitor

    c. Disk Usage

    d. all of the above

    e. only b and c

DISCOVERY EXERCISES

1. Start the X Window system on your computer. Open the GNOME Project window, and perform these window operations:

    ❐ Shade and unshade the window

    ❐ Maximize the window

    ❐ Minimize the window

    ❐ Iconify the window

    ❐ Restore the window from the Pager

    ❐ Close the window

2. Open the GNOME Project window while the upper-left quadrant of the Pager's virtual desktop view is active. Describe how the icon for the current desktop changes.

3. Activate the upper-right quadrant of the Pager's desktop view, and open a Terminal window. Practice a shell command, such as ls.

4. Activate the lower-left quadrant of the Pager's desktop view, and open another Terminal window. Use the who command to see a list of current users. Note how many times you are listed.

5. Change the Clock applet so that the time appears in 24-hour format and the date does not appear.

6. Open a Terminal window in the current desktop. Next, open a Nautilus window in the same desktop. How does the icon for the current desktop indicate that two windows are open?

7. With the Terminal window and Nautilus still open, note the button icons in the Pager's application view. Change your current desktop by selecting the lower-right quadrant of the Pager's desktop view. Describe the contents of the Application view now.

8. With the Nautilus window open, use the mouse to resize the window as small as possible. Next, use the Minimize/Maximize button to expand the window to full screen. Click the Minimize/Maximize button again. To what size did the window shrink?

9. Display the contents of the /etc/inittab file. What comments describe the available run levels?

10. Open a Terminal window and create these empty files in your home directory: file1, file2, and file3. Next perform these activities:

    ◻ Use Nautilus to create the old_files directory, and then to copy the files you created (file1, file2, and file3) into the old_files directory.

    ◻ Use Nautilus to move the files that are in the old_files directory into the new_files directory (create the new_files directory first).

    ◻ Use Nautilus to delete file1, file2, and file3 in your home directory.

11. Change Nautilus so that you view files in a list instead of as icons (or vice versa).

12. Change the preferences in Nautilus so that the application has a different appearance.

13. Reconfigure the desktop background so it is your favorite color, and configure a gradient.

14. Open the Calendar application and add these appointments:

   ❏ Meeting with insurance agent, today at 4:30 PM

   ❏ Meeting with VP of sales tomorrow at 10:00 AM

   ❏ Meeting with Jim today at 11:00 AM

   ❏ Meeting with Sally tomorrow at 2:00 PM

15. After you enter the appointments listed in Discovery Exercise 14, look at them in the Day, Week, and Month Views.

16. Think of two errands that you have to perform tomorrow, and enter them in the Calendar's to-do list.

17. Use vi or Emacs to create a script file called list. The file should contain the commands -l. Then do the following:

   ❏ Create an icon on the Panel that launches the list script file you created.

   ❏ Run the list script file from the icon you created on the Panel. Does the directory listing scroll by too fast to see? Modify the script file so the user must press Enter after the list is displayed. This pauses the output, so you have time to see it.

   ❏ Add an entry to the Main Menu under Programs and Applications for the list script file.

18. Add the CPU/MEM Usage and MemLoad applets to the Panel. What are some other applets that you can add?

19. Remove the MemLoad applet from the Panel that you added in Discovery Exercise 18.

20. Open the Gnumeric Spreadsheet, create a spreadsheet named ss_practice, and enter these values:

   ❏ 492.8 in cell A1

   ❏ 224.7 in cell A2

   ❏ 881.5 in cell A3

   ❏ 42 in cell A4

   ❏ 95.18 in cell A5

   ❏ 7822.10 in cell A6

   ❏ 172.54 in cell A7

   In cell B1, enter the function that sums cells A1 through A7.

21. After you enter the spreadsheet values listed in Discovery Exercise 20, experiment with the Accounting, Date, Time, Percentage, Fraction, and Scientific formats.

22. Find a screen saver that you have not used before, and configure it for use. Set up the screen saver to have a password and to start after 15 minutes of inactivity.

11

A

HOW TO ACCESS A UNIX/LINUX OPERATING SYSTEM

This appendix explains your options for using the Telnet protocol to remotely access a computer running UNIX or Linux. Applications or programs that can be used in a Telnet session are not graphical, use text only, and tend to be either administrative tools or older applications.

As an example of using the Telnet protocol, many universities have a class scheduling system that requires a student to sign onto the system and set his or her schedule. This access is provided via the Telnet protocol. As another example, many businesses use the Telnet protocol when they need to centralize a particular text-mode application, such as the ones banks use for their tellers. Additionally, administrators use the Telnet protocol for remote access to systems for configuring, troubleshooting, and system administration.

In this appendix, you'll learn how to access a UNIX/Linux system using the following:

♦ A dumb terminal

♦ A computer running a Microsoft Windows OS

♦ A computer running UNIX or Linux

Before we jump into these different uses, a review of Telnet is in order. Let's do that next.

OVERVIEW OF TELNET

The Telnet protocol specifies how sessions are created, how data is passed, and how an interactive shell or prompt is displayed to the remote user. Telnet has been around a long time, with relatively few changes to the protocol.

Telnet has been implemented on a huge variety of systems for the express purpose of establishing a session on a remote host. The disparate systems that use Telnet all adhere to a standard that determines how a system sends or generates the correct signals from the Telnet client to the corresponding Telnet daemon or server. Both the client and the server must understand and support at least a base level of the protocol in order for communications to be established and a session granted.

Systems normally run Telnet over TCP/IP connections, with a few systems supporting Telnet over IPX (Novell's base networking protocol). Regardless of the traditional role of the systems, such as a user's workstation and a file server, all UNIX/Linux systems have the capability to be used as a client and to perform the role of a server. In fact, it's very common for an administrator to connect from a server-class machine to another server-class machine using a Telnet client for administrative work. The only restrictions that exist are the software running on the machines and the security measures that have been implemented.

Telnet uses TCP/IP port 23 to send and receive its data. A Windows NT 4.0, Windows 2000, or Windows XP computer commonly stores its port and procotol information in the %systemroot%\system32\drivers\etc\services file. This file shows the name of a given service, the port(s) it uses, and the Transport layer protocols associated with it (UDP or TCP). Most services that make a session, transfer data, or need some certainty of delivery use TCP. Services that don't need any guarantee of delivery, such as broadcasts or multicasts, use the UDP protocol.

ACCESSING UNIX/LINUX COMPUTERS FROM AN ATTACHED TERMINAL

When you use a terminal to access a UNIX/Linux system, you only need to turn on the terminal and press a key on the keyboard to begin your session. At the login prompt, enter your assigned user name and password to begin your session. Depending on your terminal and administrator, you may see either a graphical user interface (GUI) or text-mode login screen.

One advantage of using a terminal is the relative ease of beginning the session. Another advantage is how convenient it is to replace a malfunctioning terminal and have the user continue a session, virtually uninterrupted.

ACCESSING A UNIX/LINUX SYSTEM FROM A MICROSOFT WINDOWS COMPUTER

When accessing a UNIX/Linux system from a computer running Microsoft Windows, you can use various utilities to help you. They range from simple and free to complex and expensive. Let's discuss each in turn.

Simple and Free

All versions of Microsoft Windows, from Windows for Workgroups to Windows XP, have access to TCP/IP networking, either natively or as an add-on. If the computer already has TCP/IP loaded, you can use the existing address and utilities to attach to a remote UNIX/Linux computer.

For example, if you are using a Microsoft Windows 98 computer in the computer lab at your school to access the Internet, it's very likely that computer can also be used, as is, to Telnet to a remote host. To successfully connect, you would need to know the IP address of the UNIX/Linux computer that allows Telnet sessions.

In the following steps, you practice connecting to a Red Hat Linux computer on your network. To accomplish this project, a computer running Red Hat Linux needs to be connected to the network, with the firewall on the medium setting and customized for FTP access, or with no firewall set up at all. The system administrator can configure the firewall from the root account by running the lokkit program from the command prompt. In addition, you will need an account on the Red Hat Linux computer to which you connect. You can use Windows 95, Windows 98, Windows NT, Windows 2000, or Windows XP on the workstation that you use to remotely connect to the Red Hat Linux computer.

To connect to a Red Hat Linux computer from a Windows-based client over a network:

1. Find out the IP address, such as 127.0.10.4, of the Red Hat Linux computer to which you will connect, or determine the host name of the computer. (If you have access to the root account for the computer, log onto the console as **root**, open a Terminal window, and type **ifconfig**. Look for the data area that starts with eth0. The inet addr field contains the IP address. Log off the root account.)

2. In your Windows-based client, such as Windows XP Professional, click the **Start** button, and then click **Run** to open the Run dialog box.

3. In the Run dialog box, type **telnet *IPaddress***, where *IPaddress* is the IP address you determined in Step 1, and then press **Enter**. See Figure A-1.

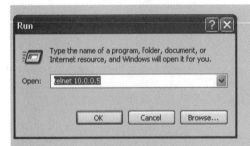

Figure A-1   Starting up telnet

4. You can see the connection being made, and then a login prompt appears. The prompt is similar to the one shown in Figure A-2.

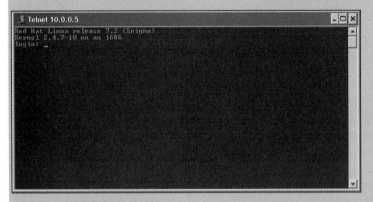

Figure A-2   Login prompt for a remote session

5. Type your user account name and press **Enter**.

6. Next, type your password and press **Enter**.

7. Type **ls –l** and press **Enter** at the command prompt to view files in your home directory.

8. Type **exit** at the command prompt and press **Enter** to close the session.

If you do not have access to a Red Hat Linux computer on your network, try Telneting to Detriot Free-Net at *http://detriot.freenet.org*. There you can create a new account using the instructions on the login screen.

More Features, But Still Free

Microsoft's included Telnet client is very simple, with almost no options, and it works for simple tasks. However, there are times when you are connected to a computer that has some special font requirements or terminal types. In this situation, you want to use a more full-featured client—such as PuTTY—to connect.

PuTTY is free and licensed under the Massachusetts Institute of Technology's MIT License. You can modify, alter, and redistribute it as long as you follow the restrictions for the license. You can download the program at *www.chiark.greenend.org.uk/~sgtatham/putty/*. After you have downloaded the Puttytel.exe file, place the program in its own directory, preferably c:\putty.

Using PuTTY to connect to a remote system:

1. Click **Start**, click **Run**, and then type **c:\putty\puttytel** to start the program. See Figure A-3 to make sure you've got the right tool.

2. Click the **Session** item in the left panel under Category. This shows the basic options for running PuTTY.

3. In the Host Name dialog box, type the host name or IP address of the Red Hat computer you connected to in the previous Hands-on Project in this appendix. You can also type **detroit.freenet.org**, if you connected to that computer. Leave the port set to 23.

4. Leave the Protocol option button set to Telnet.

5. Click the **Saved Sessions** text box, and type **Test session**.

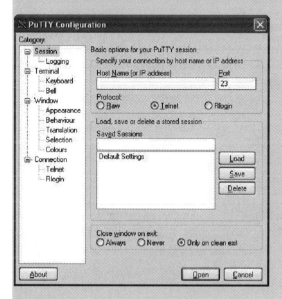

Figure A-3   PuTTY Configuration Screen

6. Now click the **Window** item in the left panel under Category. This shows the options for the number of rows and columns. We we won't change this information.

7. To make viewing long listings much easier, change the Lines of Scrollback text box from 200 to **500**.

8. Click the **Appearance** item under Window in the left panel for more options.

9. Click the **Change** button to see the available fonts and sizes.

10. Choose a font size of **12** point. Click **OK** to return the Appearance dialog box. Switch to the Session window.

11. Click the **Save** button to save your settings.

12. At this point, your selection should appear in the list for Saved Sessions. You can click the **Open** button to initiate your session with the Detroit Free-Net.

13. If you want to alter any of your settings, click the upper-left corner of the program window and you see the menu shown in Figure A-4.

14. Exit the session.

Figure A-4 Accessing the settings menu

While still free, PuTTY makes life a lot easier by allowing you to use fonts, colors, descriptive titles, and many other options. You can also download the source code, and modify it to suit your needs.

Commercial Telnet Options

Many vendors offer a suite of remote access tools, usually consisting of a NFS client or server and Telnet and File Transfer Protocol (FTP) utilities. Some of the best are WRQ's Reflection suite, Hummingbird's Exceed and Host Explorer suites, and Attachmate's EXTRA series of applications. These range from less than $100 to over $500 per client.

USING A UNIX/LINUX COMPUTER TO ACCESS OTHER UNIX/LINUX COMPUTERS VIA TELNET

Because you are using the same general program and access structure, connecting to a UNIX/Linux Telnet server from a UNIX/Linux client is relatively uncomplicated. The Telnet client application is almost always installed and available on the workstation, unless specifically uninstalled or removed as a security measure.

Where is My Telnet Client Program?

Finding the Telnet client on your UNIX/Linux computer is quite simple. On a UNIX/Linux computer, use the which command to see the first occurrence of a Telnet executable in your path. The which command also shows you all instances of any queried command in your path, for example:

```
[root@localhost root]# which -a telnet
/usr/kerberos/bin/telnet
/usr/bin/telnet
[root@localhost root]#
```

The output from this command shows two instances of the telnet command. The first in the path (the Kerberos version) is executed by default. The Telnet binary in the /usr/bin location exists for systems that don't have Kerberos installed. Kerberos is a security mechanism that helps systems and users authenticate their username and password across a wide area network (WAN) or the Internet, without the usual security risks associated with programs such as Telnet and FTP.

Connecting to the Remote Server

In this project, you connect to a remote computer from a UNIX/Linux client. When you make your connection, use the IP address of the remote Red Hat Linux computer from the first Hands-on Project in this appendix. You can also log on to *http://detroit.freenet.org*, if you connected to that remote site earlier.

To connect using a UNIX/Linux Telnet client:

1. Open a Terminal window on your UNIX/Linux system. Type **telnet** plus the IP address of the Red Hat Linux computer you connected to earlier, or type **detroit.freenet.org**. Press **Enter**.

2. You see the welcome and login screens as in previous examples. If you are asked for the terminal type, it will be similar to the cryptic message in Figure A-5. The reason for the confusion is that your computer may have a value in its environment that doesn't match a defined terminal type on the remote host. Type a valid terminal type, such as **vt220** or **vt100** and then press **Enter**.

Figure A-5   Type prompt from *http://detroit.freenet.org*

3. On most Linux systems, you can set your default session's terminal type by opening the .bash_profile file in your home directory and then adding the line shown in Figure A-6. When you connect, your terminal type, which is stored in the $TERM variable, is passed to the remote system, allowing you to connect normally.

Figure A-6   Editing the .bash_profile

4. End the session.

As we have just seen in the previous exercises, connecting to remote computers via Telnet is a valuable way to gain access to services located on remote computers. Many system administrators and users check their e-mail, perform administrative tasks, and compile programs via such remote connections.

A

Appendix

B

Syntax Guide to UNIX Commands

This appendix is a quick reference for essential Unix utilities available on most systems.

Table B-1 lists the commands alphabetically, including the command name, its purpose, and any useful options. Table B-2 lists the UNIX utilities by category. Table B-3 summarizes the vi editor commands, while Table B-4 summarizes the emacs editor commands. The UNIX command syntax uses the format diagrammed in Figure B-1.

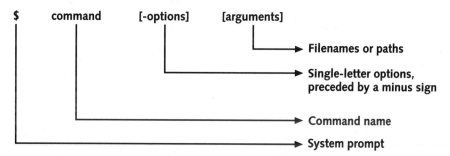

Figure B-1 Command syntax format

Table B-1   Common UNIX commands

Command	Purpose	Useful Options and Examples
alias	Create an alias for a command	Created by editing the .bashrc file; example: **alias dir='ls -1'**
awk	Invoke a pattern-scanning and processing language operation	**-f** indicates code is coming from a disk file, not the keyboard **-F** specifies the field separator
cal	Show the system calendar for a specified year or month	**-1** shows a single month **-3** shows three months beginning with the previous month **-j** displays the calendar in Julian date format
cat	Concatenate or display files	**-n** displays line numbers
cd	Change directories	**cd** by itself takes the user to his or her home directory
chmod	Change security mode of a file or directory (r: read, w: write, x: executable); set file permissions for specified users (u: user, g: group, o: others, a: all)	**chmod a+x** sets the execute bit for owner, group, and other (all)
clear	Clear the screen	Commonly aliased to **cls**; see the alias command
comm	Compare sorted files and show differences	**comm *file1* *file2*** compares the files line by line **-1** does not display unique lines in the first file **-2** does not display unique lines in the second file **-3** does not display unique lines in both files
cp	Copy files from one directory to another	**-i** requests confirmation if the target file already exists **-r** copies directories to a new directory
cut	Select and extract columns or fields from a file	**-c** specifies the character position **-d** specifies the field separator **-f** specifies the field position
date	Display the system date	**-u** displays the time in Greenwich Mean Time
diff	Compare and select differences in two files or directories	**diff *ic1* *dir2*** compares the file entries in both directories and shows only the missing files for each directory
. (dot)	Represents the current directory (the "." is a link to the inode for the current directory)	Used mostly in specifying that something happen in the current directory; example: **cp *dir/file* .** copies the file to the current director

Table B-1   Common UNIX commands (continued)

Command	Purpose	Useful Options and Examples
.. (dot dot)	Represents the parent directory (the ".." is a link to the inode for the parent directory)	Used for changing to a different directory, either the parent of the current (**cd ..**) or up one directory and down a different tree (**cd ../dir2/dir3**)
echo	Display the specified arguments on the output device	**echo $VAR**, where *VAR* is the variable name, echos the data from an environment variable to standard output; can also be used in scripts and programs
emacs	Start the emacs editor	
exit or logout	Log out of your current session	**Ctrl+d** also logs the user out of a session or a subshell and back to the parent shell
export	Export a specified list of variables to other shells Make a variable an environment variable	
find	Locate files that match a given value	**-amin *n*** finds files accessed more recently than *n* minutes ago **-atime *n*** finds files last accessed *n**24 hours ago **-fstype *type*** finds files that exist only on the specified file system type, such as ext3 **-iname *pattern*** finds files with names that match a pattern **-inum *inode#*** finds files with inodes that match *inode#* **-user *uname*** finds files owned by user matching *uname*
fuser	Displays the Process ID (PID) of processes using a given resource	Useful for finding which users have mounted a drive that needs maintenance; example: **fuser –vu /mnt** shows all processes accessing a resource and their associated usernames
grep	Select lines or rows that match a specified pattern	**-c** displays the count of matching lines **-i** ignores case **-l** lists only filenames that contain the pattern **-L** lists only filenames that do not contain the pattern **-n** displays line numbers **-v** displays line numbers of lines in a file that do not match the specified pattern
head	Display the first few lines of a file	Shows the first 10 lines by default; **-n *n*** displays the first *n* lines of the specified file

B

Table B-1   Common UNIX commands (continued)

Command	Purpose	Useful Options and Examples
history	List all the commands contained in the bash history file	Bash history file is .bash_history by default and resides in the user's home directory; default number of last commands kept in the history file is 500
join	Join two files, matching row by row	**-a** *n* produces a line for each unpairable line in file *n*, where *n* = 1 or 2 **-e** *string* replaces the empty fields for the unpairable line with the string specified by str. **-j** specifies the common fields on which the join is to be made. **-o** specifies a list of fields to be output. **-t** specifies the field separator character. By default, this is a blank, tab, or new-line character. Multiple blanks and tabs count as one field separator.
kill	End a process	**-9** destructively ends a process **-HUP** causes the service or daemon to stop (hangup) and restart, which causes the rereading of its configuration files; often used to make changes to a running service
last	Shows the login history of all users on the system	**-a** displays the hostname from which the user connected **-d** shows the corresponding IP address for remotes
lastcomm	Shows log of last executed commands from the acct logfile	**lastcomm** *username* shows all commands executed by the specified user; **lastcomm** *command* shows all users who have executed the specified command
less	To scroll long files to screen	Allows for scrolling up and down in a file, where the more command only allows advancing down a file
let	Store the results of arithmetic operations in a variable	
ln	Create symbolic or hard links to files	By default, creates a hard link, which is another name for a particular inode; **-s** creates a symlink to a file, like a shortcut
lpr	Print a file	**-d** prints on a specified printer **-n** prints a specified number of copies of the file

Table B-1   Common UNIX commands (continued)

Command	Purpose	Useful Options and Examples
ls	List a directory's contents, including its files and subdirectories	**-a** lists hidden files **-l** lists files in long format, showing detailed information **-r** lists files in reverse alphabetic order **-s** shows the size of each file
lspci	Displays information about all PCI buses on the system (but you must be logged on as root)	**-v** is verbose output **-vv** is very verbose output **-t** shows a tree-like structure of PCI bus/devices
man	Display the online manual for the specified command	**-k** searches for the following pattern in the man pages **-t** formats the output for printing using ghostscript
mkdir	Make a new directory	
more	Display a long file one screen at a time	Pressing the spacebar advances a screen at a time; pressing Enter advances one line at a time
mount	Connect the file system to the directory tree in the specified location	**-r** indicates that the mounted partition's device is read-only **-a** mounts all possible file systems from /etc/fstab **-t** specifies the type of file system
mv	Move or rename files	**-f** never prompt before overwrite of existing files and directories **-i** prompts before overwriting files and directories
passwd	Change your UNIX password	When used by a user, can change only own password; root user can change other's passwords
paste	Paste multiple files, column by column	
pr	Format a specified file before printing or viewing	**-a** displays output in columns across the page, one line per column **-d** doublespaces the output **-h** customizes the header line **-l***n* sets the number of lines per page
printenv	Print a list of environment variables	
printf	Tell the awk program what action to take	

B

Table B-1   Common UNIX commands (continued)

Command	Purpose	Useful Options and Examples
ps	Shows processes on a system	**-a** shows all running processes **-u** shows user associated with a process **-x** shows background system processes
pwd	Display your current path	
rm	Remove a file	**-i** requests confirmation before deleting a file **-r** deletes a specified directory and its contents
rmdir	Remove a directory	
sed	Specify an editing command	**-a ** appends text after a line or a script file containing sed commands **-d** deletes specified text **-e** specifies multiple commands on one line **-n** indicates line numbers **-p** displays lines **-s** substitutes specified text
set –o noclobber	Prevents files from being overwritten by the > operator	Can negatively interact or affect other operations, notably some desktop managers
sh	Execute a shell script	Makes using *./* or *#!/bin/sh* unnecessary; *-n* reads commands without executing them **-v** displays lines of code as executed **-x** displays commands and arguments as executed
sort	Sort and merge multiple files	**.+** designates the position that follows an offset (+) as a character position, not a field position **+n** sorts on the field specified by *n* **-b** ignores leading blank characters **-d** sorts in dictionary order **-f** indicates that a specified character separates the fields **-m** merges files before sorting **-n** sorts numbers arithmetically **-o** directs the sorted output to a specified file
tail	Display the last few lines of a file	By default, displays the last 10 lines of a file; **-n** *n* displays the last *n* lines of the specified file

Table B-1   Common UNIX commands (continued)

Command	Purpose	Useful Options and Examples
test	Compare values and validate file existence	**!** logical negation **-a** logical AND **-b** tests if a file exists and is a block special file (which is a block-oriented device, such as a disk or tape drive) **-c** tests if a file exists and is a character special file (that is, a character-oriented device, such as a terminal or printer) **-d** true if a file exists and is a directory **-e** true if a file exists **-eq** equal to **-f** tests if a file exists and is a regular file **-ge** greater than or equal to **-gt** greater than **-le** less than or equal to **-lt** less than **-n** tests for a nonzero string length **-ne** not equal to **-o** logical OR **-r** true if a file exists and is readable **-s** true if a file exists and its size is greater than zero **string** tests for a nonzero string length **string1 = string2** tests two strings for equality **string1 != string2** tests two strings for inequality **-w** true if a file exists and is writeable **-x** true if a file exists and is executable **-z** tests for a zero-length string
top	Display a list of the most CPU-intensive tasks	**-c** displays the command that initiated each process **-I** ignores any idle processes **-q** displays output continually, with no delay between outputs (Use with caution! Try the spacebar for periodic updates) **-s** causes the top command to run in secure mode, disabling its interactive commands **-S** runs top in cumulative mode, which displays the cumulative CPU time used by a process
touch	Change a file's time and date stamp	**-a** updates access time only **-c** prevents touch from creating a file that does not already exist **-m** updates the modification time only

B

Table B-1   Common UNIX commands (continued)

Command	Purpose	Useful Options and Examples
tput	Format screen text	**clear** clears the screen **cols** prints the number of columns on the current terminal **cup** moves the screen cursor to a specified row and column **rmso** disables boldface output **smso** enables boldface output
tr	Translate characters	**-d** deletes input characters found in string1 from the output **-s** checks for sequences of string1 repeated consecutive times
trap	Execute a command when a specified signal is received from the operating system	
tty	Display terminal pathname	
umount	Disconnect the file system partitions from the directory tree	If mounted or being accessed by another user, see the fuser command to force unmounting of the resource
uniq	Select unique lines or rows	**-d** writes one copy of each line that has a duplicate **-u** writes only the lines of the source file that are not duplicated
wc	Count the number of lines, bytes, or words in a file	**-c** counts the number of bytes or characters **-l** counts the number of lines **-w** counts the number of words
whatis	Display a brief description of a command	
whereis	Locates source, binary and manual entries for the specified string or command	**-b** search for binary entries only **-m** search for manual entries only **-s** search for source entries only
w	Display users currently on the system	Shows user's originating host, idle time, his or her current command, CPU utilization, and login time
who	Shows who is currently logged onto a system	**-H** displays column headings **-i** displays session idle times **-q** displays a quick list of users

Table B-2   UNIX utilities by category

B

Command	Purpose
File-Processing Utilities	
afio	Creates an archive or restores files from archive
awk	Processes files
cat	Displays files and is used with other tools to concatenate files
cmp	Compares two files
comm	Compares sorted files and shows differences
cp	Copies files
cpio	Copies and backs up files to an archive
cut	Selects characters or fields from input lines
dd	Copies and converts input records
diff	Compares two text files and shows differences
dump	Backs up files
fdformat	Formats a floppy disk at a low level
find	Finds files within a file tree
fmt	Formats text very simply
grep	Matches patterns in a file
groff	Processes embedded text formatting codes
gzip	Compresses or decompresses files
head	Displays the first part of a file (first 10 lines by default)
ispell	Checks one or more files for spelling errors
less	Displays files allowing for scrolling forward and backward (pauses when screen is full)
ln	Creates a link to a file
lpr	Prints a file (hard copy)
ls	Lists file and directory names and attributes
man	Displays documentation for commands
mkdir	Creates a new directory
mkfs	Builds a UNIX file system
mv	Renames and moves files and directories
od	Formats and displays data from a file in octal, hexadecimal, and ASCII formats
paste	Concatenates files horizontally
pr	Formats text files for printing and displays them
pwd	Shows the directory you are in
rdev	Queries or sets the root image device
restore	Restores files (from a dump)
rm	Removes files
rmdir	Removes a directory
sed	Edits streams (non-interactive)

Table B-2 UNIX utilities by category (continued)

Command	Purpose
File-Processing Utilities	
sort	Sorts or merges files
tail	Displays the last lines of files (last 10 lines by default)
tar	Copies and backs up files to a tape archive
touch	Changes file modification dates
uniq	Displays unique lines of a sorted file
wc	Counts lines, words, and bytes
System Status Utilities	
chgrp	Changes the group associated with a file or the file's group ownership
chmod	Changes the access permissions of a file
chown	Changes the owner of a file
date	Sets and displays date and time
df	Displays the amount of free space remaining on a disk
du	Summarizes file space usage
file	Determines file type (such as shell script, executable, ASCII text, or others)
finger	Displays detailed information about users who are logged on
free	Displays amount of free and used memory in the system
edquota	Displays user disk quotas and enables them to be changed
kill	Terminates a running process
ps	Displays process status by process identification number and name
sleep	Suspends execution for a specified time
top	Dynamically displays the status of processes in real time, focusing on those processes that are using the most CPU resources
w	Displays detailed information about the users who are logged on
who	Displays brief information about the users who are logged on
Network Utilities	
ftp	Transfers files over a network
ifconfig	Used to set up a network interface
netstat	Shows network connection information
ping	Used to poll another network station (using the TCP/IP protocol); great for a fast determination about whether your network connection is working
rcp	Remotely copies a file from a network computer
rlogin	Logs on to a remote computer
rsh	Executes commands on a remote computer
rwho	Displays the names of users attached to a network
showmount	Lists clients that have mounted volumes on a server
telnet	Connects to a remote computer on a network
wvdial	Controls a modem dialer for dial-up connections over a phone line

Table B-2 UNIX utilities by category (continued)

Command	Purpose
Communications Utilities	
mail	Sends electronic mail messages
mesg	Denies (mesg n) or accepts (mesg y) messages
pine	Sends and receives electronic mail and news
talk	Lets users simultaneously type messages to each other
wall	Sends a message to all logged-on users (who have permissions set to receive messages)
write	Sends a message to another user
Programming Utilities	
configure	Configures program source code automatically
gcc	Compiles C and C++ programs
make	Maintains program source code
patch	Updates source code
Source Code Management Utilities	
ci	Creates changes in Revision Control Systems (RCS)
co	Retrieves an unencoded revision of an RCS file
cvs	Manages concurrent access to files in a hierarchy
rcs	Creates or changes the attributes of an RCS file
rlog	Prints a summary of the history of an RCS file
Miscellaneous Utilities	
at	Executes a command or script at a specified time
atq	Shows the jobs (commands or scripts) already scheduled to run
atrm	Enables you to remove a job (command or script) that is scheduled to run
batch	Runs a command or script and is a subset of the at command that takes you to the at> prompt, if you type only *batch* (in Red Hat Linux, a command or script is run when the system load is at an acceptable level)
cal	Displays a calendar for a month or year
crontab	Schedules a command to run at a preset time
expr	Evaluates expressions (used for arithmetic and string manipulations)
fsck	Checks and fixes problems on a file system (repairs damages)
tee	Clones output stream to one or more files
tr	Replaces specified characters (a translation filter)
tty	Displays a terminal path name
xargs	Converts standard output of one command into arguments for another

B

Table B-3   vi editor commands

Command	Purpose
!	Leave vi temporarily
:!	leave vi temporarily
$	Go to the end of the line
. (repeat)	Repeat your most recent change
/	Search forward for a pattern of characters
0 (zero)	Go to the beginning of the line
d$ or D	Delete from the cursor to the end of the line
d0	Delete from the cursor to the start of the line
dd	Delete the current line
dw	Delete the word starting at the cursor; if the cursor is in the middle of the word, delete from the cursor to the end of the line
H	Go to the upper-left corner of the screen
i	Switch to insert mode
L	Go to the last line on the screen
p	Paste text from the clipboard
q	Cancel an editing session
:q!	Cancel an editing session and exit
:r	Read text from one file, and add it to another
:set	Turn on certain options, such as line numbering
u	Undo your most recent change
:w	Save a file and continue working
:wq	Write changes to disk and exit vi
:x	Save changes and exit vi
x	Delete the character at the cursor location
yy	Copy (yank) text to the clipboard
ZZ	In command mode, save changes and exit vi

Table B-4   emacs editor commands

Alt Commands	Purpose
Alt+<	Move cursor to start of file
Alt+>	Move cursor to end of file
Alt+B	Move cursor back one word
Alt+D	Delete current word
Alt+F	Move cursor forward one word
Alt+Q	Reformat current paragraph using word wrap so that lines are full
Alt+T	If the cursor is under the first character of the word, transpose the word with the preceding word

B

Table B-4 emacs editor commands (continued)

Alt Commands	Purpose
Alt+U	Capitalize all letters of the current word
Alt+W	Scroll up one screen
Alt+X doctor	Enter doctor mode to play a game in which emacs responds to your statements with questions; save your work first, not all versions support this mode
emacs editor Ctrl commands	
Ctrl+@	Put a mark at the cursor location; after moving the cursor, you can move or copy text to the mark
Ctrl+A	Move cursor to start of line
Ctrl+B	Move cursor back one character
Ctrl+D	Delete the character under cursor
Ctrl+E	Move cursor to end of line
Ctrl+F	Move cursor forward one character
Ctrl+G	Cancel the current command
Ctrl+H	Use online help
emacs editor Ctrl commands	
Ctrl+K	Delete text to the end of the line
Ctrl+N	Move cursor to next line
Ctrl+P	Move cursor to preceding line
Ctrl+T	Transpose the character before the cursor with the one under the cursor
Ctrl+V	Scroll down one screen
Ctrl+W	Delete marked text; see Ctrl+@ (kept in buffer)
Ctrl+Y	Insert text from the buffer, and place it after the cursor
Ctrl Combinations	
Ctrl+H+C	Display the command that runs when you press a particular key
Ctrl+H+T	Run an emacs tutorial
Ctrl+X, Ctrl+C	Exit emacs
Ctrl+X, Ctrl+S	Save the file
Ctrl+X, U	Undo the last change
Ctrl+Del	Delete the character under the cursor

C

HOW TO INSTALL RED HAT LINUX 7.2 AND APACHE WEB SERVER

Depending on your preference and the capabilities of your hardware, you can perform a GUI or text-mode installation of Red Hat Linux 7.2. For most computers, you will likely prefer to use a GUI installation, which requires at least 32 MB of memory. If your computer has less than 32 MB of memory, the Red Hat installation process may force you to use a text mode installation. In this appendix, we teach you how to do the GUI installation because it's the easiest option for a newcomer to Linux. Note that your installation is a **workstation-class** installation, which means that you are performing an installation that has been predefined by Red Hat to include the most useful options for a typical user's workstation.

After you complete the installation of Red Hat Linux 7.2, you have the opportunity to install Apache Web Server. You need Apache Web Server to complete some of the exercises included in your book. Additionally, having the software installed on your computer allows you to experiment with using it as a Web server for your intranet or local workgroup.

INSTALLATION NOTES FOR RED HAT LINUX 7.2

The installation instructions in this appendix are written for a computer that is currently running Windows 95, Windows 98, or Windows Me. These steps and the selections that they contain create the simplest and easiest installation experience for first-time users.

If you are replacing an operating system other than Windows 95, Windows 98, or Windows Me, or if you wish to perform a server-class installation, you need to become familiar with issues such as accessing data and partitions formatted with the New Technology File System (NTFS). NTFS is compatible with Windows NT, Windows 2000, Windows XP, and Windows .NET Server. You also need to be aware of potential boot-loader issues. In such situations, we recommend that you visit these Red Hat Web sites for additional information:

- *www.redhat.com*
- *www.redhat.com/corp/support/manuals*

Successfully completing the steps in this appendix completely removes the existing operating system from your computer and installs Red Hat Linux 7.2. That is, this installation erases everything on your hard drive. If you have data you wish to keep, make a backup, or copy the data to a safe place so that you can restore the data back to your computer when the installation is done. You cannot recover data from the disk after you perform the installation!

OUTLINE OF AN INSTALLATION OF RED HAT LINUX 7.2

There are three major groups of steps in this appendix:

- Gather information about your computer hardware and network
- Create a Red Hat Linux 7.2 boot disk
- Install Red Hat Linux 7.2

You must follow the steps in the order they are listed. The three groups of steps are presented to you here to familiarize you with the process.

GATHER INFORMATION ABOUT YOUR COMPUTER HARDWARE AND NETWORK

The minimum recommended hardware for this Red Hat Linux 7.2 installation is as follows:

- An Intel 486 or higher processor
- 32 MB of RAM (preferably 64 MB or higher)
- 1.2 GB hard drive or larger
- 3.5-inch floppy disk
- CD-ROM drive

In the past, you had little help in gathering the above information. Now, you have more help in the form of informative prompts that are built into the installation routine.

Although the installation routine is helpful, there are still some specific facts you need to gather by hand to assist you in making choices before and during the installation procedure itself:

- The type and size of your hard drive

- The amount of memory in your system

- The type of CD-ROM drive in your system (specifically if it has an IDE, SCSI, or other interface)

- The brand and model of your video card

- The amount of video memory on your video card

- The brand and model of your monitor, as well as the monitor's vertical and horizontal sync ranges (found in the monitor's manual)

- The type of mouse you are using (PS/2 or serial, two buttons or three)

- If your computer has a SCSI adapter, its brand and model

- The printer type you use, if any; you also need to know how the printer connects to the computer

If your computer is on a network, you need to find out the following:

- The network connection information for your printer, if you print through a network

- The type of network card your computer has; you also need to determine configuration information the card's driver may require

- Your computer's IP address configuration information. You need to determine if your computer has a static IP address or if it uses BOOTP or DHCP. You also need to know the IP address of your default gateway and primary name server. (If you have a secondary and tertiary name server, you need their IP addresses as well.) Your network administrator can provide all this information.

After you collect the required information, you should compare it with the information contained within the Red Hat Linux Hardware Compatibility Lists, which are found at *www.redhat.com/hardware*. These lists show all the devices that Red Hat Linux supports. If any piece of your hardware does not appear on the respective list, Red Hat Linux may not run on your system.

After you determine that Red Hat Linux 7.2 supports your hardware, continue to the next installation phase.

CREATING THE RED HAT LINUX 7.2 BOOT DISK

You can start a Red Hat Linux 7.2 installation by booting your computer from Red Hat Linux 7.2 CD 1 or from a Red Hat Linux 7.2 floppy boot disk. If your system can boot from the CD-ROM drive (which includes most modern computers), you *do not* need to make a floppy boot disk from which to boot for the initial installation. However, if your system cannot boot from the CD-ROM drive, you *do* need to make a floppy boot disk. You use a program named rawrite.exe on the Red Hat Linux 7.2 CD-ROM to make the boot disk.

To make the Red Hat Linux 7.2 boot disk:

1. Insert the Red Hat Linux 7.2 CD-ROM into the CD drive.

2. Insert a blank floppy disk in drive A.

3. Click the **Start** button, and then point to **Programs**.

4. Click **MS-DOS Prompt** on the Programs menu. An MS-DOS window opens.

5. Change the default drive to the CD-ROM drive. If the CD-ROM drive is drive D, type **D:** and press **Enter**. (Likewise, if the CD-ROM drive is drive E, type **E:** and press **Enter**.)

6. Type **cd \dosutils** and press **Enter**.

7. Type **rawrite** and press **Enter**. You see this message:

   Enter disk image source file name:

8. Type **..\images\boot.img** and press **Enter**. You see this message:

   Enter target diskette drive:

9. Type **A:** and press **Enter**. You see this message:

   Please insert a formatted diskette into drive A: and press -ENTER- :

10. Because the disk is already in the drive, press **Enter**.

11. There is a short delay while the program creates the boot disk. When the program ends, you see a DOS prompt. You now have a Red Hat boot disk.

12. Type **exit** and press **Enter** to close the window.

INSTALLING RED HAT LINUX 7.2

Your installation of Red Hat Linux 7.2 can take anywhere from 30–90 minutes, depending on the processor speed, CD-ROM drive speed, and RAM of your computer. Also, you may need to set your computer's BIOS to boot from the floppy or CD-ROM drive, depending on which method you are using. Consult your computer's documentation to determine how to configure the boot sequence in the BIOS. (In many cases, your computer is already configured to boot from the floppy drive first, then from the hard drive, and then the CD-ROM drive.) Further, if you want to boot from the CD-ROM drive first, your computer may support pressing a particular Ctrl-key sequence at start up for the boot sequence.

To perform the final phase of the Red Hat Linux 7.2 installation:

1. Remove all diskettes and CD-ROMs from your computer. If your computer supports booting from CD-ROM, insert the Red Hat Linux 7.2 CD 1 disc. If it does not support booting from CD-ROM, insert the floppy boot disk you made in the previous steps and also insert the Red Hat Linux 7.2 CD 1 disc.

2. Reboot or turn on your computer. When the system starts, you see a Welcome to Red Hat Linux 7.2! screen, which lists several installation options. See Figure C-1.

![Welcome screen showing Red Hat Linux 7.2 boot options with text listing install or upgrade modes including graphical mode, text mode, lowres, nofb, expert, linux rescue, and linux dd.]

Figure C-1 Welcome screen

3. Press **Enter** to select the first option. The installation program takes several minutes to load. As it loads, various messages appear on the screen.

4. When the installation program loads, your screen should resemble Figure C-2. As shown in Figure C-3, the next screen asks you what language you want to use for the installation. Choose a language, and click **Next** to continue.

(C) 2001 Red Hat, Inc.

Figure C-2   Red Hat Logo screen

5. You next choose the configuration of your keyboard, as shown in Figure C–4, leaving the defaults selected if you don't need to make any changes for the installation. Click **Next** to continue.

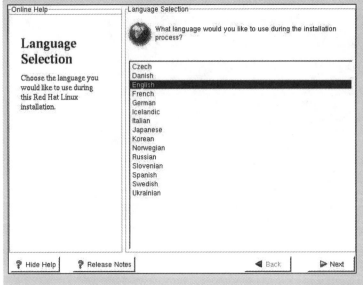

Figure C-3   Language Selection screen

C

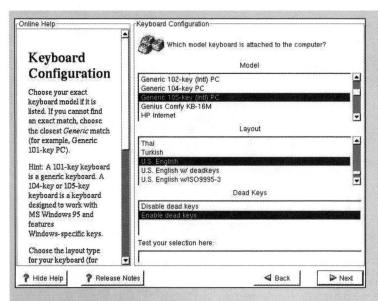

Figure C-4   Keyboard Configuration screen

6. The mouse configuration screen appears next, and in it, you can fine-tune the detected mouse. If you don't have a three-button mouse, you can check the Emulate three-buttons checkbox, which enables you to emulate a three-button mouse by pressing both the left and right mouse buttons simultaneously. Click **Next** to continue, as shown in Figure C-5.

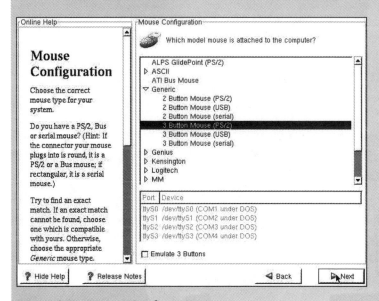

Figure C-5   Mouse Configuration screen

7. Your screen should resemble Figure C-6, which has an outline of the installation process and some opportunities for viewing the release notes for the distribution. Click **Next** to continue.

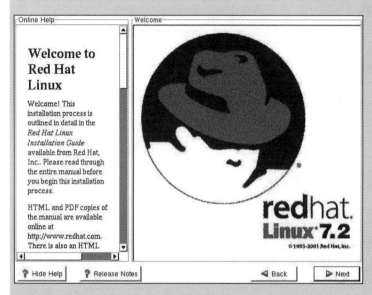

Figure C-6   Welcome to Red Hat Linux screen

8. In Figure C-7, choose the Workstation installation option. This selection installs the most popular and likely options for a user's workstation. Click **Next** to continue.

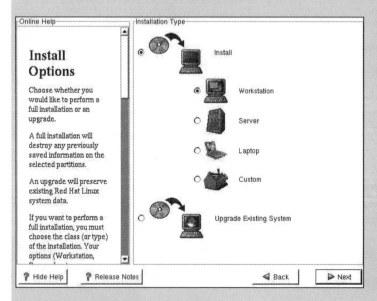

Figure C-7   Install Options screen

C

9. Figure C-8 shows various options, including having the installation program automatically partition your system for you. Choose this option and click **Next** to continue.

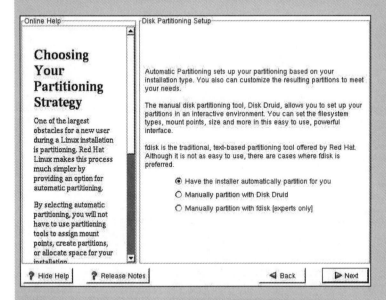

Figure C-8 Choosing Your Partitioning Strategy screen

 Remember when we mentioned how you lose the data on your drive when you do this installation? Don't proceed with the next step unless you've done the backup that we recommended.

10. In Figure C-9, you are prompted to decide what to do with the existing partitions on the drive. Because this is a fresh install, you should click the Remove all partitions on this system option button, and then click **Next** to continue.

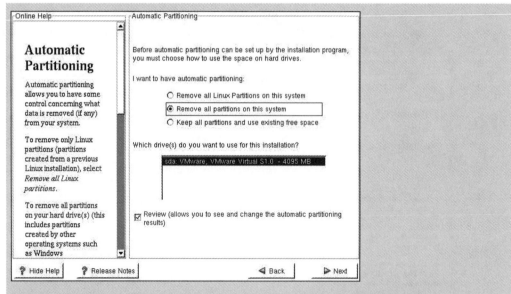

Figure C-9 Automatic Partitioning screen

11. In Figure C-10, you see yet another warning about losing all data on this drive. After reassuring yourself that you did indeed make backups of the necessary data, click **Yes** to continue.

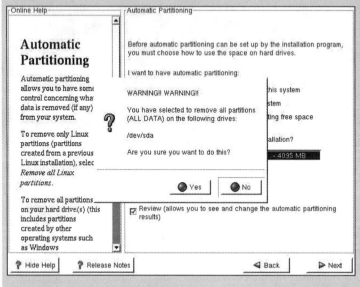

Figure C-10 Warning dialog box

12. Figure C-11 shows you how the drive is being partitioned and its geometry. Take note that the /boot partition is fairly small and is mostly present to ensure that you don't have any problems with your root partition extending past the one thousand twenty-fourth cylinder of the drive. Click **Next** to continue.

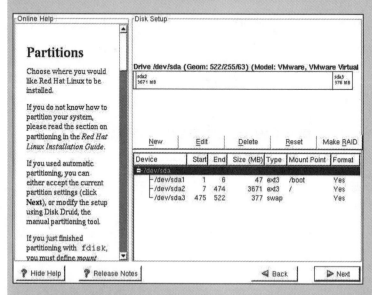

Figure C-11   Partitions screen

13. In Figure C-12, you can choose to use either GRUB (Grand Unified Boot Loader) or LILO (Linux Loader). For support and familiarity with the majority of systems installed, it's recommended that you choose the LILO option; it's been around a lot longer and is considered more stable. You won't need to alter any of the other information. Click **Next** to continue.

14. Next you see the Network Configuration screen, as shown in Figure C-13, which allows you to set up your network card and how you will be using TCP/IP addressing. If your network supports DHCP and you know the system can get an address, leave that option selected. If for some reason you don't want your network card to be active when you boot your computer, unselect the option. If you choose to set your IP address manually, make sure to use a valid one and to include a netmask (subnet mask) and other information needed to fully participate on your network. Click **Next** to continue.

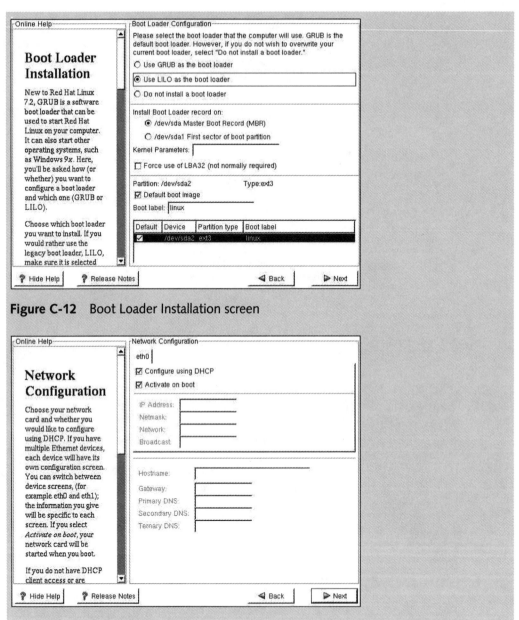

Figure C-12   Boot Loader Installation screen

Figure C-13   Network Configuration screen

C

15. When Figure C-14 appears, you will likely not change any settings. However, if you know you will be trying to connect to services such as Telnet and Secure Shell on this machine, you may want to click the No Firewall option button. You may need to alter these options if your computer will be securely behind a firewall. Click **Next** to continue.

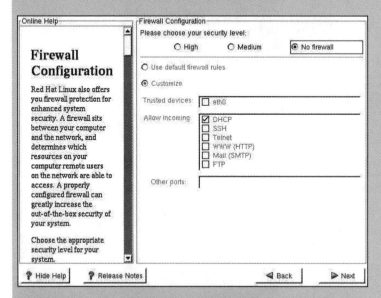

Figure C-14   Firewall Configuration screen

16. Next you may see the Language Support Selection screen, where can you choose the language(s) supported on your system. If shown, choose the appropriate language(s), and click **Next** to continue.

17. When the Time Zone Selection screen appears, as shown in Figure C-15, you should use the mouse to either click the world map to set the time zone or scroll through the prodigious amount of selections in the list. You might want to move to the bottom of the list and scroll slowly up to find the CST, MST, and EST types of entries. Make your choice, and click **Next** to continue.

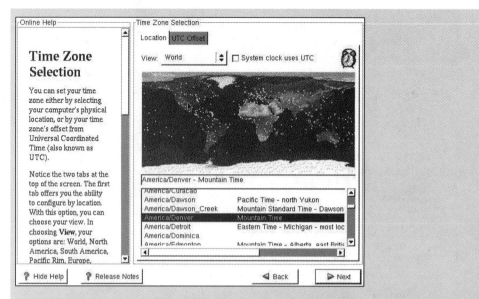

Figure C-15   Time Zone Selection screen

18. Configuring the root password and a user account is next, as shown in Figure C-16. Enter the same root user password twice, and then click the **Add** button to enter the information for a regular user account, as shown in Figure C-17. When finished with the user's information, click **OK**, and then click **Next** to continue.

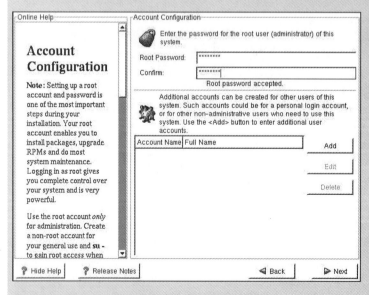

Figure C-16   Account Configuration screen

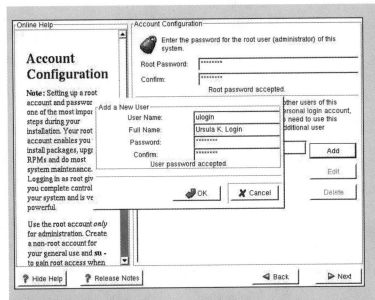

Figure C-17   Adding a New User dialog box

19. Next you choose any optional package groups, as shown in Figure C-18. Make sure that you at least select GNOME for the projects in this book. Click **Next** to continue.

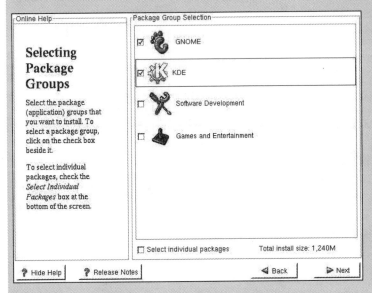

Figure C-18   Selecting Package Groups screen

20. The Video Configuration screen, as shown in Figure C-19, can be one of the most difficult and vexing items in your installation. If your hardware video card and monitor are detected, you can have an easier installation. If not, you may have to manually choose a video card and a monitor later. This is where you look at the information you gathered prior to this installation and find the video card specification. If for some reason you don't want to fully install the X Window System, you can choose to skip it. In any case, make your choices, and click **Next** to continue.

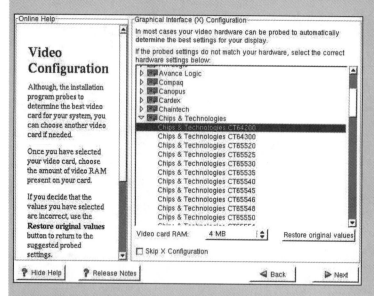

Figure C-19   Video Configuration screen

21. The About to Install screen, which is shown in Figure C-20, is little more than an information screen; it just lets you know you are ready to install and how to abort the installation if needed. Click **Next** to continue.

22. After the files from disc 1 are loaded (which can take 15 minutes or much longer), you are prompted, as shown in Figure C-21, to insert a disc 2 to continue the installation. Insert the requested item, and when the drive has spun up, click **OK** to continue.

C

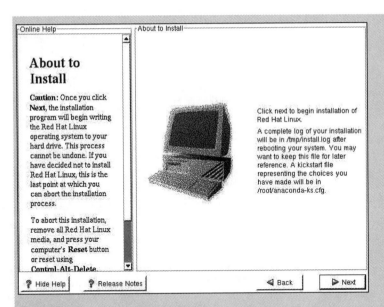

Figure C-20   About to Install screen

Figure C-21   Insert prompt

23. When the installation is finished, you see Figure C-22, where you can choose to create a boot disk. It's highly recommended that you create one; you need it if there are any problems with the installation. Place a blank floppy disk in the drive, and click **Next** to continue.

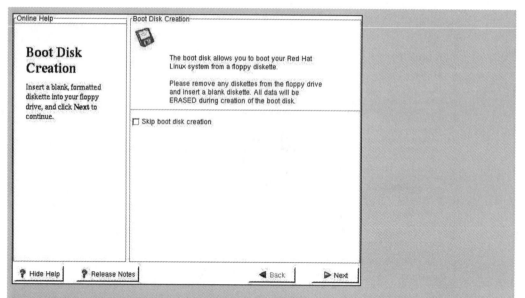

Figure C-22   Boot Disk Creation screen

24. After your boot disk is created, remove it and choose your monitor make and model from the list on the Monitor Selection screen, as shown in Figure C-23. If your make and model are automatically detected, they are selected and you can simply click **Next** to continue. If not, do some experimenting with monitors from the same manufacturer, but don't stray too far; you can physically damage monitors with the wrong settings in Linux. Click **Next** to continue.

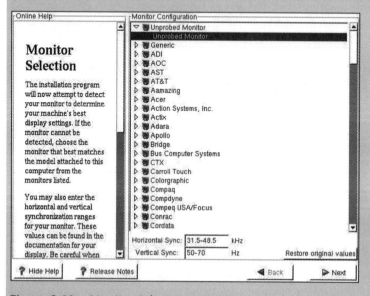

Figure C-23   Monitor Selection screen

C

25. The final configuration screen, which is shown in Figure C-24, is where you set the color depth and screen resolution, the default desktop, and set whether your machine will use a graphical login dialog box. After making your choices, click **Next** to continue.

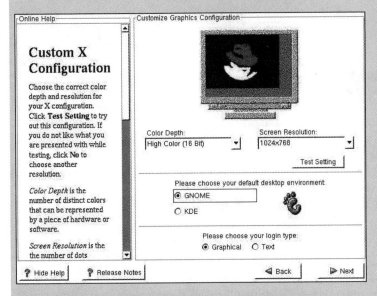

Figure C-24 Custom X Configuration screen

26. Finally, you are presented with the Congratulations screen, as shown in Figure C-25. This is a sign that your installation is finished and that the machine is ready to reboot and start Red Hat Linux 7.2. Make sure to remove the CD-ROM from its tray. The tray might get pulled back into the drive when the machine reboots and cause you to have to reboot again. Last, make sure to remove the boot diskette that you created in Step 23. Store the boot diskette in a safe place. If the boot loader or another system file is corrupted on your hard drive, the boot diskette can be vital because it gives you the option to boot into your system from the floppy drive and then fix the problem.

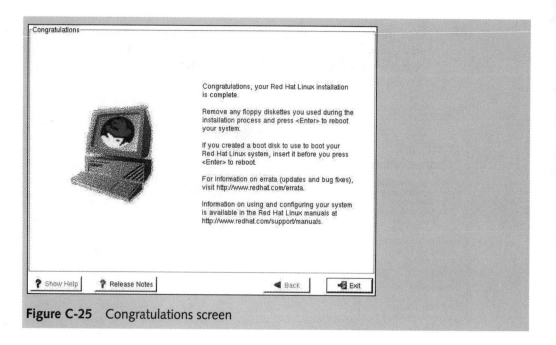

Figure C-25   Congratulations screen

INSTALLING APACHE WEB SERVER

To develop and test Web pages with CGI scripts as discussed in Chapter 9, you must install the Apache Web Server software. You can always obtain the latest version of the Apache Web Server software by visiting *www.apache.org*.

Red Hat Package Manager files (which have the .rpm extension) are an important part of your Apache Web Server software installation and are used to manage your Apache installation. Sometimes, the Apache Web Server software is upgraded faster than the Red Hat Package Manager files (.rpm). If you try to use outdated Red Hat Package Manager files (.rpm), unpredictable things such as crashes and library dependency errors may occur. If your main concern is stability and consistency, it's best to wait until you can get the current files at *www.apache.org* or from the Red Hat Web site.

To install the Apache Web Server software:

1. Make sure you are logged in to your workstation as root.
2. Insert the Red Hat Linux 7.2 CD-ROM 1 into the CD-ROM drive.
3. Mount the CD-ROM drive by typing **mount /mnt/cdrom** and pressing **Enter**.
4. Type **cd /mnt/cdrom/RedHat/RPMS** and press **Enter**.
5. Type **ls mm*.rpm** and press **Enter**. The output of this command should show the file mm-1.1.3-1.i386.rpm, which contains library files (much like a .dll files in Windows) that Apache needs to function.

C

6. Install the package mm-1.1.3-1.i386.rpm by typing **rpm –ivh mm-1.1.3-1.i386.rpm** and pressing **Enter**. The rpm command only needs the -i option and the filename, but we add the "v" and "h" to verbosely inform us of the installation's progress and other information.

> The term "verbosely" means to give more information than the default messages. In this case, it means that hash (#) marks show the progress of the installation and that the package's executable or primary filename is echoed to the screen.

7. Now type **ls apache*.rpm** and press **Enter**. The output of the command should be the names of two files, in the form of apache-*X.X.X-X*.i386.rpm and apacheconf-*X.X.X-X*.noarch.rpm (where the *X*s are numbers that represent the major, minor, and patch versions; note that on your CD-ROM, noarch.rpm may be i386.rpm). The filenames are similar to the following: apache-1.3.20-16.i386.rpm and apacheconf-0.8.1-1.noarch.rpm.

8. Type **rpm –ivh apache-*X.X.X-X*.noarch.rpm** (where the *X*s are the numbers you saw in the filename as a result of the command in Step 7), and press **Enter**. For example, if you saw apache-1.3.20-16.noarch.rpm when you typed the command in Step 7, you type **rpm –ivh apache-1.3.20-16.noarch.rpm** and press **Enter**.

9. Type **rpm –ivh apacheconf-*X.X.X-X*.noarch.rpm** (where the *X*s are the numbers you saw in the file name as a result of the command in Step 7) and press **Enter**. For example, if you saw apacheconf-0.8.1-1.noarch.rpm when you typed the command in Step 7, you type **rpm –ivh apacheconf-0.8.1-1.noarch.rpm** and press **Enter**.

10. Apache is not set to start automatically, by default. To start it now without rebooting, type **/etc/rc.d/init.d/httpd start** and press Enter.

11. To have Apache start automatically every time your machine is rebooted, type **ntsysv** and press **Enter**. This loads the ntsysv program, as shown in Figure C-26. ntsysv is a simplified and menu-based method of editing the complex system initialization scripts.

12. Scroll down the list of available daemons and services until you find the httpd selection, and then use the spacebar to place an asterisk in the brackets [*]. This signifies the service is started each time the system is brought up in this runlevel.

13. Press **Tab** to move the focus to the OK button, and then press **Enter** to save your changes and exit the ntsysv program

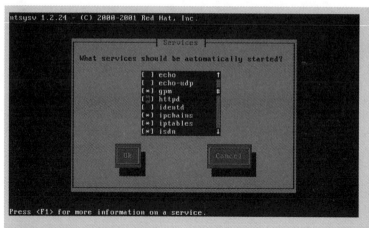

Figure C-26 Services screen

In Steps 11-13, you set Apache to start only for a particular runlevel. If you want Apache to start in a different runlevel in the future, you may have to use the ntsysv program while in that runlevel. You then would repeat your actions precisely as done in Steps 11-13 above.

You can specify the runlevel(s) to edit as an option to the ntsysv command. For example, you could type **ntsysv —level 35** to edit the service startup information for both runlevel 3 and 5 at the same time. To alter a single runlevel's information, type **ntsysv —level X**, where the X is the runlevel you want to change.

D

UNIX VARIANTS

A UNIX variant is simply one of the many different versions or distributions of UNIX. According to one count by the UNIX Guru Universe, which is an organization of UNIX administrators, there are about 80 UNIX variants that run on different kinds of computers. This appendix does not attempt to list all 80 variants, but instead focuses on providing an overview of some of the most popular.

One reason why UNIX has proliferated into so many variants is because much of the operating system kernel and UNIX software are written in portable languages, such as C. Another reason for UNIX's popularity is that TCP/IP (Transmission Control Protocol/Internet Protocol), the main protocol of the Internet and of general networking, was built into UNIX systems in the early 1980s—at the same time TCP/IP was adopted for the international network that has become the Internet. Most other operating systems did not implement full TCP/IP capabilities until much later. A third reason why UNIX has evolved into so many variants is that the basic kernel source code is publicly available, instead of being a trade secret, as it true of proprietary operating systems such as Windows-based systems. This characteristic makes it easier for vendors to adapt hardware to UNIX systems and for software creators to offer a huge range of applications, many of which are free.

POPULAR VERSIONS OF UNIX

Most versions of UNIX follow one (or a combination) of two standards: the Berkeley System Distribution (BSD) standard and the System V release 4 (SVR4) standard.

The BSD standard grew out of the efforts of several professors and students at the University of California at Berkeley. This group of professors and students developed the BSD 3 version of UNIX and then the BSD 4 version. In the early 1990s, their work evolved into a commercial enterprise through the newly formed company, Berkeley Software Design. Two popular features of UNIX that you have learned about in this text, the vi editor and the C shell, grew out of the BSD version of UNIX.

The System V version has roots in the work done by Bell Labs at AT&T. From the mid-1970s through the late 1980s, Bell Labs and AT&T developed System V. Eventually this version of UNIX was taken over by an AT&T subsidiary company called UNIX Systems Laboratories. In the early 1990s, UNIX Systems Laboratories joined with Novell to port a version of UNIX to Intel processors. Not only was UNIX ported to popular PCs through their work, but also this version of UNIX initiated a GUI interface for UNIX, called UNIX Desktop. Before long, UNIX Systems Laboratories was taken over by Novell. In the mid-1990s, Novell decided to deemphasize its UNIX operations and sold them to a company called Santa Cruz Operation (SCO), which today offers a System V commercial product called UnixWare.

Today, many computer and operating system vendors provide commercial UNIX distributions. In addition, independent groups provide free UNIX systems. Table D-1 lists a sampling of the popular commercial systems and Table D-2 lists some of the free systems.

Table D-1   Popular commercial UNIX variants

Version	Manufacturer	Origin	Information on the Web
AIX	IBM	A combination of SVR4 and BSD	*www.ibm.org* or *www-1.ibm.com/servers/aix*
Digital Equipment UNIX (previously called Ultrix)	Compaq/Digital (which at this writing is being purchased by Hewlett Packard)	BSD	*www.compaq.com* or *www.tru64unix.compaq.com*
Hewlett Packard UNIX (HP-UX)	Hewlett Packard	SVR4	*www.hp.com*
Irix	Silicon Graphics	SVR4	*www.sgi.com*
Mac OS X	Apple	BSD	*www.apple.com*
Red Hat Linux	Red Hat	SVR4	*www.redhat.com*
OSF1	Compaq/Digital (which at this writing is being purchased by Hewlett Packard)	SVR4	*www.compaq.com* or *www.tru64unix.compaq.com*

Table D-1 Popular commercial UNIX variants (continued)

Version	Manufacturer	Origin	Information on the Web
OpenServer (new versions now integrated into UnixWare and not sold as OpenServer)	Santa Cruz Operation, Inc.	SVR4	*www.sco.com*
SINIX	Siemens Nixdorf	SVR4	*www.siemens.com*
Solaris	Sun Microsystems	BSD	*www.sun.com*
SunOS	Sun Microsystems	BSD	*www.sun.com*
SuSE Linux	SuSE (German for Software and System Development)— providing international distributions	SVR4	*www.suse.com*
Turbo Linux	Turbolinux, Inc.	SVR4	*www.turbolinux.com*
UnixWare	Santa Cruz Operation, Inc.	SVR4	*www.sco.com*

Table D-2 Popular free UNIX variants

Version	Source	Origin	Information on the Web
FreeBSD	FreeBSD	BSD	*www.freebsd.org*
Linux	Available from many sources depending on your language and country	SVR4	*www.linux.org*
HURD	GNU	BSD	*www.gnu.ai.mit.edu/ software/hurd/hurd.html*
NetBSD	NetBSD Project	BSD	*www.netbsd.org*
OpenBSD	OpenBSD Project	BSD	*www.openbsd.org*

There are many similarities between versions of UNIX. For example, they all offer full TCP/IP network compatibility. All versions of UNIX have layered components that make up the operating system (see Chapter 1), and they all use shells as command-line interpreters. In fact, virtually every version of UNIX supports the Bourne shell, and many support the C and Bash shells.

All UNIX versions come with at lease one text editor, such as vi, Emacs, or both, and they use similar file and text manipulation utilities. UNIX variants use a similar hierarchical file system that employs permissions for file security. In addition, UNIX systems support a variety of software compilers, particularly C, C++, LISP, and Pascal. They also permit shell scripting and enable Perl and CGI scripts.

The differences between versions of UNIX are generally evident in some differences in commands and in the hardware platforms they use. These differences are explored in the next two sections.

UNIX Command Differences

Many of the UNIX command differences stem from whether a system is based on BSD or System V. However, command differences are also related to enhancements or changes that particular vendors have made to commands. For example, in IBM's AIX, the command to create a new user is mkuser; in FreeBSD, the command is adduser, and in Red Hat Linux 7.2, the command is useradd. To delete a user in these systems, you would use rmuser in AIX, rmuser in FreeBSD, and userdel in Red Hat 7.2 Linux.

Sometimes the command line differences are not in the commands that are supported, but in the options associated with a command. For example, in BSD-based systems, the ls –s command usually shows the file size in kilobytes while the same command shows the file size in 512 blocks in SVR4 systems. To display the processor type in Red Hat Linux 7.2, you type uname –m, but in Solaris, you type uname –imp.

Table D-3 gives you a small taste of how commands can be similar or different among these systems: AIX (based on BSD and SVR4), Red Hat Linux 7.2 (based on SVR4), and Solaris (based on BSD).

Table D-3   UNIX commands of AIX, Red Hat Linux, and Solaris

Activity	Command in AIX	Command in Red Hat Linux	Command in Solaris
Print a file	lp, lpr, enq, qprt	lpr	lp, lpr
Show the size of the swap file	lsps -a, vmstat	free, vmstat	swap -l, vmstat
Show processes	ps	ps	ps
Configure a network interface card	ifconfig	ifconfig	ifconfig
Change information associated with a user's account	chuser -a	usermod	usermod
View information in a print queue	lpq, lpstat, qchk, enq -A	lpq	lpstat
List all of the software packages installed	lslpp -L all	rmp -qa	pkginfo
Initiate paging (virtual memory)	swapon -a	swapon -a	swap -a

In some instances in Table D-3, there are several commands that accomplish the same purpose in a single operating system. In these cases, the commands are separated by commas. For example, there are four commands that can be used to print a file in AIX: lp, lpr, enq, and qprt.

UNIX Hardware Platforms

Some of the UNIX variants, such as Hewlett Packard's HP-UX, are particularly targeted for high-end powerful RISC (Reduced Instruction Set Computer) processors or the new supercharged Intel Itanium processors.

A RISC processor is fast and powerful because it requires fewer instructions for common operations and it has portions of the CPU that are dedicated to specific functions. The Itanium processor is built from the basic RISC architecture, but it includes EPIC (Explicitly Parallel Instruction Computing)—which is the capability to predict upcoming processor operations on the basis of tracking previous operations. The Itanium processor also has larger processor work areas than non–EPIC RISC processors.

 Both the RISC and Itanium processors have a 64-bit architecture instead of the slower 32-bit architecture of non-Itanium Intel-class processors.

Other UNIX variants, such as Red Hat Linux 7.2, function well on Intel-class servers and workstations. Still other versions of UNIX, such as Compaq/Digital Equipment Corporation's UNIX, are particularly targeted at computers with the alpha processor, which is a powerful, but specialized, RISC processor originally developed for use in Compaq/Digital Equipment Corporation computers. However, following Digital Equipment Corporation's purchase by Compaq, the alpha processor computers are being replaced by computers that use the new Itanium processor.

Of the UNIX variants, distributions of Linux have proven to be especially versatile in terms of hardware compatibility. Besides Intel-class processors, Linux has been adapted to run on IBM mainframe and minicomputers, Hewlett Packard RISC-based computers, Sun workstations, the Compaq/DEC alpha computers, Silicon Graphics workstations, and many others.

Table D-4 is a list of some typical hardware configurations that can be used with UNIX operating systems. Note that as each UNIX version evolves, more scalability is built in so that different processors can be used.

Table D-4   A sampling of UNIX systems and typical hardware compatibility

UNIX Version	Typical Hardware
AIX	IBM RISC-based pSeries servers and RS/6000 workstations and servers
Digital Equipment UNIX and Ultrix	DEC alpha and DEC VAX computers
HP-UX	RISC-based and Itanium processors in HP workstations and servers
IRIX	Silicon Graphics RISC-based MIPS processor in the Silicon Graphics Fuel, O2, and Octane2 workstations and servers

Table D-4 A sampling of UNIX systems and typical hardware compatibility (continued)

UNIX Version	Typical Hardware
Linux from Silicon Graphics	Intel Itanium processor in the Silicon Graphics 750 computer
Mac OS X	Apple RISC-based G4 (fourth generation) PowerPCs
Red Hat Linux	Intel-class processors
Sun Solaris	RISC-based UltraSPARC III processor in Sun UltraSPARC workstations and servers
SuSE Linux	Intel-class processors
Turbo Linux	Intel-class processors
UnixWare and OpenServer	Intel-based processors

CHOOSING A UNIX VARIANT

When it comes to selecting any operating system, the best advice is to:

1. Understand the requirements of what you want to accomplish and what application software is needed to meet those requirements.

2. Select the operating system on which the software can run.

3. Select the hardware that is appropriate to the operating system and software needs.

For example, if you need to perform professional computing that requires using lots of graphics for publishing, one good choice is a Mac OS X system. If you are engaging in personal computing and want to use an Intel-based computer, then a free or commercial distribution of Linux is often an appropriate selection. If the application requirement is to have a powerful server for an accounting system, then AIX, HP-UX, or Sun Solaris on a RISC or Itanium computer might be needed.

One significant advantage to selecting any UNIX variant is the element of portability. If you start with one UNIX variant and its associated hardware platform, but later find you need to scale up to a different UNIX variant and platform, the chances are very good that you can port most or all of your initial investment in application software. Another advantage is that users trained in one UNIX variant can quickly adapt to a different variant, so you do not lose your training investment either.

As you can see, there is a variant of UNIX to help you accomplish nearly any type of computing task and on a wide range of computers—which is the single, most impressive advantage of UNIX.

E

LINUX SECURITY: NETWORK AND INTERNET CONNECTIVITY

With the running of a powerful and flexible system comes the responsibility to ensure that the system is not easily broken into and misused.
Toward that end, this appendix is designed to inform you about the security
risks of running a standard Linux installation and the steps you can take to
make your computer more secure without severely disabling its functionality.

 If you are going to be using Linux as a firewall computer, you have much
reading and investigation to do. Visit such sites as *linuxsecurity.org* and
www.securityfocus.org. Again, this appendix is written toward only the
standard Linux installation.

Security hardening is the process of taking a default system installation and making that system more secure, harder to break into, and less likely to be exploited for some nefarious purpose. You should understand the different levels of security hardening available. Toward that end, we focus on localhost security as the most likely and efficient way for you to protect the systems for which you are personally responsible. The other types of security—network and organizational—are beyond the scope of this book.

Steps to secure your systems at the localhost level include the following:

1. Implementing physical system security

2. Defining and publishing the security policy

3. Ensuring password security

4. Managing unnecessary services

5. Viewing log files on a regular basis

6. Keeping up with security fixes and patches

7. Monitoring your system automatically

We discuss each in turn.

Step # 1 – Implementing Physical System Security

Can a person who is not a system administrator walk up to your server and physically touch it? If yes, why? If a computer is important and you want it to be as secure as possible, it should be secured in a cabinet or other enclosure such as a locked room. Setting a BIOS password, locking the case, putting up a security camera that is above and pointing down at the computer, disabling the floppy and CD-ROM internally, and keeping the cleaning staff out of the server room are great ways to increase your physical system security.

Physical and programmatic security is just as important for desktop users as it is for server operators. Although you normally would not turn off a server computer at night due to its role, you can shut down a desktop computer, log off your session, or use a locking screensaver to secure your desktop at night or when you are away for more than a moment.

Step # 2 – Defining and Publishing the Security Policy

If an action is not allowed, it's denied. This should be your standard security policy. There are numerous examples of well-constructed security policies available on the Internet and in security manuals. Use them as reference as you build your own.

Building your own security policy is easy when you take it task by task. For each of the following sections about localhost security, we include relevant sections from sample security policies. One of the best resources for security information and policy templates is the SANS Institute, which is at *www.sans.org*.

Your policy should be reasonable and regularly seen by the subjects who are governed by it. Post a copy in the breakroom and one on your door. Then email the entire company your online version of it (as a password-protected Acrobat PDF file) and remind them regularly that this is where they should look to see what is acceptable and unacceptable.

Step # 3 – Ensuring Password Security

One of the most important keys to system security is having hard-to-guess passwords. Any user who has a common password with another user is putting your system at risk. In spite of the danger, some organizations make almost no use of password-based security and put their entire network and corporate data at risk by being so lax. Don't be one of them.

In some UNIX systems, but not in Red Hat Linux 7.2, a user's password is stored in the /etc/passwd file in an encrypted form. UNIX and Linux systems require the passwd file to be readable by all users of the system, as shown in Figure E-1, and available for query by outsiders presenting themselves for possible login. The system compares the entered username and password against the relevant entry in the passwd file and either admits or rejects the attempted login. Because this read access is granted to all users, a vulnerability exists for systems that store the actual encrypted password in the /etc/passwd file. Once a password file containing encrypted passwords has been copied, that system is only a few hours or days from being fully compromised.

Figure E-1   /etc/passwd file permissions

Obviously this is not a desirable situation for a security-minded administrator to be in. Fortunately, you can use the Shadow Suite, which is a suite of tools and files that replaces the generic security setup for the computer's password and group databases with one that keeps normal users from seeing the hashed or encrypted passwords in these files.

When the Shadow Suite is installed, several changes occur in the contents of the /etc/passwd and /etc/group files. On some systems, when the second field of a /etc/passwd file contains a string of characters that represent the user's password, the installation of the Shadow Suite causes an "x" to be placed in the second field, replacing the encrypted password and indicating that the system should look for the encrypted password in the /etc/shadow file. (Red Hat Linux 7.2 has this password protection built in, without the use of a third-party tool such as Shadow Suite.) The /etc/shadow file contains the username and actual encrypted password, and other fields that determine a user's password age and frequency of change. The /etc/shadow file has the added security benefit of being only readable by the root user, and by processes that can assume the root user's role. See Figure E-2 for the shadow file's permissions.

E

Figure E-2   /etc/shadow permissions

Additionally the Shadow Suite moves any passwords that are assigned to groups in the /etc/group file to the /etc/gshadow file. The same rules apply to these two files as applied to the /etc/passwd and /etc/shadow files.

You can also set the defaults for the user's login experience in the /etc/login.defs file. This file contains the default login settings for all users. It's arranged in sections, the pertinent one dealing with user passwords. Figure E-3 below shows the section's contents and explanations.

```
#     PASS_MAX_DAYS    Maximum number of days a password may be used.
#     PASS_MIN_DAYS    Minimum number of days allowed between password changes.
#     PASS_MIN_LEN     Minimum acceptable password length.
#     PASS_WARN_AGE    Number of days warning given before a password expires.
#
PASS_MAX_DAYS    99999
PASS_MIN_DAYS    0
PASS_MIN_LEN     5
PASS_WARN_AGE    7
```

Figure E-3   /etc/login.defs file detail

As you can see, the system is relatively lenient in allowing users to have 99,999 days before they have to change their passwords. Add the fact of a minimum password length of six characters, and you have a system waiting to be broken into by brute force. As a minimum, you should set the PASS_MAX_DAYS variable to no more than 60 days, and set the PASS_MIN_LEN to at least seven or eight characters. The PASS_MIN_DAYS variable governs how often the user can change his or her password and should be set between five and fifteen days. This keeps the user from constantly changing their password, or trying to get the same password by altering it several times in a row. In Figure E-3, the default PASS_WARN_AGE value of seven is fine. You want the user to be notified of the approaching need to change his or her password, and seven days is ample warning time.

 A word to the wise: it's not a good idea to set the PASS_MAX_DAYS to less than 30 days and the minimum length to nine or above. If you do, you may find your users writing down their passwords in desk drawers, on their calendars, or in other conspicuous locations. Most system administrators choose a 45 to 60 day password change time frame. This is frequent enough to be acceptable for security, and it doesn't place undue memory strain on the users.

Step # 4 – Managing Unnecessary Services

In this section, we focus on how to disable a service, tools you can use to manage services, and services you should avoid putting on your system altogether.

How to Disable Running Services

Linux uses either the /etc/rc.d tree or the /etc/rc.d tree to store the runlevels and their scripts, depending on the distribution. You can edit these scripts manually, although it is not recommended. The rc0.d through rc6.d directories contain symbolic links to scripts that are kept in the /etc/rc.d/init.d folder. Scripts that begin with an "S" are to be started when that particular runlevel is begun, and scripts that begin with a "K" are to be stopped or killed when that runlevel is exited.

Red Hat systems have a user-friendly menu-based tool for enabling and disabling services: the ntsysv tool. It is a text-mode, yet graphical-appearing, tool. You use the space-bar to both place an asterisk next to those services you want to run and to remove the asterisk from those you want disabled, as shown in Figure E-4.

E

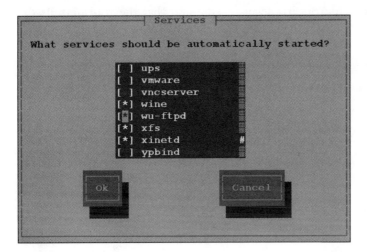

Figure E-4   Using ntsysv

Disabling a service using ntsysv:

1. Log in to your system as the root user by opening a shell in your X Window session, typing **su –** and then entering the password at the prompt.

2. You need to know what runlevel you are editing, so type **runlevel** and press **Enter** to display your current runlevel. You see two characters, the first is most likely the letter N, and the second, a numeral, in our case a 5, that denotes your current runlevel.

3. To begin editing your system initialization scripts, type **ntsysv** and press **Enter**.

4. In the list of services, use your cursor keys to find either the selection for isdn or the selection for wine and deselect the service by pressing the space-bar. The asterisk (*) in the brackets should disappear. This means the service is disabled or left off when you reboot your machine.

Neither service is necessary for your machine at this time; isdn is the connection service to use Integrated Serviced Digital Network connections and wine is a Windows emulation product.

5. You should close the tool at this time by pressing the **Tab** key until the OK button is highlighted. Press **Enter** to save your changes, and exit the tool.

6. It's a good idea to reboot your machine to make the changes take effect, so save any data files, close and type **reboot** to reinitialize your machine.

You can also use X Window system tools to manipulate your runlevels. For example, you can use the KDE Sysv-Init Editor, which is shown in Figure E-5. Notice you can select all, some, or only one runlevel to edit, and that the tool permits dragging and dropping services to and from the desired runlevel dialog.

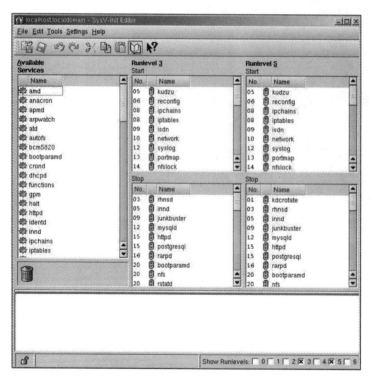

Figure E-5   Using the Sysv-Init Editor

Using the tksysv Tool

Another system initialization editor that's been around for a while and works well in the GNOME environment is tksysv. The tool is written in TCL/TK, a programming language pronounced "tickle" and defined as a "tool command language." Although not installed by default in Red Hat 7.2, you can obtain the tksysv-1.3-2.noarch.rpm file from *www.rpmfind.net*.

The "noarch" section of the tksysv-1.3-2.noarch.rpm filename means it doesn't depend on any particular processor or architecture. It is written in a script language and run by the local systems interpreter.

Installing the tksysv tool:

1. Log in as root and switch to the download directory, or whichever directory contains the tksysv-1.3-2.noarch.rpm file you downloaded from www.rpmfind.net. Type **rpm –ivh tksysv-1.3-2.noarch.rpm**.

2. Type **tksysv** to start the runlevel editor. See Figure E-6.

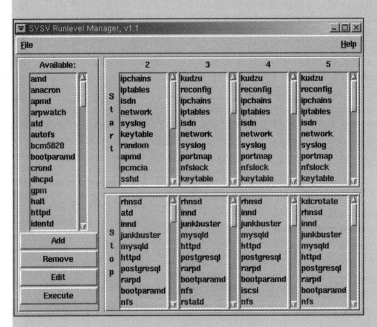

Figure E-6   The installed tool

Services to Avoid

A Web and FTP server should never run telnet, the finger daemon, Samba, Network File System (NFS), or anything else that's classically used in a normal user environment. Many services such as Telnet and FTP send the user's keystrokes, commands, and even passwords in clear-text or in easily crackable simple encryption algorithms. Thus, most system administrators use the SCP (Secure Copy) application to transfer files.

E

Step # 5 – Viewing Log Files on a Regular Basis

Linux has many useful log files that provide all kinds of informaiton about your system and about security. Some show only boot messages, some warn of security issues, and many simply write to the log file when a given action, error, or event occurs. All are valuable sources of system information and should be examined regularly.

The default location for log files in Linux is the /var/log/ directory. Because our focus is on security, let's look at some of the most useful logs your system keeps by default:

- */var/log/wtmp*—This log shows the login time and duration of the login for each and every user. You can view this information raw by using the less command to view the logfile, or you can use the last command to see what your users have been up to recently. See Figure E-7 for a sample of the last commands's output. In the figure, you can see when the system has been rebooted, who has logged in on what port and from what address, and the daemon used to control that session (in this case, the FTP daemon).

- */var/log/utmp*—This log shows information about currently logged-in users. When you suspect an attack, this can be an important log—you need to know if the attacker is still on the system. Normally accessed by the who, w, and finger commands, the output can show you not only who is currently logged in, but in the case of the w command, what the user is currently running or executing. See Figure E-8 for a view of the w command's output on a system. In Figure E-8, you can see that a couple of users are running the bash shell, one is running telnet to connect to another computer, and the root user is running the w command.

- */var/log/lastlog*—This log file is designed to show you the last time a user has logged in, from what address, and from what port. It also tells you if a user has never logged in. See Figure E-9 for sample lastlog output. Examining this output on a regular basis is particularly important when you consider that most system accounts should not be used to log in to a system. System accounts run background services such as FTP and the daemons, plus keep ownership secure for various directories on the system, such as /bin.

```
[root@localhost root]# last
ulogin    ftpd14815    192.168.1.100    Wed Feb 27 10:07 - 10:07  (00:00)
rbrunson   ftpd14809    192.168.1.100    Wed Feb 27 10:06 - 10:07  (00:00)
rbrunson   ftpd14498    192.168.1.100    Wed Feb 27 09:46 - 10:03  (00:16)
rbrunson   ftpd14265    192.168.1.100    Wed Feb 27 09:25 - 09:26  (00:01)
rbrunson   pts/1        192.168.1.100    Wed Feb 27 08:26   still logged in
rbrunson   pts/0        :0               Wed Feb 27 08:19   still logged in
rbrunson   pts/0        :0               Wed Feb 27 07:30 - 07:30  (00:00)
rbrunson   pts/0        :0               Tue Feb 26 14:55 - 15:10  (00:14)
rbrunson   pts/0        :0               Tue Feb 26 14:40 - 14:41  (00:00)
rbrunson   pts/0        :0               Tue Feb 26 14:38 - 14:38  (00:00)
rbrunson   :0                            Tue Feb 26 14:37   gone  - no logout
reboot     system boot  2.4.7-10         Tue Feb 26 14:36          (19:30)
```

Figure E-7   Output from the last command

```
10:15am  up 19:39,  5 users,  load average: 0.00, 0.00, 0.00
USER      TTY       FROM           LOGIN@    IDLE    JCPU    PCPU  WHAT
ulogin    pts/2     192.168.1.101  10:14am   1:14    0.07s   0.05s -bash
rbrunson  pts/0     :0             8:19am    28:52   3.08s   2.96s ksysv
linust    pts/1     192.168.1.103  8:26am    1:14    0.28s   0.04s telnet 192.168.
billg     pts/3     192.168.1.106  10:14am   44.00s  0.05s   0.05s -bash
root      pts/4     192.168.1.109  10:15am   0.00s   0.09s   0.03s w
```

Figure E-8   Output from the w command

```
Username    Port    From           Latest
root        pts/4   192.168.1.100  Wed Feb 27 10:15:00 -0700 2002
bin                                **Never logged in**
daemon                             **Never logged in**
adm                                **Never logged in**
mysql                              **Never logged in**
ldap                               **Never logged in**
pvm                                **Never logged in**
rbrunson    ftp     192.168.1.100  Wed Feb 27 10:06:50 -0700 2002
monique     pts/3   192.168.1.100  Wed Feb 27 10:14:47 -0700 2002
ulogin      pts/2   192.168.1.101  Wed Feb 27 10:14:17 -0700 2002
```

Figure E-9   Output from the lastlog command

If a system account has logged on, you've got serious troubles. The account has been hacked and used for system access! You should immediately disable the account by typing usermod -L to l ock it out. Then investigate what's happened to that account. (You can enable the account when you are done checking by typing usermod -U.)

Step # 6 – Keeping up with Security Fixes and Patches

Although it's possible to monitor all the Web sites and email lists that post security fixes for your system, you can spend a lot of time downloading and installing all these fixes manually. There's no doubt about it—updating systems manually is a lot of work, enough that you should consider an automated service to keep up with security fixes.

There are different methods of handling updates. These methods include the Red Hat Update Agent tool, as shown in Figure E-10, the MandrakeUpdate tool as shown in Figure E-11, and the Debian Apt-Get tool, which, although totally free, offers little in the way of organized management of a network of computers or servers. When using these tools, be aware that although a single user may be able to access the services for free, the use of the product for a network of computers might require some sort of purchased support contract.

Some of the update tools work in either X sessions or in text mode; a couple of them have both options. The option to run in text-only mode is particularly important on computers that do not run X. These computers include dedicated servers, headless special-purpose computers, and most normal servers.

Using the text version of the Red Hat Network can be as simple as typing up2date -u, in which case you are then prompted for the root user's password. You then can perform a download and installation of all new and updated packages from the Red Hat network. You can configure the tool by typing up2date –configure, which allows you to set whether updates are automatically installed and whether a proxy server configuration is needed to access the Internet. You can also set your encryption and security options.

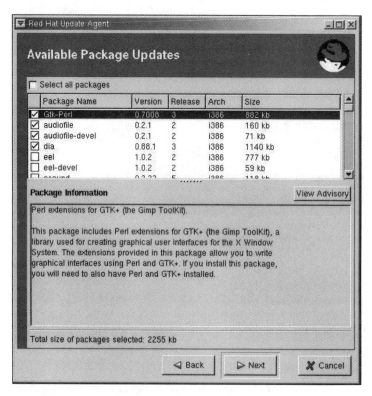

Figure E-10   Red Hat Update Agent tool

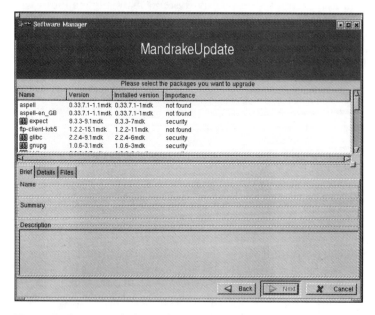

Figure E-11   MandrakeUpdate tool

Step # 7 - Monitoring Your System Automatically

You can automate many of the functions of monitoring by using the tools already installed on your systems. To illustrate, this last section walks you through the automation of one such task.

To get a system snapshot on an hourly basis using the crontab utility, the top utility, and the mail command:

1. Log in as the root user.

2. Edit the crontab file by typing **crontab -e**.

3. When the file opens in vi, press the **I** on your keyboard to begin inserting text.

4. On a single line, type the following (the period is not part of the command): *** 0-23 * * 1-5 top -nl | mail root**.

   This causes the system to run the top command one time every hour, Monday through Friday, for every week in the month and year. The system e-mails the output of this command to you, the root user. Be sure to check your inbox using your favorite e-mail reader.

5. Press the **Esc** key, type **:wq** and then press **Enter** to exit the file.

6. Your system should return a text message similar to the following:

   ```
   crontab:  installing new crontab
   ```

You can also use many other commands in the place of the top command. Here is a list of the more useful commands:

- *vmstat*—The vmstat command shows the current state of the processor, the memory, the swap space, the I/O system, the system, and the CPU.

- *netstat*—The netstat command can show you many things about the network connections to your computer, most notably the use of the "–s" option for statistics on all loaded protocols. The command can also show the users connecting, their originating addresses, and the ports and protocols they are using to connect.

- *ps*—This command is used with the aux options. It can show the current state of all system processes, including all background processes that are being run by daemons.

- *pstree*—This command is used with various options. It can show all processes in a tree-like format that helps you visualize what's responsible for what processes. It also assists in eliminating some security risks associated with giving too many permissions to users. See Figure E-12 for an example of how pstree shows processes.

```
[root@localhost root]# pstree
init-+-apmd
     |-atd
     |-4*[bonobo-moniker-]
     |-cpumemusage_app
     |-crond
     |-deskguide_apple
     |-dhcpcd
     |-drivemount_appl
     |-evolution-alarm
     |-gconfd-1
     |-gdm---gdm-+-X
     |                `-gnome-session
     |-gmc
     |-gnome-name-serv
     |-gnome-smproxy
     |-gnome-terminal-+-bash---su---bash
     |                `-gnome-pty-helpe
     |-gpm
     |-kapm-idled
     |-4*[kdeinit]
     |-keventd
     |-khubd
```

Figure E-12   Output from the pstree command

Glossary

.bashrc file — A file in your home directory that you can use to customize your work environment and specify what occurs each time you log on. Each time you start a shell, that shell executes the commands in .bashrc.

/boot — A partition that is used to store the operating system files that compose the kernel.

/home partition — A partition, which is on the home directory, that provides storage space for all users' directories. A separate section of the hard disk, it protects and insulates users' personal files from the UNIX operating system software.

/lib directory — Directory that houses kernel modules, security information, and the shared library images, which are files that programmers generally use to share code in the libraries rather than creating copies of this code in their programs.

/mnt directory — Mount points for temporary mounts by the system administrator reside in this directory, often divided into subdirectories to clearly specify device types.

/proc directory — Occupies no space on the disk; it is a virtual file system allocated in memory only.

/root directory — The home directory for the root user—the system administrator.

/sbin directory — Reserved for the system administrator to house programs that start the system, programs needed for file system repair, and essential network programs are stored here.

/tmp directory — A temporary place to store data during processing cycles.

/usr — Partition in which to store some or all of the non-kernel operating system programs that will be accessed by users.

/usr partition — A large section of the hard disk that stores all non-kernel operating system

programs that make the computer useful: software development packages, networking, Internet access, graphical screen (including X-Windows), and a large number of UNIX utilities.

/var directory — Holds subdirectories whose sizes often change. These subdirectories contain files such as error logs and other system performance logs that are useful to the system administrator.

absolute path — A pathname that begins at the root directory and lists all subdirectories to the destination file.

address — An exact location in a file or in memory.

algorithm — A sequence of instruction or commands that produce a desirable result. You develop an algorithm by following the logic flow expressed in flowcharts and pseudocode.

alias — A name that represents a command. Aliases are helpful in simplifying and automating frequently used commands.

applet — Usually a program or system monitor software application that is represented by an icon. In the X Window GNOME desktop, an applet can be placed on the Panel for fast access.

argument — Provides UNIX and other operating systems with additional information for executing a command. On the command line, an argument name follows an option name, and a space separates the two. Examples of arguments are file and directory names.

arithmetic operator — A character that represents a mathematical activity. Arithmetic operators include + (addition), - (subtraction), * (multiplication), / (division), > (greater than), < (less than), and a number of other characters.

array — A variable that stores an ordered list of scalar values that are accessed with numeric subscripts, starting as zero.

ASCII — An acronym for American Standard Code for Information Interchange, a standard set of bit patterns organized and interpreted as alphabetic characters, decimal numbers, punctuation marks, and special characters. The code is used to translate binary numbers into ordinary language and therefore makes information stored in files accessible.

assembler — Called by the compiler to convert the lines of code in a source file into object code.

assembly language — A low-level language that provides maximum access to all the computer's devices, both internal and external. Writing an assembly language program requires a great deal of coding and time. UNIX was originally written in assembly language.

automatic variable — A variable declared inside a function and local to the function in which it is declared.

Awk — A pattern-scanning and processing utility that helps to produce professional-looking reports.

B — A forerunner of C, this programming language was developed in 1970 for the first UNIX system to run on the DEC PDP-7 mini-computer. Its developer is Ken Thompson, a Bell Labs employee.

backquote (') operator — Encloses UNIX commands whose output becomes the contents of a variable. For example, TODAY='date' creates the variable TODAY, executes the date command, and stores the command's output in the TODAY variable.

bash — The default Linux shell.

Bash shell — Linux's default command interpreter. Incorporating the best features of the Bourne shell and the Korn shell, its name is an acronym for "Bourne Again Shell."

binaries — The programs residing in the /bin directory and elsewhere that are needed to start the system and perform other essential tasks. Also called executables.

binary digit — A number composed of two numbers, 0 and 1. UNIX stores all data in the form of binary digits. Because the computer consists of

electronic circuits in either an on or off state, binary digits are perfect for representing these states. Binary digits are also called bits.

binary file — A file containing non-ASCII characters (such as machine instructions).

bit — A short term for binary digit.

bitmap — Rows and columns of dots or bit patterns that graphics software transforms into an infinite variety of images. *See also* GUI.

block special file — A file related to devices, such as disks.

body — One of two parts of HTML code. (The other part is the head.) The body defines what appears within the browser window.

bootstrap loader — A utility residing in the /boot directory that starts the operating system.

Bourne shell — The first UNIX command interpreter, developed at AT&T Bell Laboratories by Steve Bourne.

buffers — When used in an editor, enable you to open any of the editor's storage buffers that currently hold information, including the text that is already in the file.

byte — An acronym for binary term, a string of eight binary numbers. These numbers can be configured into patterns of bits, which in turn can be interpreted as alphabetic characters, decimal numbers, punctuation marks, and special characters. This is the basis for ASCII code.

C — A programming language developed in part to overcome the disadvantages of assembly language programming, which requires a great deal of coding and time. The result is a high-level set of easy-to-understand instructions. UNIX was originally written in assembly language but further developed and refined in C, largely due to the efforts of Dennis Ritchie and Brian Kernighan of Bell Labs.

C++ — A programming language developed by Bjarne Stroustrup of AT&T Bell Labs, who added object-oriented capabilities and other features to the C language.

C library — A collection of functions that perform file, screen, and keyboard operations, and many other tasks. To perform or include one of these functions in your program, you insert a function call at the appropriate location in your file.

C shell — A UNIX command interpreter designed for C programmers.

cal — Command to show the system calendar.

case logic — One of the four basic shell logic structures necessary for program development. Using case logic, a program can perform one of many actions, depending on the value of a variable and matching results to a test.

case-sensitive — A property that distinguishes uppercase letters from lowercase letters (John differs from john). UNIX is case sensitive.

cat — A command that displays a whole file at one time. *See also* concatenate.

cc — The compiler's name in some UNIX versions. In Linux, it is gcc.

CC — The C++ compiler's name in some UNIX versions. In Linux, it is g++.

CGI programming — An acronym for Common Gateway Interface programming.

character special file — A file related to serial input/output devices, such as printers.

child — A subdirectory created and stored within a (parent) directory.

chmod command — A command that is used to set the security permissions associated with a file or directory.

clear command — A command that clears your screen of commands you previously entered and their output. A useful housekeeping utility for clearing the screen before new screens appear (which happens frequently in shell scripts). The output of the clear command can be stored in a shell variable.

clients — Computers in a network running programs that depend on the network's server or host computer.

cmp command — A utility used to compare the contents of two files and report the first difference between them.

code — A synonym for "binary term" or "byte," most often used in the context of ASCII codes.

comm command — Command that identifies duplicate lines in two files.

command — Text typed after the command-line prompt that requests that the computer take a specific action.

command line — The on-screen location for typing commands.

command line history — List of your recently used commands that allows you to recall a command without retyping it.

command mode — A feature of a modal editor that lets you enter commands to perform editing tasks, such as moving through the file and deleting text. The UNIX vi editor is a modal editor.

command_name — Specifies what operation to perform.

Common Gateway Interface (CGI) — A protocol or set of rules governing how browsers and servers communicate. Any script that sends information to or receives information from a server must follow these rules.

compiler — A program that reads the lines of code in a source file, converts them to machine-language instructions or calls the assembler to convert them into object code, and creates a machine-language file.

concatenate — To link. For example, by typing the cat command and then typing several filenames separated by single spaces, you can display the contents of all the files.

configuration variable — A variable that stores information about the operating system and does not change value.

console — The monitor connected directly to a computer.

constant — A value in program code that does not change when the program runs.

control string — Specifies how formatting should occur when using the screen output library function printf.

core file — A type of garbage file created when an executing program attempts to do something illegal, such as accessing another user's memory.

cua — Callout device used in conjunction with a serial port.

cua1 — Device used to access serial ports. For example, /dev/ttyS1 refers to COM2, the communication port on your PC.

current line — The line containing the cursor

date and time — Critical for smooth processing, only the system administrator can change the date and time.

decision logic — One of the four basic shell logic structures necessary for program development. Decision logic states that commands execute only if a certain condition exists. In this type of logic the if statement sets the condition(s) for execution.

decrement operator (--) — A C arithmetic operator that decreases the value of a variable by a specified amount.

decryption operation — An operation that restores an encrypted file to its original state.

default prompt — The prompt the system generated when the system administrator created a login account.

dependent file — A source code file listed within a makefile.

diamond operator (<>) — Accesses data from an open file. Each time the diamond operator is used, it returns the next line from the file.

diff command — A command that finds differences between the contents of two files.

directory — A special type of file that can contain other files and directories. Directory files store the names of regular files and other directories, called subdirectories.

domain name — A set of characters separated by periods and used to identify and access remote systems. An example is (Lunar.campus.edu).

dot — A character that signifies the current directory. Two dot characters (with no space between them) signify the root directory. A dot used as the first character of the filename indicates the file is hidden.

dot dot (two consecutive dots) — To mean the parent directory.

editor — A program for creating and modifying computer documents, such as program and data files.

electronic interfaces — The means for connecting peripherals to computers.

Emacs — A UNIX text editor.

environment variable — A variable that UNIX reads when you log on, which stores information about the characteristics of your work session. For example, the PS1 environment variable determines how your prompt appears. Other environment variables tell UNIX where to look for programs, which shell to use, and the path to your home directory. You can change the value of an environment variable as needed.

EOF (end-of-file marker) — A character that shows the location of the end of a file.

equal sign (=) operator — Sets a value in a variable.

ex mode — A text editing command mode, currently used in the vi editor, that employs an extended set of commands initially used in an early UNIX editor called ex.

executable file — A useable program, the result of the program development cycle.

executable program file — A compiled file (from a programming language) or an interpreted file (from a script) that can be run on the computer.

executables — The programs residing in the /bin directory needed to start the system and perform other essential tasks. Also called binaries.

exit status — A numeric value that tests the command returns to the operating system when it finishes indicating the result of the test. If the exit status is 0 (zero), the test result is true. An exit status of 1 indicates the test result is false.

false value — A value returned from a program function indicating that the function was not carried out successfully. A 0 represents a false value.

file — The basic component for data storage.

file decryption — An operation that restores a file to the state it was in before file encryption.

file encryption — An operation that scrambles a file's contents into secret code and is a useful security measure.

file system — A system's way of organizing files on mass storage devices, such as hard and floppy disks. Its organization is hierarchical and resembles an inverted tree: in the branching structure, top-level files (or folders or directories) contain other files, which in turn contain other files.

File Transfer Protocol (FTP) — An Internet protocol for sending files.

filehandle — An input/output connection between a Perl program and the operating system. It can be used inside a program to open, read, write, and close the file.

flat ASCII file — A file that you can create, manipulate, and use to store data such as letters, product reports, or vendor records. Its organization as an unstructured sequence of bytes is typical of a text file and lends flexibility in data entry because it can store any kind of data in any order. Any operating system can read this file type. However, because you can retrieve data only in the order you entered it, this file type's usefulness is limited. Also called an ordinary file or regular file.

flowchart — A logic diagram that uses a set of standard symbols to explain a program's sequence and each action it takes.

foot icon — The Main Menu icon in the Panel at the bottom of the screen.

for loop — Command statement in a program used for looping through a range of values. A variable takes on each value in a specified set individually, and performs an action while the variable contains each individual value. The loop stops after the variable has taken on the last value in the set and performed the specified action.

FORM tag — In HTML specifies how you wish to receive information users entered as responses to your document. You can choose one of two methods: GET or POST.

foundation layer — Hardware that supports the entire UNIX structure.

fstab — A file used for mapping information about filesystems to devices (such as hard disks and CD-ROMs).

FTP — *See* File Transfer Protocol.

function — A separate body of code designed to contribute to the execution of a single task. You can put together a number of functions to create a program. In some languages, functions are called subroutines or procedures.

function call — A feature that you insert in the appropriate location of a program file to specify and use one of the functions in the C library.

function overloading — A feature of the C++ programming language that lets functions respond to more than one set of criteria and conditions.

g++ — The C++ compiler's name in UNIX and Linux.

garbage file — A temporary file, such as a core file, that loses its usefulness after several days.

gcc — The C compiler's name in Linux.

GET — A method for receiving information users entered as responses to your HTML document. It transfers data within the URL itself.

glob — Similar to a wildcard, a glob character is used to find or match filenames. Glob characters are part of glob patterns.

glob pattern — A combination of glob characters used to find or match multiple filenames.

GNU Network Object Model Environment (GNOME) — Produced by the GNU project, GNOME is a desktop environment that must be used with a Windows Manager.

GNU project — An organization created to develop a free, UNIX-like, operating system named GNU.

graphical user interface (GUI) — Software that transforms bitmaps into an infinite variety of images.

grep command — Command to search for a specified pattern in a file, such as a particular word or phrase.

group id (GID) — A number used to identify a group of users.

GUI — *See* graphical user interface.

hash — A variable representing a set of key value pairs. A percent sign (%) precedes a hash variable.

hd — Device names beginning with this, access IDE hard drives.

head — One of two parts of HTML code. (The other part is body.) The head contains the title, which appears on the top bar of your browser window.

header file — A file containing the information the compiler needs to process standard input or output statements.

hidden file — A file that the operating system uses to keep configuration information and for other purposes. The name of a hidden file begins with a dot.

high-level language — A computer language that uses English-like expressions. COBOL, C, and C++ are high-level languages.

host — *See* server.

Hyper Text Markup Language (HTML) — A format for creating documents and Web pages with embedded codes known as tags.

hyperlink — Text or an object in a Web document. When you click a hyperlink, another document loads and appears in the browser.

icon — A small graphics symbol in a graphical user interface that represents a program or an action that can be started by clicking or double-clicking the symbol.

IDE — Integrated drive electronics, the most popular electronic hard disk interface for personal computers.

identifiers — Names given to variables and functions.

if statement — A primary decision-making control structure used in programming.

increment operator (++) — A C arithmetic operator that increases the value of a variable by a specified amount.

init program — A program that performs essential chores, such as reading startup parameters in the inittab file, when a UNIX system starts.

inittab — The configuration file for the init program that performs essential chores when the system starts

inline sort block — A compact Perl notation that replaces an if-else statement and eliminates the need for a separate subroutine.

inode (information node) — A system for storing key information about UNIX-based files. Inode information includes the inode number, the owner of the file, the file group, the file size, the change date of the inode, the file creation date, the date the file was last modified and last read, the number of links to this inode, and information regarding the location of the blocks in the file system in which the file is stored.

input validation — A process a program performs to ensure that the user has entered acceptable information.

insert mode — A feature of a modal editor that lets you enter text. The UNIX vi editor is a modal editor.

Internet Protocol (IP) address — A set of four numbers separated by periods (123.456.678.90) used to identify and access remote systems.

Internet Protocol (IP) — A protocol that enables packets (small data packages) to reach a destination on a local or remote network by using dotted decimal addressing.

interpreter — A UNIX feature that reads statements in a program file, immediately translates them into executable instructions, and then runs the instructions. Unlike a compiler, an interpreter does not produce a binary, an executable file because it translates the instructions and runs them a single step.

IP — *See* Internet Protocol.

KDE — An example of an X Windows desktop.

kernel — The basic operating system, which interacts directly with the hardware and services user programs.

kernel mode — A means of accessing the kernel. Its use is limited to the system administrator to prevent unauthorized data from damaging the hardware that supports the entire UNIX structure.

key — A common field that each of the linked files share.

key words — Components of all programming languages, these words have special meaning and must not be used as variable or function names.

Korn shell — A UNIX command interpreter that offers more features than the original Bourne shell. David Korn developed it at AT&T Bell Laboratories.

layering — A method of organizing software so that it surrounds the computer system's inner core, protecting its vital hardware and software and insulating the core and its users.

line editor — An editor that lets you work with only one line or a group of lines at once. Although you cannot see the context of your file, you may find a line editor useful for tasks like searching, replacing, and copying blocks of text.

line-oriented command — A command that can perform more than one action, such as searching and replacing, in more than one place in a file. When using a line-oriented command, you must specify the exact location where the action is to occur. These commands differ from screen-oriented commands, which execute relative to the location of the cursor.

link — A means of joining multiple files that share a common field.

linker — In program development, used after the compiler to link all object files that belong to the program and any library programs the program may use.

log in — Users log in by typing a user name and password before they are allowed to use a multi-user system.

log on — A process that protects privacy and safeguards a multi-user system by requiring each user to type a user name and password before using the system.

logging out — A process that tells a system that a user has finished using it. Commands for logging out vary from system to system; exit, Ctrl+D, and logout are examples.

logical structure — The organization of information in files, records, and fields, each of which represents a logical entity such as a payroll file, an employee's pay record, or an employee social security number.

login script — A script that runs just after you log into your account.

loopback — A feature that helps you experiment with and test HTML documents, or Web pages, using a UNIX or Linux system. To use localhost, you need not be connected to the Internet. Located on your PC, localhost also accesses your PC's internal network. Use localhost to ensure that networking is properly configured.

looping logic — One of the four basic shell logic structures necessary for program development. In looping logic a control structure (or loop) repeats until some condition exists or some action occurs.

lp — Device names beginning with this access parallel ports. The lp0 device refers to LPT1, the line printer.

ls command — Command to display a directory's contents, including files and other directories.

machine language — The exclusive use of 0s (which mean off) and 1s (which mean on) to communicate with the computer. Years ago, programmers had to write programs in machine language, a tedious and time-consuming process.

macro — A set of commands that automates a complex task. A macro is sometimes called a super instruction.

main — C programs are made up of one or more functions. Every function must have a name, and every C program must have a function called main.

mainframe system — A large computer system with multiple processors that conducts input, output, processing, and storage operations for many users. Most widely used in large corporations and industrial computing.

make utility — A UNIX utility that controls changes and additions to programs during program development. It tracks what needs to be recompiled using the time stamp file stored in all source files.

makefile — A control file you create and the make utility uses. The file includes a list of all your source files and their relationship to each other, expressed as targets and dependencies.

man page directory — A directory for an online manual that contains all commands, including their options and arguments.

manipulation and transformation commands — A group of commands that alter and format extracted information so that it's useful and appealing.

methods — Part of the new data class, objects, introduced in the C++ programming language. Methods are a set of operations that manipulate data.

modal editor — A text editor that enables you to work in different modes. For example, the vi editor has three modes: insert, command, and ex.

motd — The message of the day file.

mount — To connect a file system to the directory tree structure, making it accessible.

MS-DOS — An operating systems for desktop personal computers.

Multipurpose Internet Mail Extensions (MIME) — A communications utility that supports sending and receiving binary files in mail messages.

multitasking system — A system that lets a user work with more than one program at a time. UNIX is a multitasking system.

multi-user system — A system in which many people can simultaneously access and share a server computer's resources. To protect privacy and safeguard the system, each user must type a user name and password in order to use, or log on to, the system. UNIX is a multi-user system.

network — A group of computers wired together to let many users share computer resources and files. Combines the convenience and familiarity of the personal computer with the processing power of a mainframe.

network operating system — Controls the operations of a server or host computer, which accepts and responds to requests from user programs running on other computers on the network called clients.

null — A "black hole"; any data sent to this device is gone forever, a single byte where all bits are set to zero. Use this device when you want to suppress the output of a command appearing on your screen.

null character — A single byte whose bits are all set to zero.

-o noclobber option — Using the set command with this option will prevent a file from being overwritten.

object code — Binary instructions translated from program source code by a compiler.

object-oriented programming — Uses objects for handling data—allowing the data to be described by name and type anywhere in the program.

objects — A new data class introduced in the C++ programming language. Objects are a collection of data and a set of operations called methods that manipulate data.

operand — The variable name that appears to the left of an operator or the variable value that appears to the right of an operator. For example, in NAME=Becky, NAME is the variable name, = is the operator, and Becky is the variable value. Note that no spaces separate the operator and operands.

operating system (OS) — The most fundamental computer program—it controls all the computer's resources and provides the base upon which application programs can be used or written.

option — Directs UNIX and other operating systems to execute a command in a specific way. On the command line, an option name follows a command name, and a space separates the two. In UNIX option names begin with a hyphen and are case sensitive.

ordinary files — Files that you can create and manipulate. Includes ASCII files and binary files. Also called regular files or flat ASCII files.

ordinary users — All persons who use the system, except the system administrator or superuser.

parent — The directory in which a subdirectory (child) is created and stored.

partition — A separate section of a disk, created so activity and problems occurring in other partitions do not affect it.

passwd command — Command used to change your password or to create one.

paste command — Combines files side-by-side, whereas the cat command combines files end to end.

PATH variable — Identifies a path and provides a list of directory locations where UNIX looks for executable programs.

pathname — A means of specifying a file or directory that includes the names of directories and subdirectories on the branches of the tree-structure. A forward slash (/) separates each directory name. For example, the pathname of the file phones (the destination file) in the source directory of Jean's directory within the /home directory is /home/jean/source/phones.

PC — *See* personal computer.

peer-to-peer network — A networking configuration in which each computer system on the network is both a client and a server. Data and programs reside on individual systems, so users do not depend on a central server. The advantage of a peer-to-peer network is that if one computer fails, the others continue to operate.

peripherals — Equipment connected to a computer via electronic interfaces. Examples include hard and floppy disk drives, printers, and keyboards.

Perl — An acronym for Practical Extraction and Report Language, a UNIX programming language similar to C that uses features from the Awk and shell programs. Created by Larry Wall in 1986 as a simple report generator, Perl has evolved to become a powerful and popular tool for creating interactive Web pages.

personal computer — A single, standalone machine, like a desktop or laptop computer, that performs all input, output, processing, and storage operations.

physical file system — A section of the hard disk that has been formatted to hold files.

pipe (|) — Redirects the output of one command to the input of another command.

port — Adapting software so that it can be moved from one type of computer or operating system to another.

portability — A characteristic of an operating system that allows the system to be used in a number of different environments. UNIX is a portable operating system.

POST — A method for receiving information users entered as responses to your HTML document. It uses the body of the HTTP request to transfer data.

pr command — Prints the specified files on the standard output in paginated form.

preprocessor — Used after initial application development and before the compiler to make necessary modifications to the program and to include the contents of other files.

preprocessor directive — A statement that you place in your program to instruct the preprocessor to modify your source code in some way. A preprocessor directive always begins with the # symbol. An example is #include, which tells the preprocessor to include another file in your program.

process — To receive data from the standard input device (your keyboard) and then send output to the standard output device (your monitor).

print working directory (pwd) — UNIX command to display your current path.

printcap — The printer capability information file.

printenv command — Command used to see a list of your environment variables.

printf — A print formatting function from the C language. It lets you specify an edit pattern for the output.

profile — Files executed at logon that let the system administrator set global defaults for all users.

program development cycle — The process of developing a program, which includes (1) creating program specification, (2) the design process, (3) writing code, (4) testing, (5) debugging, and (6) correcting errors.

protocol — A set of rules governing communication and the transfer of data between computers.

prototype — A running model, which lets programmers review a program before committing to its design.

pseudocode — Instructions similar to actual programming statements. Used to create a model that may later become the basis for an actual program.

pty — Device names beginning with this are "pseudo-terminals." They are used to provide a terminal to remote login sessions.

pwd (print working directory) — Command used to display your current path.

record layout — The first task in the process of designing a new program, in which each field is named and identified by data type (for example, numeric or nonnumeric).

redirection symbol — The greater than sign (>). Typing > after a command that produces output creates a new file or overwrites an existing file and then sends output to a disk file, rather than the monitor.

regular files — Files that you can create and manipulate. Includes ASCII files and binary files. Also called ordinary files or flat ASCII files.

relational database — Contains files that UNIX treats as tables, records that UNIX treats as rows, and fields that UNIX treats as columns that can be joined to create new records. Using the join command, you can extract information from two files in a relational database that share a common field.

relative path — A pathname that begins at the current working directory and lists all subdirectories to the destination file.

RGB color code — A set of three numbers that specify a colors red, green, and blue components.

root — The basis of the tree-like structure of the file system and the name of the file (root directory) located at this level. The slash character (/) denotes this file. Also, the system administrator's unique user name, a reference to the system administrator's ownership of the root account and unlimited system privileges.

root device — The hard disk partition that houses the UNIX root file system.

root directory — The most basic file in the tree-like structure of the file system. The slash character (/) denotes this file.

run level — Mode of operation for a system, such as run level 3 for full multi-user mode or run level 5 to invoke an X Window. The system boots into this mode.

scalability — Ability for a computer operating system to be used on smaller computers, such as those with a single Intel-based processor, and on larger computers, such as those with multiple Intel or RISC processors.

scalar — A simple variable that holds a number or a string. Scalar variables' names begin with a dollar sign ($).

scope — The part of the program where a variable is defined and accessible. The scope can be either inside or outside of a function.

screen editor — An editor supplied by the operating system that displays text one screen at a time and lets you move around the screen to add and change text. UNIX has two screen editors: vi and Emacs.

screen-oriented command — A command that executes relative to the position of the cursor. Screen-oriented commands are easy to type, and you can readily see their result on the screen. These commands differ from line-oriented commands, which execute independently of the location of the cursor.

SCSI — Small computer system interfaces, pronounced *scuzzy*, a popular electronic hard disk interface commonly used on local-network servers.

sd — Device names beginning with this are SCSI drives.

sed — A powerful UNIX stream editor used to make global changes to large files.

select commands — File processing commands which extract information.

sequential logic — One of four basic shell logic structures necessary for program development. Sequential logic states that commands execute in the order they appear in the program. An exception occurs when a branch instruction changes the flow of execution.

server — The computer that houses the network operating system and, as a result, can accept and respond to requests from user programs running on other computers in the network called clients. Also called the host.

server-based network — A centralized approach to networking, in which all client computers' data and programs reside on the server.

shared library images — Files residing in the /lib directory that programmers use to share code, rather than copying this code into their programs. Doing so makes their programs smaller and faster.

shell — A required interface between the user and the UNIX operating system. It interprets commands entered from the keyboard.

shell function — A group of commands stored in memory and assigned a name. Shell functions simplify the program code. For example, you can include a function's name within a shell script so the function's commands execute as part of the script. You can also use shell functions to store reusable code sections, so that you do not need to duplicate them.

shell script — Text file that contains sequences of UNIX commands which do not need to be converted into machine language by a compiler.

shell script file — A file type based on the UNIX command-line history feature that recalls and reexecutes the commands you enter. The file contains command-line entries that you and others can repeatedly access and run sequentially as a set. Similar to an MS-DOS batch file.

shell variable — A variable you create at the command line or in a shell script. Valuable for use in shell scripts for storing information temporarily.

source file — A file containing source code, created by an editor such as vi or Emacs, and used for storing a program's high-level language statements. To execute, a source file must be converted to a low-level machine language file consisting of object code.

spaceship operator <=> — A special Perl operator for numeric sorts that reduces coding requirements.

sorting key — A field position within each line. The sort command sorts the lines based on the sorting key.

standard error (stderr) — A type of output that results when UNIX detects errors in processing systems tasks and user programs and sends the error to the screen by default.

standard input — Data received from the standard input device (the keyboard).

standard output — Data sent to the standard output device (the monitor).

status line — File status information that appears at the bottom of the screen. The vi editor's status line provides information on patterns you are searching for, line-oriented commands, and error messages.

stderr — An acronym for standard error.

stdin — An acronym for standard input.

stdio.h — A header file that is part of the C programming language development system. This file contains information the compiler needs to process standard input or output statements. Any C program that performs standard input or output must include the stdio.h header file.

stdout — An acronym for standard output.

string — A nonnumeric field of information treated simply as a group of characters. Numbers in a string are considered characters rather than digits.

subdirectory — A directory created and stored within another directory. The subdirectory is considered the child of the parent directory.

superuser — *See* system administrator.

swap — Acts like an extension of memory, so that there is more room to run large programs.

swap partition — A section of the hard disk, separated from other sections so that it functions as an extension of memory; that is, it supports virtual memory. A computer system can use the space in this partition to swap information between disk and RAM so the computer runs faster and more efficiently.

symbolic link — A name that points to and provides access to a file located in another directory. Many files in the /lib directory are symbolic links to files in system libraries. A 1 to the left of a filename in a long directory listing identifies a symbolic link file.

syntax — A command's format, wording, options and arguments.

syntax error — A grammatical mistake in a source file. Such mistakes prevent the compiler from converting the file into an executable file.

system administrator — Manages the system by adding new users, deleting old accounts, and ensuring that the system performs services well and efficiently for all users.

tags — Code embedded in a document or Web page created with Hyper Text Markup Language (HTML). When the document is viewed with a Web browser like Netscape Navigator or Internet Explorer, the tags give the document special properties like foreground and background colors, font size, and the placement of graphical elements. You can also use tags to place hyperlinks in a document.

target file — A file listed within a makefile. It depends on another file to determine if the make utility needs to take action to rebuild the target file.

tcsh — A free, shareware UNIX command interpreter based on the C shell.

Telnet — An Internet terminal emulation program.

termcap — The terminal capability information file.

test command — Makes preliminary checks of the UNIX internal environment and other useful comparisons (beyond those that the if command alone can perform).

text editor — A simplified word processor used to create and edit documents but has no formatting features for boldfacing and centering text, for example.

text file — Computer file composed entirely of ASCII characters.

tput command — Initializes the terminal display and cursor placement to respond to a setting that the user chooses.

transformation commands — Alter and transform extracted information into useful and appealing formats.

translate utility (tr) — A utility that copies data from the standard input to the standard output, substituting or deleting characters specified by options and patterns.

trap command — Specifies that a command, listed as the argument to trap, is read and executed when the shell receives a specified system signal. It is useful when you want your shell program to automatically remove any temporary files that are created when the shell script runs.

true value — A value returned from a program function indicating that the function was carried out successfully. A 1 usually represents a true value, but sometimes any non-zero value represents a true value.

tty — Device names beginning with this refer to terminals or consoles.

ttyS1 — Device used to access serial ports. For example, /dev/ttyS1 refers to COM2, the communication port on your PC.

uniq command — Command that removes duplicate lines from a file.

user mode — A means of accessing the areas of a system where all program software resides.

utility — A program that performs useful operations like copying files, listing directories, and communicating with other users. Unlike other operating system programs, a utility is an add-on and not part of the UNIX shell, nor a component of the kernel.

variables — Symbolic names that represent values stored in memory.

vi editor — A screen editor that displays on screen the changes you make to text.

virtual file system — A system that occupies no disk space, such as the /proc directory. The system

references and lets you obtain information about which programs and processes are running on a computer.

virtual memory — A seemingly unlimited memory resource supported by the swap partition, where the system can swap information between disk and RAM, allowing the computer to run faster and more efficiently.

wallpaper — A graphic image you can choose to use as the background of your desktop area.

wc command — Command to count the number of lines (option -l), words (option -w), and bytes or characters (option -c) in text files.

Web server — A system connected to the Internet running Web server software, such as Apache. The Web server software lets other users access the HTML document via the Internet.

whatis command — Displays a brief summary of a command.

who command — Command to see who is using the system and their current location.

wildcard — A special character used to represent any other character or, sometimes, a group of characters. Wildcards help you work with files whose names are similar or find a file whose exact name you cannot remember. Wildcard characters are also called glob characters.

Window Manager — The top layer of the X Window system and the user's interface to the system's components. It controls how windows appear and how users control them.

workstation — A computer that has its own CPU and that may be used as a standalone computer for word processing, spreadsheet creation, or other software applications. It also may be used to access another computer such as a mainframe computer or a network server, as long as the necessary network hardware and software are installed.

workstation-class installation — Performing an installation that has been predefined by Red Hat to include the most useful options for a typical user's workstation.

X11 — The eleventh version of the X Window system.

X client — In X Window network terminology, the system that hosts and executes a program.

XFree86 — A version of X11 that was ported to the PC and on Linux.

X server — In X Window network terminology, the desktop system from which the user runs a program.

X Window system — A graphical user interface (GUI) that runs on Linux and many UNIX operating systems.

zsh — A free, shareware UNIX command interpreter based on the Korn shell.

Index

Symbol index

; (semicolon)
in ending Perl statements, 320
to separate commands on same line, 19, 204

* (asterisk), 202
as multiplication operator, 200, 323, 368–369
as wildcard, 55–56, 62, 200, 202

- (minus operator), 169, 200, 259, 260, 323, 368–369

( ) parentheses
in C language programming, 363, 376
in Perl, 268

' (single quotation mark)
in defining and evaluating operators, 198
to delimit string literals, 325
in shell scripting, 217

! = (not-equal operator) in while loop, 211

! operator in negating the value of an expression, 247

"" (quotation marks)
in decision logic, 204
in defining and evaluating operators, 198
to delimit string literals, 325
enclosing argument in, 260

(pound sign), 330
to mark comments, 173
in Perl programs, 320
for preprocessor directives, 365
as system administrator prompt, 24

$ (dollar sign)
in arrays, 327
as command prompt, 24
for scalar variable names, 324

% (percent sign)
in formatting output, 169
to precede hash variables, 327

*/ to denote end of comment, 364, 396

++ (increment operators), 336, 369

+ (plus operator), 61, 200, 368–369

, (comma) as list separator, 325

— (decrement operator), 369

./ (dot slash), 131, 199
to indicate current directory, 192

. (repeat) command, to repeat most recent changes, 76–77

[ ] (brackets)
for command options, 14
in decision logic, 205

/ (division), 38, 200, 323, 368–369

/ (forward slash), 200, 325
to denote root directory, 38, 39, 40
in searching for pattern, 81
to separate subdirectory names, 49
in separating directory names, 47

/* to denote beginning of comment, 364, 396

// to denote comment line, 396

: (colon)
in adding current directory to search path, 200
to enter extended commands, 74
in preceding line-oriented commands, 83
in separating fields, 287
in separating variable-length fields, 222

;; (semicolons) to terminate action, 212

<=> (spaceship operator), 337, 339

<> (diamond operator), 330, 332, 333

< > (angled brackets) in creating web pages, 341

< (redirection operator), 108–109, 149, 251

==> (arrow operator), to define key/value pairs, 327

== in testing numeric values for equality, 322

= operator
in defining and evaluating operators, 197
in if statement's test expression, 205

>> (redirection operator), 108–109
to append output to existing file, 27
with paste command, 119

> (redirection operator), 59, 108–109, 149, 202
to create new file or overwrite existing file, 27

? (question mark), 202
as wildcard, 55, 56

@ (at sign) in arrays, 327

\$), 48

_ (underscore)
in identifiers, 367
in Perl, 325

` (backquote operator), enclosing command in, 198, 258

{} (braces)
with awk command, 136–137
in C language programming, 363
to open and close blocks, 268
in Perl, 322
in shell functions, 268

~ (tilde), 258
to denote user's home directory, 50, 58
in shell scripting, 217

| (pipe operator)
in formatting record output, 252
to redirect output, 149–150, 161

|| (vertical bar), 333

2> (redirection operator), 108–109

A

absolute path, 50, 192
address, 83
advanced file processing, 147–180
selecting, manipulating, and formatting information, 147–162
comm command, 153–155
diff command, 155
grep command, 150–152
pipes, 149–150
pr command, 161–162
sed, 156–159
tr command, 160–161
unrq command, 152–153
wc command, 155–156
UNIX file processing tools to create applications
creating programs and project files, 165–167
cutting and sorting, 170–172
designing records, 163–164
formatting output, 168–170